Hands-On Graph Analysis with Neo4j

Perform graph processing and visualization techniques using connected data across your enterprise

Estelle Scifo

BIRMINGHAM - MUMBAI

Hands-On Graph Analytics with Neo4j

Copyright © 2020 Packt Publishing

All rights reserved. No part of this book may be reproduced, stored in a retrieval system, or transmitted in any form or by any means, without the prior written permission of the publisher, except in the case of brief quotations embedded in critical articles or reviews.

Every effort has been made in the preparation of this book to ensure the accuracy of the information presented. However, the information contained in this book is sold without warranty, either express or implied. Neither the author(s), nor Packt Publishing or its dealers and distributors, will be held liable for any damages caused or alleged to have been caused directly or indirectly by this book.

Packt Publishing has endeavored to provide trademark information about all of the companies and products mentioned in this book by the appropriate use of capitals. However, Packt Publishing cannot guarantee the accuracy of this information.

Commissioning Editor: Sunith Shetty
Acquisition Editor: Ali Abidi
Content Development Editor: Sean Lobo
Senior Editor: Roshan Kumar
Technical Editor: Sonam Pandey
Copy Editor: Safis Editing
Language Support Editors: Martin Whittemore, Annie Whittemore
Project Coordinator: Aishwarya Mohan
Proofreader: Safis Editing
Indexer: Priyanka Dhadke
Production Designer: Nilesh Mohite

First published: August 2020

Production reference: 1210820

Published by Packt Publishing Ltd.
Livery Place
35 Livery Street
Birmingham
B3 2PB, UK.

ISBN 978-1-83921-261-1

www.packt.com

Packt.com

Subscribe to our online digital library for full access to over 7,000 books and videos, as well as industry leading tools to help you plan your personal development and advance your career. For more information, please visit our website.

Why subscribe?

- Spend less time learning and more time coding with practical eBooks and Videos from over 4,000 industry professionals

- Improve your learning with Skill Plans built especially for you

- Get a free eBook or video every month

- Fully searchable for easy access to vital information

- Copy and paste, print, and bookmark content

Did you know that Packt offers eBook versions of every book published, with PDF and ePub files available? You can upgrade to the eBook version at www.packt.com and as a print book customer, you are entitled to a discount on the eBook copy. Get in touch with us at customercare@packtpub.com for more details.

At www.packt.com, you can also read a collection of free technical articles, sign up for a range of free newsletters, and receive exclusive discounts and offers on Packt books and eBooks.

Contributors

About the author

Estelle Scifo possesses over 7 years' experience as a data scientist, having received her PhD from the Laboratoire de l'Accélérateur Linéaire, Orsay (affiliated to CERN in Geneva). As a Neo4j-certified professional, she uses graph databases on a daily basis and takes full advantage of its features to build efficient machine learning models from this data. In addition, she is also a data science mentor to newcomers to the field. Her domain expertise and deep insights into the perspective of the needs of beginners make her an excellent teacher.

About the reviewers

Aaron Ploetz has been a professional software developer since 1997, and has several years of experience as a technical lead for both start-ups and Fortune 500 enterprises. He has previously worked as an author on distributed database titles such as *Mastering Apache Cassandra 3.x* and *Seven NoSQL Databases in a Week*. Aaron earned a B.Sc. in management/computer systems from the University of Wisconsin-Whitewater, an M.Sc. in software engineering (focusing on database technology) from Regis University, and has been named a DataStax MVP for Apache Cassandra on three occasions.

Sonal Raj is a Pythonista, engineer, and writer who has carved his niche in the financial technology domain. He currently heads the data analytics and research division of a high-frequency trading firm. He is a Goldman Sachs and D. E. Shaw alumnus, with expertise in electronic trading algorithms. He holds dual masters degrees in IT and business management and is a former research fellow at the Indian Institute of Science, where he worked on real-time graph processing with Neo4j. He has authored the books *Neo4j High Performance* and *The Pythonic Way*. His published works focus on image processing, SDLC models, and mobile communications. When not engrossed in fiction books or symphonies on the piano, he spends far too much time watching rockets lift off!

Packt is searching for authors like you

If you're interested in becoming an author for Packt, please visit authors.packtpub.com and apply today. We have worked with thousands of developers and tech professionals, just like you, to help them share their insight with the global tech community. You can make a general application, apply for a specific hot topic that we are recruiting an author for, or submit your own idea.

Table of Contents

Preface — 1

Section 1: Graph Modeling with Neo4j

Chapter 1: Graph Databases — 9
Graph definition and examples — 10
Graph theory — 10
   A bit of history: the Seven Bridges of Königsberg problem — 10
   Graph definition — 12
   Visualization — 12
Examples of graphs — 14
   Networks — 14
      Road networks — 14
      Computer networks — 16
      Social networks — 16
   Your data is also a graph — 19
Moving from SQL to graph databases — 20
Database models — 20
SQL and joins — 21
It's all about relationships — 23
Neo4j – the nodes, relationships, and properties model — 24
Building blocks — 24
   Nodes — 25
   Relationships — 25
   Properties — 25
SQL to Neo4j translator — 26
Neo4j use cases — 27
Understanding graph properties — 27
Directed versus undirected — 28
Weighted versus unweighted — 28
Cyclic versus acyclic — 29
Dense versus sparse — 30
   Graph traversal — 30
Connected versus disconnected — 31
Considerations for graph modeling in Neo4j — 31
Relationship orientation — 32
Node or property? — 32
Summary — 33
Further reading — 33

Chapter 2: The Cypher Query Language — 35
Technical requirements — 36

Creating nodes and relationships — 36
Managing databases with Neo4j Desktop — 36
Creating a node — 37
Selecting nodes — 39
Filtering — 39
Returning properties — 40
Creating a relationship — 40
Selecting relationships — 42
The MERGE keyword — 43
Updating and deleting nodes and relationships — 44
Updating objects — 44
Updating an existing property or creating a new one — 44
Updating all properties of the node — 44
Updating node labels — 45
Deleting a node property — 46
Deleting objects — 47
Pattern matching and data retrieval — 48
Pattern matching — 48
Test data — 49
Graph traversal — 50
Orientation — 50
The number of hops — 51
Variable-length patterns — 52
Optional matches — 53
Using aggregation functions — 53
Count, sum, and average — 54
Creating a list of objects — 55
Unnesting objects — 55
Importing data from CSV or JSON — 56
Data import from Cypher — 56
File location — 56
Local file: the import folder — 56
Changing the default configuration to import a file from another directory — 58
CSV files — 58
CSV files without headers — 58
CSV files with headers — 58
Eager operations — 62
Data import from the command line — 64
APOC utilities for imports — 64
CSV files — 65
JSON files — 66
Importing data from a web API — 69
Setting parameters — 69
Calling the GitHub web API — 70
Summary of import methods — 72
Measuring performance and tuning your query for speed — 72
Cypher query planner — 72

Neo4j indexing	75
Back to LOAD CSV	75
The friend-of-friend example	77
Summary	79
Questions	80
Further reading	81

Chapter 3: Empowering Your Business with Pure Cypher — 83

Technical requirements	83
Knowledge graphs	84
Attempting a definition of knowledge graphs	84
Building a knowledge graph from structured data	85
Building a knowledge graph from unstructured data using NLP	86
NLP	86
Neo4j tools for NLP	87
GraphAware NLP library	87
Importing test data from the GitHub API	89
Enriching the graph with NLP	90
Adding context to a knowledge graph from Wikidata	92
Introducing RDF and SPARQL	92
Querying Wikidata	93
Importing Wikidata into Neo4j	96
Enhancing a knowledge graph from semantic graphs	99
Graph-based search	101
Search methods	101
Manually building Cypher queries	103
Automating the English to Cypher translation	104
Using NLP	104
Using translation-like models	107
Recommendation engine	109
Product similarity recommendations	109
Products in the same category	110
Products frequently bought together	112
Recommendation ordering	113
Social recommendations	113
Products bought by a friend of mine	114
Summary	115
Questions	115
Further reading	115

Section 2: Graph Algorithms

Chapter 4: The Graph Data Science Library and Path Finding — 119

Technical requirements	120
Introducing the Graph Data Science plugin	120
Extending Neo4j with custom functions and procedures	121
The difference between procedures and functions	121

[iii]

Table of Contents

Functions	121
Procedures	121
Writing a custom function in Neo4j	122
GDS library content	123
Defining the projected graph	124
Native projections	125
Cypher projections	127
Streaming or writing results back to the graph	128
Understanding the importance of shortest path algorithms through their applications	129
Routing within a network	129
GPS	129
The shortest path within a social network	130
Other applications	130
Video games	130
Science	130
Dijkstra's shortest paths algorithm	131
Understanding the algorithm	131
Running Dijkstra's algorithm on a simple graph	132
Example implementation	135
Graph representation	135
Algorithm	136
Displaying the full path from A to E	138
Using the shortest path algorithm within Neo4j	139
Path visualization	145
Understanding relationship direction	146
Finding the shortest path with the A* algorithm and its heuristics	149
Algorithm principles	150
Defining the heuristics for A*	150
Using A* within the Neo4j GDS plugin	152
Discovering the other path-related algorithms in the GDS plugin	152
K-shortest path	153
Single Source Shortest Path (SSSP)	154
All-pairs shortest path	155
Optimizing processes using graphs	157
The traveling-salesman problem	158
Spanning trees	160
Prim's algorithm	161
Finding the minimum spanning tree in a Neo4j graph	162
Summary	163
Questions	164
Further reading	165
Chapter 5: Spatial Data	167
Technical requirements	168
Representing spatial attributes	168
Understanding geographic coordinate systems	168

Using the Neo4j built-in spatial types	172
Creating points	172
Querying by distance	174
Creating a geometry layer in Neo4j with neo4j-spatial	**175**
Introducing the neo4j-spatial library	175
A note on spatial indexes	176
Creating a spatial layer of points	177
Defining the spatial layer	177
Adding points to a spatial layer	178
Defining the type of spatial data	178
Creating layers with polygon geometries	179
Getting the data	179
Creating the layer	181
Performing spatial queries	**182**
Finding the distance between two spatial objects	182
Finding objects contained within other objects	184
Finding the shortest path based on distance	**184**
Importing the data	185
Preparing the data	186
Importing data	186
Creating a spatial layer	188
Running the shortest path algorithm	188
Visualizing spatial data with Neo4j	**194**
neomap – a Neo4j Desktop application for spatial data	194
Visualizing nodes with simple layers	195
Visualizing paths with advanced layer	195
Using the JavaScript Neo4j driver to visualize shortest paths	196
Neo4j JS driver	197
Leaflet and GeoJSON	198
Summary	**202**
Questions	**202**
Further reading	**203**
Chapter 6: Node Importance	**205**
Technical requirements	**205**
Defining importance	**206**
Popularity and information spread	207
Critical or bridging nodes	207
Computing degree centrality	**209**
Formula	209
Computing degree centrality in Neo4j	210
Computing the outgoing degree using GDS	211
Computing the incoming degree using GDS	212
Using a named projected graph	212
Using an anonymous projected graph	213
Understanding the PageRank algorithm	**214**
Building the formula	215

[v]

Table of Contents

The damping factor	216
Normalization	216
Running the algorithm on an example graph	217
Implementing the PageRank algorithm using Python	219
Using GDS to assess PageRank centrality in Neo4j	221
Comparing degree centrality and the PageRank results	222
Variants	222
ArticleRank	222
Personalized PageRank	223
Eigenvector centrality	224
The adjacency matrix	224
PageRank with matrix notation	225
Eigenvector centrality	227
Computing eigenvector centrality in GDS	227
Path-based centrality metrics	**227**
Closeness centrality	228
Normalization	228
Computing closeness from the shortest path algorithms	228
The closeness centrality algorithm	230
Closeness centrality in multiple-component graphs	231
Betweenness centrality	231
Comparing centrality metrics	232
Applying centrality to fraud detection	**234**
Detecting fraud using Neo4j	234
Using centrality to assess fraud	235
Creating a projected graph with Cypher projection	236
Other applications of centrality algorithms	239
Summary	**239**
Exercises	**240**
Further reading	**240**
Chapter 7: Community Detection and Similarity Measures	**243**
Technical requirements	**244**
Introducing community detection and its applications	**244**
Identifying clusters of nodes	245
Applications of the community detection method	246
Recommendation engines and targeted marketing	246
Clusters of products	246
Clusters of users	247
Fraud detection	247
Predicting properties or links	247
A brief overview of community detection techniques	248
Detecting graph components and visualizing communities	**249**
Weakly connected components	251
Strongly connected components	252
Writing the GDS results in the graph	254
Visualizing a graph with neovis.js	256
Using NEuler, the Graph Data Science Playground	258

Usage for community detection visualization	259
Running the Label Propagation algorithm	262
Defining Label Propagation	263
Weighted nodes and relationships	264
Semi-supervised learning	264
Implementing Label Propagation in Python	264
Using the Label Propagation algorithm from the GDS	267
Using seeds	268
Writing results to the graph	269
Understanding the Louvain algorithm	270
Defining modularity	270
All nodes are in their own community	271
All nodes are in the same community	271
Optimal partition	272
Steps to reproduce the Louvain algorithm	273
The Louvain algorithm in the GDS	273
Syntax	273
The aggregation method in relationship projection	274
Intermediate steps	275
A comparison between Label Propagation and Louvain on the Zachary's karate club graph	276
Going beyond Louvain for overlapping community detection	278
A caveat of the Louvain algorithm	278
Resolution limit	279
Alternatives to Louvain	280
Overlapping community detection	281
Dynamic networks	282
Measuring the similarity between nodes	283
Set-based similarities	283
Overlapping	283
Definition	283
Quantifying user similarity in the GitHub graph	284
Jaccard similarity	286
Vector-based similarities	286
Euclidean distance	287
Cosine similarity	288
Summary	290
Questions	290
Further reading	291

Section 3: Machine Learning on Graphs

Chapter 8: Using Graph-based Features in Machine Learning	295
Technical requirements	296
Building a data science project	296
Problem definition – asking the right question	297
Supervised versus unsupervised learning	298

Regression versus classification	299
Introducing the problem for this chapter	300
Getting and cleaning data	300
Data characterization	301
Quantifying the dataset size	301
Labels	301
Columns	303
Data visualization	306
Data cleaning	308
Outliers detection	308
Missing data	310
Correlation between variables	311
Data enrichment	311
Feature engineering	312
Building the model	313
Train/test split and cross-validation	313
Creating the train and test samples with scikit-learn	314
Training a model	315
Evaluating model performances	316
The steps toward graph machine learning	**319**
Building a (knowledge) graph	319
Creating relationships from existing data	319
Creating relationships from relational data	319
Creating relationships from Neo4j	320
Using an external data source	321
Importing the data into Neo4j	321
Graph characterization	321
The number of nodes and edges	322
The number of components	323
Extracting graph-based features	325
Using graph-based features with pandas and scikit-learn	**326**
Extracting graph-based features from Neo4j Browser	326
Creating the projected graph	327
Running one or several algorithms	327
Dropping the projected graph	328
Extracting the data	328
Automating graph-based feature creation with the Neo4j Python driver	**328**
Discovering the Neo4j Python driver	329
Basic usage	329
Transactions	330
Automating graph-based feature creation with Python	331
Creating the projected graph	332
Calling the GDS procedures	334
Writing results back to the graph	335
Dropping the projected graph	338
Exporting the data from Neo4j to pandas	338
Training a scikit-learn model	341
Introducing community features	341
Using both community and centrality features	343

Summary	344
Questions	345
Further reading	345

Chapter 9: Predicting Relationships — 347
Technical requirements — 347
Why use link prediction? — 348
- Dynamic graphs — 348
- Applications — 350
  - Recovering missing data — 350
    - Fighting crime — 350
    - Research — 350
  - Making recommendations — 350
    - Social links (Facebook friends, LinkedIn contacts...) — 351
    - Product recommendations — 351
  - Making recommendations using a link prediction algorithm — 352

Creating link prediction metrics with Neo4j — 354
- Community-based metrics — 355
- Path-related metrics — 355
  - Distance between nodes — 356
  - The Katz index — 357
- Using local neighborhood information — 358
  - Common neighbors — 358
  - Adamic-Adar — 359
  - Total neighbors — 359
  - Preferential attachment — 360
- Other metrics — 360

Building a link prediction model using an ROC curve — 361
- Importing the data into Neo4j — 361
- Splitting the graph and computing the score for each edge — 362
- Measuring binary classification model performance — 363
  - Understanding ROC curves — 364
  - Extracting features and labels — 368
  - Drawing the ROC curve — 369
    - Creating the DataFrame — 369
    - Plotting the ROC curve — 371
  - Determining the optimal cutoff and computing performances — 372
- Building a more complex model using scikit-learn — 374
- Saving link prediction results into Neo4j — 374
- Predicting relationships in bipartite graphs — 375

Summary — 380
Questions — 380
Further reading — 380

Chapter 10: Graph Embedding - from Graphs to Matrices — 381
Technical requirements — 382
Why do we need embedding? — 382
- Why is embedding needed? — 382

Table of Contents

One-hot encoding	383
Creating features for words – the manual way	385
Embedding specifications	387
The graph embedding landscape	388
Adjacency-based embedding	**389**
The adjacency matrix and graph Laplacian	389
Eigenvectors embedding	390
Locally linear embedding	390
Similarity-based embedding	391
High-Order Proximity preserved Embedding (HOPE)	391
Computing node embedding with Python	391
Creating a networkx graph	392
The Neo4j test graph	392
Extracting the edge list data from Neo4j	392
Creating a networkx graph matrix from pandas	393
Fitting a node embedding algorithm	394
Extracting embeddings from artificial neural networks	**396**
Artificial neural networks in a nutshell	396
A reminder about neural network principles	397
Neurons, layers, and forward propagation	397
Different types of neural networks	399
Skip-graph model	400
Fake task	401
Input	401
Word representation before embedding	401
Target	401
Hidden layer	403
Output layer	403
DeepWalk node embedding	404
Generating node context through random walks	404
Generating random walks from the GDS	405
DeepWalk embedding with karateclub	406
Node2vec, a DeepWalk alternative	407
Node2vec from the GDS (≥ 1.3)	408
Getting the embedding results from Python	408
Graph neural networks	**409**
Extending the principles of CNNs and RNNs to build GNNs	410
Message propagation and aggregation	410
Taking into account node properties	412
Applications of GNNs	412
Image analysis	412
Video analysis	413
Zero-shot learning	413
Text analysis	413
And there's more...	414
Using GNNs in practice	414
GNNs from the GDS – GraphSAGE	414
Going further with graph algorithms	**415**
State-of-the-art graph algorithms	415

[x]

Summary	416
Questions	417
Further reading	417

Section 4: Neo4j for Production

Chapter 11: Using Neo4j in Your Web Application — 421
Technical requirements — 422
Creating a full-stack web application using Python and Graph Object Mappers — 422
  Toying with neomodel — 422
    Defining the properties of structured nodes — 423
      StructuredNode versus SemiStructuredNode — 423
      Adding properties — 424
    Creating nodes — 425
    Querying nodes — 425
      Filtering nodes — 426
    Integrating relationship knowledge — 427
      Simple relationship — 427
      Relationship with properties — 428
  Building a web application backed by Neo4j using Flask and neomodel — 429
    Creating toy data — 429
    Login page — 430
      Creating the Flask application — 430
      Adapting the model — 430
      The login form — 431
      The login template — 432
      The login view — 433
    Reading data – listing owned repositories — 435
    Altering the graph – adding a contribution — 436
Understanding GraphQL APIs by example – GitHub API v4 — 438
  Endpoints — 439
  Returned attributes — 440
  Query parameters — 441
  Mutations — 443
Developing a React application using GRANDstack — 444
  GRANDstack – GraphQL, React, Apollo, and Neo4j Database — 444
  Creating the API — 445
    Writing the GraphQL schema — 445
      Defining types — 445
    Starting the application — 446
      Testing with the GraphQL playground — 447
      Calling the API from Python — 448
      Using variables — 449
  Mutations — 450
  Building the user interface — 452
    Creating a simple component — 453
      Getting data from the GraphQL API — 453
      Writing a simple component — 453

Adding navigation	457
Mutation	459
Refreshing data after the mutation	461
Summary	**461**
Questions	**462**
Further reading	**462**
Chapter 12: Neo4j at Scale	**463**
Technical requirements	**463**
Measuring GDS performance	**464**
Estimating memory usage with the estimate procedures	464
Estimating projected graph memory usage	464
Fictive graph	465
Graph defined by native or Cypher projection	466
Estimating algorithm memory usage	467
The stats running mode	467
Measuring time performances for some of the algorithms	468
Configuring Neo4j 4.0 for big data	**469**
The landscape prior to Neo4j 4.0	469
Memory settings	469
Neo4j in the cloud	470
Sharding with Neo4j 4.0	470
Defining shards	471
Creating the databases	472
Querying a sharded graph	472
The USE statement	473
Querying all databases	473
Summary	**475**
Other Books You May Enjoy	**477**
Index	**479**

Preface

Interest in graph databases and especially Neo4j is increasing, both because of the naturalness of a graph data model and the range of data analyses they permit. This book is a journey inside the world of graphs and Neo4j. We will explore Neo4j and Cypher, but also different plugins (officially supported or from third parties), to extend database capabilities in terms of data types (APOC or Neo4j Spatial) or Data Science and Machine Learning applications using the Graph Data Science (GDS) plugin or the GraphAware NLP plugins.

A large part of the book covers graph algorithms. You will learn both **how they work** by running through an example implementation in python for the most famous algorithms (shortest path, PageRank or Label Propagation) and **how to use them** in practice from a Neo4j graph. We will also give some example applications to inspire you about when to use these algorithms for your use-cases.

Once you will be more familiar with the different types of algorithms that can be run on a graph to extract information about its individual components (nodes) or the overall graph structure, we will switch to some Data Science problems and lean how a graph structure and graph algorithms can enhance a model predictive power.

Finally, we will see that Neo4j, on top of being a fantastic tool for data analysis, can also be used to expose the data in a web application for our analysis to go live.

Who this book is for

This book is for data analysts, business analysts, graph analysts, and database developers looking to store and process graph data to reveal key data insights. This book will also appeal to data scientists who want to build intelligent graph applications catering to different domains. Some experience with Neo4j is required.

Although Python is used to demonstrate some algorithms in "Section 2: Graph Algorithms", we have kept the implementation simple (without any "Python magic") such that it should be accessible to you even if you are not familiar with Python. The following sections however requires some more experience with this language, especially its Data Science ecosystem, including `scikit-learn`, `pandas` or `seaborn` would be a plus.

Preface

What this book covers

Chapter 1, *Graph Databases*, provides a review of graph database concepts, starting from graph theory and important definitions to the node and relationship model of Neo4j.

Chapter 2, *The Cypher Query Language*, covers the basics of Cypher, the query language used by Neo4j, which will be used throughout this book for data import and pattern matching. APOC utilities for data import are also studied. In this chapter, we will start building the graph of Neo4j contributors on GitHub, which will be used elsewhere in this book.

Chapter 3, *Empowering Your Business with Pure Cypher*, explains how to build a knowledge graph from structured and unstructured data (using NLP) and start applying it from graph-based search or recommendation engines. We will use the graph of Neo4j contributors on GitHub and extend this thanks to natural language analysis and external publicly available knowledge graphs (namely, Wikidata).

Chapter 4, *The Graph Data Science Library and Path Finding*, explains the main principles of the graph data science plugin for Neo4j and uses our first algorithms with the shortest path-finding applications.

Chapter 5, *Spatial Data*, explains how, thanks to the Neo4j Spatial plugin, we will be able to store and query spatial data (points, lines, and polygons). Coupling Neo4j Spatial with the graph data science plugin, we will create a routing engine in Manhattan, New York.

Chapter 6, *Node Importance*, covers the different centrality algorithms, depending on how you define node importance, their applications, and usage from the GDS.

Chapter 7, *Community Detection and Similarity Measures*, covers the different algorithms to detect structures in a graph and how to visualize them using JavaScript libraries.

Chapter 8, *Using Graph-Based Features in Machine Learning*, explains how, starting from a flat CSV file, we will build a full machine learning project, reviewing the different steps required to build a predictive pipeline (feature engineering, model training, and model evaluation). We will then transform our flat CSV data to a graph using extra knowledge of our data and learn how graph algorithms can enhance the performance of a classification task.

Chapter 9, *Predicting Relationships*, explains how, in a time-evolving graph, we will formulate a link prediction problem as a machine learning problem with a training and test set.

Chapter 10, *Graph Embedding – from Graphs to Matrices*, explains how algorithms can automatically learn features for each node in a graph. Using an analogy with word embedding, we will learn how the DeepWalk algorithm works. We will then go even deeper and learn about graph neural networks and their use cases. Applications will be given using both Python and some dependencies and the GDS implementation of node2vec and GraphSAGE.

Chapter 11, *Using Neo4j in Your Web Application*, covers how, in order to use Neo4j and the tools we have studied in the previous chapter in a live application, we will create a web application using either Python and its popular Flask framework, or JavaScript and a GraphQL API.

Chapter 12, *Neo4j at Scale*, provides an overview of the possibilities offered by the GDS and Neo4j 4 in order to manage big data.

To get the most out of this book

You will need to have access to a Neo4j database that you can manage (that is, update settings and add plugins). The recommended way is to use Neo4j Desktop, which you can download from `https://neo4j.com/download/`.

You can create one graph per chapter. Only the "GitHub" graph we will start creating in chapter 2 and enrich in chapter 3 will be reused later in the book, but instructions will be given to recreate it in case you have not read the preceding chapters. You are also given a set of questions at the end of every chapter for self-learning.

All codes, except those in *Chapter 5*, *Spatial Data* and *Chapter 11*, *Using Neo4j in Your Web Application*, are compatible with both Neo4j 3.5 and Neo4j 4.x.

Regarding *Chapter 5*, since Neo4j Spatial is not yet compatible with Neo4j 4.x (the most recent version at the time of writing is `0.26.2`), the code in this chapter is only valid for Neo4j 3.5. Similarly, for *Chapter 11*, we will rely on the `neomodel` package (last version at the time of writing is `3.3.2`), not yet compatible with Neo4j 4.

Software/hardware covered in the book	OS requirements
Neo4j ≥ 3.5	Windows, Linux, or macOS; a minimum of 8 GB of RAM
APOC (Neo4j plugin) ≥ 3.5.0.11	Windows, Linux, or macOS; a minimum of 8 GB of RAM
neo4j-spatial (plugin)	Windows, Linux, or macOS; a minimum of 8 GB of RAM
Neo4j Graph Data Science plugin (GDS) ≥ 1.0	Windows, Linux, or macOS; a minimum of 8 GB of RAM
Python ≥ 3.6	Windows, Linux, or macOS; a minimum of 8 GB of RAM

Preface

Software/hardware covered in the book	OS requirements
Node.js ≥ v10 & npm (Second part of chapter 11 only)	Windows, Linux, or macOS; a minimum of 8 GB of RAM

For the second part of Chapter 11, where we will create a React application with the GRANDstack, you will also need `Node.js` and `npm` installed on your system.

If you are using the digital version of this book, we advise you to type the code yourself or access the code via the GitHub repository (link available in the next section). Doing so will help you avoid any potential errors related to the copying and pasting of code.

Download the example code files

You can download the example code files for this book from your account at `www.packt.com`. If you purchased this book elsewhere, you can visit `www.packtpub.com/support` and register to have the files emailed directly to you.

You can download the code files by following these steps:

1. Log in or register at `www.packt.com`.
2. Select the **Support** tab.
3. Click on **Code Downloads**.
4. Enter the name of the book in the **Search** box and follow the onscreen instructions.

Once the file is downloaded, please make sure that you unzip or extract the folder using the latest version of:

- WinRAR/7-Zip for Windows
- Zipeg/iZip/UnRarX for Mac
- 7-Zip/PeaZip for Linux

The code bundle for the book is also hosted on GitHub at `https://github.com/PacktPublishing/Hands-On-Graph-Analytics-with-Neo4j`. In case there's an update to the code, it will be updated on the existing GitHub repository.

We also have other code bundles from our rich catalog of books and videos available at `https://github.com/PacktPublishing/`. Check them out!

[4]

Download the color images

We also provide a PDF file that has color images of the screenshots/diagrams used in this book. You can download it here: https://static.packt-cdn.com/downloads/9781839212611_ColorImages.pdf

Conventions used

There are a number of text conventions used throughout this book.

`CodeInText`: Indicates code words in text, database table names, folder names, filenames, file extensions, pathnames, dummy URLs, user input, and Twitter handles. Here is an example: "Mount the downloaded `WebStorm-10*.dmg` disk image file as another disk in your system."

A block of code is set as follows:

```
submit = SubmitField('Submit')
```

When we wish to draw your attention to a particular part of a code block, the relevant lines or items are set in bold:

```
password = StringField('Password', validators=[DataRequired()],
                       widget=PasswordInput(hide_value=False)
)
```

Any command-line input or output is written as follows:

```
python models.py
```

Bold: Indicates a new term, an important word, or words that you see on screen. For example, words in menus or dialog boxes appear in the text like this. Here is an example: "Select **System info** from the **Administration** panel."

> Warnings or important notes appear like this.

> Tips and tricks appear like this.

[5]

Get in touch

Feedback from our readers is always welcome.

General feedback: If you have questions about any aspect of this book, mention the book title in the subject of your message and email us at `customercare@packtpub.com`.

Errata: Although we have taken every care to ensure the accuracy of our content, mistakes do happen. If you have found a mistake in this book, we would be grateful if you would report this to us. Please visit `www.packtpub.com/support/errata`, selecting your book, clicking on the Errata Submission Form link, and entering the details.

Piracy: If you come across any illegal copies of our works in any form on the internet, we would be grateful if you would provide us with the location address or website name. Please contact us at `copyright@packt.com` with a link to the material.

If you are interested in becoming an author: If there is a topic that you have expertise in, and you are interested in either writing or contributing to a book, please visit `authors.packtpub.com`.

Reviews

Please leave a review. Once you have read and used this book, why not leave a review on the site that you purchased it from? Potential readers can then see and use your unbiased opinion to make purchase decisions, we at Packt can understand what you think about our products, and our authors can see your feedback on their book. Thank you!

For more information about Packt, please visit `packt.com`.

Section 1: Graph Modeling with Neo4j

This part will review the basics of Neo4j and Cypher needed for this book. We will then explore a classic application of graph modeling: recommendation engines.

This section consists of the following chapters:

- Chapter 1, *Graph Databases*
- Chapter 2, *The Cypher Query Language*
- Chapter 3, *Empowering Your Business with Pure Cypher*

1
Graph Databases

Graph databases have gained increasing attention in the last few years. Data models built from graphs bring together the simplicity of document-oriented databases and the clarity of SQL tables. Among others, Neo4j is a database that comes with a large ecosystem, including the database, but also tools to build web applications, such as the GRANDstack, and tools to use graph data in a machine learning pipeline, as well as the Graph Data Science Library. This book will discuss those tools, but let's first start from the beginning.

Talking about graph databases means talking about graphs. Even if you do not need to know all the details about graph theory, it's always a good idea to learn some of the basic concepts underlying the tool you are using. In this chapter, we will start by defining graphs and giving some simple and less simple examples of graphs and their applications. We will then see how to move from the well-known SQL tables to graph data modeling. We'll conclude by introducing Neo4j and its building blocks, and review some design principles to understand what can and can't be done with Neo4j.

This chapter will cover the following topics:

- Graph definition and examples
- Moving from SQL to graph databases
- Neo4j: the nodes, relationships, and properties model
- Understanding graph properties
- Considerations for graph modeling in Neo4j

Graph definition and examples

The question you may ask at this point is "Why should I care about graphs? After all, my company/business/interest is not about graphs or networks of any kind. I know my data model, well arranged into SQL tables or NoSQL documents, and I can retrieve the information I want when I want." This book will teach you how to empower your data by looking at it in a different way. Surprisingly enough, graphs can be used to model a lot of processes, from the more obvious ones such as road networks, to less intuitive use cases such as video games or credit card fraud detection, among many others.

Graph theory

Let's start from the beginning and answer the question "What is a graph?"

A bit of history: the Seven Bridges of Königsberg problem

Graph studies originate back to Leonhard Euler, a prolific Swiss mathematician who lived in the eighteenth century. In 1735, he published a paper proposing a solution to the Seven Bridges of Königsberg problem. The problem is the following:

Given the city whose geography is depicted in the following image, is there a way to walk across each of the seven bridges of the city once and only once, and return to our starting point?

As you can see, this city is crossed by a river that splits the city into two banks, *A* and *B*. The river meander additionally creates two islands, *C* and *D*, also part of the city. Those two banks and two islands are connected by a total of seven bridges: two bridges between *A* and *C*, two other bridges between *C* and *B*, one between *C* and *D*, one between *B* and *D*, and a last one between *D* and *A*:

Chapter 1

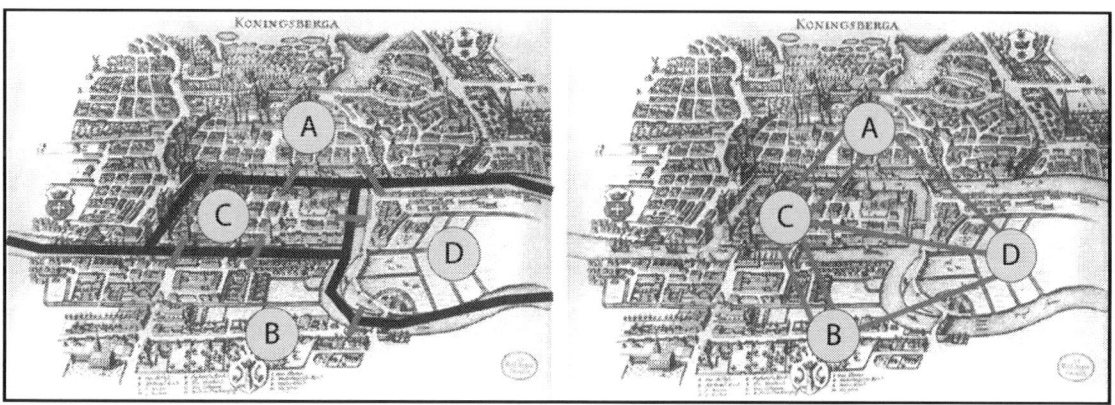

Euler's reasoning (on the right side) was to reduce this complex geography to the most simple drawing, like the one you can see on the right of the previous image, since the route used within each island is not relevant. Each island then becomes a single point, or node, connected to another by one or several links, or edges, representing the bridges.

With this simple visualization, the mathematician was able to solve the initial problem by noting that, if you arrive at an island (vertex) via one bridge, you will need to leave it using another bridge (except for the start and end vertices). In other words, all vertices but two need to be connected to an even number of relationships. This is not the case in the Königsberg graph, since we have the following:

```
A: 3 connections (to C twice, and to D once)
B: 3 connections (to C twice, and to D once)
C: 5 connections (to A twice, to B twice and to D once)
D: 3 connections (to A once, to C once and to D once)
```

This kind of path, where each edge is used once and only once, is called a **Eulerian cycle** and it can be said that a graph has a Eulerian cycle if and only if all of its vertices have even degrees.

 The number of connections for a node is called the **degree** of the node.

[11]

Graph Databases

Graph definition

This leads us to the mathematical definition of a graph:

A graph G = (V, E) is a pair of:

- V, a set of **nodes** or vertices: the islands in our previous example
- E, a set of **edges** connecting nodes: the bridges

The Königsberg graph illustrated on the right of the preceding image can then be defined as follows:

```
V = [A, B, C, D]
E = [
      (A, C),
      (A, C),
      (C, B),
      (C, B),
      (A, D),
      (C, D),
      (B, D)
    ]
```

Graphs, like many mathematical objects, are well defined. While it can be difficult to find a good visualization for some of those objects, graphs, on the other hand, suffer from the almost infinite number of ways to draw them.

Visualization

Apart from very special cases, there is no single way to draw a graph and visualize it. Indeed, graphs are most often an abstract representation of reality. For instance, all four graphs depicted in the following image represent the exact same set of nodes and edges, so, by definition, the same *mathematical* graph:

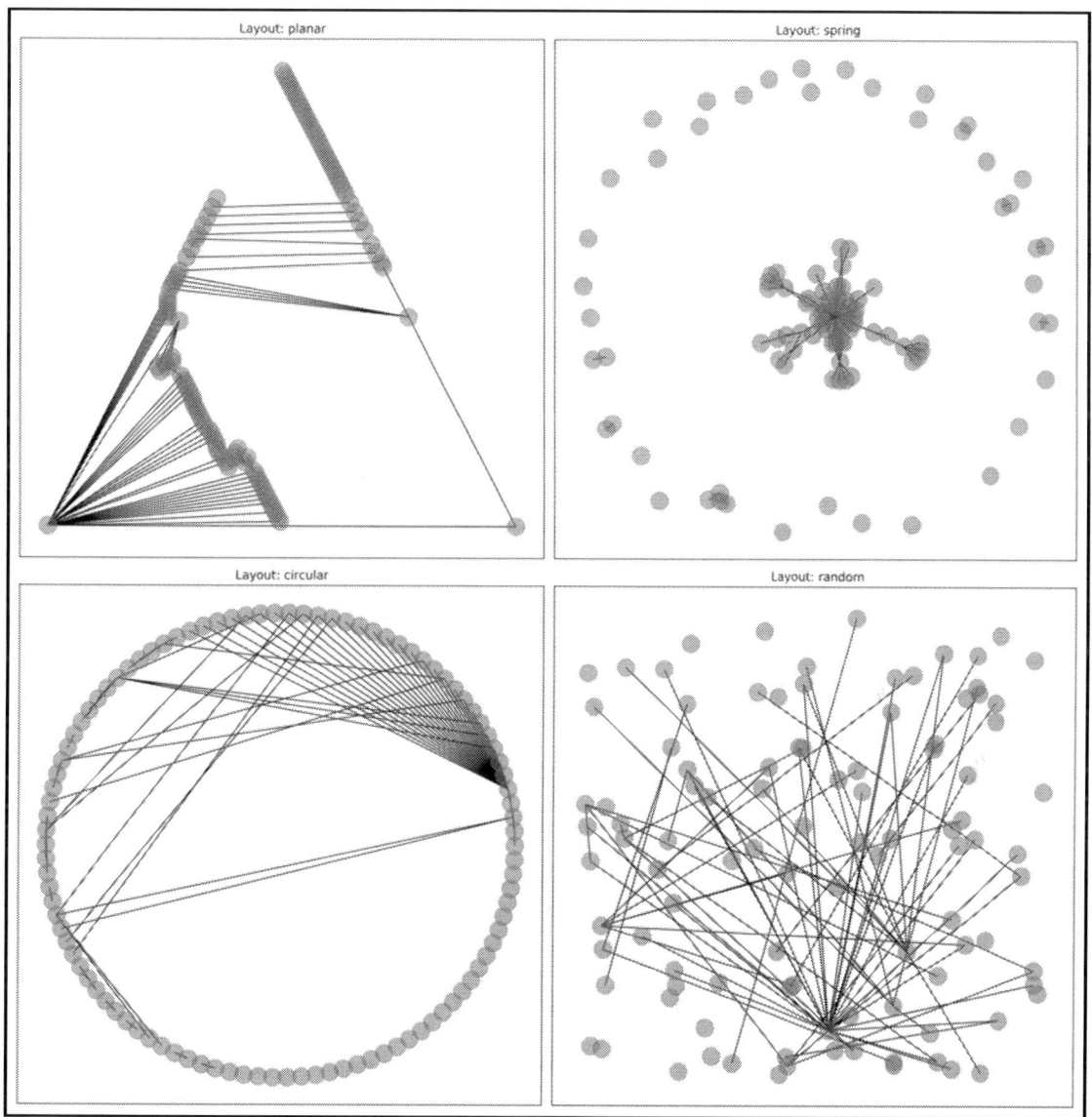

We cannot rely only on our eyes to find patterns within graphs. For instance, looking only at the lower-right plot, it would be impossible to see the pattern that is visible in the upper-right plot. That's where graph algorithms enter into the game, which will be discussed in more detail in Chapter 6, *Node Importance*, and Chapter 7, *Community Detection and Similarity Measures*.

Examples of graphs

Now that we have a better idea of what a graph is, it's time to discover some more examples to understand which purposes graphs can be useful for.

Networks

With the graph definition in mind (a set of nodes connected to each other via edges) and the bridges example from the last section, we can easily imagine how all kinds of networks can be seen as graphs, including road networks, computer networks, or even social networks.

Road networks

Road networks are a perfect example of graphs. In such networks, the nodes are the road intersections, and edges are the roads themselves, as you can see in the following image:

Chapter 1

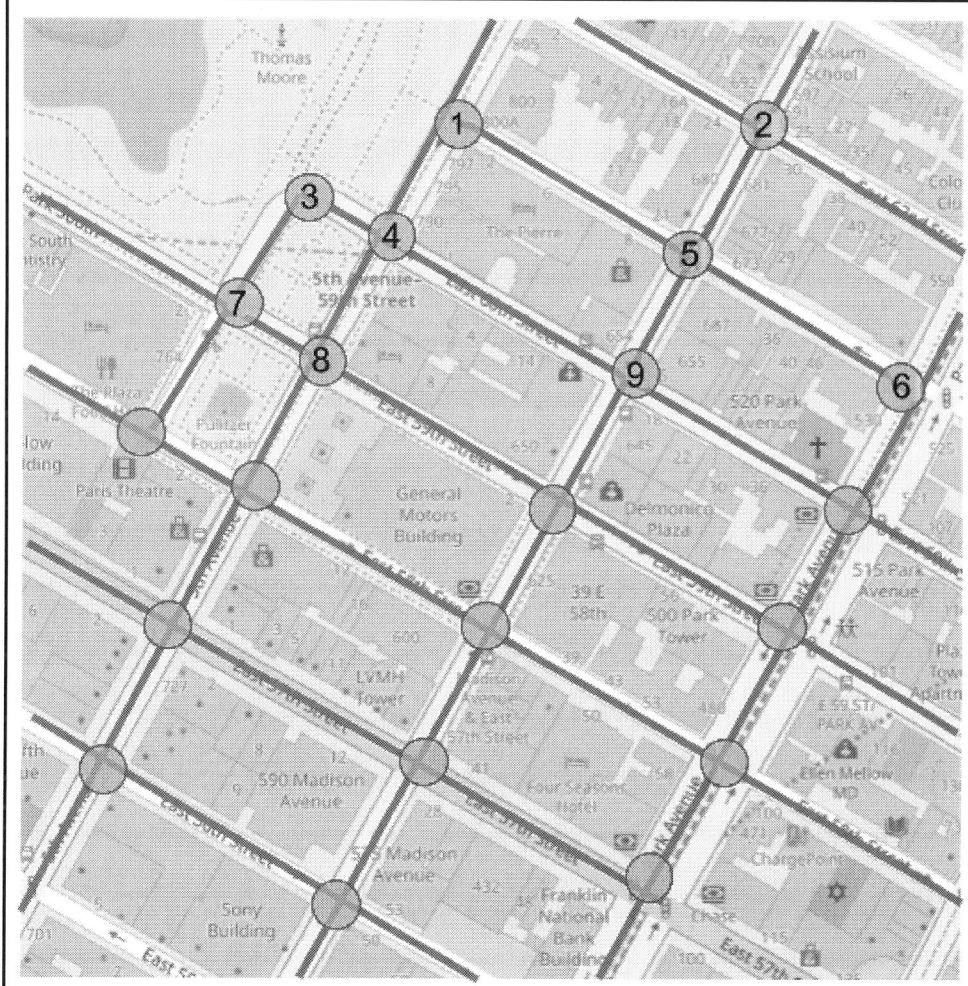

This image shows the road network around Central Park in New York City, wherein streets are edges between junctions representing nodes

With road networks, many questions can be answered with graph analysis, such as the following:

- What is the shortest path between two points (nodes)?
- How long is this shortest path?
- Are there alternative routes?
- How can you visit all nodes within a list in a minimal amount of time?

Graph Databases

This last question is especially important for parcel delivery, in order to minimize the number of driven miles to maximize the number of delivered parcels and satisfied customers.

We will go into more detail about this topic in `Chapter 4`, *The Graph Data Science Library and Path Finding*.

Computer networks

In a computer network, each computer/router is a node and the cables between them are the edges. The following image illustrates some possible topologies used for a computer network (credit: `https://commons.wikimedia.org/wiki/File:NetworkTopologies.svg`):

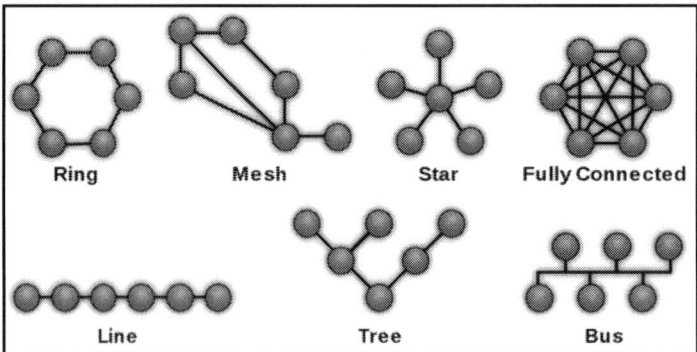

You can now draw the parallel with the graph definition we discovered in the last section. Here again, the graph structure helps in answering some common questions you may ask yourself about your network:

- How fast will this information be transferred from A to B? This sounds like a shortest path issue.
- Which of my nodes is the most critical one? By critical, we mean that if this node is not working for some reason, the whole network will be impacted. Not all nodes have the same impact on the network. That's where centrality algorithms come into the game (see `Chapter 6`, *Node Importance*).

Social networks

Facebook, LinkedIn, and all of our favorite social networks use graphs to model their users and interactions. In the most basic example of a social graph, nodes represent people, and edges the *friendship* or *professional* relationship between them, as illustrated in the following image:

Chapter 1

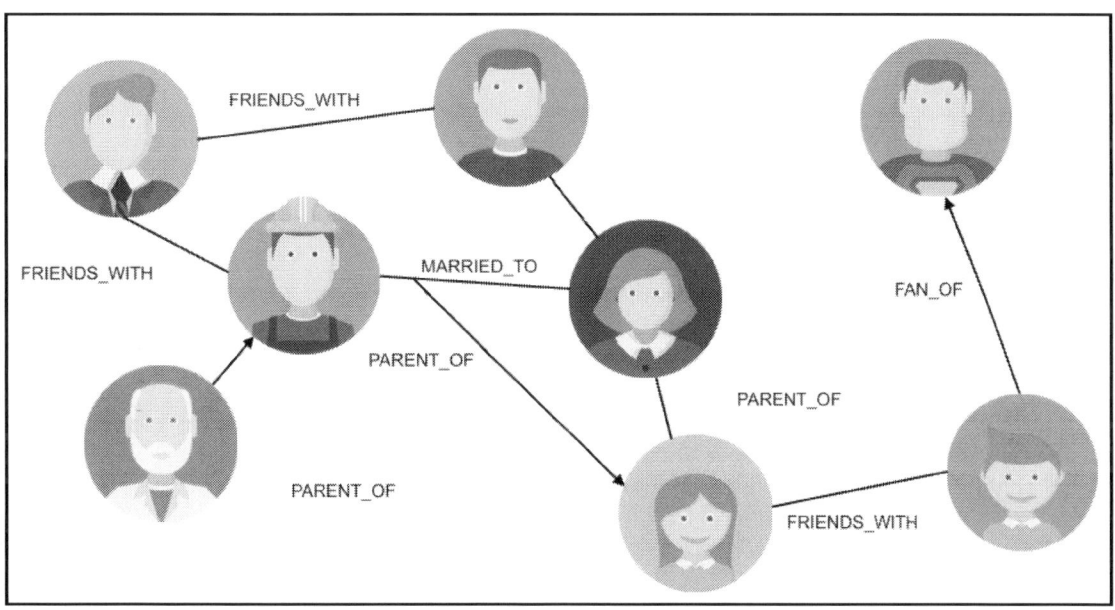

Here again, graphs allow us to see the data from a different perspective. For instance, we have seen this kind of information when looking at someone's profile on LinkedIn:

In that case, it tells us that the connected user (me) is just two connections away from Clark Kent. In other words, one person in my network is already connected to a person who is connected to Clark Kent. The following image illustrates this more clearly, in terms of **degrees of separation**:

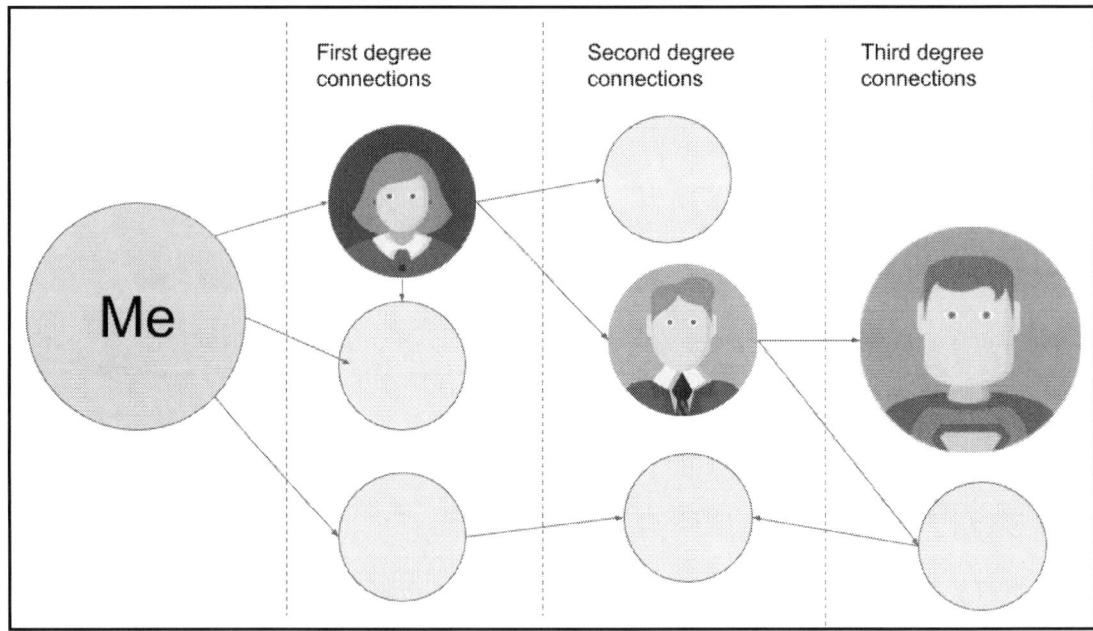

You've probably heard about the *Six Degrees of Separation* theory. In 1929, the Hungarian journalist Frigyes Karinthy proposed a theory according to which each person on Earth is at most six connections away from any other person. In other words, if you want to talk to one person, say Barack Obama, a friend of yours has a friend whose friend has a friend... who knows Barack Obama and can introduce you to him. According to Karinthy, this connection chain must contain less than six connections, or seven people in total, including you and Barack Obama.

Given that there are more than 7 billion human beings on Earth, that's a surprisingly small number! With the large databases that are available nowadays, such as the friendship connections from Facebook or email exchanges from Microsoft, researchers have tried to prove the preceding statement. From the Microsoft email database, for instance, it was shown in 2008 that the average degree of separation between 180 billion distinct pairs of people was around 6.6. But this is just an average, and the number of hops to connect two people could go up to 29 with that dataset.

Many other kinds of analyses can be performed over social graphs:

- **Node importance**: Again, it might be very useful to have an idea of which nodes (persons) are the most important. However, the definition of importance here will be different than in the case of a computer network, since it is very unlikely that a single person's retirement from social media makes the whole world collapse. However, *influencers* have a particular interest for marketing experts.
- **Community detection**: Also called clustering, is a way to find a group of nodes sharing some characteristics. For instance, finding users who share the same interests, or visit the same places, can be used to recommend products to them.
- **Link prediction**: With a graph, you can think of creating intelligent models to predict whether two entities are likely to be connected in the future. Here again, recommendation engines are one possible application of such a tool.

> You can find more information about the Facebook graph as an example at `https://developers.facebook.com/docs/graph-api`.

As you can see, networks of all kinds are very well suited to graph databases. But we can go far beyond that view and imagine all kinds of data as a graph, which will open up a lot of new perspectives.

Your data is also a graph

You may have noticed that in the previous image of a social graph, the edges have names. Indeed, some people are friends, while some others have a father/son relationship. Now, let's imagine we can have any kind of relationship, meaning we can start connecting different kinds of entities. For instance, a person is living in a particular country, so (s)he is connected to that country with a relationship of type `LIVES_IN`. Are you beginning to see the point? With that kind of reasoning, the world itself is a graph and your business is a subpart of it.

Graphs are about relationships, and the world is connected, meaning there are relationships everywhere. We'll talk about this in more detail in `Chapter 3`, *Empowering Your Business with Pure Cypher*, which is dedicated to knowledge graphs.

Graph databases allow you to model the data in that way: nodes, connected by relationships of some type. Let's see how to migrate data stored in relational databases to graph databases.

Moving from SQL to graph databases

Before going into detail about Neo4j, let's first have a look at the existing database models. We'll then focus on the most famous one, the relational model, and learn how to migrate from SQL to a graph database model.

Database models

Think about water: depending on the end goal, you will not use the same container. If you want to drink, you might use a glass of water but if you want to have a bath, you will probably choose another one. The choice of container will be different in each scenario. The problem is similar for data: without a proper container, there is nothing we can do with it and we need a proper container depending on the situation, which will not only store data but also contribute to solve the problem we have. This data container is the database.

Drawing an exhaustive list of database types on the market is not impossible but would go far beyond the scope of this book. However, I want to give some examples of the most popular ones, so that you can see where graph databases stand in the big picture:

- **Relational databases**: They are by far the most well known type of database. From *SQLite* to *MySQL* or *PostgreSQL*, they use a common query language, called **Structured Query Language (SQL)**, with some variations among the different implementations. They are well established and allow a clear *structure* of the data. However, they suffer from performance issues when the data grows and are surprisingly not that good at managing complex relationships, since the relationships require many joins between tables.
- **Document-oriented databases**: Document-oriented databases, part of the NoSQL (Not Only SQL) era, have gained increasing interest during the last few years. Contrary to relational databases, they can manage *flexible* data models and are known for better scaling with a large amount of data. Examples of NoSQL databases include *MongoDB* and *Cassandra*, but you can find many more on the market.
- **Key-value stores**: *Redis*, *RocksDB*, and *Amazon DynamoDB* are examples of key-value databases. They are very simple and known to be very fast, but are not well suited to store complex data.

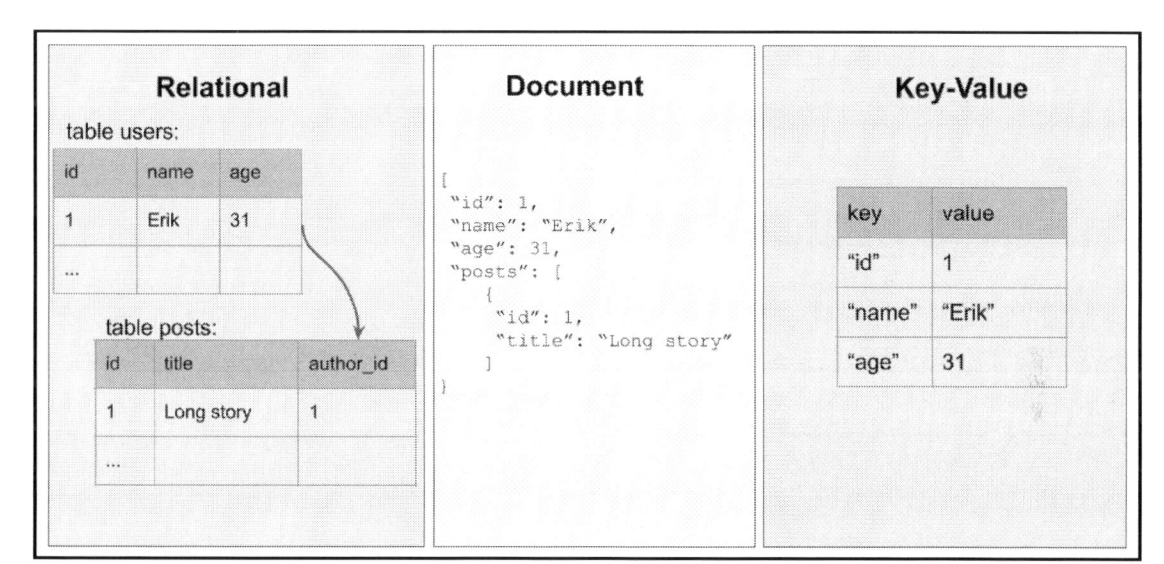

Here is how the different databases can be viewed in a figurative representation:

Relational

table users:

id	name	age
1	Erik	31
...		

table posts:

id	title	author_id
1	Long story	1
...		

Document

```
{
  "id": 1,
  "name": "Erik",
  "age": 31,
  "posts": [
    {
      "id": 1,
      "title": "Long story"
    }
  ]
}
```

Key-Value

key	value
"id"	1
"name"	"Erik"
"age"	31

Graph databases try to bring the best of each world into a single place by being quite simple to use, flexible, and very performant when it comes to relationships.

SQL and joins

Let's briefly focus on relational databases. Imagine we want to create a *Question and Answer* website (similar to the invaluable Stack Overflow). The requirements are the following:

- Users should be able to log in.
- Once logged in, users can post questions.
- Users can post answers to existing questions.
- Questions need to have *tags* to better identify which question is relevant for which user.

Graph Databases

As developers or data scientists, who are used to SQL, we would then naturally start thinking in terms of tables. Which table(s) should I create to store this data? Well, first we will look for *entities* that seem to be the core of the business. In this QA website, we can identify the following:

- **Users**, with attributes: ID, name, email, password
- **Questions**: ID, title, text
- **Answers**: ID, text
- **Tags**: ID, text

With those entities, we now need to create the *relationships* between them. To do so, we can use *foreign keys*. For instance, the question has been asked by a given user, so we can just add a new column to the `question` table, `author_id`, referencing the `user` table. The same applies for the answers: they are written by a given user, so we add an `author_id` column to the `Answer` table:

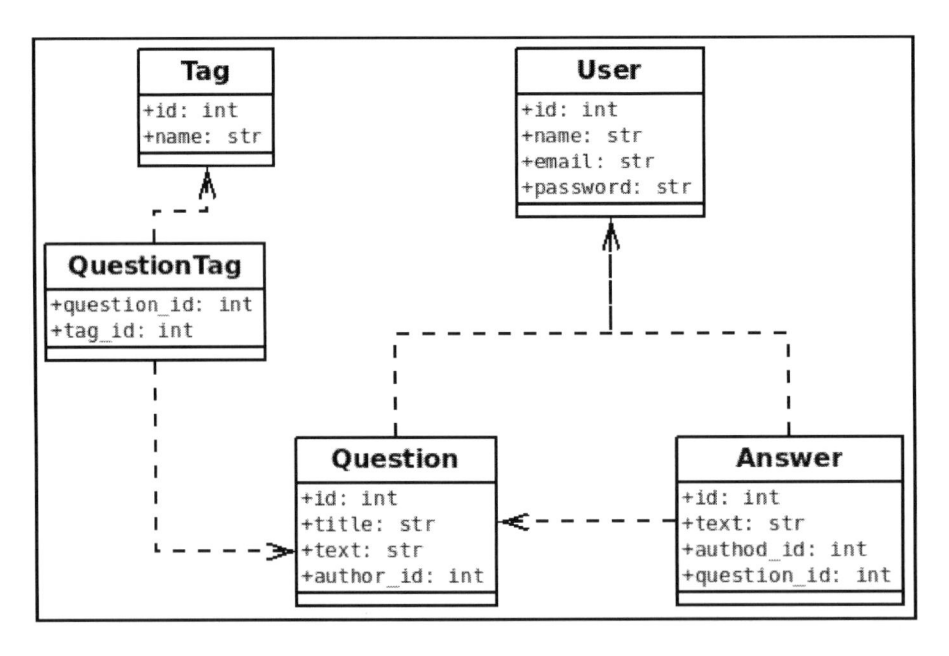

```
Tag
+id: int
+name: str

User
+id: int
+name: str
+email: str
+password: str

QuestionTag
+question_id: int
+tag_id: int

Question
+id: int
+title: str
+text: str
+author_id: int

Answer
+id: int
+text: str
+authod_id: int
+question_id: int
```

It becomes more complicated for tags, since one question can have multiple tags and a single tag can be assigned to many questions. We are in the many-to-many relationship type, which requires adding a *join table*, a table that is just there to remember that kind of relationship. This is the case of the `QuestionTag` table in the preceding diagram; it just holds the relationship between tags and questions.

[22]

It's all about relationships

The previous exercise probably looks easy to you, because you have followed lectures or tutorials about SQL and use it pretty often in your daily work. But let's be honest, the first time you face a problem and have to create the data model that will allow you to solve it, you will probably draw something that looks like the diagram in the following image, right?

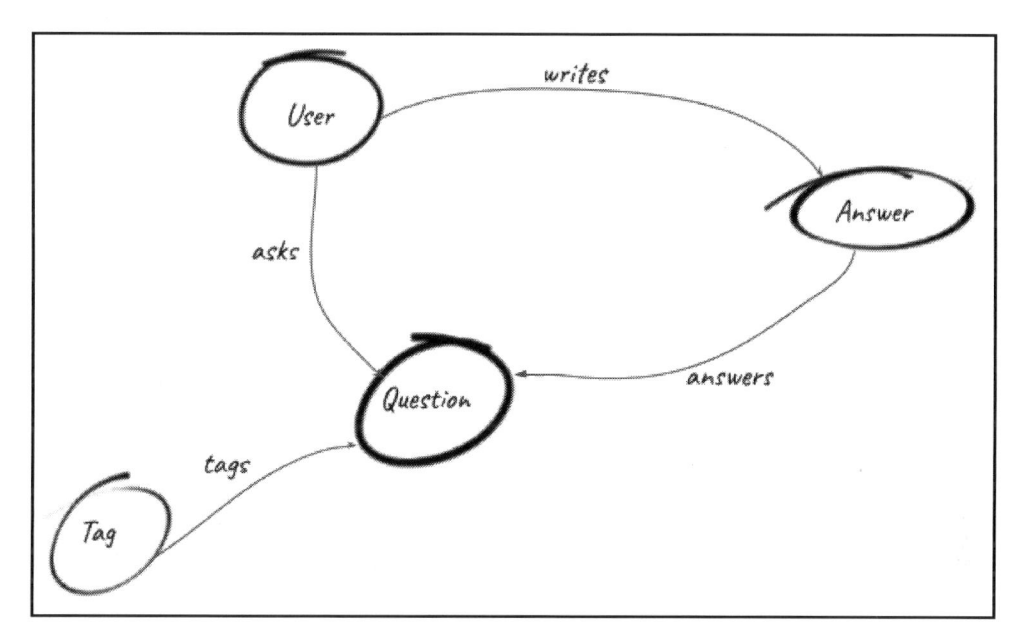

This is one of the powers of graph databases:

Neo4j, as a graph database, allows you to create vertices, or nodes, and the relationships connecting them. The next section summarizes how the different entities in the Neo4j ecosystem are related to each other and how we can structure our data in a graph.

> **TIP:** The whiteboard model is your data model.

Neo4j – the nodes, relationships, and properties model

Neo4j is a Java-based highly scalable graph database whose code is publicly available on GitHub at `github.com/neo4j/neo4j`. This section describes its building blocks and its main cases, but also the cases where it won't perform well because no system is perfect.

Building blocks

As we discussed with graph theory, a graph database such as Neo4j is made of at least two essential building blocks:

- Nodes
- Relationships between nodes:

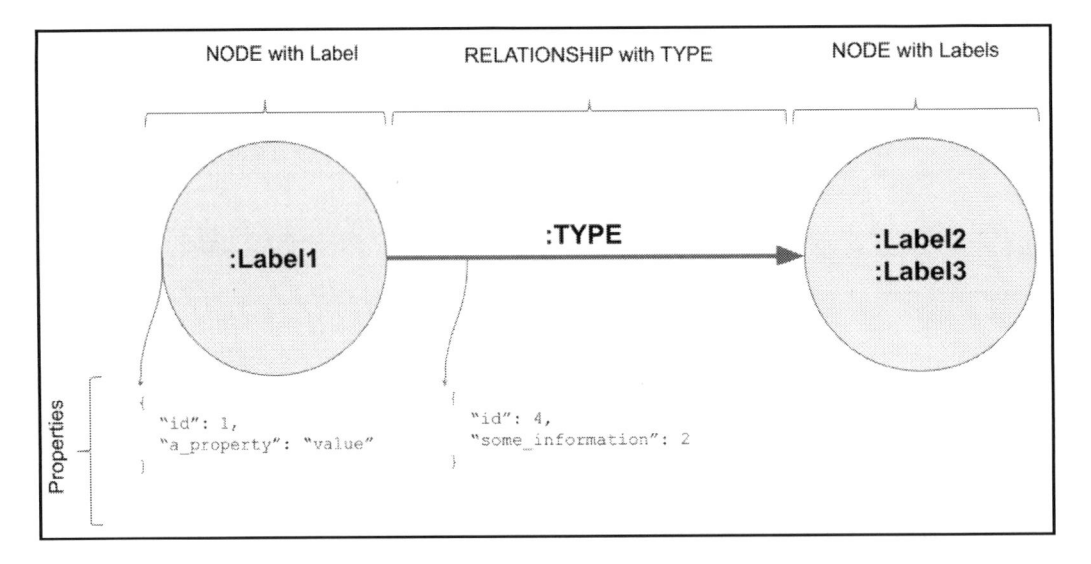

> **TIP:** Unlike SQL, Neo4j does not require a fixed and predetermined schema: nodes and relationships can be added on demand.

Let's look at each of of these in detail.

Nodes

In Neo4j, vertices are called **nodes**. Nodes can be of different types, like `Question` and `Answer` were in our former example. In order to differentiate those entities, nodes can have a **label**. If we continue the parallel with SQL, all nodes with a given label would be in the same table. But the analogy ends here, because nodes can have **multiple labels**. For instance, Clark Kent is a journalist, but he is also a superhero; the node representing this person can then have the two labels: `Journalist` and `SuperHero`.

Labels define the kind of entity the node belongs to. It is also important to store the characteristics of that entity. In Neo4j, this is done by attaching **properties** to nodes.

Relationships

Like nodes, relationships carry different pieces of information. A relationship between two persons can be of type `MARRIED_TO` or `FRIEND_WITH` or many other types of relationship. That's why Neo4j's relationships must have one and only one **type**.

One of the main powers of Neo4j is that relationships also have properties. For instance, when adding the relationship `MARRIED_TO` between two persons, we could add the wedding date, place, whether they signed a prenuptial agreement, and so on, as relationship properties.

> Be careful: even though we discussed undirected graphs earlier, in Neo4j, all relationships are oriented!

Properties

Properties are saved as key-value pairs where the key is a string capturing the property name. Each value can then be of any of the following types:

- Number: *Integer* or *Float*
- Text: *String*
- Boolean: *Boolean*
- Time properties: *Date*, *Time*, *DateTime*, *LocalTime*, *LocalDateTime*, or *Duration*
- Spatial: *Point*

Internally, properties are saved as a `LinkedList`, each element containing a key-value pair. The node or relationship is then linked to the first element of its property list.

> Naming conventions: Node labels are written in *UpperCamelCase* while relationship names use UPPER_CASE with words separated by an underscore. Property names usually use the *lowerCamelCase* convention.

SQL to Neo4j translator

Here are a few guidelines to be able to easily go from your relational model to a graph model:

SQL world	Neo4j world
Table	Node label
Row	Node
Column	Node property
Foreign key	Relationship
Join table	Relationship
NULL	Do not store null values inside properties; just omit the property

Applying those guidelines to the SQL model in the question and answer table diagram, we built up the graph model displayed in the whiteboard model for our simple Q&A website, earlier in the chapter. The full graph model can be seen as follows:

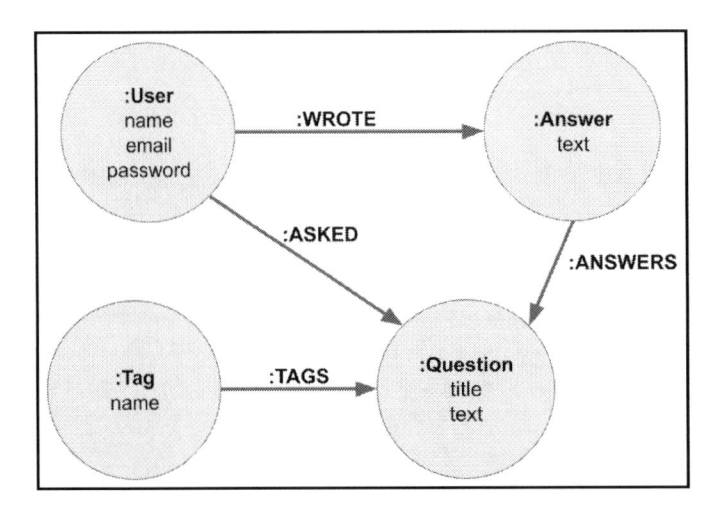

> **TIP:** You can use the online tool **Arrows**, which enables you to draw a graph diagram and export it to Cypher, the Neo4j query language:
> `http://www.apcjones.com/arrows`.

Neo4j use cases

Like any other tool, Neo4j is very good in some situations, but not well suited to others. The basic principle is that Neo4j provides amazing performance for graph traversal. Everything requiring jumping from one node to another is incredibly fast.

On the other hand, Neo4j is probably not the best tool if you want to do the following:

- Perform full DB scans, for instance, answering the question "What is?"
- Do full table aggregates
- Store large documents: the key-values properties list needs to be kept small (let's say no more than around 10 properties)

Some of those pain points can be addressed with a proper graph model. For instance, instead of saving all information as node properties, can we consider moving some of them to another node with a relationship between them? Depending on the kind of requests you are interested in, the graph schema most suited to your application may differ. Before going into the details of graph modeling, we need to stop briefly and and talk about the different kinds of graph properties which will also influence our choice.

Understanding graph properties

Graphs are classified into several categories, depending on the properties of the connections between nodes. These categories are important to consider when modeling your data as a graph, and even more so when you want to run algorithms on them, because the behavior of the algorithm might change and create unexpected results in some situations. Let's discover some of those properties with examples.

Graph Databases

Directed versus undirected

So far, we've only talked about graphs as a set of connected nodes. Those connections can be different depending on whether you are going from node *A* to node *B* or vice versa. For instance, some streets can only be driven in one direction, right? Or, the fact that you are following someone on Twitter (there is a *Follows* relationship from you to that user) doesn't mean that user is also following you. That's the reason why some relationships are **directed**. On the contrary, a relationship of type *married to* is naturally **undirected**, if *A* is married to *B*, usually *B* is also married to *A*:

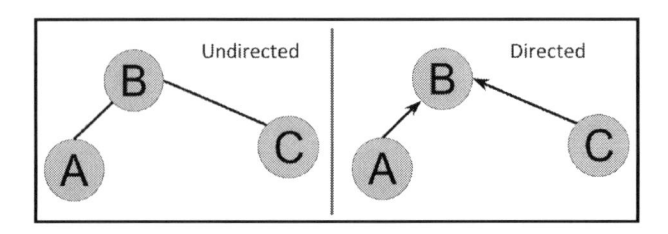

In the right-hand side graph, directed, the transition between B and A is not allowed in that direction

> In Neo4j, all relationships are directed. However, Cypher allows you to take this direction into account, or not. That will be explained in more detail in Chapter 2, *The Cypher Query Language*.

Weighted versus unweighted

As well as direction, relationships can also carry more information. Indeed, in a road network for instance, not all streets have the same importance in a routing system. They have different lengths or occupancy during peak hours, meaning the travel time will be very different from one street to another. The way to model this fact with graphs is to assign a **weight** to each edge:

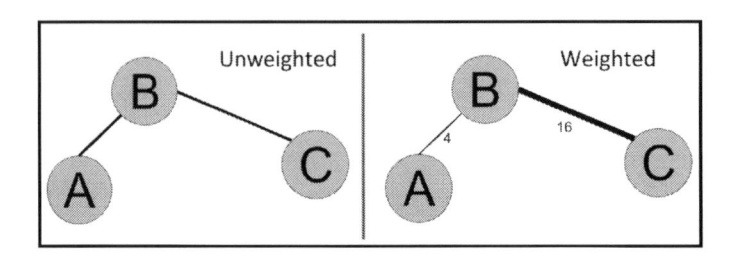

Chapter 1

In the weighted graph, relationships have weights 16 and 4

Algorithms such as shortest path algorithms take this weight into account to compute a *shortest weighted path*.

This is not only important for road networks. In a computer network, the distance between units may also have its own importance in terms of connection speed. In social networks, distance is often not the most important property to quantify the strength of a relationship, but we can think of other metrics. For instance, how long have those two people been connected? Or when was the last time user *A* reacted to a post of user *B*?

> Weights can represent anything related to the relationship between two nodes, such as distance, time, or field-dependent metrics such as the interaction strength between two atoms in a molecule.

Cyclic versus acyclic

A cycle is a loop. A graph is cyclic if you can find at least one path starting from one node and going back to that exact same node.

As you can imagine, it's important to be aware of the presence of cycles in a graph, since they can create infinite loops in a graph traversal algorithm, if we do not pay enough attention to it. The following image shows an acyclic graph versus a cyclic graph:

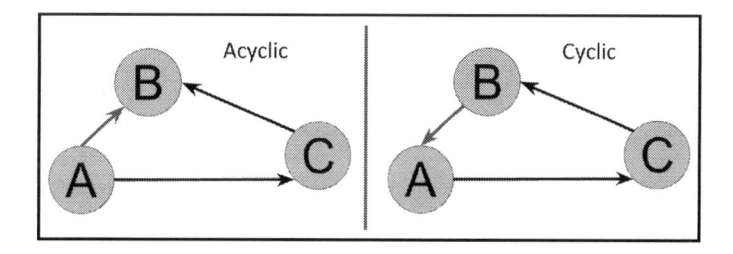

> All those properties are not self-exclusive and can be combined. Especially, we can have **directed acyclic graphs (DAG)**, which usually behave nicely.

Graph Databases

Dense versus sparse

Graph density is another property that is important to have in mind. It is related to the average number of connections for each node. In the next diagram, the left graph only has three connections for four nodes, whereas the right graph has six connections for the same amount of nodes, meaning the latter is denser than the former:

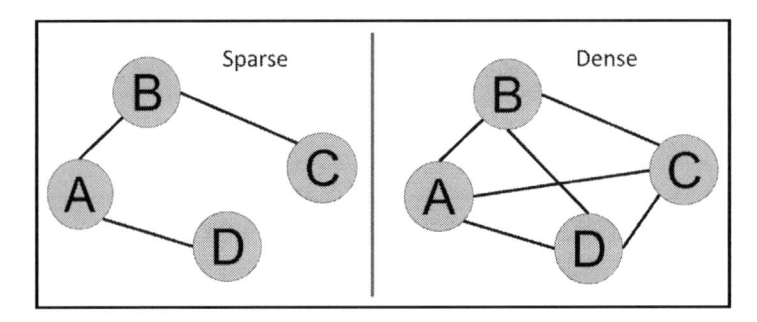

Graph traversal

But why worry about density? It is important to realize that everything within graph databases is about **graph traversal**, *jumping* from one node to another by following an edge. This can become very time-consuming with a very dense graph, especially when traversing the graph in a breadth-first way. The following image shows the graph traversals in which breadth-first search is compared to depth-first search:

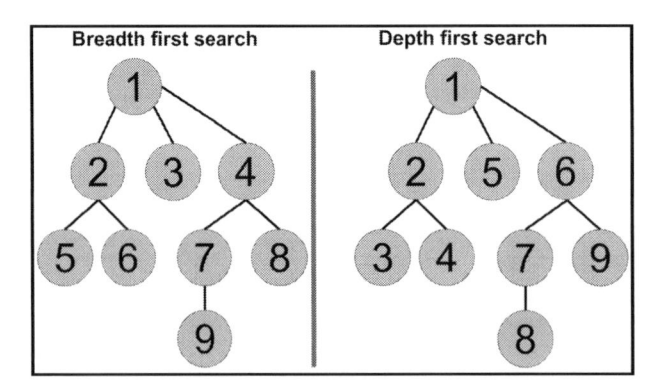

[30]

Connected versus disconnected

Last but not least is the notion of connectivity or a connected graph. In the next diagram, it is always possible to go from one vertex to another, whatever pair of vertices is considered. This graph is said to be *connected*. On the other side of the figure, you can see that D is isolated - there is no way to go from D to A, for example. This graph is disconnected, and we can even say that it has two *components*. We will cover the analysis of this kind of structure in Chapter 7, *Community Detection and Similarity Measures*. The following image shows connected versus disconnected graphs:

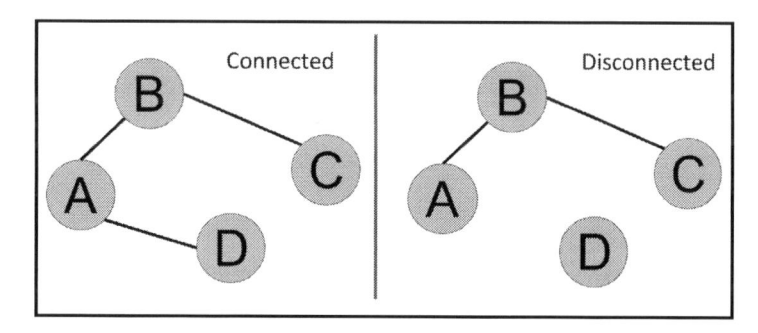

This is a non-exhaustive list of graph properties, but they are the main ones we will have to worry about within our graph database adventure. Some of them are important when creating the whiteboard graph model for our data, as we will discuss in the next section.

Considerations for graph modeling in Neo4j

The whiteboard model for our simple Q&A website is the very first approach to this problem. Depending on the kind of questions you want your application to answer, and in order to take full advantage of Neo4j, the schema can be very different.

> **TIP**
> As a rule of thumb, we consider nodes as entities or objects, while relationships are verbs.

Relationship orientation

As we discussed earlier in the chapter, relationships in Neo4j are oriented. However, with Cypher, we can build queries that are orientation-independent (see `Chapter 2`, *The Cypher Query Language*). In that scenario, a relationship that is imperatively bijective should not be stored twice in the database. In short, a friendship relationship should be created only in one direction, as illustrated in the following image:

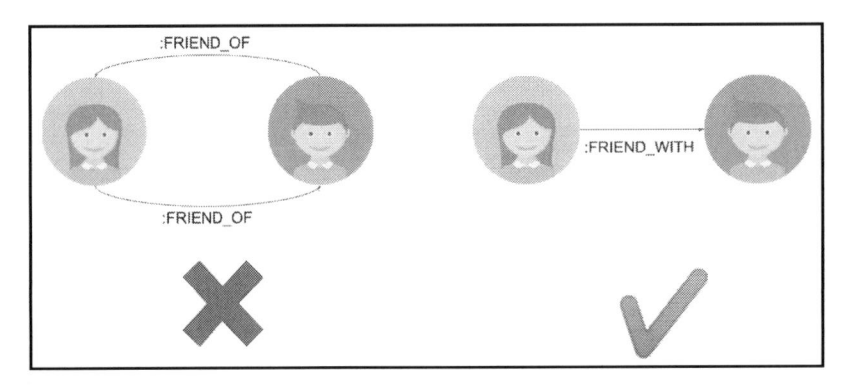

Node or property?

Another question that arises quite often and early in the choice of graph model is whether a (categorical) characteristic should be stored as a node property, or whether it should have its own node.

Nodes are the following:

- **Explicit**: Nodes appear in the graph schema, which makes them more visible than properties.
- **Performant**: If we need to find nodes sharing the same characteristics, it will be much faster with a node than by filtering on properties.

On the other hand, properties are the following:

- **Simpler**: It's just a property with a value, not a complex node and relationship structure. If you don't need to perform special analysis on the property and just want it to be available when working on the node it belongs to, a property is just fine.

- **Indexable**: Neo4j supports indexing for properties. It is used to find the first node in a graph traversal and is very efficient (more details in `Chapter 2`, *The Cypher Query Language*).

As you can see, there is no universal answer to this question, and the solution will depend on your use case. It is usually recommended to list them and try to write and test the associated queries in order to make sure you are not falling into a Neo4j pitfall.

For more information and more examples on graph modeling, I encourage you to have a look at *Neo4j Graph Data Modeling* (see the *Further reading* section).

Summary

In this chapter, we discussed the mathematical definition of a graph and how it is related to graph databases. We then moved on to the specific instance of graph databases we will use throughout this book, Neo4j. We've learned about its building blocks, nodes having labels and properties, and relationships that must have a type and, optionally, some properties as well. We concluded with some important explanations about different types of graphs, weighted, directed, cyclic, or connected, and how this can help in defining the data model best suited to a given use case.

In the next chapter, we are going to look at **Cypher**, the query language used by Neo4j, and how we can feed the database and retrieve data from it.

Further reading

- If you want to learn more about the mathematics behind graph theory, you can start with *Graph Theory with Applications, J.A. Bondy and U.S.R. Murty, Elsevier*, whose first edition is available for free on the web, for instance at `https://www.freetechbooks.com/graph-theory-with-applications-t559`.
- For more information about choosing the appropriate schema for your graph data, see *Neo4j Graph Data Modeling, M. Lal, Packt Publishing*.
- Some references to learn more about degrees of separation:
    - Paper about the Microsoft study: *Planetary-Scale Views on an Instant-Messaging Network* by Jure Leskovec and Eric Horvitz
    - Facebook research blog post: `https://research.fb.com/blog/2016/02/three-and-a-half-degrees-of-separation/`

2
The Cypher Query Language

Cypher is the language used to interact with Neo4j. Originally created by Neo4j for Neo4j, it has been open sourced as openCypher and is now used by other graph database engines such as `RedisGraph`. It is also part of the **Graph Query Language (GQL)** association, whose goal is to build a common graph database query language – like SQL is for relational databases. In any case, it is a good starting point to understand how to query graph databases due to its visual aspect: nodes and relationships can be identified quickly by looking at the query.

In this chapter, we will review the basics of Cypher, which will be used in this book: CRUD methods, bulk importing data with various formats, and pattern matching to extract exactly the data we need from a graph. It is a good place to introduce the **Awesome Procedures On Cypher (APOC)** plugin, which is an extension of Cypher introducing powerful methods for data imports, and more. We will also take a look at more advanced tools such as the Cypher query planner. It will help us to understand the different steps of a query and how we can tune it for faster execution. Finally, we'll discuss Neo4j and Cypher performance with a social (Facebook-like) graph.

The following topics will be covered in this chapter:

- Creating nodes and relationships
- Updating and deleting nodes and relationships
- Using the aggregation function
- Importing data from CSV or JSON
- Measuring performance and tuning your query for speed

The Cypher Query Language

Technical requirements

The required technologies and installations for this chapter are as follows:

- Neo4j 3.5
- Neo4j Desktop 1.2
- The `APOC` plugin installation instructions are available here: https://neo4j.com/docs/labs/apoc/current/introduction/. We recommend installing directly via Neo4j Desktop, the easiest method (version ≥ 3.5.0.3).
- Neo4j Python driver (optional): `pip install neo4j`
- The data files used in this chapter are available at https://github.com/PacktPublishing/Hands-On-Graph-Analytics-with-Neo4j/tree/master/ch2.

Creating nodes and relationships

Unlike other query languages for graph databases such as Gremlin (https://tinkerpop.apache.org/gremlin.html) or AQL (ArangoDB), Cypher was built to have a syntax similar to SQL, in order to ease the transition for developers and data scientists used to the structured query language.

> Like many tools in the Neo4j universe, Cypher's name comes from the movie *The Matrix* released in 1999: Neo is the main character. Apoc is also a character from this movie.

Managing databases with Neo4j Desktop

It is assumed you already have experience with Neo4j Desktop. This is the easiest tool to manage your Neo4j graphs, the installed plugins, and applications. I recommend creating a new project for this book, in which we are going to create several databases. In the following screenshot, I have created a project named **Hands-On-Graph-Analytics-with-Neo4j**, containing two databases: **Test graph** and **USA**:

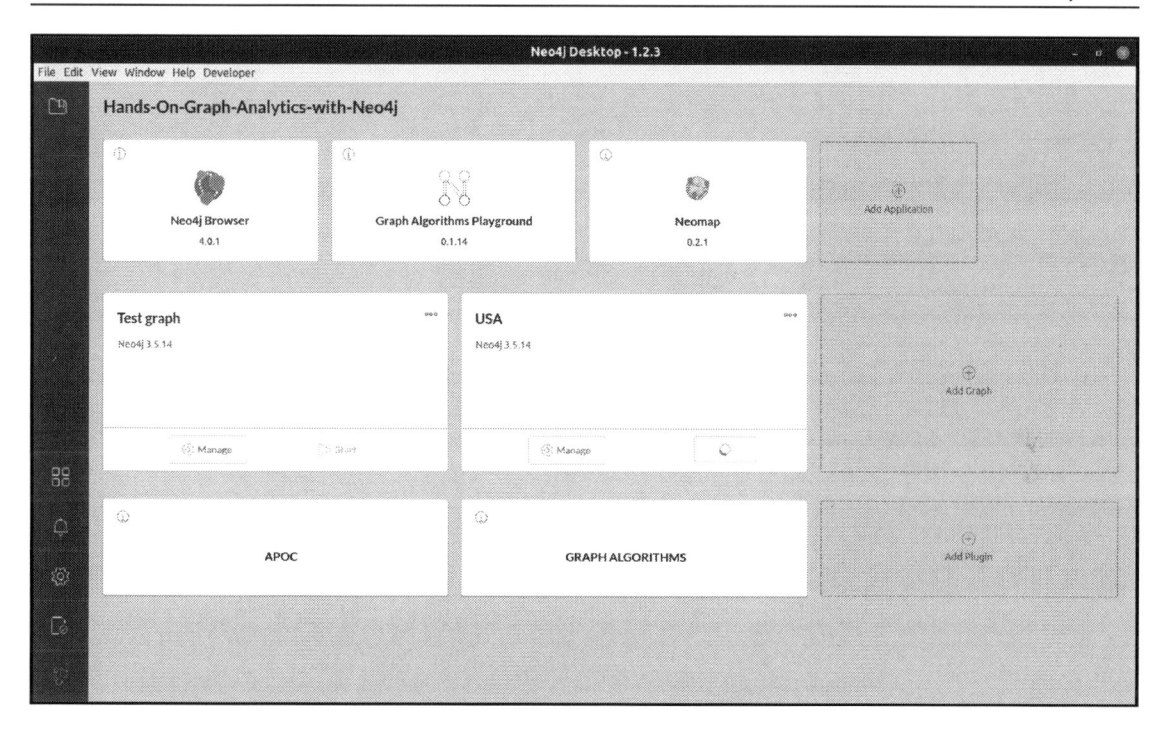

Throughout this book, we will use Neo4j Browser, which is an application installed by default in Neo4j Desktop. Within this application, you can write and execute Cypher queries, but also visualize the results in different formats: a visual graph, JSON, or tabular data.

Creating a node

The simplest instruction to create a node is the following:

```
CREATE ()
```

It creates a node, without a label or a relationship.

> **TIP**
> We can recognize the () pattern that is used to identify nodes within Cypher. Every time you want a node, you will have to use brackets.

The Cypher Query Language

We can check the content of the database after this statement with a simple `MATCH` query that will return all nodes of the graph:

```
MATCH (n)
RETURN n
```

Here, we are selecting nodes (because of the use of `()`), and we are also giving a name, an alias, to these nodes: n. Thanks to this alias, we can refer to those nodes in later parts of the query, here only in the `RETURN` statement.

The result of this query is shown here:

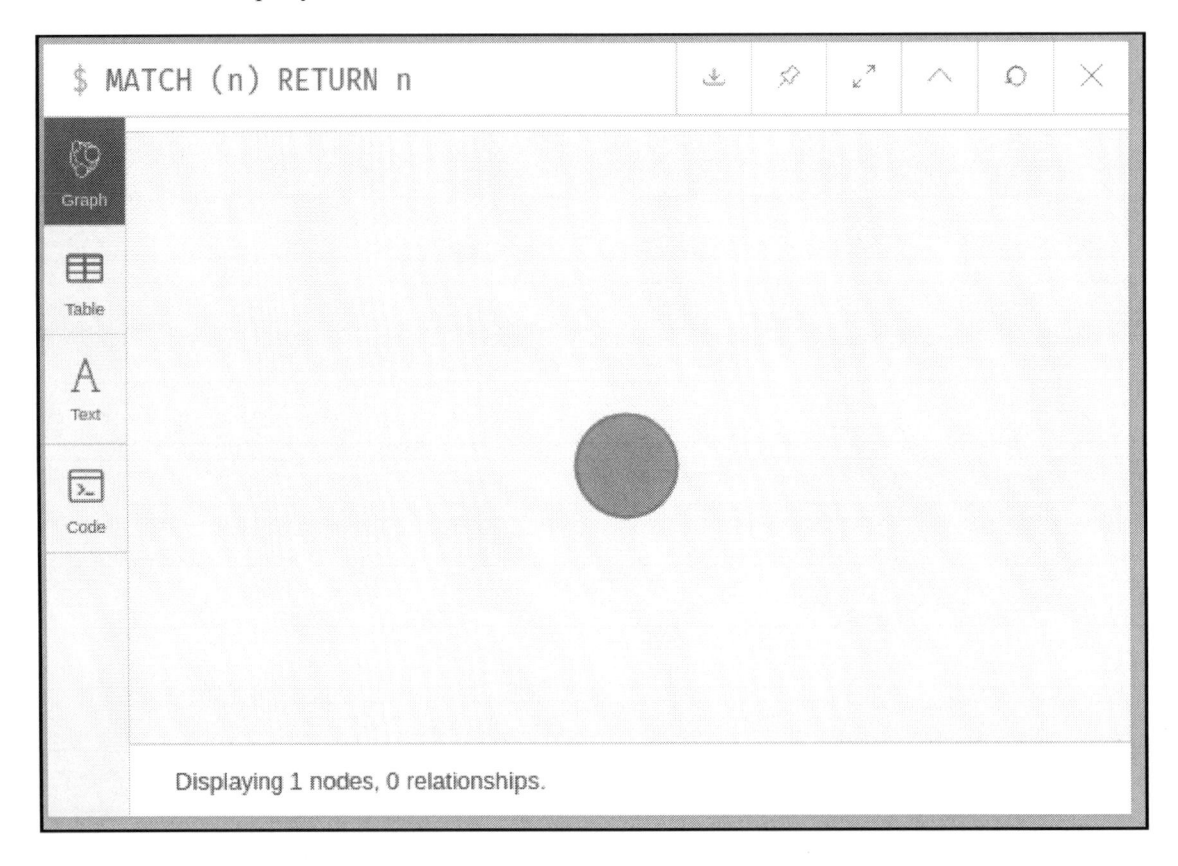

OK, great. But a single node with no label nor properties is not sufficient for most use cases. If we want to assign a label to a node when creating it, here is the syntax to use:

```
CREATE (:Label)
```

That's already better! Now, let's create properties when creating the node:

```
CREATE (:Label {property1: "value", property2: 13})
```

We'll see in later sections how to modify an existing node: adding or removing labels, and adding, updating, or deleting properties.

Selecting nodes

We've already talked about the simple query here, which selects all nodes inside the database:

```
MATCH (n)
RETURN n
```

> **TIP**
> Be careful, if your database is large, this query is likely to make your browser or application crash. It is better to do what you would do with SQL, and add a `LIMIT` statement:
>
> ```
> MATCH (n)
> RETURN n
> LIMIT 10
> ```

Let's try to be more specific in the data we want to select (filter) and the properties we need in the `RETURN` statement.

Filtering

Usually, we don't want to select *all* nodes of the database, but only those matching some criteria. For instance, we might want to retrieve only the nodes with a given label. In that case, we'd use this:

```
MATCH (n:Label)
RETURN n
```

Or, if you want to select only nodes with a given property, use this:

```
MATCH (n {id: 1})
RETURN n
```

The Cypher Query Language

The `WHERE` statement is also useful for filtering nodes. It actually allows more complex comparisons compared to the `{ }` notation. We can, for instance, use inequality comparison (greater than >, lower than <, greater or equal to >=, or lower or equal to <= statements), but also Boolean operations like `AND` and `OR`:

```
MATCH (n:Label)
WHERE n.property > 1 AND n.otherProperty <= 0.8
RETURN n
```

> It might be surprising to you that when selecting nodes, the browser also displays relationships between them when we have not asked it to do so. This comes from a setting in Neo4j Browser, whose default behavior is to enable the visualization of node connections. This can be disabled by unchecking the **Connect result nodes** setting.

Returning properties

So far, we've returned the whole node, with all properties associated with it. If for your application, you are interested only in some properties of the matched nodes, you can reduce the size of the result set by specifying the properties to return by using the following query:

```
MATCH (n)
RETURN n.property1, n.property2
```

With this syntax, we don't have access to the graph output in Neo4j Browser anymore, as it cannot access the node object, but we have a much simpler table output.

Creating a relationship

In order to create a relationship, we have to tell Neo4j about its start and end node, meaning the nodes need to be already in the database when creating the relationship. There are two possible solutions:

- Create nodes and the relationship(s) between them in one pass:

    ```
    CREATE (n:Label {id: 1})
    CREATE (m:Label {id: 2})
    CREATE (n)-[:RELATED_TO]->(m)
    ```

- Create the nodes (if they don't already exist):

    ```
    CREATE (:Label {id: 3})
    CREATE (:Label {id: 4})
    ```

And then create the relationship. In that case, since the relationship is created in another query (another namespace), we need to first MATCH the nodes of interest:

```
MATCH (a {id: 3})
MATCH (b {id: 4})
CREATE (a)-[:RELATED_TO]->(b)
```

> **TIP**: While nodes are identified with brackets, (), relationships are characterized by square brackets, [].

If we check the content of our graph after the first query, here is the result:

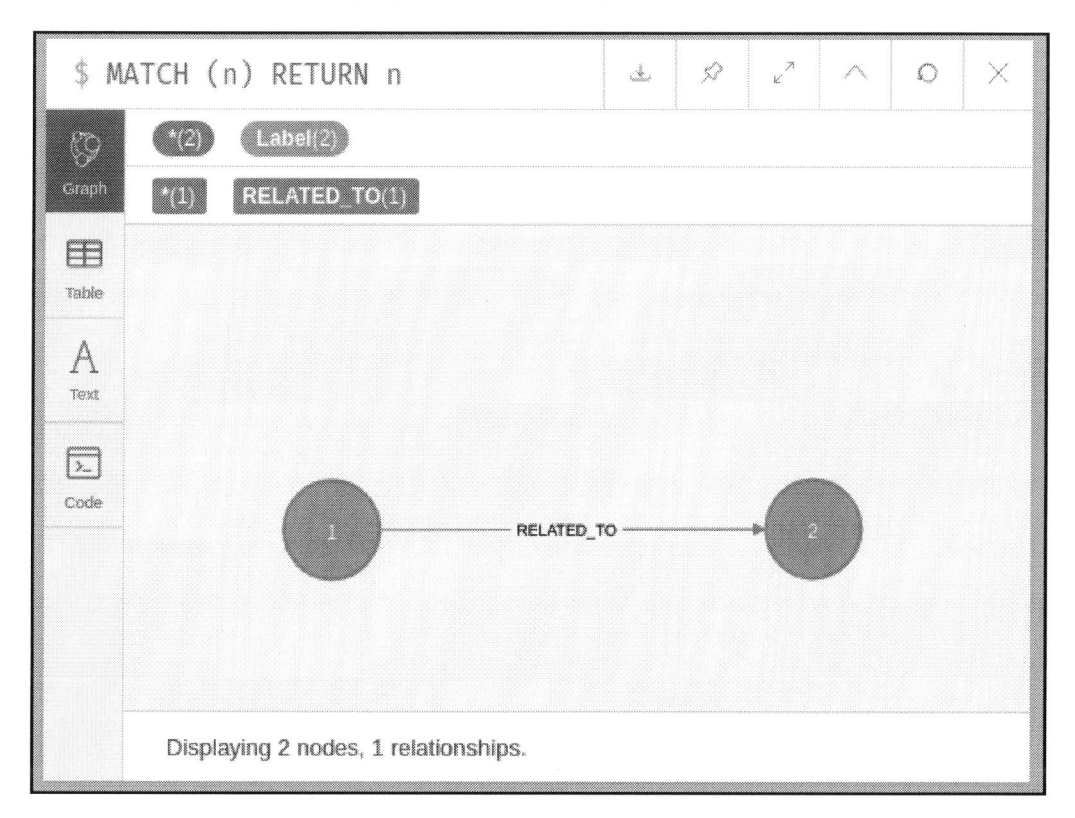

The Cypher Query Language

Reminder: while specifying a node label when creating a node is not mandatory, relationships *must* have a type. The following query is invalid: `CREATE (n)-[]->(m)` and leads to following `Neo.ClientError.Statement.SyntaxError`:

```
Exactly one relationship type must be specified for CREATE. Did you forget
to prefix your relationship type with a : (line 3, column 11 (offset: 60))?
```

Selecting relationships

We would like to write queries such as the following one, similar to the one we write for nodes but with square brackets, `[]`, instead of brackets, `()`:

```
MATCH [r]
RETURN r
```

But this query results in an error. Relationships cannot be retrieved in the same way as nodes. If you want to see the relationship properties in a simple way, you can use either of the following syntaxes:

```
// no filtering
MATCH ()-[r]-()
RETURN r

// filtering on relationship type
MATCH ()-[r:REL_TYPE]-()
RETURN r

// filtering on relationship property and returning a subset of its
properties
MATCH ()-[r]-()
WHERE r.property > 10
RETURN r.property
```

We will see how this works in detail in the *Pattern matching and data retrieval* section later on.

The MERGE keyword

The Cypher documentation describes the behavior of the MERGE command very well:

> MERGE *either matches existing nodes and binds them, or it creates new data and binds that. It's like a combination of* MATCH *and* CREATE *that additionally allows you to specify what happens if the data was matched or created.*

Let's see an example:

```
MERGE (n:Label {id: 1})
ON CREATE SET n.timestamp_created = timestamp()
ON MATCH SET n.timestamp_last_update = timestamp()
```

Here, we are trying to access a node with Label and a single property id, with a value of 1. If such a node already exists in the graph, the subsequent operations will be performed using that node. This statement is then equivalent to a MATCH in that case. However, if the node with label Label and id=1 doesn't exist, then it will be created, hence the parallel with the CREATE statement.

The two other optional statements are also important:

- ON CREATE SET will be executed if and only if the node was not found in the database and a creation process had to be performed.
- ON MATCH SET will only be executed if the node already exists in the graph.

In this example, I use those two statements to remember when the node was created and when it was last seen in such a query.

You are now able to create nodes and relationships, assigning label(s) and properties to them. The next section will be dedicated to other kinds of CRUD operations that can be performed on these objects: *update* and *delete*.

Updating and deleting nodes and relationships

Creating objects is not sufficient for a database to be useful. It also needs to be able to do the following:

- Update existing objects with new information
- Delete objects that are no longer relevant
- Read data from the database

This section deals with the first two bullet points, while the last one will be covered in the following section.

Updating objects

There is no `UPDATE` keyword with Cypher. To update an object, node, or relationship, we'll use the `SET` statement only.

Updating an existing property or creating a new one

If you want to update an existing property or add a new one, it's as simple as the following:

```
MATCH (n {id: 1})
SET n.name = "Node 1"
RETURN n
```

The `RETURN` statement is not mandatory, but it is a way to check the query went well, for instance, checking the `Table` tab of the result cell:

```
{
  "name": "Node 1",
  "id": 1
}
```

Updating all properties of the node

If we want to update all properties of the node, there is a practical shortcut:

```
MATCH (n {id: 1})
SET n = {id: 1, name: "My name", age: 30, address: "Earth, Universe"}
RETURN n
```

[44]

This leads to the following result:

```
{
    "name": "My name",
    "address": "Earth, Universe",
    "id": 1,
    "age": 30
}
```

In some cases, it might be painful to repeat existing properties to be sure not to erase the `id`, for instance. In that case, the `+=` syntax is the way to go:

```
MATCH (n {id: 1})
SET n += {gender: "F", name: "Another name"}
RETURN n
```

This again works as expected, adding the `gender` property and updating the value of the `name` field:

```
{
    "name": "Another name",
    "address": "Earth, Universe",
    "id": 1,
    "gender": "F",
    "age": 30
}
```

Updating node labels

On top of adding, updating, and deleting properties, we can do the same with node labels. If you need to add a label to an existing node, you can use the following syntax:

```
MATCH (n {id: 1})
SET n:AnotherLabel
RETURN labels(n)
```

Here, again, the RETURN statement is just there to make sure everything went well. The result is as follows:

```
["Label", "AnotherLabel"]
```

On the contrary, if you mistakenly set a label to a node, you can REMOVE it:

```
MATCH (n {id: 1})
REMOVE n:AnotherLabel
RETURN labels(n)
```

And we are back to the situation where the node with `id:1` has a single label called `Label`.

Deleting a node property

We briefly talked about `NULL` values in the previous chapter. In Neo4j, `NULL` values are not saved in the properties list. An absence of a property means it's null. So, deleting a property is as simple as setting it to a `NULL` value:

```
MATCH (n {id: 1})
SET n.age = NULL
RETURN n
```

Here's the result:

```
{
  "name": "Another name",
  "address": "Earth, Universe",
  "id": 1,
  "gender": "F"
}
```

The other solution is to use the `REMOVE` keyword:

```
MATCH (n {id: 1})
REMOVE n.address
RETURN n
```

The result would be as follows:

```
{
 "gender": "F",
 "name": "Another name",
 "id": 1
}
```

If you want to remove all properties from the node, you will have to assign it an empty map like so:

```
MATCH (n {id: 2})
SET n = {}
RETURN n
```

Deleting objects

To delete an object, we will use the `DELETE` statement:

- For a relationship:

  ```
  MATCH ()-[r:REL_TYPE {id: 1}]-()
  DELETE r
  ```

- For a node:

  ```
  MATCH (n {id: 1})
  DELETE n
  ```

> Deleting a node requires it to be detached from any relationship (Neo4j can't contain a relationship with a `NULL` extremum).

If you try to delete a node that is still involved in a relationship, you will receive a `Neo.ClientError.Schema.ConstraintValidationFailed` error, with the following message:

```
Cannot delete node<41>, because it still has relationships. To delete this
node, you must first delete its relationships.
```

We need to first delete the relationship, and then the node in this way:

```
MATCH (n {id:1})-[r:REL_TYPE]-()
DELETE r, n
```

But here again, Cypher provides a practical shortcut for this – `DETACH DELETE` – which will perform the preceding operation:

```
MATCH (n {id: 1})
DETACH DELETE n
```

You now have all the tools to in hand to create, update, delete, and read simple patterns from Neo4j. In the next section, we will focus on the pattern matching technique, to read data from Neo4j in the most effective way.

Pattern matching and data retrieval

The full power of graph databases, and Neo4j in particular, lies in their ability to go from one node to another by following relationships in a super-fast way. In this section, we explain how to read data from Neo4j through pattern matching and hence take full advantage of the graph structure.

Pattern matching

Let's take the following query:

```
MATCH ()-[r]-()
RETURN r
```

When we write these kinds of queries, we are actually performing what is called *pattern matching* with graph databases. The following schema explains this concept:

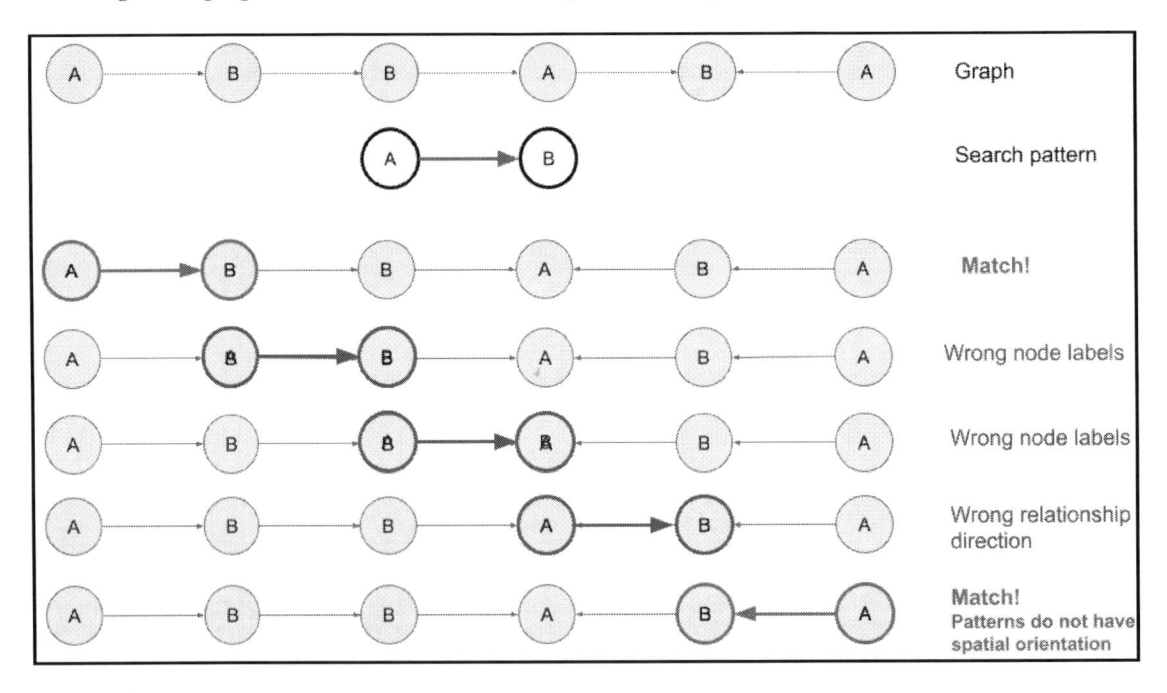

Chapter 2

In this scenario, we have a directed graph made of nodes with labels *A* or *B*. We are looking for the sequence *A -> B*. Pattern matching consists of moving a stencil along the graph and seeing which pairs of nodes and relationships are consistent with it. On the first iteration, both the node labels and the relationship direction matches the search pattern. But on the second and third iterations, the node labels are not the expected ones, and these patterns are rejected. On iteration four, the labels are right, but the relationship orientation is reversed, which makes the matching fail again. Finally, on the last iteration, the pattern is respected even if not drawn in the right order: we have a node *A* connected with an **outbound relationship** to a node *B*.

Test data

Let's first create some test data to experiment with. We'll use the states of the United States as a playground. A node in our graph will be a state, with its two-letter code, name, and rounded population as properties. Those states are connected when they share a common border through a relationship of type SHARE_BORDER_WITH:

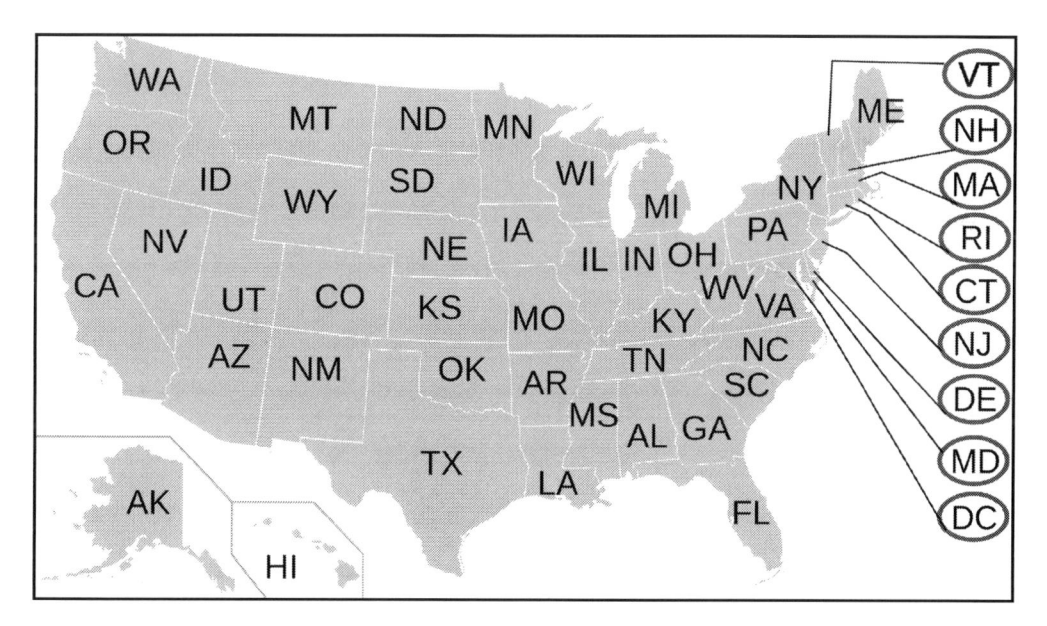

Image credit: https://commons.wikimedia.org/wiki/File:Labelled_US_map.svg

The Cypher Query Language

Here is our sample data, created from the preceding image, using only states up to two degrees of separation away from Florida (FL):

```
CREATE (FL:State {code: "FL", name: "Florida", population: 21500000})
CREATE (AL:State {code: "AL", name: "Alabama", population: 4900000})
CREATE (GA:State {code: "GA", name: "Georgia", population: 10600000})
CREATE (MS:State {code: "MS", name: "Mississippi", population: 3000000})
CREATE (TN:State {code: "TN", name: "Tennessee", population: 6800000})
CREATE (NC:State {code: "NC", name: "North Carolina", population: 10500000})
CREATE (SC:State {code: "SC", name: "South Carolina", population: 5100000})


CREATE (FL)-[:SHARE_BORDER_WITH]->(AL)
CREATE (FL)-[:SHARE_BORDER_WITH]->(GA)
CREATE (AL)-[:SHARE_BORDER_WITH]->(MS)
CREATE (AL)-[:SHARE_BORDER_WITH]->(TN)
CREATE (GA)-[:SHARE_BORDER_WITH]->(AL)
CREATE (GA)-[:SHARE_BORDER_WITH]->(NC)
CREATE (GA)-[:SHARE_BORDER_WITH]->(SC)
CREATE (SC)-[:SHARE_BORDER_WITH]->(NC)
CREATE (TN)-[:SHARE_BORDER_WITH]->(MS)
CREATE (NC)-[:SHARE_BORDER_WITH]->(TN)
```

We will now use this data to understand graph traversal.

Graph traversal

Graph traversal consists of going from one node to its neighbors by following an edge (relationship) in a given direction.

Orientation

While relationships must be oriented when creating them, pattern matching can be performed by taking this orientation into account or not. The relationship between two nodes, a and b, can be of three kinds (with respect to a):

```
OUTBOUND:  (a) -[r]->(b)
INBOUND:   (a)<-[r]- (b)
BOTH:      (a) -[r]- (b)
```

Our USA states graph is undirected, so we will only use the BOTH relationship syntax. For instance, let's find the direct neighbors of Florida and return their names:

```
MATCH (:State {code: "FL"})-[:SHARE_BORDER_WITH]-(n)
RETURN n.name
```

This leads to the following result:

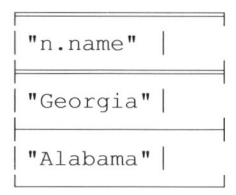

"n.name"
"Georgia"
"Alabama"

It would be interesting to also see the state population, and order the result by this value, wouldn't it?

```
MATCH (:State {code: "FL"})-[:SHARE_BORDER_WITH]-(n)
RETURN n.name as state_name, n.population as state_population
ORDER BY n.population DESC
```

Here's the corresponding result:

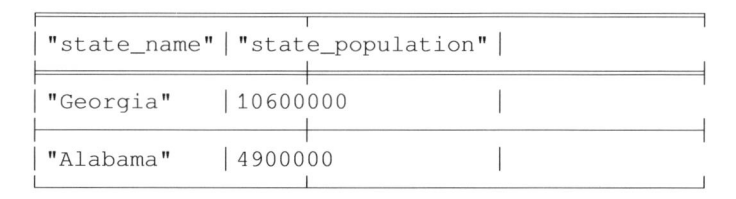

"state_name"	"state_population"
"Georgia"	10600000
"Alabama"	4900000

In this query, we are only interested in the direct neighbors of Florida, meaning only one hop from the starting node. But with Cypher, we can traverse more relationships.

The number of hops

For instance, if we also want the neighbors of the neighbors of Florida, we could use this:

```
MATCH (:State {code: "FL"})-[:SHARE_BORDER_WITH]-(neighbor)-
[:SHARE_BORDER_WITH]-(neighbor_of_neighbor)
RETURN neighbor_of_neighbor
```

The Cypher Query Language

This returns six nodes. If you check the result carefully, you will possibly be surprised to realize that it contains Alabama, for example, which is a direct neighbor of Florida. That's true, but Alabama is also a neighbor of Tennessee, which is a neighbor of Florida, so Alabama is also a neighbor of a neighbor of Florida. If we only want the neighbors of neighbors that are not direct neighbors of Florida, we have to explicitly exclude them:

```
MATCH (FL:State {code: "FL"})-[:SHARE_BORDER_WITH]-(neighbor)-
[:SHARE_BORDER_WITH]-(neighbor_of_neighbor)
WHERE NOT (FL)-[:SHARE_BORDER_WITH]-(neighbor_of_neighbor)
RETURN neighbor_of_neighbor
```

This time, the query returns only four results: South Carolina, North Carolina, Tennessee, and Mississippi.

Variable-length patterns

When the relationship is of the same type, as in our example, or, if we do not care about the relationship type, we can use the following shortcut:

```
MATCH (:State {code: "FL"})-[:SHARE_BORDER_WITH*2]-(neighbor_of_neighbor)
RETURN neighbor_of_neighbor
```

This will return the same six results that we have already seen in the previous section with this query:

```
(FL:State {code: "FL"})-[:SHARE_BORDER_WITH]-(neighbor)-
[:SHARE_BORDER_WITH]-(neighbor_of_neighbor)
```

You can give lower and upper values for the number of hops with this syntax:

```
[:SHARE_BORDER_WITH*<lower_value>..<upper_value>]
```

For instance, `[:SHARE_BORDER_WITH*2..3]` will return the neighbors with two or three degrees of separation.

It is even possible to use whatever path length using the * notation, like so:

```
[:SHARE_BORDER_WITH*]
```

This will match paths regardless of the number of relationships. However, this syntax is not recommended since it can create a huge performance decrease.

Optional matches

Some states do not share any borders with another US state. Let's add Alaska to our test graph:

```
CREATE (CA:State {code: "AK", name: "Alaska", population: 700000 })
```

In the case of Alaska, the query we wrote before to get the neighbors will actually return zero results:

```
MATCH (n:State {code: "AK"})-[:SHARE_BORDER_WITH]-(m)
RETURN n, m
```

Indeed, no pattern matches the sequence ("AK")-SHARE_BORDER_WITH-().

In some cases, we might want to see Alaska in the results anyway. For instance, knowing that Alaska has zero neighbors is information in itself. In that case, we would use OPTIONAL MATCH pattern matching:

```
MATCH (n:State {code: "AK"})
OPTIONAL MATCH (n)-[:SHARE_BORDER_WITH]-(m)
RETURN n.name, m.name
```

This query returns the following result:

"n.name"	"m.name"
"Alaska"	null

The neighbor name, m.name, is NULL because no neighbor was found, but Alaska is part of the result.

We now have a better view of the way Cypher performs pattern matching. The next section will show how to perform aggregations such as count or sum, and handle lists of objects.

Using aggregation functions

It is often very useful to compute some aggregated quantities for the entities in our database, such as the number of friends in a social graph or the total price of an order for an e-commerce website. We will discover here how to do those calculations with Cypher.

Count, sum, and average

In a similar way to SQL, you can compute aggregates with Cypher. The main difference with SQL is that there is no need to use a `GROUP BY` statement; all fields that are not in an aggregation function will be used to create groups:

```
MATCH (FL:State {code: "FL"})-[:SHARE_BORDER_WITH]-(n)
RETURN FL.name as state_name, COUNT(n.code) as number_of_neighbors
```

The result is the following one, as expected:

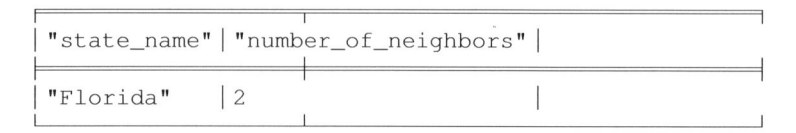

"state_name"	"number_of_neighbors"
"Florida"	2

The following aggregate functions are available:

- `AVG(expr)`: available for numeric values and durations
- `COUNT(expr)`: the number of rows with non-null `expr`
- `MAX(expr)`: the maximum value of `expr` over the group
- `MIN(expr)`: the minimum value of `expr` over the group
- `percentileCont(expr, p)`: the p (percentage) of `expr` over the group, interpolated
- `percentileDisc(expr, p)`: the p (percentage) of `expr` over the group
- `stDev(expr)`: the standard deviation of `expr` over the group
- `stDevP(expr)`: the population standard deviation of `expr` over the group
- `SUM(expr)`: available for numeric values and duration
- `COLLECT(expr)`: see the next section

For instance, we can compute the ratio between a state population and the sum of all people living in its neighboring states like so:

```
MATCH (s:State)-[:SHARE_BORDER_WITH]-(n)
WITH s.name as state, toFloat(SUM(n.population)) as neighbor_population,
s.population as pop
RETURN state, pop, neighbor_population, pop / neighbor_population as f
ORDER BY f desc
```

> The `WITH` keyword is used to perform *intermediate* operations.

Creating a list of objects

It is sometimes useful to aggregate several rows into a single list of objects. In that case, we will use the following:

```
COLLECT
```

For instance, if we want to create a list containing the code of the states sharing a border with Colorado:

```
MATCH (:State {code: "FL"})-[:SHARE_BORDER_WITH]-(n)
RETURN COLLECT(n.code)
```

This returns the following result:

```
["GA","AL"]
```

Unnesting objects

Unnesting consists of converting a list of objects into rows, each row containing an item of the list. It is the exact opposite of COLLECT, which groups objects together into a list.

With Cypher, we will use the following statement:

```
UNWIND
```

For instance, the following two queries are equivalent:

```
MATCH (:State {code: "FL"})-[:SHARE_BORDER_WITH]-(n)
WITH COLLECT(n.code) as codes
UNWIND codes as c
RETURN c

// is equivalent to, since COLLECT and UNWIND cancel each other:
MATCH (CO:State {code: "FL"})-[:SHARE_BORDER_WITH]-(n)
RETURN n.cod
```

This returns our well-known two state codes.

[55]

The `UNWIND` operation will be useful for data imports, since some files are formatted in a way that several pieces of information can be aggregated on a single row. Depending on the data format, this function can be useful when importing data into Neo4j, as we will see in the next section.

Importing data from CSV or JSON

Even if you start your business with Neo4j as a core database, it is very likely you will have to import some static data into your graph. We will also need to perform that kind of operation within this book. In this section, we detail several ways of bulk-feeding Neo4j with different tools and different input data formats.

Data import from Cypher

Cypher itself contains utilities to import data in CSV format from a local or remote file.

File location

Whether importing CSV, JSON, or another file format, this file can be located in the following places:

- Online and reachable through a public URL: `'http://example.com/data.csv'`
- On your local disk: `'files:///data.csv'`

Local file: the import folder

In the latter case, with default Neo4j configuration, the file has to be in the `/imports` folder. Finding this folder is straightforward with Neo4j Desktop:

1. Click on the **Manage** button on the graph you are interested in.
2. Identify the **Open folder** button at the top of the new window.
3. Click on the arrow next to this button and select **Import**.

This will open your file browser inside your graph import folder.

If you prefer the command line, instead of clicking on **Open Folder**, you can use the **Open Terminal** button. In my local Ubuntu installation, it opens a session whose working directory is as follows:

```
~/.config/Neo4j Desktop/Application/neo4jDatabases/database-c83f9dc8-
f2fe-4e5a-8243-2e9ee29e67aa/installation-3.5.14
```

The path on your system will be different since you will have a different database ID and maybe a different Neo4j version.

This directory structure is as follows:

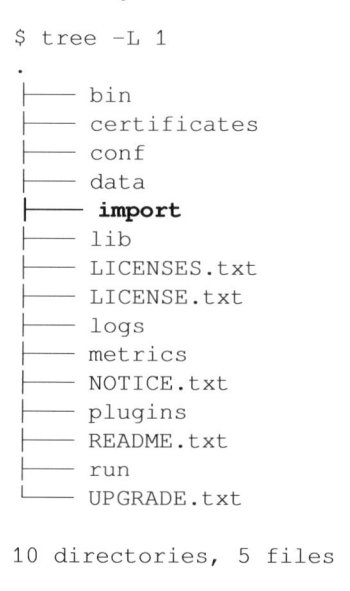

```
$ tree -L 1
.
├── bin
├── certificates
├── conf
├── data
├── import
├── lib
├── LICENSES.txt
├── LICENSE.txt
├── logs
├── metrics
├── NOTICE.txt
├── plugins
├── README.txt
├── run
└── UPGRADE.txt

10 directories, 5 files
```

Here's some notes about the content of this directory:

- data: Actually contains your data, especially data/databases/graph.db/ – the folder you can copy from one computer to another to retrieve your graph data.
- bin: Contains some useful executables such as the import tool we'll discuss in the next section.
- import: Put the files you want to import into your graph here.
- plugins: if you have installed the APOC plugin, you should see apoc-<version>.jar in that folder. All plugins will be downloaded here, and if we want to add plugins not officially supported by Neo4j Desktop, it is enough to copy the jar file in this directory.

Changing the default configuration to import a file from another directory

The default import folder can be configured by changing the `dbms.directories.import` parameter in the `conf/neo4j.conf` configuration file:

```
# This setting constrains all `LOAD CSV` import files to be under the
`import` directory. Remove or comment it out to
# allow files to be loaded from anywhere in the filesystem; this introduces
possible security problems. See the
# `LOAD CSV` section of the manual for details.
dbms.directories.import=import
```

CSV files

CSV files are imported using the `LOAD CSV` Cypher statement. Depending on whether you can/want to use the headers, the syntax is slightly different.

CSV files without headers

If your file does not contain column headers, or you prefer ignoring them, you can refer to columns by indexes:

```
LOAD CSV FROM 'path/to/file.csv' AS row
CREATE (:Node {name: row[1]}
```

> Column indexes start with 0.

CSV files with headers

However, in most cases, you will have a CSV file with named columns. In that case, it is much more convenient to use a column header as a reference instead of numbers. This is possible with Cypher by specifying the `WITH HEADERS` option in the `LOAD CSV` query:

```
LOAD CSV WITH HEADERS FROM '<path/to/file.csv>' AS row
CREATE (:Node {name: row.name})
```

Let's practice with an example. The `usa_state_neighbors_edges.csv` CSV file has the following structure:

```
code;neighbor_code
NE;SD
NE;WY
NM;TX
...
```

This can be explained as follows:

- `code` is the two-letter state identifier (for example, CO for Colorado).
- `neighbor_code` is the two-letter identifier of a state sharing a border with the current state.

Our goal is to create a graph where each state is a node, and we create a relationship between two states if they share a common border.

So, let's get started:

- Fields in this CSV file are delimited with semi-colons, `;`, so we have to use the `FIELDTERMINATOR` option (the default is a comma, `,`).
- The first column contains a state code; we need to create the associated node.
- The last column also contains a state code, so we have to check whether this state already exists and create it if not.
- Finally, we can create a relationship between the two states, arbitrarily chosen to be oriented from the first state to the second one:

```
LOAD CSV WITH HEADERS FROM "file:///usa_state_neighbors_edges.csv" AS row
FIELDTERMINATOR ';'
MERGE (n:State {code: row.code})
MERGE (m:State {code: row.neighbor_code})
MERGE (n)-[:SHARE_BORDER_WITH]->(m)
```

The Cypher Query Language

This results in the graph displayed here, which is a representation of the United States:

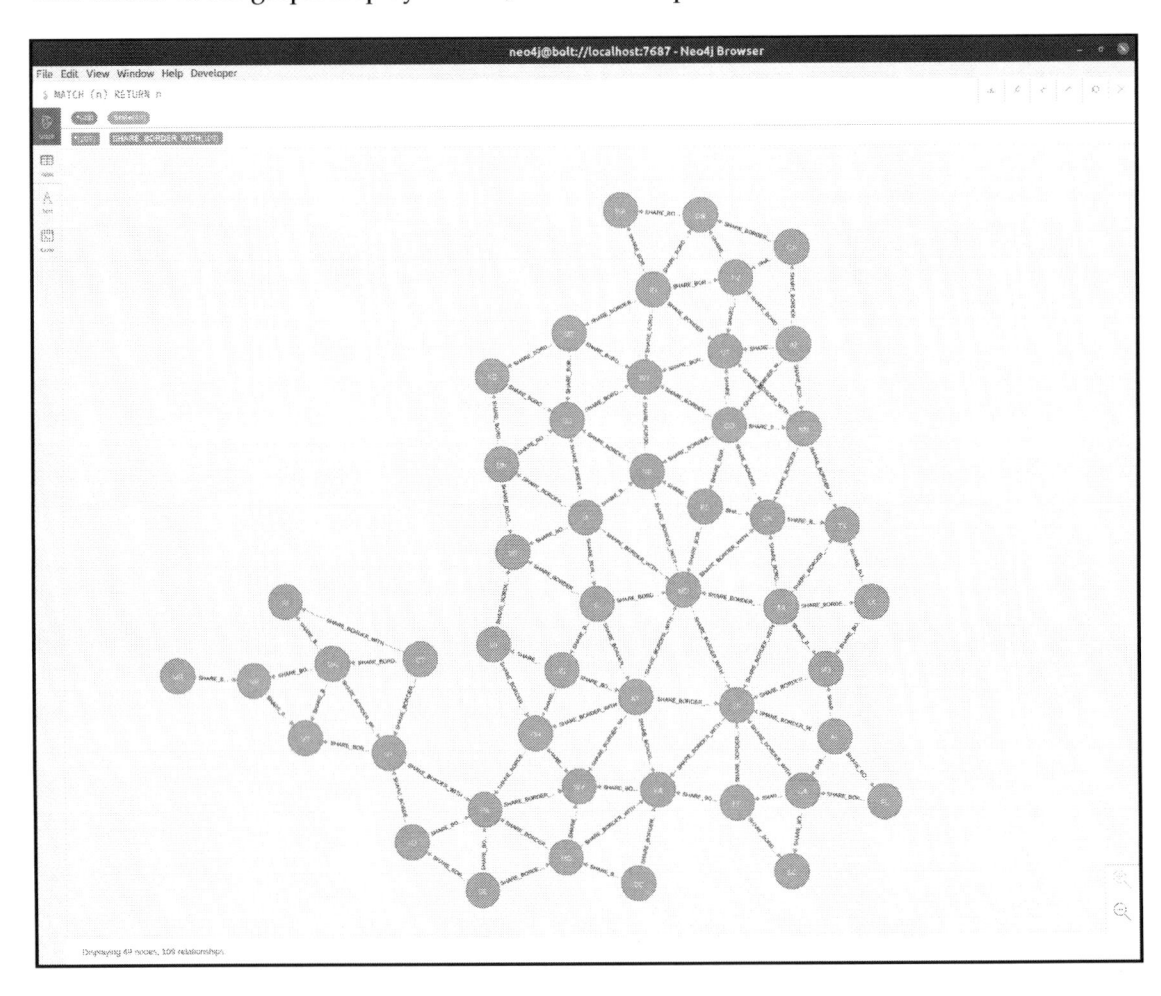

It is interesting to note the special role of New York state, which completely splits the graph into two parts: states on one side of NY are never connected to a state from the other side of NY. Chapter 6, *Node Importance*, will describe the algorithms able to detect such nodes.

Our current graph structure has at least one problem: it does not contain states with no common borders, such as Alaska and Hawaii. To fix this issue, we will use another data file with a different format but that also contains the states without shared borders:

```
code;neighbors
CA;OR,NV,AZ
NH;VT,MA,ME
```

Chapter 2

```
OR;WA,CA,ID,NV
...
AK;""
...
```

As you can see, we now have one row per state that contains a list of its neighbors. If the state does not have any neighbors, it is present in the file but the `neighbors` column contains a null value.

> **TIP**
> In reality, to prevent adding a relationship between states A and B and a second relationship between states B and A, the `neighbors` column only contains the neighbors with `name < state_name`. That's the reason why we have the row `TX;""`, while we know that Texas does have neighbors.

The query to import this file can be written as follows:

```
LOAD CSV WITH HEADERS FROM "file:///usa_state_neighbors_all.csv" AS row
FIELDTERMINATOR ';'
WITH row.code as state, split(row.neighbors, ',') as neighbors
MERGE (a:State {code: state})
WITH a, neighbors
UNWIND neighbors as neighbor
WITH a, neighbor
WHERE neighbor <> ""
MERGE (b:State {code: neighbor})
CREATE (a)-[:SHARE_BORDER_WITH]->(b)
```

A few notes to better understand this query:

- We use the `split()` function to create a list from a comma-separated list of state codes.
- The `UNWIND` operator creates one *row* for each element in the list of neighbor codes.
- We need to filter out the states with no neighbors from the rest of the query since Cypher cannot use a `NULL` value as an identifier when merging nodes. However, since the `WHERE` clause happens after the first `MERGE`, states without neighbors will still be created.

If you see an error or unexpected results when using `LOAD CSV`, you can debug by returning intermediate results. This can be achieved, for instance, like this:

```
LOAD CSV WITH HEADERS FROM "file:///usa_state_neighbors_all.csv" AS row
FIELDTERMINATOR ';'
WITH row LIMIT 10
RETURN row
```

Using a `LIMIT` function is not mandatory but can be better for performance if you are using a very large file.

Eager operations

If you look closely, Neo4j Desktop is showing a small *warning* sign next to the query text editor. If you click on this warning, it will show an explanation about it. In our case, it says this:

```
The execution plan for this query contains the Eager operator, which forces
all dependent data to be materialized in main memory before proceeding
```

This is not directly related to a data import, but this is often the first time we face this warning message, so let's try to understand it.

The Neo4j documentation defines the `Eager` operator in this sentence:

> *For isolation purposes, the operator ensures that operations affecting subsequent operations are executed fully for the whole dataset before continuing execution.*

In other words, each statement of the query is executed for each row of the file, before moving to the other row. This is usually not a problem because a Cypher statement will deal with a hundred nodes or so, but when importing large data files, the overhead is noticeable and may even lead to `OutOfMemory` errors. This then needs to be taken into account.

In the case of a data import, the `Eager` operator is used because we are using `MERGE` statements, which forces Cypher to check whether the nodes and relationships exist for the whole data file.

To overcome this issue, several solutions are possible, depending on the input data:

- If we are sure the data file does not contain duplicates, we can replace `MERGE` operations with `CREATE`.
- But most of the time, we will instead need to split the `import` statement into two or more parts.

The solution to load the US states would be to use three consecutive queries:

```
// first create starting state node if it does not already exist
LOAD CSV WITH HEADERS FROM "file:///usa_state_neighbors_edges.csv" AS row
FIELDTERMINATOR ';'
MERGE (:State {code: row.code})

// then create the end state node if it does not already exist
LOAD CSV WITH HEADERS FROM "file:///usa_state_neighbors_edges.csv" AS row
FIELDTERMINATOR ';'
MERGE (:State {code: row.neighbor_code})

// then create relationships
LOAD CSV WITH HEADERS FROM "file:///usa_state_neighbors_edges.csv" AS row
FIELDTERMINATOR ';'
MATCH (n:State {code: row.code})
MATCH (m:State {code: row.neighbor_code})
MERGE (n)-[:SHARE_BORDER_WITH]->(m)
```

The first two queries create the State nodes. If a state code appears several times in the file, the MERGE operation will take note of creating two distinct nodes with the same code.

Once this is done, we again read the same file to create the neighborhood relationships: we start from reading the State node from the graph with a MATCH operation and then create a unique relationship between them. Here, again, we used the MERGE operation rather than CREATE to prevent having the same relationship twice between the same two nodes.

We had to split the first two statements into two separate queries because they are acting on the same node label. However, a statement like the following one will not rely on the Eager operator:

```
LOAD CSV WITH HEADERS FROM "file:///data.csv" AS row
MERGE (:User {id: row.user_id})
MERGE (:Product {id: row.product_id})
```

Indeed, since the two MERGE nodes involve two different node labels, Cypher does not have to execute all the operations for the first line to make sure there is no conflict with the second one; the operations are independent.

In the *APOC utilities for imports* section, we will study another representation of the US dataset, which we will be able to import without writing three different queries.

Before that, let's have a look at the built-in Neo4j import tool.

The Cypher Query Language

Data import from the command line

Neo4j also provides a command-line import tool. The executable is located in `$NEO4J_HOME/bin/import`. It requires several CSV files:

- One or several CSV file(s) for nodes with the following format:

    ```
    id:ID,:LABEL,code,name,population_estimate_2019:int
    1,State,CA,California,40000000
    2,State,OR,Oregon,4000000
    3,State,AZ,Arizona,7000000
    ```

- It is mandatory to have a unique identifier for nodes. This identifier must be identified with the `:ID` keyword.
- All fields are parsed as a string, unless the type is specified in the header with the `:type` syntax.
- One or several CSV file(s) for relationships with the following format:

    ```
    :START_ID,:END_ID,:TYPE,year:int
    1,2,SHARE_BORDER_WITH,2019
    1,3,SHARE_BORDER_WITH,2019
    ```

Once the data files are created and located in the `import` folder, you can run the following:

```
bin/neo4j-admin import --nodes=import/states.csv --relationships=import/rel.csv
```

If you have very large files, the import tool can be much more convenient since it can manage compressed files (`.tar`, `.gz`, or `.zip`) and also understand header definitions in separate files, which makes it easier to open and update.

The full documentation about the import tool can be found at `https://neo4j.com/docs/operations-manual/current/tutorial/import-tool/`.

APOC utilities for imports

The APOC library is a Neo4j extension that contains several tools to ease working with this database:

- **Data import and export**: from and to different formats like CSV and JSON but also HTML or a web API
- **Data structure**: advanced data manipulation, including type conversion functions, maps, and collections management

- **Advanced graph querying functions**: tools to enhance pattern matching, including more conditions
- **Graph projections**: with virtual nodes and/or relationships

The first implementations of graph algorithms were done within that library, even if they have now been deprecated in favor of a dedicated plugin we will discover in part 2 of this book.

> We will only detail in this section the tools related to data import, but I encourage you to take a look at the documentation to learn what can be achieved with this plugin: `https://neo4j.com/docs/labs/apoc/current/`

When executing the code in the rest of this chapter, you may get an error saying the following:

```
There is no procedure with the name apoc.load.jsonParams registered for this database instance
```

If so, you will have to add the following line to your `neo4j.conf` setting(the **Settings** tab in the **Graph Management** area in Neo4j Desktop):

```
dbms.security.procedures.whitelist= apoc.load.*
```

CSV files

The APOC library contains a procedure to import CSV files. The syntax is the following:

```
CALL apoc.load.csv('')
YIELD name, age
CREATE (:None {name: name, age: age})
```

As an exercise, try and import the USA state data with this procedure.

> **TIP**: Similar to the `LOAD CSV` statement, the file to be updated needs to be inside the `import` folder of your graph. However, you should not include the `file://` descriptor, which would trigger an error.

JSON files

More importantly, APOC also contains a procedure to import data from JSON, which is not possible yet with vanilla Cypher. The structure of the query is as follows:

```
CALL apoc.load.json('http://...') AS value
UNWIND value.items AS item
CREATE (:Node {name: item.name}
```

As an example, we will import some data from GitHub using the GitHub API: https://developer.github.com/v3/.

We can get the list of repositories owned by the organization Neo4j with this request:

```
curl -u "<your_github_username>" https://api.github.com/orgs/neo4j/repos
```

Here is a sample of the data you can get for the given repository (with chosen fields):

```
{
  "id": 34007506,
  "node_id": "MDEwOlJlcG9zaXRvcnkzNDAwNzUwNg==",
  "name": "neo4j-java-driver",
  "full_name": "neo4j/neo4j-java-driver",
  "private": false,
  "owner": {
    "login": "neo4j",
    "id": 201120,
    "node_id": "MDEyOk9yZ2FuaXphdGlvbjIwMTEyMA==",
    "html_url": "https://github.com/neo4j",
    "followers_url": "https://api.github.com/users/neo4j/followers",
    "following_url": "https://api.github.com/users/neo4j/following{/other_user}",
    "repos_url": "https://api.github.com/users/neo4j/repos",
    "type": "Organization"
  },
  "html_url": "https://github.com/neo4j/neo4j-java-driver",
  "description": "Neo4j Bolt driver for Java",
  "contributors_url": "https://api.github.com/repos/neo4j/neo4j-java-driver/contributors",
  "subscribers_url": "https://api.github.com/repos/neo4j/neo4j-java-driver/subscribers",
  "commits_url": "https://api.github.com/repos/neo4j/neo4j-java-driver/commits{/sha}",
  "issues_url": "https://api.github.com/repos/neo4j/neo4j-java-driver/issues{/number}",
  "created_at": "2015-04-15T17:08:15Z",
  "updated_at": "2020-01-02T10:20:45Z",
  "homepage": "",
```

```
    "size": 8700,
    "stargazers_count": 199,
    "language": "Java",
    "license": {
      "key": "apache-2.0",
      "name": "Apache License 2.0",
      "spdx_id": "Apache-2.0",
      "node_id": "MDc6TGljZW5zZTI="
    },
    "default_branch": "4.0"
}
```

We will import this data into a new graph, using APOC. To do so, we have to enable file import with APOC by adding the following line to the Neo4j configuration file (`neo4j.conf`):

```
apoc.import.file.enabled=true
```

Let's now read this data. You can see the result of the `apoc.load.json` procedure with the following:

```
CALL apoc.load.json("neo4j_repos_github.json") YIELD value AS item
RETURN item
LIMIT 1
```

This query produces a result similar to the preceding sample JSON. To access the fields in each JSON file, we can use the `item.<field>` notation. So, here is how to create a node for each repository and owner, and a relationship between the owner and the repository:

```
CALL apoc.load.json("neo4j_repos_github.json") YIELD value AS item
CREATE (r:Repository {name: item.name, created_at: item.created_at, contributors_url: item.contributors_url} )
MERGE (u:User {login: item.owner.login})
CREATE (u)-[:OWNS]->(r)
```

The Cypher Query Language

Checking the content of the graph, we can see this kind of pattern:

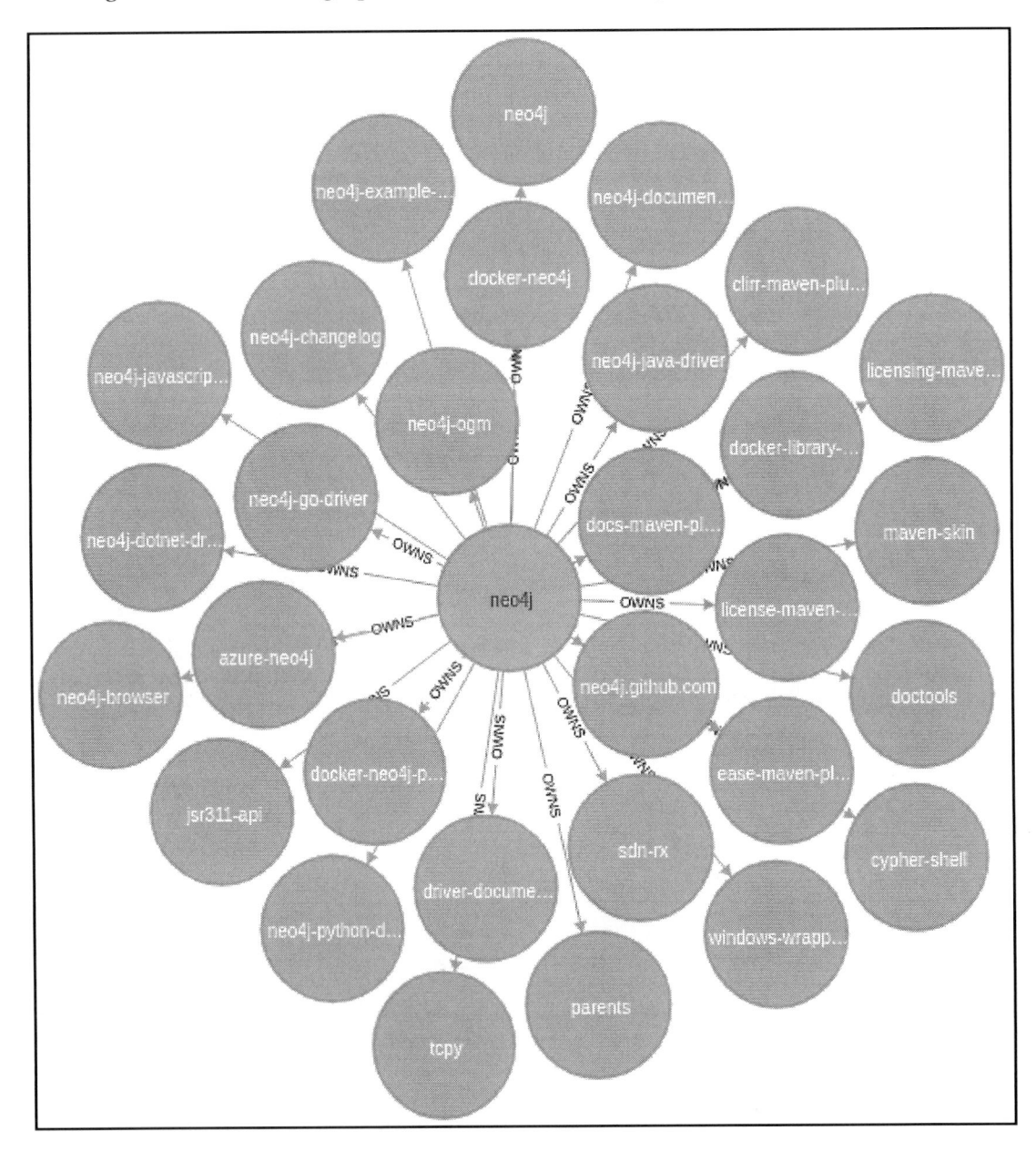

We can do the same to import all the contributors to the Neo4j repository:

```
CALL apoc.load.json("neo4j_neo4j_contributors_github.json")
YIELD value AS item
MATCH (r:Repository {name: "neo4j"})
MERGE (u:User {login: item.login})
CREATE (u)-[:CONTRIBUTED_TO]->(r)
```

Importing data from a web API

You may have noticed that the JSON returned by GitHub contains a URL to extend our knowledge about repositories or users. For instance, in the `neo4j_neo4j_contributors_github.json` file, there is a followers URL. Let's see how to use APOC to feed the graph with the result of this API call.

Setting parameters

We can set parameters within Neo4j Browser with the following syntax:

```
:params {"repo_name": "neo4j"}
```

The parameters can then be referred to in later queries with the `$repo_name` notation:

```
MATCH (r:Repository {name: $repo_name}) RETURN r
```

This can be very useful when the parameter is used in multiple places in the query.

In the next section, we will perform HTTP requests to the GitHub API directly from Cypher. You'll need a GitHub token to authenticate and save in as a parameter:

```
:params {"token": "<your_token>"}
```

The Cypher Query Language

> ℹ The token is not required but the rate limits for unauthorized requests are much lower so it will be easier to create one by following the instructions here: https://help.github.com/en/github/authenticating-to-github/creating-a-personal-access-token-for-the-command-line#creating-a-token.

Calling the GitHub web API

We can use `apoc.load.jsonParams` to load a JSON file from a web API, setting the HTTP request headers in the second parameter of this procedure:

```
CALL apoc.load.json("neo4j_neo4j_contributors_github.json") YIELD value AS item
MATCH (u:User {login: item.login})
CALL apoc.load.jsonParams(item.followers_url, {Authorization: 'Token ' + $token}, null) YIELD value AS contrib
MERGE (f:User {login: contrib.login})
CREATE (f)-[:FOLLOWS]->(u)
```

When performing the import, I got the following results:

```
Added 439 labels, created 439 nodes, set 439 properties, created 601 relationships, completed after 12652 ms.
```

This may vary when you run this since a given user's followers evolve over time. Here is the resulting graph, where users are shown in green and repositories in blue:

Chapter 2

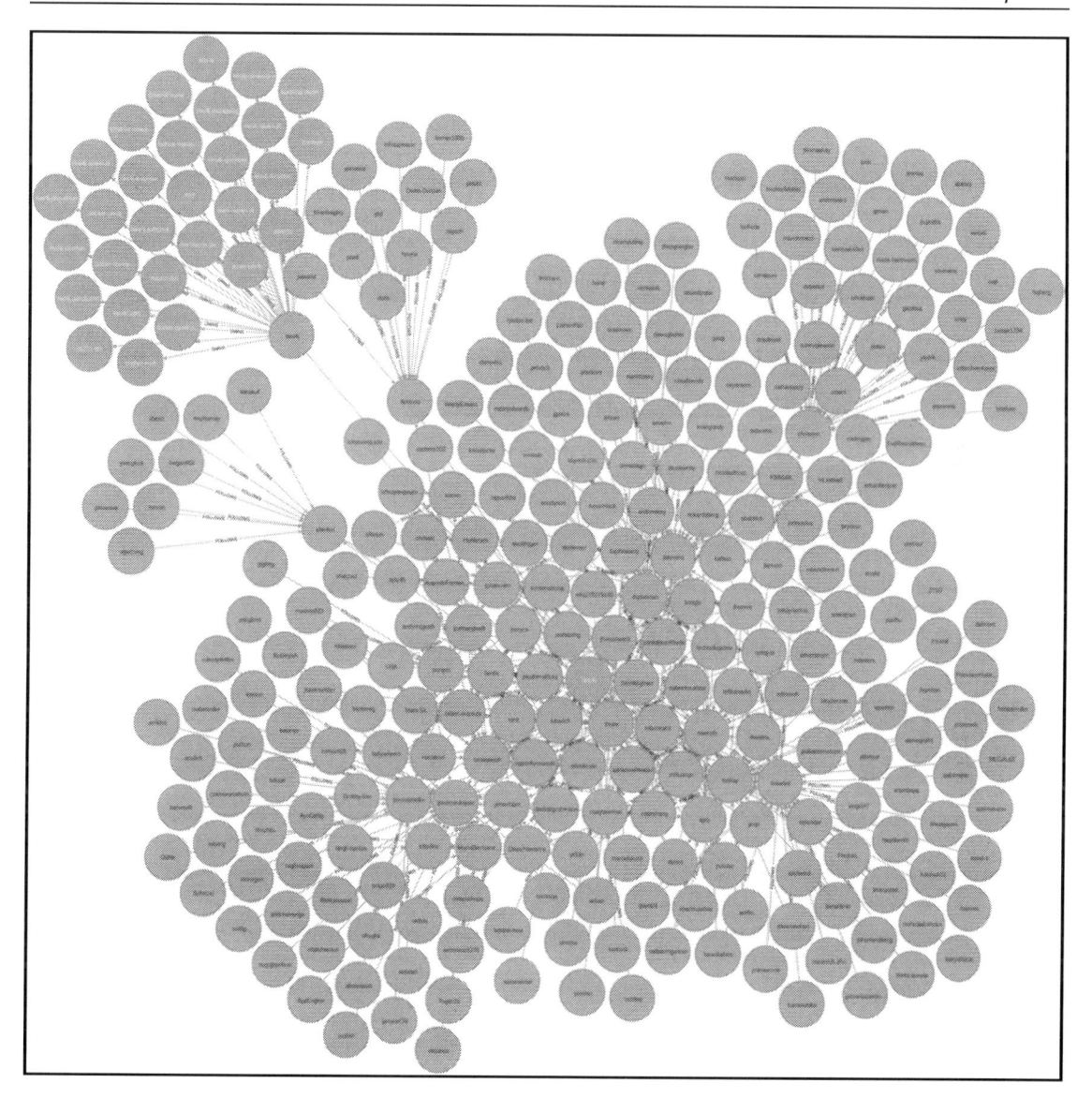

You can use any of the provided URLs to enrich your graph, depending on the kind of analysis you want to perform: you can add commits, contributors, issues, and so on.

[71]

Summary of import methods

Choosing the right tool to import your data mainly depends on its format. Here are some overall recommendations:

- If you only have JSON files, then `apoc.load.json` is your only option.
- If you are using CSV files, then:
    - If your data is big, use the import tool from the command line.
    - If your data is small or medium-sized, you can use APOC or Cypher, `LOAD CSV`.

This closes our section about data imports, where we learned how to feed a Neo4j graph with existing data, from CSV, JSON, or even via a direct call to a web API. We will use those tools all through this book to have meaningful data to run the algorithms on.

Before moving on to those algorithms, a final step is needed. Indeed, as with SQL, there are often several Cypher queries producing the same result, but not all of them have the same efficiency. The next section will show you how to measure efficiency and deal with some good practices to avoid the main caveats.

Measuring performance and tuning your query for speed

In order to measure a Cypher query performance, we will have to look at the Cypher query planner, which details the operations performed under the hood. In this section, we introduce the notions to learn how to access the Cypher execution plan. We will also deal with some good practices to avoid the worst operations in terms of performance, before concluding with a well-known example.

Cypher query planner

As you would do with SQL, you can check the Cypher query planner to understand what happens under the hood and how to improve your query. Two options are possible:

- `EXPLAIN`: If you do not want the query to be run, `EXPLAIN` won't make any changes to your graph.
- `PROFILE`: This will actually run the query and alter your graph, together with measuring performance.

In the rest of this chapter, we will use a dataset released by Facebook in 2012 for a recruiting competition hosted by Kaggle. The dataset can be downloaded here: `https://www.kaggle.com/c/FacebookRecruiting/data`. I have only used the training sample, containing a list of connections between anonymized people. It contains 1,867,425 nodes and 9,437,519 edges.

We already talked about one of the operations that can be identified in the query planner: `Eager` operations, which we need to avoid as much as possible since they really hurt performance. Let's see some more operators and how to tune our queries for performance.

A simple query to select a node with a given `id` and get Cypher query explanations could be written as follows:

```
PROFILE
MATCH (p { id: 1000})
RETURN p
```

When executing this query, a new tab is available in the result cell called **Plan**, shown in the following screenshot:

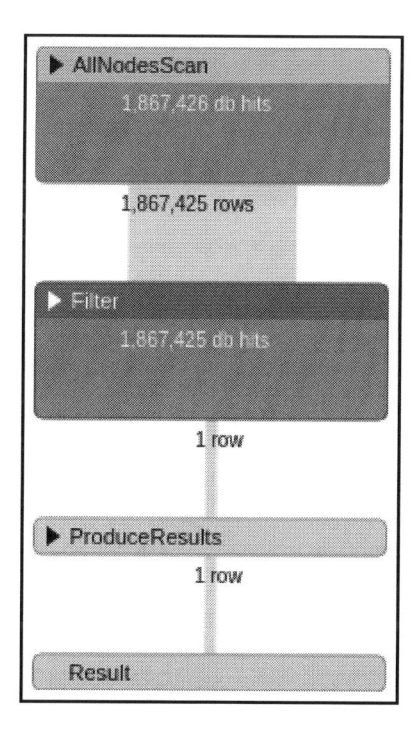

The Cypher Query Language

The query profile shows the use of the `AllNodesScan` operator, which performs a search on `ALL` nodes of the graph. In this specific case, this won't have a big impact since we have only one node label, `Person`. But if your graph happens to have many different labels, performing a scan on all nodes can be horribly slow. For this reason, it is highly recommended to explicitly set the node labels and relationship types of interest in our queries:

```
PROFILE
MATCH (p:Person { id: 1000})
RETURN p
```

In that case, Cypher uses the `NodeByLabelScan` operation as can be seen in the following screenshot:

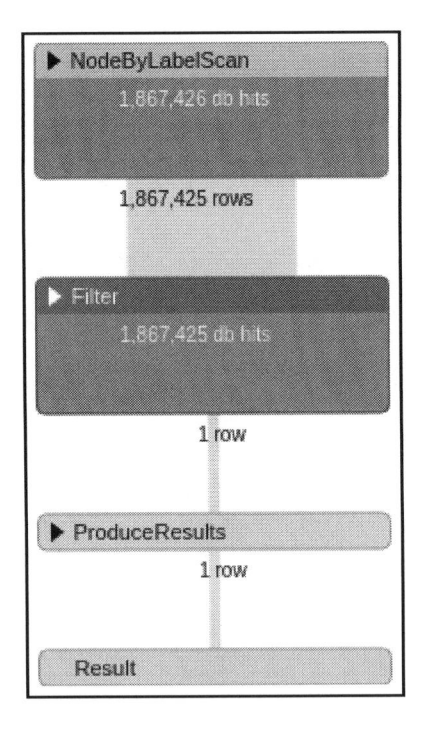

In terms of performance, this query is executed in approximately 650 ms on my laptop, in both cases. In some cases, performance can be increased even more thanks to Neo4j indexing.

Neo4j indexing

Neo4j indexes are used to easily find the start node of a pattern matching query. Let's see the impact of creating an index on the execution plan and execution time:

```
CREATE INDEX ON :Person(id)
```

And let's run our query again:

```
PROFILE
MATCH (p:Person { id: 1000})
RETURN p
```

You can see that the query is now using our index through the `NodeIndexSeek` operation, which reduces the execution time to 1 ms:

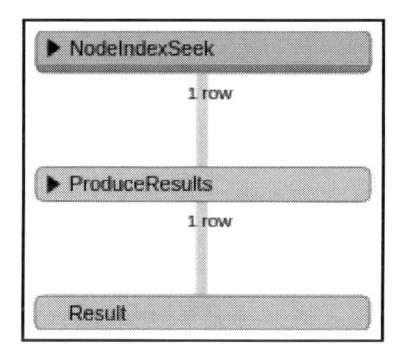

An index can also be dropped with the following statement:

```
DROP INDEX ON :Person(id)
```

The Neo4j indexing system also supports combined indexes and full-text indexes. Check https://neo4j.com/docs/cypher-manual/current/schema/index/ for more information.

Back to LOAD CSV

Remember we talked about the `Eager` operator earlier in this chapter. We are importing US states with the `LOAD CSV` statement:

```
LOAD CSV WITH HEADERS FROM "file:///usa_state_neighbors_edges.csv" AS row
FIELDTERMINATOR ';'
MERGE (n:State {code: row.code})
MERGE (m:State {code: row.neighbor_code})
MERGE (n)-[:SHARE_BORDER_WITH]->(m)
```

[75]

The Cypher Query Language

To better understand it and identify the root cause of this warning message, we ask Neo4j to EXPLAIN it. We would then get a complex diagram like the one displayed here:

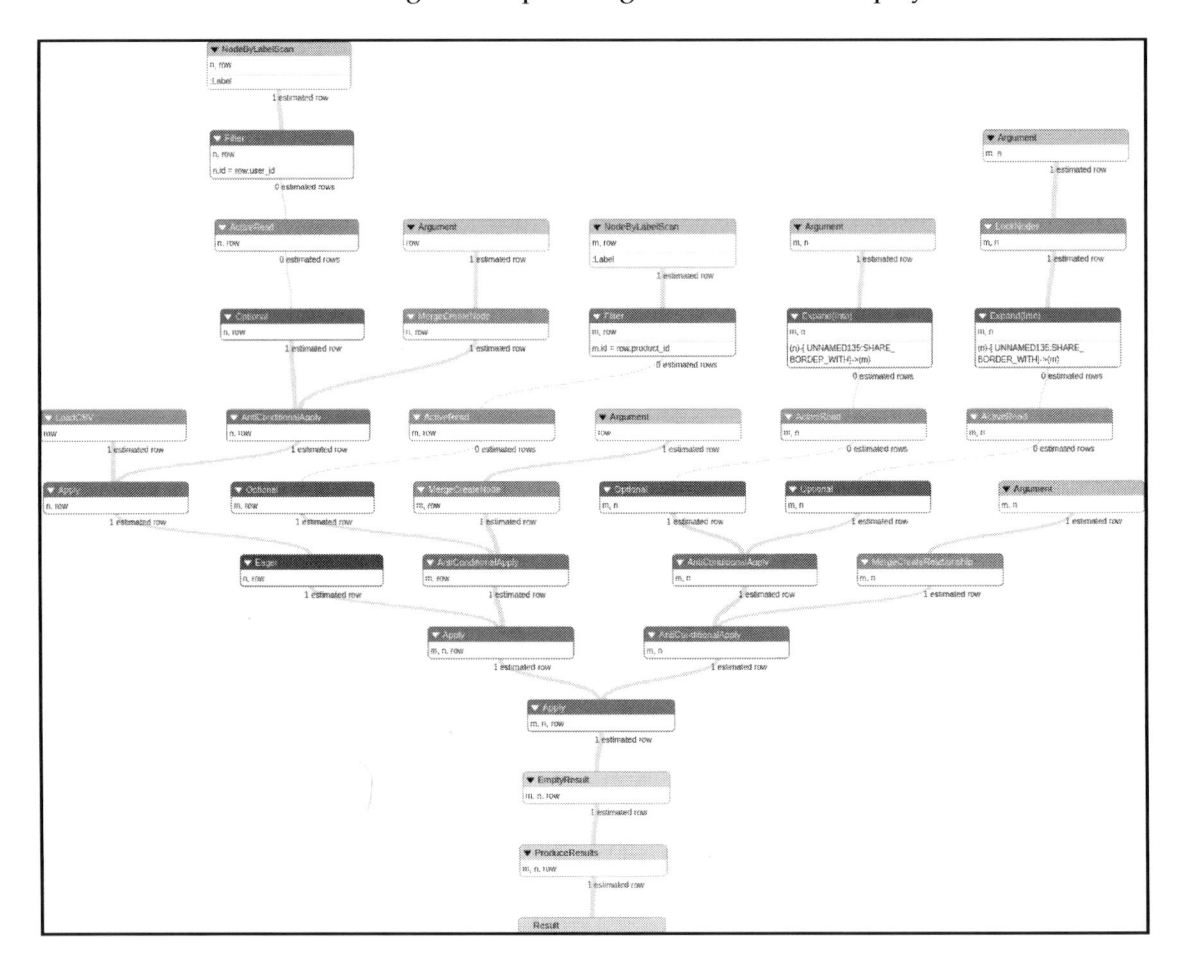

I have highlighted three elements for you:

- The violet part corresponds to the first MERGE statement.
- The green part contains the same operations for the second MERGE statement.
- The read box is the Eager operation.

From this diagram, you can see that the Eager operation is performed between step 1 (the first MERGE) and step 2 (the second MERGE). This is where your query needs to be split in order to avoid this operator.

You now know more about how to understand the operations Cypher performs when executing your query and how to identify and fix bottlenecks. It is time to actually measure query performance in terms of time. For this, we are going to use the famous *friend-of-friend* example in a social network.

The friend-of-friend example

The *friend-of-friend* example is the most famous argument in favor of Neo4j when talking about performance. Since Neo4j is known to be incredibly performant at traversing relationships, contrary to other Database engines, we expect the response time of this query to be quite low.

Neo4j Browser displays the query execution time in the result cell:

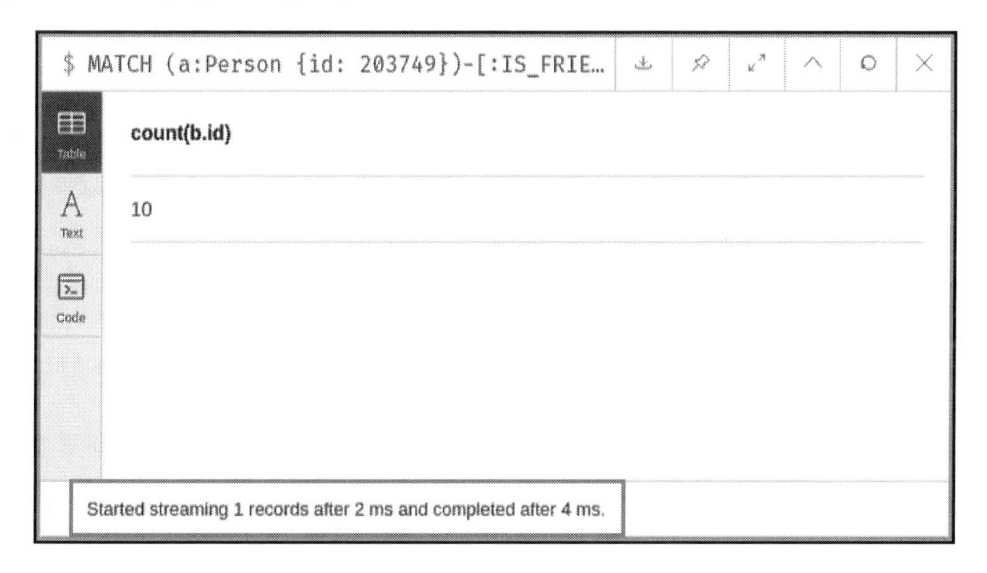

```
$ MATCH (a:Person {id: 203749})-[:IS_FRIE...

count(b.id)

10

Started streaming 1 records after 2 ms and completed after 4 ms.
```

It can also be measured programmatically. For instance, using the Neo4j Python driver from the Neo4j package, we can measure the total execution and streaming time with the following:

```
from neo4j import GraphDatabase

URL = "bolt://localhost:7687"
USER = "neo4j"
PWD = "neo4j"

driver = GraphDatabase.driver(URL, auth=(USER, PWD))
```

The Cypher Query Language

```
query = "MATCH (a:Person {id: 203749})-[:IS_FRIEND_WITH]-(b:Person) RETURN count(b.id)"

with driver.session() as session:
    with session.begin_transaction() as tx:
        result = tx.run(query)
        summary = result.summary()
        avail = summary.result_available_after   # ms
        cons = summary.result_consumed_after     # ms
        total_time = avail + cons
```

With that code, we were able to measure the total time of execution for different starting nodes, with different degrees, and different depths (first-degree friends, second degree... up to the fourth degree).

The following figure shows the results. As you can see, the amount of time before the results are made available is below 1 ms for all depth-1 queries, independently of the number of first-degree neighbors of the node:

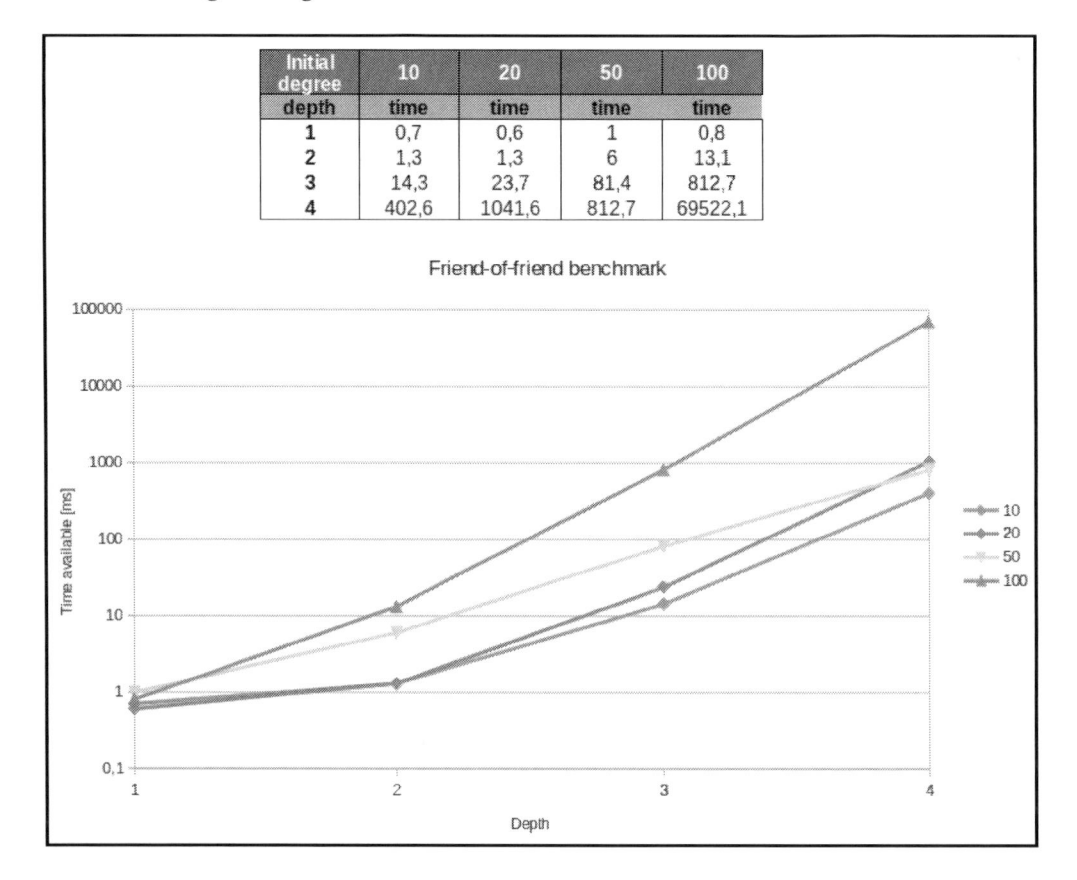

Initial degree / depth	10 time	20 time	50 time	100 time
1	0,7	0,6	1	0,8
2	1,3	1,3	6	13,1
3	14,3	23,7	81,4	812,7
4	402,6	1041,6	812,7	69522,1

Friend-of-friend benchmark

[78]

The time Neo4j needs to get the results increases with the depth of the query, as expected. However, you can see that the time difference between the number of friends for the initial node becomes really important only when having a lot of friends. When starting from the node with 100 friends at depth 4, the number of matching nodes is almost 450,000, identified within 1 minute approximately.

> This benchmark was performed without any changes to the Neo4j Community Edition default configuration. Some gain is to be expected by tuning some of those parameters, such as the maximum heap size.

More information about these configurations will be given in `Chapter 12`, *Neo4j at Scale*.

Summary

In this chapter, you learned how to navigate into your Neo4j graph. You are now able to perform CRUD operations with Cypher, creating, updating, and deleting nodes, relationships, and their properties.

But the full power of Neo4j lies in relationship traversal (going from one node to its neighbors is super fast) and pattern matching you are now able to perform with Cypher.

You have also discovered how to measure your query performance with the Cypher query planner. This can help you to avoid some pitfalls, such as the `Eager` operation when loading data. It will also help in understanding Cypher internals and tuning your query for better performance in terms of speed.

We know have all the tools in hand to start really using Neo4j and study some real-life examples. In the next chapter, we will learn about **knowledge graphs**. For many organizations, this is the first entry point to the world of graphs. With that data structure, we will be able to implement performant recommendation engines and graph-based search for your customers.

Questions

1. **US states:**
   - Find the first-degree neighbors of Colorado (code CO):
     - What are the codes of these neighbors?
     - Can you count how many there are using an aggregate function?
   - Which states have the highest number of neighbors? The lowest? Think about the ORDER BY clause.

2. **GitHub graph enhancement:**
   - From neo4j_repos_github.json, can you save the project language when provided, as a new node? You can use the new Language node label.
   - Can you also save the license, when provided, using a new node? Use a Licence node label and save all of the provided information from GitHub as properties.
   (Hint: the license is provided with the following format):

     ```
     "license": {
        "key": "other",
        "name": "Other",
        "spdx_id": "NOASSERTION",
        "url": null,
        "node_id": "MDc6TGljZW5zZTA="
     },
     ```

   - Using the GitHub API, can you save the user locations?
     Hint: the URL to get user information is https://api.github.com/users/<login>.
   - The location often contains the city and country name, separated by either a space or a comma. Can you write a query to save only the first element of this pair, assumed to be the city?
     Hint: checkout APOC text utils.
   - Using the GitHub API, can you retrieve the repositories owned by each Neo4j contributor?
     Hint: the URL to get the repositories for a given user is https://api.github.com/users/<login>/repos.
   - Which location is the most represented among Neo4j contributors?

Further reading

- The Cypher cheat sheet created by Neo4j is very informative: `https://neo4j.com/docs/cypher-refcard/current/`.
- I recommend that you take a look at the APOC plugin documentation to know what APOC is capable of and decide whether it is worth including it in your projects: `https://neo4j.com/docs/labs/apoc/current/`.
- More information about data modeling and Neo4j performance can be found in Neo4j *High Performance, S. Raj, Packt Publishing*.

3
Empowering Your Business with Pure Cypher

In the previous chapters, we introduced the concepts behind Neo4j and learned how to query it using Cypher. It is now time to build our first working application of graph databases. The first step when entering the graph database ecosystem is usually to try and build a **knowledge graph** of your business or industry. In this chapter, you will learn what a knowledge graph is and how to build one from structured or unstructured data. We will use some **Natural Language Processing** (**NLP**) techniques and query existing knowledge graphs such as Wikidata. We will then focus on two possible applications of knowledge graphs in the real world: graph-based search and recommendations.

The following topics will be covered in this chapter:

- Knowledge graphs
- Graph-based search
- Recommendation engine

Technical requirements

The required technologies and installations for this chapter are as follows:

- Neo4j 3.5
- Plugins:
    - APOC
    - GraphAware NLP library: https://github.com/graphaware/neo4j-nlp
- Some minor parts of this chapter also require Python3 to be installed; we will use the spaCy package for NLP.
- GitHub repository for this chapter: https://github.com/PacktPublishing/Hands-On-Graph-Analytics-with-Neo4j/tree/master/ch3

Knowledge graphs

If you have followed Neo4j news for the last few years, you have probably heard a lot about knowledge graphs. But it is not always clear what they are. Unfortunately, there is no universal definition of a knowledge graph, but let's try to understand which concepts are hidden behind these two words.

Attempting a definition of knowledge graphs

Modern applications produce petabytes of data every day. As an example, during the year 2019, every minute, the number of Google searches has been estimated to be more than 4.4 billion. During the same amount of time, 180 billion emails, and more than 500,000 tweets are sent, while the number of videos watched on YouTube is about 4.5 billion. Organizing this data and transforming it into knowledge is a real challenge.

Knowledge graphs try to address this challenge by storing the following in the same data structure:

- Entities related to a specific field, such as users or products
- Relationships between entities, for instance, *user A bought a surfboard*
- Context to understand the previous entities and relationships, for instance, *user A lives in Hawaii and is a surf teacher*

Graphs are the perfect structure to store all this information since it is very easy to aggregate data from different data sources: we just have to create new nodes (with maybe new labels) and the relationships. There is no need to update the existing nodes.

Those graphs can be used in many ways. We can, for instance, distinguish the following:

- **Business knowledge graph**: You can build such a graph to address some specific tasks within your enterprise, such as providing fast and accurate recommendations to your customers.
- **Enterprise knowledge graph**: To go even beyond the business knowledge graph, you can build a graph whose purpose is to support multiple units in the enterprise.
- **Field knowledge graph**: This goes further and gathers all information about a specific area such as medicine or sport.

Since 2019, knowledge graphs even have their own conference organized by the University of Columbia in New York. You can browse the past events' recordings and learn more about how organizations use knowledge graphs to empower their business at `https://www.knowledgegraph.tech/`.

In the rest of this section, we will learn how to build a knowledge graph in practice. We will study several ways:

- **Structured data**: Such data can come from a legacy database such as SQL.
- **Unstructured data**: This covers textual data that we will analyze using NLP techniques.
- **Online knowledge graphs**, especially Wikidata (`https://www.wikidata.org`).

Let's start with the structured data case.

Building a knowledge graph from structured data

A knowledge graph is then nothing more than a graph database, with well-known relationships between entities.

We have actually already started building a knowledge graph in `Chapter 2`, *Cypher Query Language*. Indeed, the graph we built there contains the Neo4j-related repositories and users on GitHub: it is a representation of the knowledge we have regarding Neo4j ecosystem.

So far, the graph only contains two kinds of information:

- The list of repositories owned by the Neo4j organization
- The list of contributors to each of these repositories

But our knowledge can be extended much beyond this. Using the GitHub API, we can go deeper and, for instance, gather the following:

- The list of repositories owned by each contributor to Neo4j, or the list of repositories they contributed to
- The list of tags assigned to each repository
- The list of users each of these contributors follow
- The list of users following each contributor

For example, let's import each repository contributor and their owned repositories in one single query:

```
MATCH (u:User)-[:OWNS]->(r:Repository)
CALL apoc.load.jsonParams("https://api.github.com/repos/" + u.login + "/" + r.name + "/contributors", {Authorization: 'Token ' + $token}, null) YIELD value AS item
MERGE (u2:User {login: item.login})
MERGE (u2)-[:CONTRIBUTED_TO]->(r)
WITH item, u2
CALL apoc.load.jsonParams(item.repos_url, {Authorization: 'Token ' + $token}, null) YIELD value AS contrib
MERGE (r2:Repository {name: contrib.name})
MERGE (u2)-[:OWNS]->(r2)
```

> **TIP**: Due to the reduced rate limit on the GitHub API, this query will fail if you are not using a GitHub token.

You can play around and extend your knowledge graph about the Neo4j community on GitHub. In the following sections, we will learn how to use NLP to extend this graph and extract information from the project's README file.

> The preceding query uses the data from `neo4j_repos_github.json` we imported in the preceding chapter. Moreover, since it sends one request per user per repository, it can take some time to complete (around 5 min).

Building a knowledge graph from unstructured data using NLP

NLP is the part of machine learning whose goal is to understand natural language. In other words, the holy grail of NLP is to make computers answer questions such as "What's the weather like today?"

NLP

In NLP, researchers and computer scientists try to make a computer understand an English (or any other human language) sentence. The result of their hard work can be seen in many modern applications, such as the voice assistants Apple Siri or Amazon Alexa.

But before going into such advanced systems, NLP can be used to do the following:

- **Perform sentiment analysis**: Is a comment about a specific brand positive or negative?
- **Named Entity Recognition (NER)**: Can we extract the name of people or locations contained within a given text, without having to list them all in a regex pattern?

These two questions, quite easy for a human being, are incredibly hard for a machine. The models used to achieve very good results are beyond the scope of this book, but you can refer to the *Further reading* section to learn more about them.

In the next section, we are going to use pre-trained models provided by the NLP research group from Stanford University, which provides state-of-the-art results, at `https://stanfordnlp.github.io/`.

Neo4j tools for NLP

Even if not officially supported by Neo4j, community members and companies using Neo4j provide some interesting plugins. One of them was developed by the GraphAware company and enables Neo4j users to use Stanford tools for NLP within Neo4j. That's the library we will use in this section.

GraphAware NLP library

If you are interested in the implementation and more detailed documentation, the code is available at `https://github.com/graphaware/neo4j-nlp`.

To install this package, you'll need to visit `https://products.graphaware.com/` and download the following JAR files:

- `framework-server-community` (if using Neo4j community edition) or `framework-server-enterprise` if using the Enterprise edition
- `nlp`
- `nlp-stanford-nlp`

You also need to download trained models from Stanford Core NLP available at `https://stanfordnlp.github.io/CoreNLP/#download`. In this book, you will only need the models for the English language.

Empowering Your Business with Pure Cypher

After all those JAR files are downloaded, you need to copy them into the `plugins` directory of the GitHub graph we started building in Chapter 2, *Cypher Query Language*. Here is the list of JAR files that you should have downloaded and that will be needed to run the code in this chapter:

```
apoc-3.5.0.6.jar
graphaware-server-community-all-3.5.11.54.jar
graphaware-nlp-3.5.4.53.16.jar
nlp-stanfordnlp-3.5.4.53.17.jar
stanford-english-corenlp-2018-10-05-models.jar
```

Once those JAR files are in your `plugins` directory, you have to restart the graph. To check that everything is working fine, you can check that GraphAware NLP procedures are available with the following query:

```
CALL dbms.procedures() YIELD name, signature, description, mode
WHERE name =~ 'ga.nlp.*'
RETURN signature, description, mode
ORDER BY name
```

You will see the following lines:

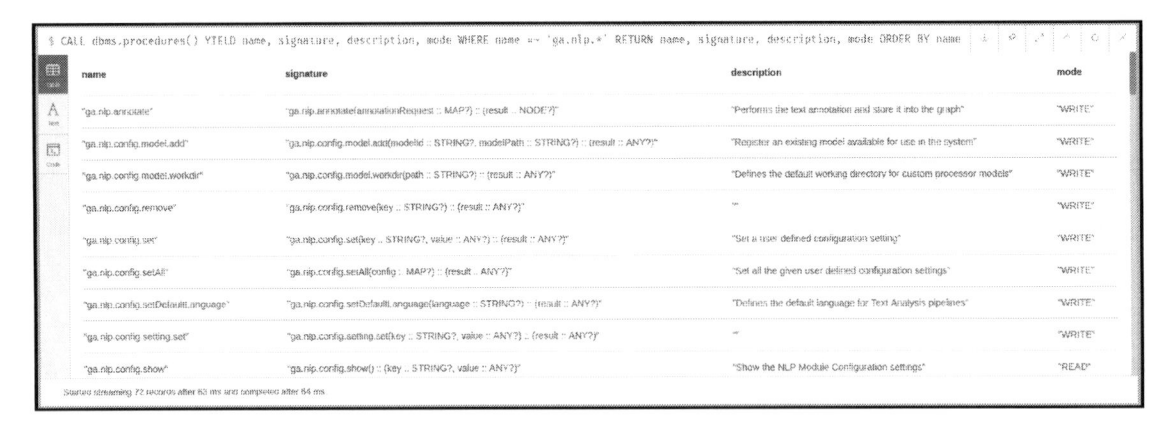

The last step before starting using the NLP library is to update some settings in `neo4j.conf`. First, trust the procedures from `ga.nlp.` and tell Neo4j where to look for the plugin:

```
dbms.security.procedures.unrestricted=apoc.*,ga.nlp.*
dbms.unmanaged_extension_classes=com.graphaware.server=/graphaware
```

[88]

Then, add the following two lines, specific to the GraphAware plugin, in the same `neo4j.conf` file:

```
com.graphaware.runtime.enabled=true
com.graphaware.module.NLP.1=com.graphaware.nlp.module.NLPBootstrapper
```

After restarting the graph, your working environment is ready. Let's import some textual data to run the NLP algorithms on.

Importing test data from the GitHub API

As test data, we will use the content of the README for each repository in our graph, and see what kind of information can be extracted from it.

The API to get the README from a repository is the following:

```
GET /repos/<owner>/<repo>/readme
```

Similarly to what we have done in the previous chapter, we are going to use `apoc.load.jsonParams` to load this data into Neo4j. First, we set our GitHub access token, if any (optional):

```
:params {"token": "8de08ffe137afb214b86af9bcac96d2a59d55d56"}
```

Then we can run the following query to retrieve the README of all repositories in our graph:

```
MATCH (u:User)-[:OWNS]->(r:Repository)
CALL apoc.load.jsonParams("https://api.github.com/repos/" + u.login + "/" +
r.name + "/readme", {Authorization: "Token " + $token}, null, null,
{failOnError: false}) YIELD value
CREATE (d:Document {name: value.name, content:value.content, encoding:
value.encoding})
CREATE (d)-[:DESCRIBES]->(r)
```

> Similarly to the previous query to fetch data from the GitHub API, the execution time of this query can be quite long (up to more than 15 minutes).

You will notice from the preceding query that we added a parameter `{failOnError: false}` to prevent APOC from raising an exception when the API returns a status code different from 200. This is the case for the https://github.com/neo4j/license-maven-plugin repository, which does not have any README file.

Empowering Your Business with Pure Cypher

Checking the content of our new document nodes, you will realize that the content is base64 encoded. In order to use NLP tools, we will have to decode it. Happily, APOC provides a procedure for that. We just need to clean our data and remove line breaks from the downloaded content and invoke `apoc.text.base64Decode` as follows:

```
MATCH (d:Document)
SET d.text = apoc.text.base64Decode(apoc.text.join(split(d.content, "\n"), ""))
RETURN d
```

> If you are not using the default `dbms.security.procedures.whitelist` parameter in `neo4j.conf`, you will need to whitelist the `apoc.text` procedure for the previous query to work:
> `dbms.security.procedures.whitelist=apoc.text.*`

Our document nodes now have a human-readable `text` property, containing the content of the `README`. Let's now see how to use NLP to learn more about our repositories.

Enriching the graph with NLP

In order to use GraphAware tools, the first step is to build an NLP pipeline:

```
CALL ga.nlp.processor.addPipeline({
 name:"named_entity_extraction",
 textProcessor:
'com.graphaware.nlp.processor.stanford.StanfordTextProcessor',
 processingSteps: {tokenize:true, ner:true}
})
```

Here, we specify the following:

- The pipeline name, `named_entity_extraction`.
- The text processor to be used. GraphAware supports both Stanford NLP and OpenNLP; here, we are using Stanford models.
- The processing steps:
    - **Tokenization**: Extract tokens from a text. As a first approximation, a token can be seen as a word.
    - **NER**: This is the key step that will identify named entities such as persons or locations.

We can now run this pipeline on the README text by calling the `ga.nlp.annotate` procedure as follows:

```
MATCH (n:Document)
CALL ga.nlp.annotate({text: n.text, id: id(n), checkLanguage: false,
pipeline : "named_entity_extraction"}) YIELD result
MERGE (n)-[:HAS_ANNOTATED_TEXT]->(result)
```

This procedure will actually update the graph and add nodes and relationships to it. The resulting graph schema is displayed here, with only some chosen nodes and relationships to make it more readable:

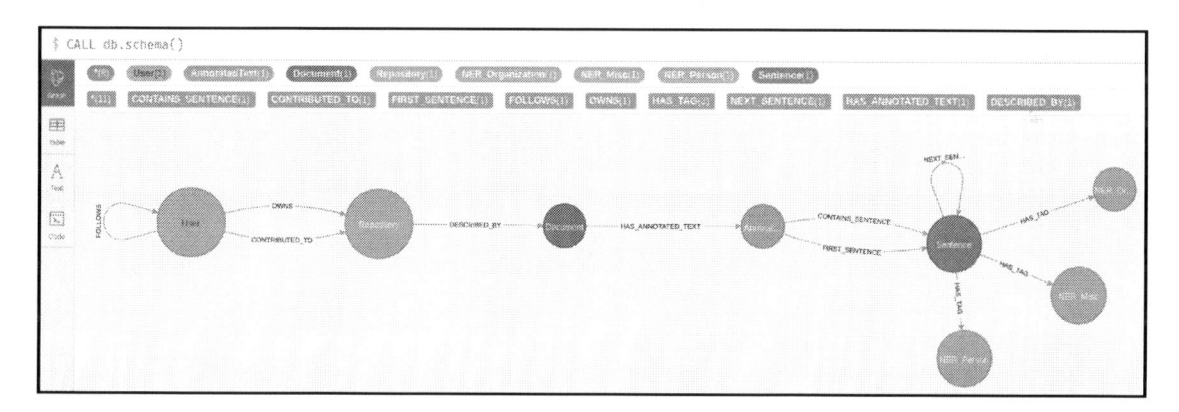

We can now check which people were identified within our repositories:

```
MATCH (n:NER_Person) RETURN n.value
```

Part of the result of this query is displayed here:

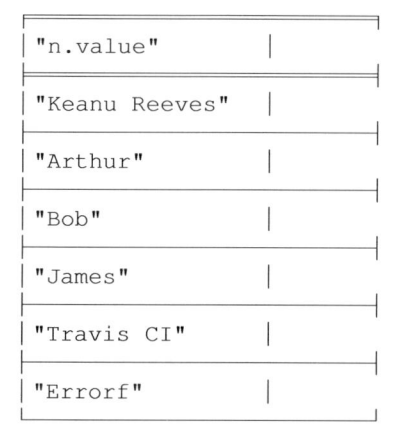

"n.value"
"Keanu Reeves"
"Arthur"
"Bob"
"James"
"Travis CI"
"Errorf"

[91]

You can see that, despite some errors with `Errorf` or `Travis CI` identified as people, the NER was able to successfully identify Keanu Reeves and other anonymous contributors.

We can also identify which repository Keanu Reeves was identified in. According to the preceding graph schema, the query we have to write is the following:

```
MATCH (r:Repository)<-[:DESCRIBES]-(:Document)-
[:HAS_ANNOTATED_TEXT]->(:AnnotatedText)-[:CONTAINS_SENTENCE]->(:Sentence)-
[:HAS_TAG]->(:NER_Person {value: 'Keanu Reeves'})
RETURN r.name
```

This query returns only one result: `neo4j-ogm`. This actor name is actually used within this `README`, for the version I downloaded (you can have different results here since `README` changes with time).

NLP is a fantastic tool to extend knowledge graphs and bring structure from unstructured textual data. But there is another source of information that we can also use to enhance a knowledge graph. Indeed, some organizations such as the Wikimedia foundation give access to their own knowledge graph. We will learn in the next section how to use the Wikidata knowledge graph to add even more context to our data.

Adding context to a knowledge graph from Wikidata

Wikidata defines itself with the following words:

> *Wikidata is a free and open knowledge base that can be read and edited by both humans and machines.*

In practice, a Wikidata page, like the one regarding Neo4j (https://www.wikidata.org/wiki/Q1628290) contains a list of properties such as *programming language* or *official website*.

Introducing RDF and SPARQL

Wikidata structure actually follows the **Resource Description Framework (RDF)**. Part of the W3C specifications since 1999, this format allows us to store data as triples:

```
(subject, predicate, object)
```

Chapter 3

For instance, the sentence `Homer is the father of Bart` is translated with RDF format as follows:

(Homer, is father of, Bart)

This RDF triple can be written with a syntax closer to Cypher:

(Homer) - [IS_FATHER] -> (Bart)

RDF data can be queried using the SPARQL query language, also standardized by the W3C.

The following will teach you how to build simple queries against Wikidata.

Querying Wikidata

All the queries we are going to write here can be tested using the online Wikidata tool at `https://query.wikidata.org/`.

If you have done the assessments at the end of `Chapter 2`, *Cypher Query Language*, your GitHub graph must have nodes with label **Location**, containing the city each user is declared to live in. If you skipped Chapter 2 or the assessment, you can find this graph in the GitHub repository for this chapter. The current graph schema is the following:

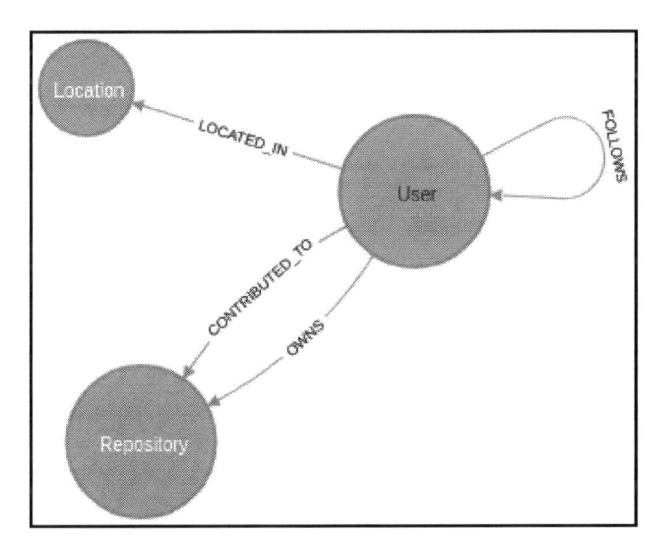

Our goal will be to assign a country to each of the locations. Let's start from the most frequent location within Neo4j contributors, Malmö. This is a city in Sweden where the company building and maintaining Neo4j, Neo Inc., has its main offices.

[93]

Empowering Your Business with Pure Cypher

How can we find the country in which Malmö is located using Wikidata? We first need to find the page regarding Malmö on Wikidata. A simple search on your favorite search engine should lead you to `https://www.wikidata.org/wiki/Q2211`. From there, two pieces of information are important to note:

- The entity identifier in the URL: `Q2211`. For Wikidata, `Q2211` means Malmö.
- If you scroll down on the page, you will find the property, `country`, which links to a `Property` page for property `P17`: `https://www.wikidata.org/wiki/Property:P17`.

With these two pieces of information, we can build and test our first SPARQL query:

```
SELECT ?country
WHERE {
    wd:Q2211 wdt:P17 ?country .
```

> Notice the final dot in the WHERE block. It is very important in SPARQL and marks the end of the **sentence**.

This query, with Cypher words, would read: starting from the entity whose identifier is Q2211 (Malmö), follow the relationship with type `P17` (country), and return the entity at the end of this relationship. To go further with the comparison to Cypher, the preceding SPARQL query could be written in Cypher as follows:

```
MATCH (n {id: wd:Q2211})-[r {id: wdt:P17}]->(country)
RETURN country
```

So, if you run the preceding SPARQL in the Wikidata online shell, you will get a result like `wd:Q34`, with a link to the Sweden page in Wikidata. So that's great, it works! However, if we want to automatize this treatment, having to click on a link to get the country name is not very convenient. Happily, we can get this information directly from SPARQL. The main difference compared to the previous query is that we have to specify in which language we want the result back. Here, I forced the language to be English:

```
SELECT ?country ?countryLabel
WHERE {
  wd:Q2211 wdt:P17 ?country .
  SERVICE wikibase:label { bd:serviceParam wikibase:language "en". }
}
```

[94]

Executing this query, you now also get the country name, Sweden, as a second column of the result.

Let's go even further. To get the city identifier, Q2211, we had to first search Wikidata and manually introduce it in the query. Can't SPARQL perform this search for us? The answer, as expected, is yes, it can:

```
SELECT ?city ?cityLabel ?countryLabel WHERE {
    ?city rdfs:label "Malmö"@en .
    ?city wdt:P17 ?country .
    SERVICE wikibase:label { bd:serviceParam wikibase:language "en". }
}
```

Instead of starting from a well-known entity, we start by performing a search within Wikidata to find the entities whose label, in English, is Malmö.

However, you'll notice that running this query now returns three rows, all having Malmö as city label, but two of them are in Sweden and the last one is in Norway. If we want to select only the Malmö we are interested in, we will have to narrow down our query and add more criteria. For instance, we can select only big cities:

```
SELECT ?city ?cityLabel ?countryLabel WHERE {
    ?city rdfs:label "Malmö"@en;
          wdt:P31 wd:Q5119 .
    ?city wdt:P17 ?country .
    SERVICE wikibase:label { bd:serviceParam wikibase:language "en". }
}
```

In this query, we see the following:

- **P31 means** instance of.
- **Q1549591 is the identifier for** big city.

So the preceding bold statement, translated to English, could be read as follows:

```
Cities
whose label in English is "Malmö"
AND that are instances of "big city"
```

Now we only select one Malmö in Sweden, which is the Q2211 entity we identified at the beginning of this section.

Next, let's see how to use this query result to extend our Neo4j knowledge graph.

Importing Wikidata into Neo4j

In order to automatize data import into Neo4j, we will use the Wikidata query API:

```
GET https://query.wikidata.org/sparql?format=json&query={SPARQL}
```

Using the `format=json` is not mandatory but it will force the API to return a JSON result instead of the default XML; it is a matter of personal preference. In that way, we will also be able to use the `apoc.load.json` procedure to parse the result and create Neo4j nodes and relationships depending on our needs. Note that if you are used to XML and prefer to manipulate this data format, APOC also has a procedure to import XML into Neo4j: `apoc.load.xml`.

The second parameter of the Wikidata API endpoint is the SPARQL query itself, such as the ones we have written in the previous section. We can run the query to ask for the country and country label of Malmö (entity Q2211):

```
https://query.wikidata.org/sparql?format=json&query=SELECT ?country
?countryLabel WHERE {wd:Q2211 wdt:P17 ?country . SERVICE wikibase:label {
bd:serviceParam wikibase:language "en". }}
```

The resulting JSON that you can directly see in your browser is the following:

```
{
  "head": {
    "vars": [
      "country",
      "countryLabel"
    ]
  },
  "results": {
    "bindings": [
      {
        "country": {
          "type": "uri",
          "value": "http://www.wikidata.org/entity/Q34"
        },
        "countryLabel": {
          "xml:lang": "en",
          "type": "literal",
          "value": "Sweden"
        }
      }
    ]
  }
}
```

If we want to handle this data with Neo4j, we can copy the result into the `wikidata_malmo_country_result.json` file (or download this file from the GitHub repository of this book), and use `apoc.load.json` to access the country name:

```
CALL apoc.load.json("wikidata_malmo_country_result.json") YIELD value as item
RETURN item.results.bindings[0].countryLabel.value
```

Remember to put the file to be imported inside the `import` folder of your active graph.

But, if you remember from Chapter 2, *Cypher Query Language*, APOC also has the ability to perform API calls by itself. It means that the two steps we've just followed – querying Wikidata and saving the result in a file, and importing this data into Neo4j – can be merged into a single step in the following way:

```
WITH 'SELECT ?countryLabel WHERE {wd:Q2211 wdt:P17 ?country. SERVICE wikibase:label { bd:serviceParam wikibase:language "en". }}' as query
CALL apoc.load.jsonParams('http://query.wikidata.org/sparql?format=json&query='
+ apoc.text.urlencode(query), {}, null) YIELD value as item
RETURN item.results.bindings[0].countryLabel.value
```

Using a `WITH` clause here is not mandatory. But if we want to run the preceding query for all `Location` nodes, it is convenient to use such a syntax:

```
MATCH (l:Location) WHERE l.name <> ""
WITH l, 'SELECT ?countryLabel WHERE { ?city rdfs:label "' + l.name + '"@en.
?city wdt:P17 ?country. SERVICE wikibase:label { bd:serviceParam
wikibase:language "en". } }' as query
CALL apoc.load.jsonParams('http://query.wikidata.org/sparql?format=json&query='
+ apoc.text.urlencode(query), {}, null) YIELD value as item
RETURN l.name, item.results.bindings[0].countryLabel.value as country_name
```

This returns a result like the following:

"l.name"	"country_name"
"Dresden"	"Germany"
"Beijing"	"People's Republic of China"
"Seoul"	"South Korea"
"Paris"	"France"

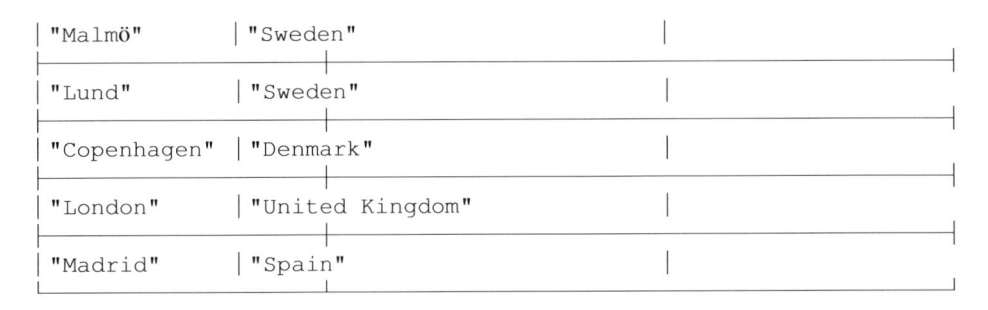

```
| "Malmö"      | "Sweden"         |
| "Lund"       | "Sweden"         |
| "Copenhagen" | "Denmark"        |
| "London"     | "United Kingdom" |
| "Madrid"     | "Spain"          |
```

This result can then be used to create new country nodes with a relationship between the city and the identified country in this way:

```
MATCH (l:Location) WHERE l.name <> ""
WITH l, 'SELECT ?countryLabel WHERE { ?city rdfs:label "' + l.name + '"@en.
?city wdt:P17 ?country. SERVICE wikibase:label { bd:serviceParam
wikibase:language "en". } }' as query
CALL
apoc.load.jsonParams('http://query.wikidata.org/sparql?format=json&query='
+ apoc.text.urlencode(query), {}, null) YIELD value as item
WITH l, item.results.bindings[0].countryLabel.value as country_name
MERGE (c:Country {name: country_name})
MERGE (l)-[:LOCATED_IN]->(c)
```

Our knowledge graph of the Neo4j community on GitHub has been extended thanks to the free online Wikidata resources.

> **TIP**
> Note that if you have to manage large RDF datasets, the neosemantics extension of Neo4j is the way to go instead of APOC:
> https://github.com/neo4j-labs/neosemantics

> The method we used to extract the city from the user-defined location from GitHub is full of broad approximations and the result is often not really accurate. We used this for teaching purposes, but in a real-life scenario, we would rather use some kind of geocoding service such as the one provided by Google or Open Street Map to get a normalized location from a free text user input.

If you navigate through Wikidata, you will see there are many other possibilities for extensions. It does not only contain information about persons and locations but also about some common words. As an example, you can search for `rake`, and you will see that it is classified as an `agricultural tool` used by `farmers` and `gardeners` that can be made out of `plastic` or `steel` or `wood`. The amount of information stored there, in a structured way, is incredible. But there are even more ways to extend a knowledge graph. We are going to take advantage of another source of data: semantic graphs.

Enhancing a knowledge graph from semantic graphs

If you had the curiosity to read the documentation of the GraphAware NLP package, you have already seen the procedures we are going to use now: the `enrich` procedure.

This procedure uses the ConceptNet graph, which relates words together with different kinds of relationships. We can find synonyms and antonyms but also *created by* or *symbol of* relationships. The full list is available at https://github.com/commonsense/conceptnet5/wiki/Relations.

Let's see ConceptNet in action. For this, we first need to select a `Tag` which is the result of the GraphAware `annotate` procedure we used previously. For this example, I will use the `Tag` corresponding to the verb "make" and look for its synonyms. The syntax is the following:

```
MATCH (t:Tag {value: "make"})
CALL ga.nlp.enrich.concept({tag: t, depth: 1,
admittedRelationships:["Synonym"]}
```

The `admittedRelationships` parameter is a list of relationships as defined in ConceptNet (check the preceding link). The procedure created new tags, and relationships of type `IS_RELATED_TO` between the new tags and the original one, "make". We can visualize the result easily with this query:

```
MATCH (t:Tag {value: "make"})-[:IS_RELATED_TO]->(n)
RETURN t, n
```

Empowering Your Business with Pure Cypher

The result is shown in the following diagram. You can see that ConceptNet knows that **produce**, **construct**, **create**, **cause**, and many other verbs are synonyms of **make**:

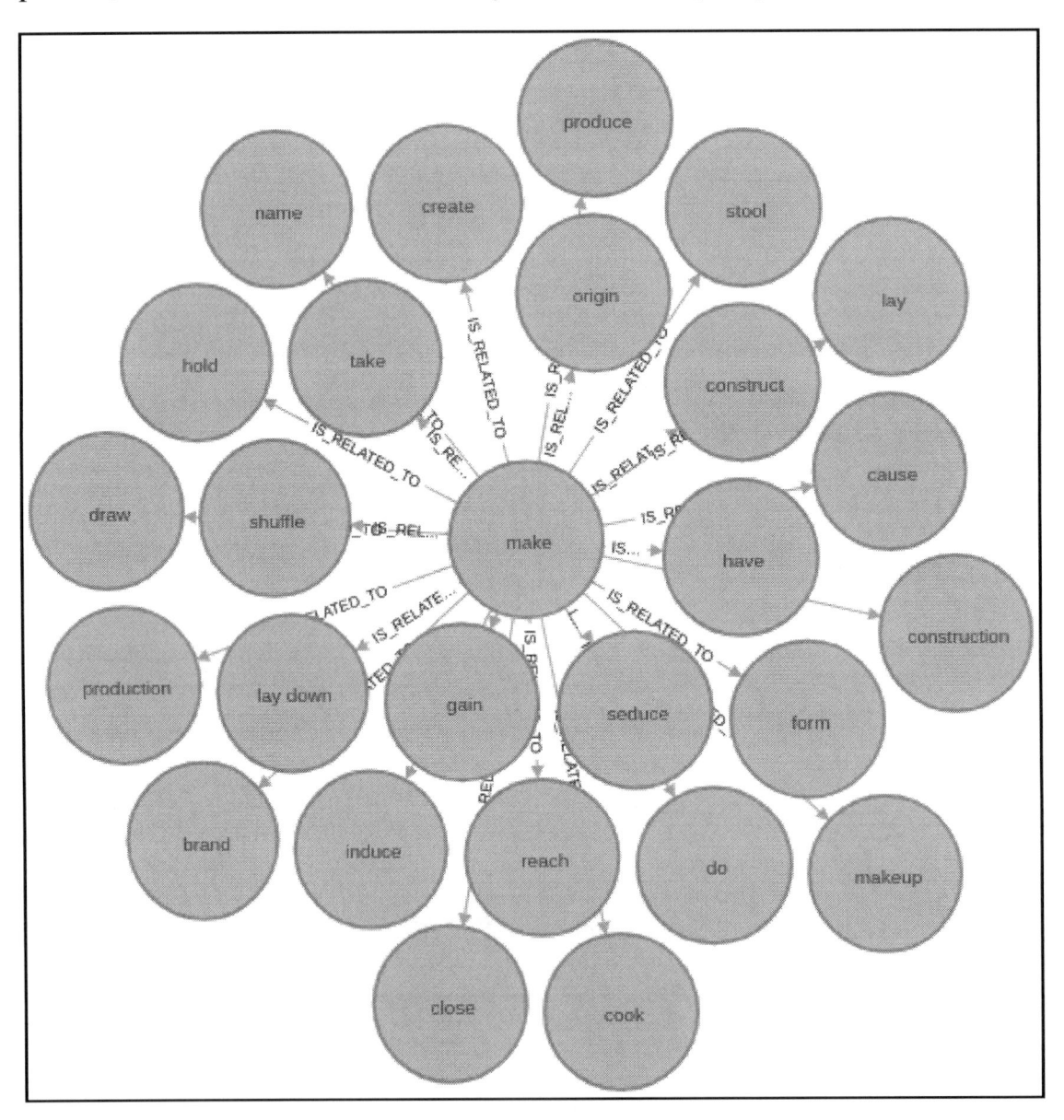

This information is very useful, especially when trying to build a system to understand the user intent. That's the first use case for knowledge graphs we are going to investigate in the next section: graph-based search.

Graph-based search

Graph-based search emerged in 2012, when Google announced its new graph-based search algorithm. It promised more accurate search results, that were closer to a human response to a human question than before. In this section, we are going to talk about the different search methods to understand how graph-based search can be a big improvement for a search engine. We will then discuss the different ways to implement a graph-based search using Neo4j and machine learning.

Search methods

Several search methods have been used since search engines exist in web applications. We can, for instance, think of tags assigned to a blog article that help in classifying the articles and allow to search for articles with a given tag. This method is also used when you assign **keywords** to a given document. This method is quite simple to implement, but is also very limited: what if you forget an important keyword?

Fortunately, one can also use **full-text search**, which consists of matching documents whose text contains the pattern entered by the user. In that case, no need to manually annotate documents with keywords, the full text of the document can be used to index it. Tools such as Elasticsearch are extremely good at indexing text documents and performing full-text searches within them.

But this method is still not perfect. What if the user chooses a different wording to the one you use, but with a similar meaning? Let's say you write about *machine learning*. Wouldn't a user typing *machine learning* be interested in your text? We all remember the times where we had to redefine the search keywords on Google until we get the desired result.

That's where graph-based search enters into the game. By adding context to your data, you will be able to identify that *data science* and *machine learning* are actually related, even if not the same thing, and that a user looking for one of those terms might be interested in articles using the other expression.

To understand better what graph-based search is, let's take a look at the definition given by Facebook in 2013:

> With Graph Search, you simply enter phrases such as "My friends who live in San Francisco", "Photos of my family taken in Copenhagen", or "Dentists my friends like", and Facebook quickly displays a page of the content you've requested.

(Source: `https://www.facebook.com/notes/facebook-engineering/under-the-hood-building-graph-search-beta/10151240856103920`)

The graph-based search was actually first implemented by Google back in 2012. Since then, you have been able to ask questions such as the following:

- *How far is New York from Australia?*
  And you directly get the answer:

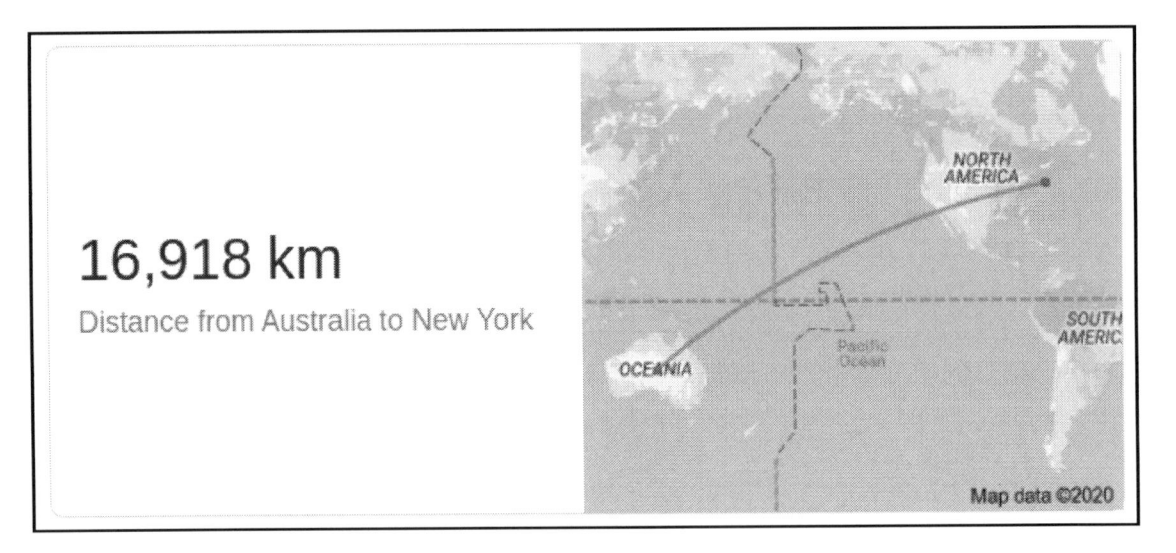

16,918 km
Distance from Australia to New York

Map data ©2020

- *Movies with Leonardo DiCaprio.*
  And you can see at the top of the result page, a list of popular movies Leonardo DiCaprio acted in:

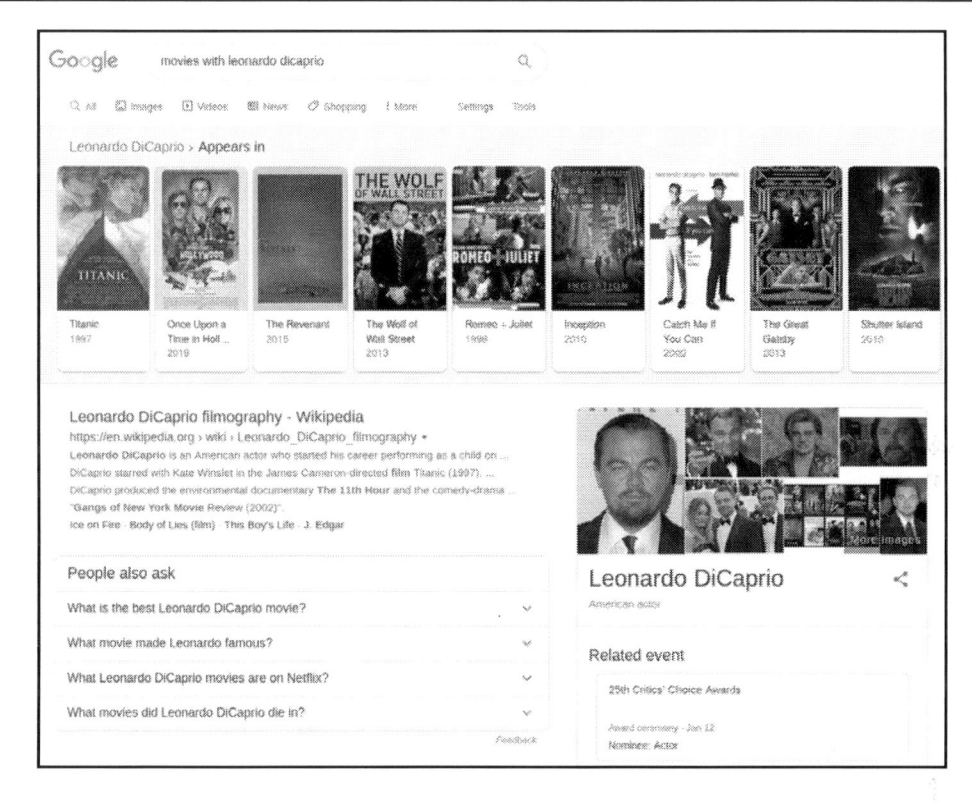

How can Neo4j help in implementing a graph-based search? We will first learn how Cypher enables it to answer complex questions like the preceding one.

Manually building Cypher queries

Firstly, and in order to understand how this search works, we are going to write some Cypher queries manually.

The next table summarizes several kinds of questions together with a possible Cypher query to get to the answer:

Question (English)	Cypher query to get the answer	Answer

When was the "neo4j" repository created?	`MATCH (r:Repository)`
	`WHERE r.name = "neo4j"`
	`RETURN r.created_at`
		2012-11-12T08:46:15Z

Question (English)	Cypher query to get the answer	Answer

Who owns the "neo4j" repository?	`MATCH (r:Repository)<-[:OWNS]-(u:User)`
	`WHERE r.name = "neo4j"`
	`RETURN u.login`
		neo4j

How many people contributed to "neo4j"?	`MATCH (r:Repository)<-[:CONTRIBUTED_TO]-`
	`(u:User)`
	`WHERE r.name = "neo4j"`
	`RETURN count(DISTINCT u.login)`
		30

Which "neo4j" contributors are living in Sweden?	`MATCH (:Country {name: "Sweden"})<-`
	`[:LOCATED_IN]-(:Location)<-`
	`[:LOCATED_IN]-(u:User)-[:CONTRIBUTED_TO]->`
	`(:Repository {name: "neo4j"})`
	`RETURN u.login`
		"sherfert", "henriknyman", "sherfert", ...

You can see that Cypher allows us to answer many different types of questions in quite a few characters. The knowledge we have built in the previous section, based on other data sources such as Wikidata, is also important.

However, so far, this process assumes a human being is reading the question and able to translate it to Cypher. This is a solution that is not scalable, as you can imagine. That's why we are now going to investigate some techniques to automate this translation, via NLP and state-of-the-art machine learning techniques used in the context of translation.

Automating the English to Cypher translation

In order to automate the English to Cypher translation, we can either use some logic based on language understanding or go even further and use machine learning techniques used for language translation.

Using NLP

In the previous section, we used some NLP techniques to enhance our knowledge graph. The same techniques can be applied in order to analyze a question written by a user and extract its meaning. Here we are going to use a small Python script to help us convert a user question to a Cypher query.

In terms of NLP, the Python ecosystem contains several packages that can be used. For our needs here, we are going to use spaCy (https://spacy.io/). It is very easy to use, especially if you don't want to bother with technical implementations. It can be easily installed via the Python package manager, pip:

```
pip install -U spacy
```

It is also available on conda-forge if you prefer to use conda.

Let's now see how spaCy can help us in building a graph-based search engine. Starting from an English sentence such as *Leonardo DiCaprio is born in Los Angeles*, spaCy can identify the different parts of the sentence and the relationship between them:

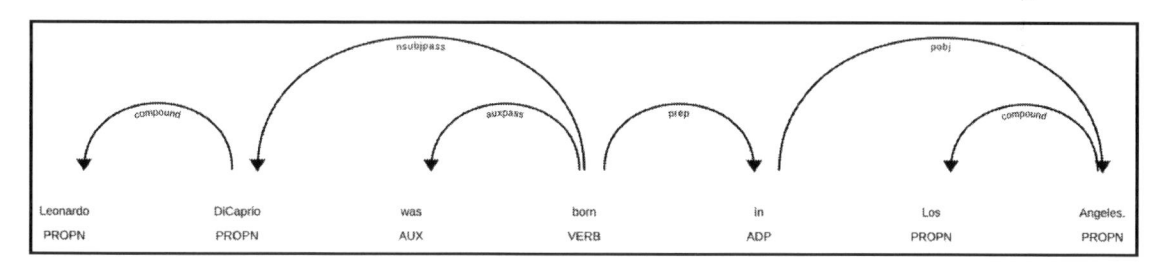

The previous diagram was generated from the following simple code snippet:

```
import spacy
// load English model
nlp = spacy.load("en_core_web_sm")

text = "Leonardo DiCaprio is born in Los Angeles."

// analyze text
document = nlp(text)

// generate svg image
svg = spacy.displacy.render(document, style="dep")
with open("dep.svg", "w") as f:
    f.write(svg)
```

On top of these relationships, we can also extract named entities, as we did with GraphAware and Stanford NLP tools in the previous section. The result of the preceding text is as follows:

This information can be accessed within `spaCy` in the following way:

```
for ent in document.ents:
    print(ent.text, ":", ent.label_)
```

This piece of code prints the following results:

```
Leonardo DiCaprio : PERSON
Los Angeles : GPE
```

Leonardo DiCaprio is well identified as a `PERSON`. And according to the documentation at `https://spacy.io/api/annotation#named-entities`, GPE stands for *Countries, cities, states*; so Los Angles was also identified correctly.

How does that help? Well, now that we have entities, we have node labels:

```
MATCH (:PERSON {name: "Leonardo DiCaprio"})
MATCH (:GPE {name: "Los Angeles"})
```

The two preceding Cypher queries can be generated from Python:

```
for ent in document.ents:
    q = f"MATCH (n:{ent.label_} {{name: '{ent.text}' }})"
    print(q)
```

> **TIP**
> Python f-strings will replace `{var}` by the value of the `var` variable in the string scope. In order for the curly brackets needed in Cypher not to be interpreted, we have to double them, hence the `{{ }}` syntax in the code, which will be printed as valid Cypher at the end.

In order to identify which relationship we should use to relate the two entities, we are going to use the verb in the sentence:

```
for token in document:
    if token.pos_ == "VERB":
        print(token.text)
```

The only printed result will be `born`, since this is the only verb in our sentence. We can update the preceding code to print the Cypher relationship:

```
for token in document:
    if token.pos_ == "VERB":
        print(f"[:{token.text.upper()}]")
```

Putting all the pieces together, we can write a query to check whether the statement is true or not:

```
MATCH (n0:PERSON {name: 'Leonardo DiCaprio' })
MATCH (n1:GPE {name: 'Los Angeles' })
RETURN EXISTS((n1)-[:BORN]-(n2))
```

This query returns `true` if the pattern we are looking for exists in our working graph, and `false` otherwise.

As you can see, NLP is very powerful and a lot can be done from it if we want to push the analysis further. But the amount of work required is incredibly high, especially if we want to cover several fields (not only people and locations but also gardening products or GitHub repositories). That's the reason why, in the next section, we are going to investigate another possibility enabled by NLP and machine learning: an automatic English to Cypher translator.

Using translation-like models

As you can see from the previous paragraph, natural language understanding helps in automating the human language to a Cypher query, but it relies on some rules. These rules have to be carefully defined and you can imagine how difficult this can be when the number of rules increases. That's the reason why we can also find help in machine learning techniques, especially those related to translation, another part of NLP.

Translation consists in taking a text in a (human) language, and outputting a text in another (human) language, as illustrated in the following diagram, where the translator is a machine learning model, usually relying on *artificial neural networks*:

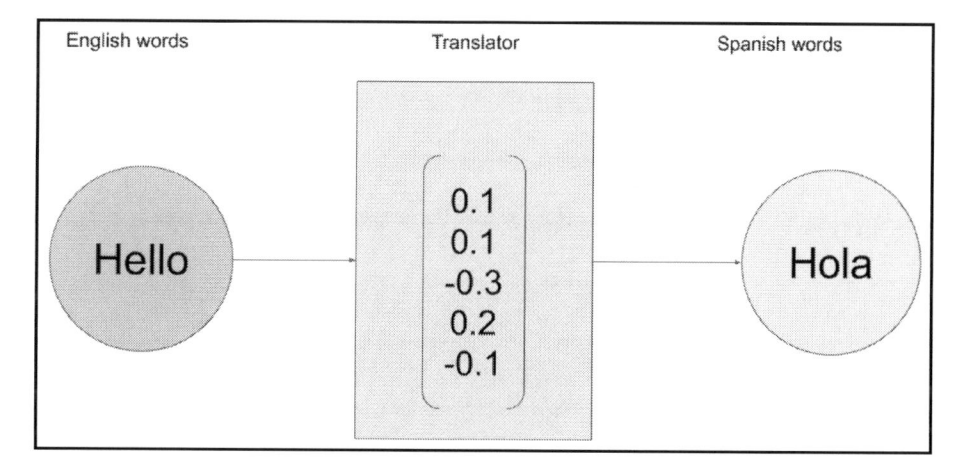

The translator's goal is to assign a value (or a vector of values) to each word, this vector carrying the meaning of the word. We will talk about this in more detail in the chapter dedicated to embedding (Chapter 10, *Graph Embedding from Graphs to Matrices*).

But without knowing the details of the process, can we imagine applying the same logic to translate a human language to Cypher? Indeed, using the same techniques as those used for human language translation, we can build models to convert English sentences (questions) to a Cypher query.

The Octavian-AI company worked on an implementation of such a model in their english2cypher package (https://github.com/Octavian-ai/english2cypher). It is a neural network model implemented with TensorFlow in Python. The model learned from a list of questions regarding the London Tube, together with their *translations* in Cypher. The training set looks like this:

```
english: How many stations are between King's Cross and Paddington?

cypher: MATCH (var1) MATCH (var2)
        MATCH tmp1 = shortestPath((var1)-[*]-(var2))
        WHERE var1.id="c2b8c082-7c5b-4f70-9b7e-2c45872a6de8"
        AND var2.id="40761fab-abd2-4acf-93ae-e8bd06f1e524"
        WITH nodes(tmp1) AS var3
        RETURN length(var3) - 2
```

Even if we have not yet studied the shortest path methods (see Chapter 4, *The Graph Data Science Library and Path Finding*), we can understand the preceding query:

1. It starts from getting the two stations mentioned in the question.
2. It then finds the shortest path between those two stations.
3. And counts the number of nodes (stations) in the shortest path.
4. The answer to the question is the length of the path, minus 2 since we do not want to count the start and end station.

But the power of machine learning models lies within their prediction: from a set of known data (the train dataset), they are able to issue **predictions** for unknown data. The preceding model would, for instance, be able to answer questions such as "How many stations are there between Liverpool Street Station and Hyde park Corner?" even if it has never seen it before.

In order to use such a model within your business, you will have to create a training sample made of a list of English questions with the corresponding Cypher queries able to answer them. This part is similar to the one we performed in the *Manually building Cypher queries* section. Then you will have to train a new model. If you are not familiar with machine learning and model training, this topic will be covered in more detail in `Chapter 8`, *Using Graph-Based Features in Machine Learning*.

You now have a better overview of how graph-based search works and why Neo4j is a good structure to hold the data if user search is an important feature for your company. But knowledge graph applications are not limited to search engines. Another interesting application of the knowledge graph is recommendations, as we will discover now.

Recommendation engine

Recommendations are now unavoidable if you work for an e-commerce website. But e-commerce is not the only use case for recommendations. You can also receive recommendations for people you may want to follow on Twitter, meetups you may attend, or repositories you might like knowing about. Knowledge graphs are a good approach to generate those recommendations.

In this section, we are going to use our GitHub graph to recommend to users new repositories they are likely to contribute to or follow. We will explore several possibilities, split into two cases: either your graph contains some social information (users can like or follow each other) or it doesn't. We'll start from the case where you do not have access to any social data since it is the most common one.

Product similarity recommendations

Recommending products, whether we are talking about movies, gardening tools, or meetups, share some common patterns. Here are some common-sense assertions that can lead to a good recommendation:

- Products in the same categories to a product already bought are more likely to be useful to the user. For instance, if you buy a rake, it probably means you like gardening, so a lawnmower could be of interest to you.
- There are some products that often get bought together, for instance, printers, ink, and paper. If you buy a printer, it is natural to recommend the ink and paper other users also bought.

We are going to see the implementations of those two approaches using Cypher. We will again use the GitHub graph as a playground. The important parts of its structure are shown in the next schema:

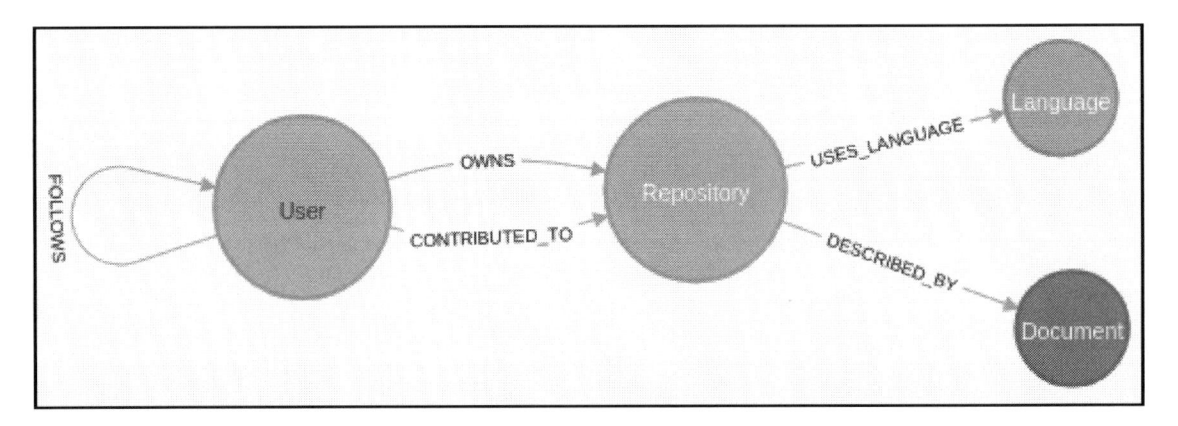

It contains the following entities:

- **Node labels:** User, Repository, Language, and Document
- **Relationships:**
  - A User node owns or contributes to one or several Repository nodes.
  - A Repository node has one or several Language nodes.
  - A User node can follow another User node.

Thanks to the GitHub API, the USES_LANGUAGE relationship even holds a property quantifying the number of bytes of code using that language.

Products in the same category

In the GitHub graph, we will consider the language as categorizing the repositories. All repositories using Scala will be in the same category. For a given user, we can get the languages used by the repositories they contributed to with the following:

```
MATCH (:User {login: "boggle"})-[:CONTRIBUTED_TO]->(repo:Repository)-
[:USES_LANGUAGE]->(lang:Language)
RETURN lang
```

If we want to find the other repositories using the same language, we can extend the path from the language node to the other repositories in this way:

```
MATCH (u:User {login: "boggle"})-[:CONTRIBUTED_TO]->(repo:Repository)-
[:USES_LANGUAGE]->(lang:Language)<-[:USES_LANGUAGE]-
(recommendation:Repository)
WHERE NOT EXISTS ((u)-[:CONTRIBUTED_TO]->(repo))
RETURN recommendation
```

For instance, the user `boggle` contributed to the `neo4j` repository, which is partly written using Scala. With that technique, we would recommend to this user the repositories `neotrients` or `JUnitSlowTestDiscovery`, also using Scala:

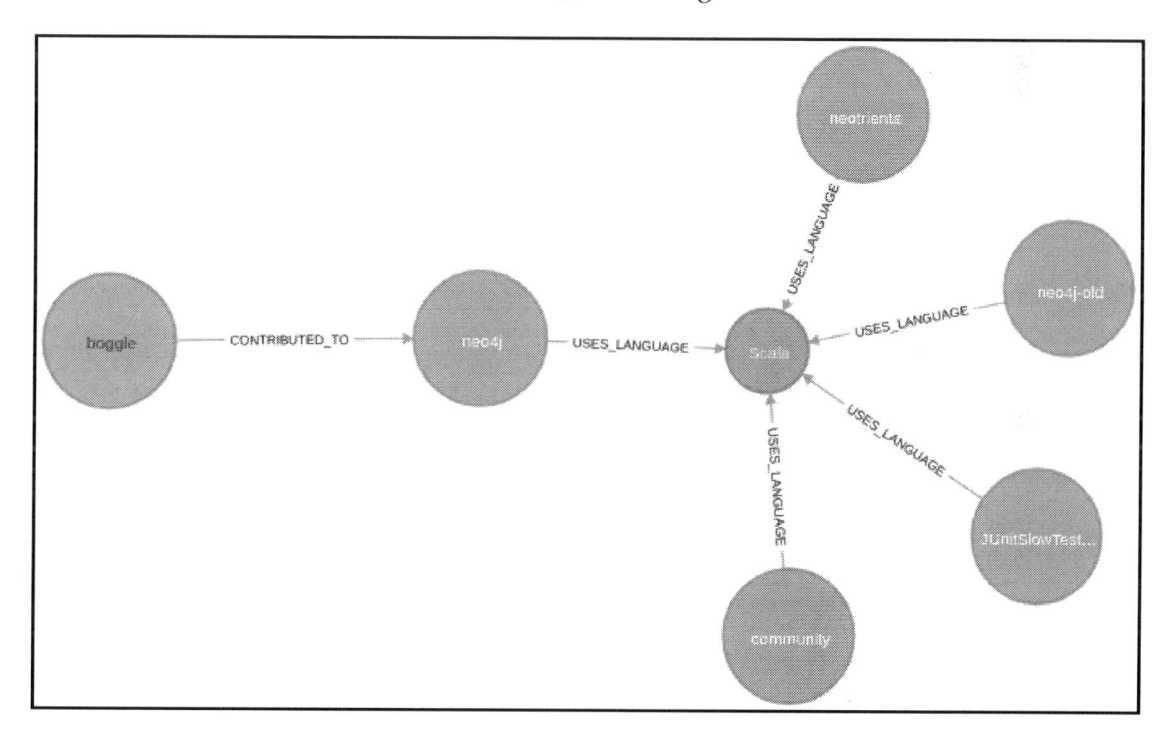

However, recommending all repositories using Scala is like recommending all gardening tools because a user bought a rake. It is maybe not accurate enough, especially when the categories contain lots of items. Let's see which other kinds of methods can be used to improve this technique.

[111]

Products frequently bought together

One possible solution is to trust your users. Information about their behavior is also valuable.

Consider the pattern in the following diagram:

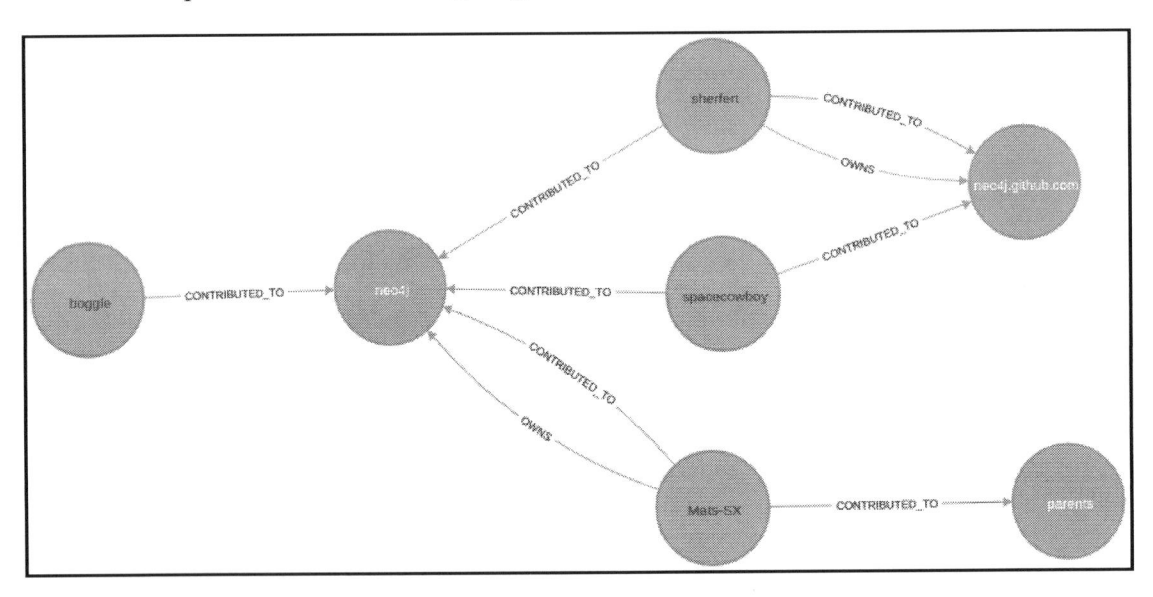

The user `boggle` contributed to the repository `neo4j`. Three more users contributed to it, and also contributed to the repositories `parents` and `neo4j.github.com`. Maybe `boggle` would be interested in contributing to one of those repositories:

```
MATCH (user:User {login: "boggle"})-
[:CONTRIBUTED_TO]->(common_repository:Repository)<-[:CONTRIBUTED_TO]-
(other_user:User)-[:CONTRIBUTED_TO]->(recommendation:Repository)
WHERE user <> other_user
RETURN recommendation
```

We can even group together this method and the preceding one, by selecting only repositories using a language the user knows and with at least one common contributor:

```
MATCH (user:User {login: "boggle"})-
[:CONTRIBUTED_TO]->(common_repository:Repository)<-[:CONTRIBUTED_TO]-
(other_user:User)-[:CONTRIBUTED_TO]->(recommendation:Repository)
MATCH (common_repository)-[:USES_LANGUAGE]->(:Language)<-[:USES_LANGUAGE]-
(recommendation)
WHERE user <> other_user
RETURN recommendation
```

When having only a few matches, we can afford to display all returned items. But if your database grows, you will find a lot of possible recommendations. In that case, finding a way to rank the recommended items would be essential.

Recommendation ordering

If you look again at the preceding image, you can see that the repository `neo4j.github.com` is shared between two people, while the `parents` repository would be recommended by only one person. This information can be used to rank the recommendations. The corresponding Cypher query would be as follows:

```
MATCH (user:User {login: "boggle"})-
[:CONTRIBUTED_TO]->(common_repository:Repository)<-[:CONTRIBUTED_TO]-
(other_user:User)-[:CONTRIBUTED_TO]->(recommendation:Repository)
WHERE user <> other_user
WITH recommendation, COUNT(other_user) as reco_importance
RETURN recommendation
ORDER BY reco_importance DESC
LIMIT 5
```

The new `WITH` clause is introduced to perform the aggregation: for each possible recommended repositories, we count how many users would recommend it.

This is the first way of using user data to provide accurate recommendations. Another way is, when possible, to take into account using social relationships, as we will see now.

Social recommendations

If your knowledge graph contains data related to social links between users, like GitHub or Medium does, a brand new field of recommendations is open to you. Because you know which person a given user likes or follows, you can have a better idea about which type of content this user is likely to appreciate. For instance, if someone you follow on Medium claps a story, it is much more likely you will also like it, compared to any other random story you can find on Medium.

Luckily, we have some social data in our GitHub knowledge graph, through the `FOLLOWS` relationships. So will use this information to provide other recommendations to our users.

Products bought by a friend of mine

If we want to recommend new repositories to our GitHub users, we can think of the following rule: repositories of a user I follow are more likely to be of interest to me, otherwise I wouldn't follow those users. We can use Cypher to identify those repositories:

```
MATCH (u:User {login: "mkhq"})-[:FOLLOWS]->(following:User)-
[:CONTRIBUTED_TO]->(recommendation:Repository)
WHERE NOT EXISTS ((u)-[:CONTRIBUTED_TO]->(recommendation))
RETURN DISTINCT recommendation
```

This query matches patterns similar to the following one:

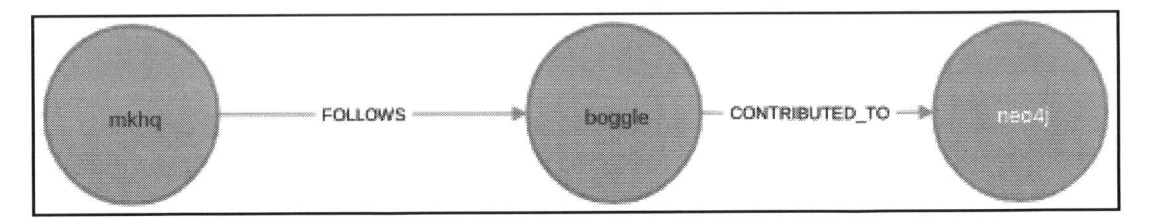

We can also use recommendation ordering here. The higher the number of people I follow that also contributed to a given repository, the higher the probability that I will also contribute to it. This translates into Cypher in the following way:

```
MATCH (u:User {login: "mkhq"})-[:FOLLOWS]->(following:User)-
[:CONTRIBUTED_TO]->(recommendation:Repository)
WHERE NOT EXISTS ((u)-[:CONTRIBUTED_TO]->(recommendation))
WITH user, recommendation, COUNT(following) as
nb_following_contributed_to_repo
RETURN recommendation
ORDER BY nb_following_contributed_to_repo DESC
LIMIT 5
```

The first part of the query is exactly the same as the previous one, while the second part is similar to the query we wrote in the previous section: for each possible recommendation, we count how many users `mkhq` is following would recommend it.

We have seen several ways of finding recommendations based on pure Cypher. They can be extended depending on your data: the more information you have about your products and customers, the more precise the recommendations can be. In the following chapters, we will discover algorithms to create clusters of nodes within the same community. This concept of community can also be used in the context of recommendations, assuming users within the same community are more likely to like or buy the same products. More details will be given in `Chapter 7`, *Community Detection and Similarity Measures*.

Summary

This chapter described in detail how to create a knowledge graph, either using already structured data, such as an API result, or an existing knowledge graph that can be queried, such as Wikidata. We also learned how to use NLP and named entity recognition in order to extract information from unstructured data, such as a human-written text, and turn this information into a structured graph. We have also learned about two important applications of knowledge graphs: graph-based search, the method used by Google to provide even more accurate results to the users, and recommendations, which are a mandatory step for e-commerce today.

All of this was done with Cypher, extended by some plugins such as APOC or the NLP GraphAware plugin. In the rest of this book, we will make extensive use of another very important library when dealing with graph analytics: the Neo4j Graph algorithms library. The next chapter will introduce it and give application examples in the context of the shortest pathfinder challenges.

Questions

Using Wikidata, what kind of contextual information can we add to the repository language?

Further reading

- If you are new to NLP and want to learn more about it, you can start with *Natural Language Processing Fundamentals*, D. Gunning and S. Ghosh, Packt Publishing.
- Then, consider checking out *Hands-On Natural Language Processing with Python*, R. Shanmugamani and R. Arumugam, Packt Publishing.
- W3C specifications:
  - RDF: https://www.w3.org/TR/rdf-concepts/
  - SPARQL: https://www.w3.org/TR/rdf-sparql-query/
- Neural Machine Translation models used by Google Translate:
  - The initial paper by Google: https://research.google/pubs/pub45610/
  - The implementation using Tensorflow: https://github.com/tensorflow/nmt

Section 2: Graph Algorithms

In part II, we will learn about specific data analysis techniques for graph data, including shortest path methods with more advanced features.

This section consists of the following chapters:

- Chapter 4, *The Graph Data Science Library and Path Finding*
- Chapter 5, *Spatial Data*
- Chapter 6, *Node Importance*
- Chapter 7, *Community Detection and Similarity Measures*

4
The Graph Data Science Library and Path Finding

In this chapter, we will use the **Graph Data Science (GDS)** library for the first time, which is the successor of the Graph Algorithm library for Neo4j. After an introduction to the main principles of the library, we will learn about the pathfinding algorithms. Following that, we will use implementations in Python and Java to understand how they work. We will then learn how to use the optimized version of these algorithms, implemented in the GDS plugin. We will cover the Dijkstra and A* shortest path algorithms, alongside other path-related methods such as the traveling-salesman problem and minimum spanning trees.

The following topics will be covered in this chapter:

- Introducing the Graph Data Science plugin
- Understanding the importance of shortest path through its applications
- Going through Dijkstra's shortest path algorithm
- Finding the shortest path with the A* algorithm and its heuristics
- Discovering the other path-related algorithms in the GDS library
- Optimizing our process using graphs

Technical requirements

The following tools will be used throughout this chapter:

- Neo4j (≥ 3.5) with the Neo4j Graph Data Science ≥ 1.0 plugin
- Some code examples will be written in Python (recommended ≥ 3.6)
- The full code files used are available at: `https://github.com/PacktPublishing/Hands-On-Graph-Analytics-with-Neo4j/ch4/`

> If you are using **Neo4j < 4.0**, then the latest compatible version of the **GDS** plugin is **1.1**, whereas if you are using **Neo4j ≥ 4.0**, then the first compatible version of the **GDS** plugin is **1.2**.

Introducing the Graph Data Science plugin

We'll start by introducing the GDS plugin. Provided by Neo4j, it extends the capabilities of its graph database for analytics purposes. In this section, we will go through naming conventions and introduce the very important concept of graph projection, which we will use intensively in the rest of this book.

The first implementation of this plugin was done in the *Graph Algorithms library*, which was first released in June 2017. In 2020, it was replaced by the GDS plugin. The GDS plugin includes performance optimization for the most used algorithms so that they can run on huge graphs (several billions of nodes). Even though I will be highlighting the optimized algorithms in this book, I would suggest you refer to the latest documentation to ensure you get the most up-to-date information (`https://neo4j.com/docs/graph-data-science/current/`).

> The full code of the GDS plugin is open source and available on GitHub at: `https://github.com/neo4j/graph-data-science`.

Extending Neo4j with custom functions and procedures

We have actually already used several Neo4j extensions in the previous chapters. APOC are neo4j-nlp are both built using the tools provided by Neo4j to access the core database from an external library. Neo4j starting offering this with its 3.0 release.

Users are given the opportunity to define custom functions and/or procedures. Let's first understand the difference between these two types of objects.

The difference between procedures and functions

The main difference between a function and a procedure is the number of results returned for each row. A function must return one and only one result per row, while procedures can return more values.

Functions

To get the list of available functions in your running Neo4j instance, you can use the following:

```
CALL dbms.functions()
```

The default installation (without plugins) already contains some functions – for instance, the `randomUUID` function.

The result of a function is accessible through a normal Cypher query. For instance, to generate a random UUID, you can use the following:

```
RETURN randomUUID()
```

This can be used to generate a random UUID when creating a node like this:

```
CREATE (:Node {uuid: randomUUID()})
```

A new node will be created with a property `uuid` containing a randomly generated UUID.

Procedures

A list of available procedures can be obtained with the following query:

```
CALL dbms.procedures()
```

The Graph Data Science Library and Path Finding

To invoke a procedure, we have to use the CALL keyword.

> **TIP**
> That means that dbms.functions and dbms.procedures are actually procedures themselves.

For instance, db.labels is a procedure available in the default installation. By using the following query, you will see a list of labels used in the active graph:

```
CALL db.labels()
```

As it returns several rows, it can't be used like the randomUUID function to set a node property. This is why it is a procedure and not a function.

Writing a custom function in Neo4j

If you are interested in writing your own custom procedure, Neo4j provides a Java API for this. In a Maven project, you will have to include the following dependency:

```
<dependency>
    <groupId>org.neo4j</groupId>
    <artifactId>neo4j</artifactId>
    <version>${neo4j.version}</version>
    <scope>provided</scope>
</dependency>
```

A user-defined function that simply multiplies two numbers together can be implemented with the following piece of code:

```
@UserFunction
@Description("packt.multiply(value, value)")
public Double multiply(
        @Name("number1") Double number1,
        @Name("number2") Double number2
) {
    if (number1 == null || number2 == null) {
        return null;
    }
    return number1 * number2;
}
```

Let's break down this code:

1. The `@UserFunction` annotation declares a user-defined function. Similarly, procedures can be declared with the `@Procedure` annotation.
2. We then declare a function named `multiply`, with the return type `Double`. This accepts two parameters: `number1` (`Double`) and `number2` (`Double`).
3. If either of these numbers is null, the function returns null, otherwise, it returns the product of the two numbers.

After building the project and copying the generated JAR into the plugins directory of our graph, we will be able to use this new function as follows:

```
RETURN packt.multiply(10.1, 2)
```

> For more information and examples, you can check the the Neo4j documentation: https://neo4j.com/docs/java-reference/current/extending-neo4j/procedures-and-functions/.

Let's now focus on the GDS plugin.

GDS library content

The GDS plugin contains several types of algorithms. In this chapter, we will focus on the shortest path algorithms, but in later chapters, we'll also learn how to do the following:

- **Measure node importance**: The algorithms we use for this are called *centrality algorithms*. They include, for example, the PageRank algorithms developed by Google to rank search results (see Chapter 5, *Node Importance*).
- **Identify communities of nodes** (see Chapter 7, *Community Detection and Similarity Measures*).
- Extract features to **perform link prediction** (see Chapter 9, *Predicting Relationships*).
- Run **graph embedding** algorithms to learn features from the graph structure (see Chapter 10, *Graph Embeddings—from Graphs to Matrices*).

The names of procedures have a common syntax:

```
gds.<tier>.<algo>.<write|stream>(graphName, configuration)
```

Let's look at each of the components in detail:

- `tier` is optional. If the procedure name doesn't contain `tier`, it means that the algorithm is fully supported and has a production-ready implementation. Other possible values are `alpha` or `beta`. The `alpha` tier contains the algorithms ported from the Graph Algorithms library, but not yet optimized.
- `algo` is the algorithm name, for instance, `shortestPath`.
- `write | stream` allows you to control the way the results will be rendered (more about this in the next section).
- `graphName` is the name of the projected graph the algorithm will be run on.
- `configuration` is a map to define the algorithm parameters.

We will detail the available options in the `configuration` map for each of the algorithms we will study in this book. But before that, we need to understand what the projected graph is.

> **TIP**: Some algorithms are likely to move from `alpha` to `beta` or production in the upcoming releases of the GDS.

To find the exact name of a procedure, you can use this query:

```
CALL gds.list() YIELD name, description, signature
WHERE name =~ ".*shortestPath.*"
RETURN name, description, signature
```

Defining the projected graph

In practice, most of the time, you do not want to run a GDS algorithm on your full Neo4j graph. You can reduce the size of the data used in the algorithm by selecting the nodes and relationships of interest to you in that particular case. The GDS plugin implements the **projected graph** concept for that purpose.

The projected graph is a lighter version of your Neo4j graph, containing only a subset of nodes, relationships, and properties. Reducing the size of the graph allows it to fit into the RAM, making access easier and faster.

We can use **named projected graphs**, defined for the length of a session, or **anonymous projected graphs**, defined on the fly when running algorithms. Although this is not mandatory, we are mainly going to use named projected graphs in this book, which allow us to split the projected graph definition and the algorithm configuration.

The projected graph is highly customizable. You can select specific label(s) and type(s), rename them, and even create new ones.

Native projections

The first way of creating a projected graph is to list the node labels, relationship types, and properties you want to include. For this, we will use the `gds.graph.create` procedure to create a **named projected graph**. Its signature is as follows:

```
CALL gds.graph.create(
    graphName::STRING,
    nodeProjection::STRING, LIST or MAP,
    relationshipProjection::STRING, LIST or MAP,
    configuration::MAP
)
```

The simplest way of using this procedure is to include all nodes and relationships like this:

```
CALL gds.graph.create("projGraphAll", "*", "*")
```

The `projGarphAll` graph is now available and we will be able to tell the graph algorithms to run on this graph.

If you need more customization, here is the full signature of a node projection:

```
{
    <node-label>: {
        label: <neo4j-label>,
        properties: {
            <property-key-1>: {
                property: <neo-property-key>,
                defaultValue: <numeric-value>
            },
            [...]
        }
    },
    [...]
}
```

The Graph Data Science Library and Path Finding

The following node projection includes nodes with the `User` label and the `name` property. If the property is missing for a given node, an empty string is used instead (default value):

```
{
    "User": {
        label: "User",
        properties: {name: {property: "name", defaultValue: ""}}
    }
}
```

Similarly, relationship projections are defined with the following:

```
{
    <relationship-type>: {
        type: <neo4j-type>,
        projection: <projection-type>,
        aggregation: <aggregation-type>,
        properties: {
            <property-key-1>: {
                property: <neo4j-property-key>,
                defaultValue: <numeric-value>,
                aggregation: <aggregation-type>
            },
            [...]
        }
    },
    [...]
}
```

Shortcuts are fortunately possible when we do not want to redefine everything. For instance, to select all nodes with the `User` label and all relationships with the `FOLLOWS` type, you can use the following:

```
CALL gds.graph.create("myProjectedGraph", "User", "FOLLOWS")
```

This syntax already allows a lot of customization for the objects to include in the projected graph. If this is not enough, the projected graph can also be defined via a Cypher query, as we will discuss now.

Cypher projections

In order to customize the projected graph even more, you can use Cypher projection. It enables us to create relationships on the fly that will only be created in the projected graph and not in the Neo4j graph. The syntax to create the projected graph is quite similar to the native projected graph syntax, except that the configuration of nodes and relationships is done through a Cypher query:

```
CALL gds.graph.create.cypher(
    graphName::STRING,
    nodeQuery::STRING,
    relationshipQuery::STRING,
    configuration::MAP
)
```

The only constraints are as follows:

- nodeQuery must return a property named id, containing a node unique identifier.
- relationshipQuery must contain two properties, source and destination, indicating the source and destination node identifiers.

The equivalent of myProjectedGraph with Cypher projection would be the following:

```
CALL gds.graph.create.cypher(
    "myProjectedCypherGraph",
    "MATCH (u:User) RETURN id(u) as id",
    "MATCH (u:User)-[:FOLLOWS]->(v:User) RETURN id(u) as source, id(v) as destination"
)
```

Cypher projections are really useful to add relationships or properties *on the fly* in the projected graph. We will see several examples of this feature later in this book (Chapter 5, *Spatial Data*, and Chapter 8, *Using Graph-Based Features in Machine Learning*).

> Be careful: projected graphs are lost if you have to restart your Neo4j instance.

Streaming or writing results back to the graph

Once we have defined the input for our graph algorithm procedure, the projected graph, we also have to decide what the plugin will do with the results. There are three possible options:

- **Stream the results**: The results will be made available as a stream, either in the Neo4j browser or readable from the Neo4j drivers in different languages (Java, Python, Go, .NET, and so on).
- **Write the results to the Neo4j graph**: If the number of affected nodes is really big, streaming the results might not be a good option. In that scenario, it is possible to write the results of the algorithm into the initial graph; for instance, adding a property to the affected nodes or adding a relationship.
- **Mutate the projected graph**: The algorithm results are saved as a new property in the in-memory graph. They will have to be copied to the Neo4j graph later on, using the `gds.graph.writeNodeProperties` procedure.

In this book, we will work with static projected graphs, either using stream or write mode. The full pipeline is summarized in the following figure:

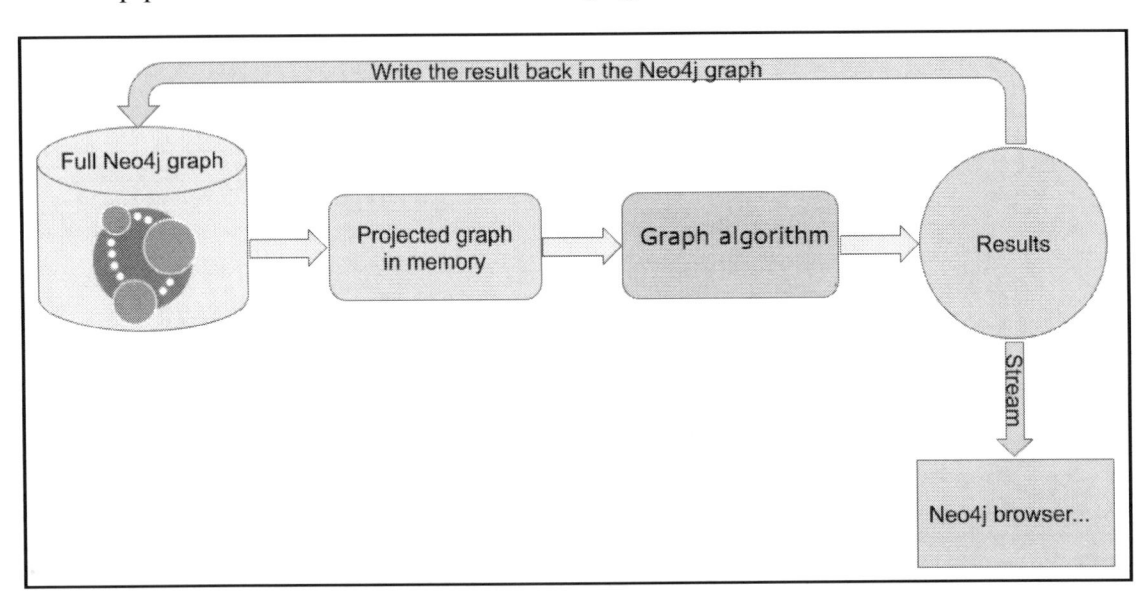

The choice between these two return modes is made via the procedure name:

- `gds.<tier>.<algo>.stream` to get streamed results
- `gds.<tier>.<algo>.write` to write the results back in the original graph

> **TIP:** Similarly, to mutate the projected graph, you would use `gds.<tier>.<algo>.mutate`.

> Some algorithms do not have both return modes available. We will highlight them in this book but always refer to the latest documentation in case of changes.

With all the principles of the GDS in mind, we can get on with our first use case: shortest path algorithms. Before going into the details of implementation, let's review some applications for pathfinding algorithms, including (but not limited to) routing applications.

Understanding the importance of shortest path algorithms through their applications

When trying to find applications for shortest pathfinders on a graph, we think of car navigation via GPS, but there are many more use cases. This section gives an overview of the different applications of pathfinding. We will talk about networks and video games, and give an introduction to the traveling-salesman problem.

Routing within a network

Routing often refers to GPS navigation, but some more surprising applications are also possible.

GPS

The name GPS is actually used for two different technologies:

- The **Global Positioning System (GPS)** itself is a way of finding your precise location on Earth. It is made possible by a constellation of satellites orbiting around the planet and sending continuous signals. Depending on which signals your device receives, an algorithm based on triangulation methods can determine your position.

The Graph Data Science Library and Path Finding

> The satellites used by the GPS system all belong to the USA. Equivalent systems have been or are being developed by other countries. For instance, Russia has GLONASS, while the European system, Galileo, is planned to be fully operational in 2020.

- **Routing algorithms**: From your position and the position of your destination, an algorithm with good knowledge about the *roads* around you should compute the shortest route from point A, your position, to point B, your destination.

The second bullet point here is made possible due to graphs. As we discussed in Chapter 1, *Graph Databases*, a road network is a perfect application for graphs, where junctions are the vertices (nodes) of the graph and the road segments between them are the edges. This chapter will discuss the shortest path algorithms and in the next chapter (Chapter 5, *Spatial Data*), we will create a routing engine.

The shortest path within a social network

Within a social network, the shortest path between two people is called a degree of separation. Studying the distribution of degrees of separation gives insights into the structure of the network.

Other applications

As is the case with graphs, there are plenty of real-world applications for pathfinding algorithms. The following sections are two examples of interesting use cases, but many more can be found in different fields.

Video games

Graphs have been frequently used in video games. The game environment can be modeled as a grid, which in turn can be seen as a graph in which each cell is a node and adjacent cells are connected through an edge. Finding paths within that graph allows the player to move around the environment, avoiding collisions with obstacles.

Science

Some applications of pathfinding within a graph have been studied in several scientific fields, especially genetics, where researchers study the relationships between genes in a given sequence.

Chapter 4

You can probably think of other applications in your field of expertise.

Let's now focus on the most famous shortest path algorithm, the Dijkstra algorithm.

Dijkstra's shortest paths algorithm

Dijkstra's algorithm was developed by the Dutch computer scientist E. W. Dijkstra in the 1950s. Its purpose is to find the shortest path between two nodes in a graph. The first subsection will guide you through how the algorithm works. The second subsection will be dedicated to the use of Dijkstra's algorithm within Neo4j and the GDS plugin.

Understanding the algorithm

Dijkstra's algorithm is probably the most famous path finding algorithm. It is a greedy algorithm that will traverse the graph breadth first (see the following figure), starting from a given node (the start node) and trying to make the optimal choice regarding the shortest path at each step:

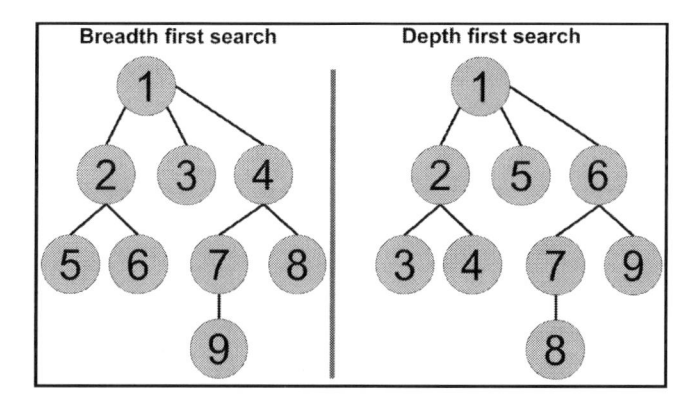

Graph traversal (reminder from Chapter 1, *Graph Databases*)

In order to understand the algorithm, let's run it on a simple graph.

Running Dijkstra's algorithm on a simple graph

As an example, we will use the following undirected weighted graph:

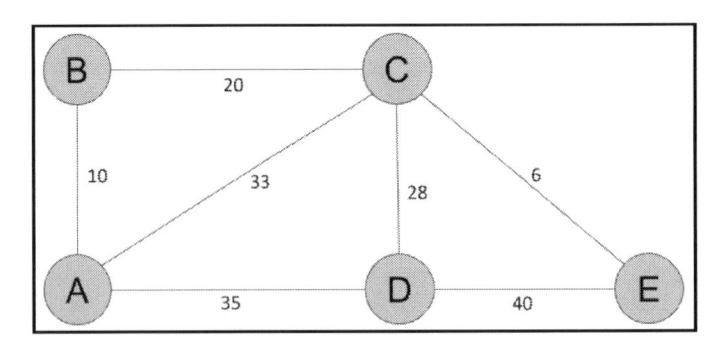

We are looking for the shortest weighted path between nodes *A* and *E*.

The different steps are as follows:

1. **Initialization** (the first row of the table): We initialize the distances between the starting node *A* and all the other nodes to infinity, except the distance from *A* to *A*, which is set to 0.
2. **The first iteration** (the second row of the following table):

    - Starting from node *A*, the algorithm traverses the graph toward each of the neighbors of *A*, *B*, *C*, and *D*.
    - It remembers the distance from the starting node *A* to each of the other nodes. If we're interested only in the shortest path length, we would only need the distance. But if we also want to know which nodes the shortest path is made of, we also need to keep the information about the incoming node (the parent). The reason will become clearer in the coming iterations. In this iteration, since we started from node *A*, all the distances computed are relative to node *A*.
    - The algorithm selects which node is closest to *A* so far. In its second iteration, it performs the same actions from this new starting node. In this case, *B* is the node closest to *A*, so the second iteration will start from *B*.

3. **The second iteration**: Starting from *B*, the algorithm visits *C* – its only neighbor that has not yet been used as a starting node in any iteration by the algorithm. The distance from *A* to *C* through *B* is as follows:

   ```
   10 (A -> B) + 20 (B -> C) = 30
   ```

   This means it is shorter to go from *A* to *C* through *B* rather than going directly from *A* to *C*. The algorithm then remembers that the shortest path from *A* to *C* is 30 and that the previous node before reaching *C* was *B*. In other words, the parent of *C* is *B*.

4. **The third iteration**: On the third iteration, the algorithm will start from node *C*, which was the closest to *A* from the previous iteration with a distance of 30. It visits *D* and *E*. The distance from *A* to *D* through *C* is 58, higher than the direct distance from *A* to *C*, so this new path is not memorized.

5. **The fourth iteration**: The fourth iteration starts from *D* and visits only node *E*, which is the only remaining node. Again, it is the second time we see node *E* in our traversal, but it appears that reaching *E* from *C* is much shorter than the path from *D*, so the algorithm will only remember the path through *C*.

The following table illustrates the steps taken:

Iteration	Start	A	B	C	D	E	Next node
0	A	0	∞	∞	∞	∞	A
1	A	x	10 - A	33 - A	35 - A	∞	B
2	B	x	x	33 - A **30 (10+20) - B**	35 - A	∞	C
3	C	x	x	x	**35 - A** 58 (30+28) - C	36 (30+4) - C	D
4	D	x	x	x	x	**36 (30+4) - C** 75 (35+40) - D	E

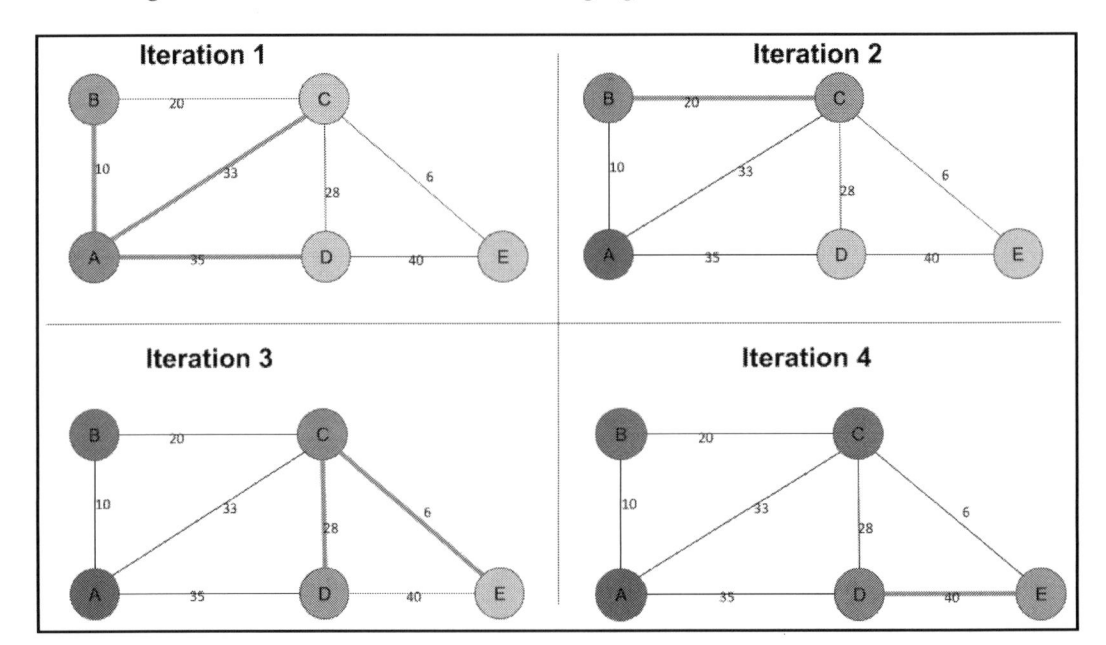

The same algorithm is illustrated in the following figure:

The green node represents the starting node for each iteration. Red nodes are the already visited nodes and the blue node is the node that will be chosen as the starting node for the next iteration.

We have now studied all the nodes in the initial graph. Let's recap the results. To do so, we are going to start from the end node, E. Column E tells us that the shortest path from A to E has a total distance of 36. In order to reconstruct the full path, we have to navigate the table in the following way:

1. Starting from column E, we look for the row with the shortest path, and we identify the previous node in the path: C.
2. We repeat the same operation from column C: we can see that the shortest path from A to C is 30, and the previous node in this path is B.
3. Finally, we can repeat the same procedure from column B, to conclude that the shortest path between A and B is the direct path, whose cost is 10.

To conclude, the shortest path between A and E is as follows:

```
A -> B -> C -> E
```

> Dijkstra's algorithm assumes that the distance between two nodes can only increase when adding a new node to the path. It means it does not support edges with negative weights.

The next section gives an example implementation of this algorithm in pure Python.

Example implementation

In order to fully understand the algorithm, we'll look at an example implementation in Python.

> **TIP**: If you are more familiar with Java, you can find an example implementation with Java using the Neo4j API for graph representation at https://github.com/stellasia/neoplus/blob/master/src/main/java/neoplus/ShortestPath.java.

Graph representation

Firstly, we have to define a structure to store the graph. There are many ways a graph can be represented for performing computations. The simplest way, for our purposes, is to use a dictionary whose keys are the graph nodes. The value associated with each key contains another dictionary, representing the edges starting from that node and its corresponding weight. For instance, the graph we have been studying in this chapter can be written as follows:

```
G = {
    'A': {'B': 10, 'C': 33, 'D': 35},
    'B': {'A': 10, 'C': 20},
    'C': {'A': 20, 'B': 33, 'D': 28, 'E': 6},
    'D': {'A': 35, 'C': 28, 'E': 40},
    'E': {'C': 6, 'D' : 40},
}
```

This means that vertex A is connected to three other vertices:

- B, with weight 10
- C, with weight 33
- D, with weight 35

This structure will be used to navigate through the graph to find the shortest path between *A* and *E*.

Algorithm

The following piece of code reproduces the steps we followed in the previous section.

Given a graph, G, the `shortest_path` function will iterate over the graph to find the shortest path between the start and end nodes.

Each iteration, starting at `step_start_node`, will do the following:

1. Find the neighbors of `step_start_node`.
2. For each neighbor, n (skip n if it has already been visited) do the following:

    - Compute the distance between n and `step_start_node` using the weight associated with the edge between n and `step_start_node`.
    - If the new distance is shorter than the previously saved one (if any), save the distance and the incoming (parent) node into the `shortest_distances` dictionary.
    - Add `step_start_node` to the list of visited nodes.

3. Update `step_start_node` for the next iteration:

    - The next iteration will start from the node closest to `start_node` that has not yet been visited.

4. Repeat until `end_node` is marked as visited.

The code should look like this:

```
def shortest_path(G, start_node, end_node):
    """Dijkstra's algorithm example implementation

    :param dict G: the graph representation
    :param str start_node: the start node name
    :param str end_node: the end node name
    """
    # initialize the shortest_distances to all nodes to Infinity
    shortest_distances = {k: (float("inf"), None) for k in G}
    # list of already visited nodes
    visited_nodes = []
    # the shortest distance to the starting node is 0
    shortest_distances[start_node] = (0, start_node)
    # first iteration starts from the start_node
    step_start_node = start_node
    while True:
        print("-"*20, "Start iteration with node", step_start_node)
```

```python
        # break condition: when the algorithm reaches the end_node
        if step_start_node == end_node:
            #return shortest_distances[end_node][0]
            return nice_path(start_node, end_node, shortest_distances)
        # loop over all the direct neighbors of the current step_start_node
        for neighbor, weight in G[step_start_node].items():
            # if neighbor already visited, do nothing
            print("-"*10, "Neighbor", neighbor, "with weight", weight)
            if neighbor in visited_nodes:
                print("\t already visited, skipping")
                continue
            # else, compare the previous distance to that node
            previous_dist = shortest_distances[neighbor][0]
            # to the new distance through the step_start_node
            new_dist = shortest_distances[step_start_node][0] + weight
            # if the new distance is shorter than the previous one
            # remember the new path
            if new_dist < previous_dist:
                shortest_distances[neighbor] = (new_dist, step_start_node)
                print("\t found new shortest path between", start_node,
"and", neighbor, ":", new_dist)
            else:
                print("\t distance", new_dist, "higher than previous one",
previous_dist, "skipping")
        visited_nodes.append(step_start_node)
        unvisited_nodes = {
            node: shortest_distances[node][0] for node in G if node not in
visited_nodes
        }
        step_start_node = min(unvisited_nodes, key=unvisited_nodes.get)
```

We can use this function using the graph defined in the previous section:

```
shortest_path(G, "A", "E")
```

This produces the following output:

```
==================== Start ====================
------------------- Start iteration with node A
---------- Neighbors B with weight 10
     found new shortest path between A and B : 10
---------- Neighbors C with weight 33
     found new shortest path between A and C : 33
---------- Neighbors D with weight 35
     found new shortest path between A and D : 35
------------------- Start iteration with node B
---------- Neighbors A with weight 10
     already visited, skipping
```

```
---------- Neighbors C with weight 20
    found new shortest path between A and C : 30
-------------------- Start iteration with node C
---------- Neighbors A with weight 20
    already visited, skipping
---------- Neighbors B with weight 33
    already visited, skipping
---------- Neighbors D with weight 28
    distance 58 higher than previous one 35 skipping
---------- Neighbors E with weight 6
    found new shortest path between A and E : 36
-------------------- Start iteration with node D
---------- Neighbors A with weight 35
    already visited, skipping
---------- Neighbors C with weight 28
    already visited, skipping
---------- Neighbors E with weight 40
    distance 75 higher than previous one 36 skipping
-------------------- Start iteration with node E
=============== Result ===============
36
==================== End ====================
```

So, we found the shortest path length of 36, consistent with our manual approach.

If we need more than the distance from A to E, such as the nodes inside this shortest path, we can retrieve this information from the shortest_distances dictionary.

Displaying the full path from A to E

The shortest_distances variable contains the following data at the end of the shortest_path function:

```
{
    'A': (0, 'A'),
    'B': (10, 'A'),
    'C': (30, 'B'),
    'D': (35, 'A'),
    'E': (36, 'C')
}
```

We can use this information to nicely display the full path between A and E. Starting from the end node, E, shortest_distances["E"][1] contains the previous node in the shortest path. Similarly, shortest_distances["C"][1] contains the previous node in the shortest path from A to E and so on.

We can write the following function to retrieve each node and distance in the path:

```
def nice_path(start_node, end_node, shortest_distances):
    node = end_node
    result = []
    while node != start_node:
        result.append((node, shortest_distances[node][0]))
        node = shortest_distances[node][1]
    result.append((start_node, 0))
    return list(reversed(result))
```

This function returns the following results:

```
=============== Result ===============
[('A', 0), ('B', 10), ('C', 30), ('E', 36)]
==================== End ====================
```

These results are consistent with the ones we found when filling in the table in the previous section.

> **TIP**: The two functions we wrote in this section, shortest_path and nice_path, could also be written in a recursive way.

This implementation was created for you to understand the principles behind the algorithm. If you intend to use this algorithm for real-life applications, state-of-the-art libraries exist with much more optimized solutions in terms of memory usage. In Python, the main graph library is called networkx: https://networkx.github.io. However, using this library or another one from data stored in Neo4j requires you to export the data out of Neo4j, process it, and maybe import the results again. With the GDS library, the process is simplified, since it allows us to run optimized algorithms directly within Neo4j.

Using the shortest path algorithm within Neo4j

In order to test that the shortest path algorithm has been implemented in the GDS library, we will use the same graph we have been using since the beginning of this chapter. So let's first create our test graph in Neo4j:

```
CREATE (A:Node {name: "A"})
CREATE (B:Node {name: "B"})
CREATE (C:Node {name: "C"})
CREATE (D:Node {name: "D"})
CREATE (E:Node {name: "E"})
```

The Graph Data Science Library and Path Finding

```
CREATE (A)-[:LINKED_TO {weight: 10}]->(B)
CREATE (A)-[:LINKED_TO {weight: 33}]->(C)
CREATE (A)-[:LINKED_TO {weight: 35}]->(D)
CREATE (B)-[:LINKED_TO {weight: 20}]->(C)
CREATE (C)-[:LINKED_TO {weight: 28}]->(D)
CREATE (C)-[:LINKED_TO {weight: 6 }]->(E)
CREATE (D)-[:LINKED_TO {weight: 40}]->(E)
```

The resulting graph in Neo4j is illustrated in the following figure:

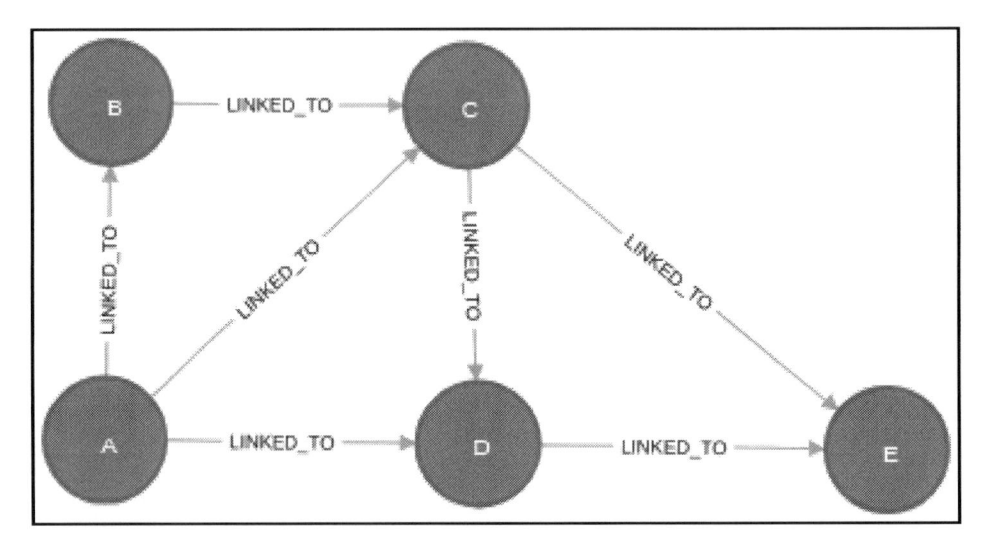

The procedure to find the shortest path between two nodes is as follows:

```
gds.alpha.shortestPath.stream(
    graphName::STRING,
    {
        startNode::NODE,
        endNode::NODE,
        relationshipWeightProperty::STRING
    }
)
(nodeId::INTEGER, cost::FLOAT)
```

The configuration parameters are the following:

- The start node
- The end node
- A string containing the relationship property to be used as the weight

Chapter 4

It returns a list of nodes in the shortest path with two elements:

- The Neo4j internal node ID
- The cost of the traversal up to that node

> All shortest path algorithms in version 1.0 of the GDS library are in the `alpha` tier, meaning they have not yet been optimized for production and changes are very likely to be made. Always check the latest documentation at https://neo4j.com/docs/graph-data-science/preview/ to check compatibility.

Let's use it on our test graph to find the shortest path between A and E. But before we do that, we need to define the projected graph. In our case, we are going to use the nodes with the `Node` label and the relationships with the `LINKED_TO` label so the procedure call to create this projected graph is as follows:

```
CALL gds.graph.create("graph", "Node", "LINKED_TO")
```

We can then use the shortest path procedure like this:

```
MATCH (A:Node {name: "A"})
MATCH (E:Node {name: "E"})
CALL gds.alpha.shortestPath.stream("graph", {startNode: A, endNode: E})
YIELD nodeId, cost
RETURN nodeId, cost
```

The result of this query looks like the following table:

"nodeId"	"cost"
45	0.0
48	1.0
49	2.0

[141]

The Graph Data Science Library and Path Finding

The `nodeId` column contains the ID given by Neo4j to the node for internal use. The values you obtain might differ from mine, but, most importantly, they are hard to interpret since we do not know which nodes they correspond with. Fortunately, the GDS plugin contains a helper function to get the node from its ID: `gds.util.asNode`. So let's update our query to return something more meaningful:

```
MATCH (A:Node {name: "A"})
MATCH (E:Node {name: "E"})
CALL gds.alpha.shortestPath.stream("graph", {startNode: A, endNode: E})
YIELD nodeId, cost
RETURN gds.util.asNode(nodeId).name as name, cost
```

This query produces the following output:

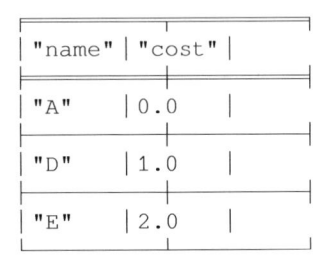

"name"	"cost"
"A"	0.0
"D"	1.0
"E"	2.0

Now the node names are understandable. However, we have another issue with this output: it does not match the one we found in the previous section. This is because the default behavior of the `shortestPath` procedure is to count the number of hops from one node to another, regardless of any weight associated with the edges. This is equivalent to setting a weight of 1 for all edges. In terms of hops, this result is correct – a possible shortest path to go from A to E is to transit by node D.

> It is important to note that Dijkstra's algorithm only returns *one* shortest path. If several solutions exist, only one will be returned.

To take into account the edge weight, or the distance between nodes, we have to use the `relationshipWeightProperty` configuration parameter:

```
MATCH (A:Node {name: "A"})
MATCH (E:Node {name: "E"})
CALL gds.alpha.shortestPath.stream("graph", {
      startNode: A,
      endNode: E,
      relationshipWeightProperty: "weight"
   }
```

```
)
YIELD nodeId, cost
RETURN gds.util.asNode(nodeId).name as name, cost
```

If you try to run this procedure, you will get the following error message:

```
Failed to invoke procedure `gds.alpha.shortestPath.stream`: Caused by:
java.lang.IllegalArgumentException: Relationship weight property `weight`
not found in graph with relationship properties: []
```

Indeed, our projected graph, graph, does not contain any relationship properties. You can check this by using the gds.graph.list procedure:

```
CALL gds.graph.list("graph")
YIELD relationshipProjection
RETURN *
```

This gives the following result:

```
{
  "LINKED_TO": {
    "aggregation": "DEFAULT",
    "projection": "NATURAL",
    "type": "LINKED_TO",
    "properties": {

    }
  }
}
```

You can identify the empty property list.

To fix this issue, let's create another projected graph, this time including the weight property:

```
CALL gds.graph.create("graph_weighted", "Node", "LINKED_TO", {
    relationshipProperties: [{weight: 'weight' }]
    }
)
```

The list procedure called on graph_weighted now tells us we have one property, weight, associated with the relationship type LINKED_TO:

```
{
  "LINKED_TO": {
    "aggregation": "DEFAULT",
    "projection": "NATURAL",
    "type": "LINKED_TO",
```

```
      "properties": {
        "weight": {
          "property": "weight",
          "defaultValue": NaN,
          "aggregation": "DEFAULT"
        }
      }
    }
  }
}
```

We can now run the shortest path procedure on this new projected graph, `graph_weighted`:

```
MATCH (A:Node {name: "A"})
MATCH (E:Node {name: "E"})
CALL gds.alpha.shortestPath.stream("graph_weighted", {
        startNode: A,
        endNode: E,
        relationshipWeightProperty: "weight"
    }
)
YIELD nodeId, cost
RETURN gds.util.asNode(nodeId).name as name, cost
```

This time, we get the results we expected:

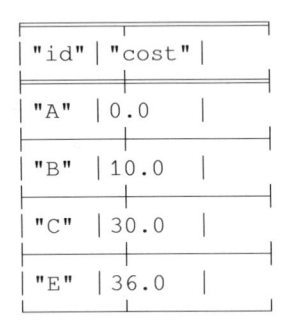

"id"	"cost"
"A"	0.0
"B"	10.0
"C"	30.0
"E"	36.0

If you check the graph visualization for this result, you will find the four nodes, A, B, C, and E, but also all the existing relationships between them, without filtering the relationships belonging to the shortest path. This means we lose the order in which the nodes need to be visited. This is due to a configuration default option in Neo4j Browser. To disable it, you need to go to the settings view in Neo4j Desktop and disable the option called **Connect result nodes**. Rerunning the previous query with that option disabled will display only the nodes. We are now going to tune this query a little bit in order to visualize the real path.

Path visualization

In order to visualize our path, we will first write the results into the graph. This is not mandatory, but will slightly simplify the following queries.

Instead of using `gds.alpha.shortestPath.stream`, we are going to call the `gds.alpha.shortestPath.write` procedure. The parameters are similar, but the returned values are completely different:

```
MATCH (A:Node {name: "A"})
MATCH (E:Node {name: "E"})
CALL gds.alpha.shortestPath.write("graph_weighted", {
        startNode: A,
        endNode: E,
        relationshipWeightProperty: "weight"
    }
) YIELD totalCost
RETURN totalCost
```

This writes the result of the shortest path algorithm into an `sssp` property on the nodes belonging to the shortest path.

> **TIP**: The name of the property used to write the result to the original graph can be configured by adding a `writeProperty` key to the configuration map.

If we want to retrieve that path, including the relationships, we have to find the relationship between two consecutive nodes in the path and return it, together with the nodes. This is exactly what the following query does:

```
MATCH (n:Node)
WHERE n.sssp IS NOT NULL
WITH n
ORDER BY n.sssp
WITH collect(n) as path
UNWIND range(0, size(path)-1) AS index
WITH path[index] AS currentNode, path[index+1] AS nextNode
MATCH (currentNode)-[r:LINKED_TO]-(nextNode)
RETURN currentNode, r, nextNode
```

This Cypher query performs the following actions:

- Selects the nodes that are part of the shortest path by keeping only the nodes with the `sssp` property and ordering them.

- Groups all those nodes into a list called `path` with the `collect` statement (see Chapter 2, *The Cypher Query Language*, if you need some reminders about it).
- Iterates over the indexes of this list, from 0 to n-1, where n is the number of nodes in `path`.
- We can then access a node (`path[index]`) and its subsequent node in the path (`path[index+1]`).
- Finally, we can find the relationship of type `LINDED_TO` between those two nodes and return it as part of the final result.

This query produces the following graph:

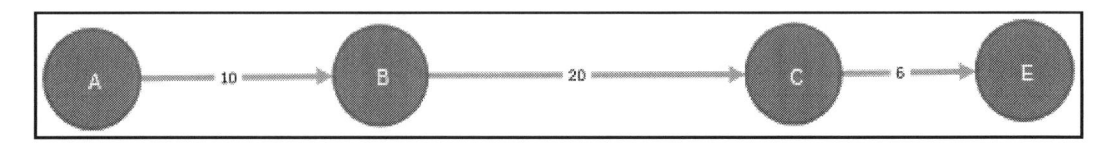

Understanding relationship direction

So far, we have used the default configuration for the direction of the projected relationship. By default, it's the same as the Neo4j graph.

The difference between outgoing and incoming relations is illustrated in the next diagram. With respect to node *A*, the relationship with *B* is outgoing, meaning it starts from *A* and ends in *B*, while the relationship with *C* is incoming, meaning *A* is the end node:

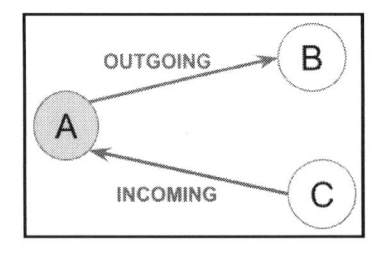

In the GDS, you can always choose whether to use only outgoing or incoming relationships or use relationships in both directions. The last case allows you to treat your graph as *undirected*, whereas all Neo4j relationships have to be directed.

To illustrate this concept, let's add a new edge to our test graph:

```
MATCH (A:Node {name: "A"})
MATCH (C:Node {name: "C"})
MATCH (E:Node {name: "E"})
CREATE (C)-[:LINKED_TO {weight: 20}]->(A)
CREATE (E)-[:LINKED_TO {weight: 5}]->(C)
```

Our graph now looks like this:

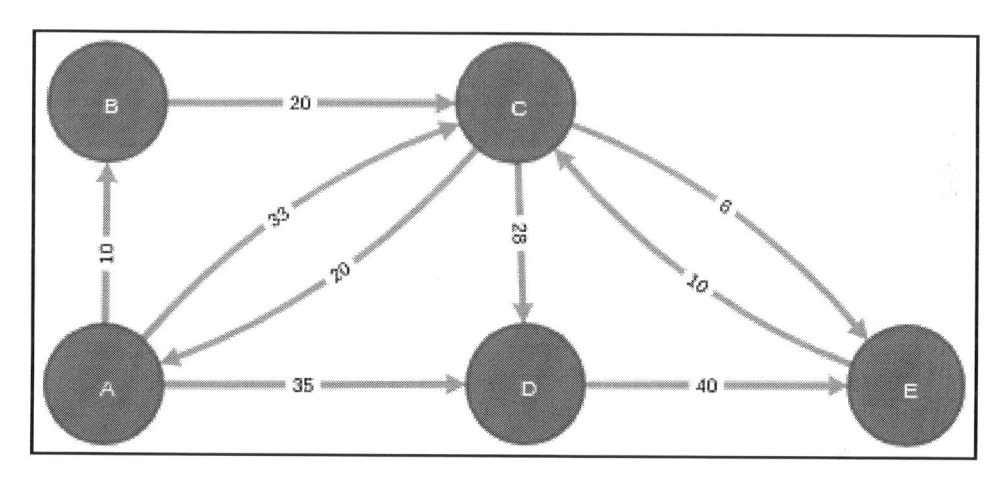

Let's now create a new projected graph, which will use relationships in the reverse direction:

```
CALL gds.graph.create("graph_weighted_reverse", "Node", {
        LINKED_TO: {
            type: 'LINKED_TO',
            projection: 'REVERSE',
            properties: "weight"
        }
    }
)
```

Note that we have also simplified the graph creation query by adding the relationship property directly into the projected relationship definition.

[147]

The Graph Data Science Library and Path Finding

We can now run the same shortest path algorithm on this newly created `graph_weighted_reverse`:

```
MATCH (A:Node {name: "A"})
MATCH (E:Node {name: "E"})
CALL gds.alpha.shortestPath.stream("graph_weighted_reverse", {
        startNode: A,
        endNode: E,
        relationshipWeightProperty: "weight"
    }
)
YIELD nodeId, cost
RETURN gds.util.asNode(nodeId).name as name, cost
```

The result is now different:

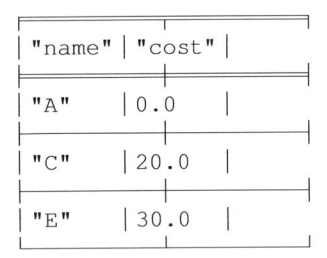

"name"	"cost"
"A"	0.0
"C"	20.0
"E"	30.0

Indeed, considering the relationships from the reverse direction, the shortest path is now going directly through C.

Last but not least, it is also possible to include in the projected graph relationships in both directions:

```
CALL gds.graph.create("graph_weighted_undirected", "Node", {
        LINKED_TO: {
            type: 'LINKED_TO',
            projection: 'UNDIRECTED',
            properties: "weight"
        }
    }
)
```

The shortest path between A and E on the `graph_weighted_undirected` projected graph is as follows:

"name"	"cost"
"A"	0.0

| "C" | 20.0 |
| "E" | 26.0 |

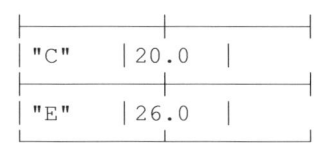

The chosen paths in both cases are illustrated in the following diagram:

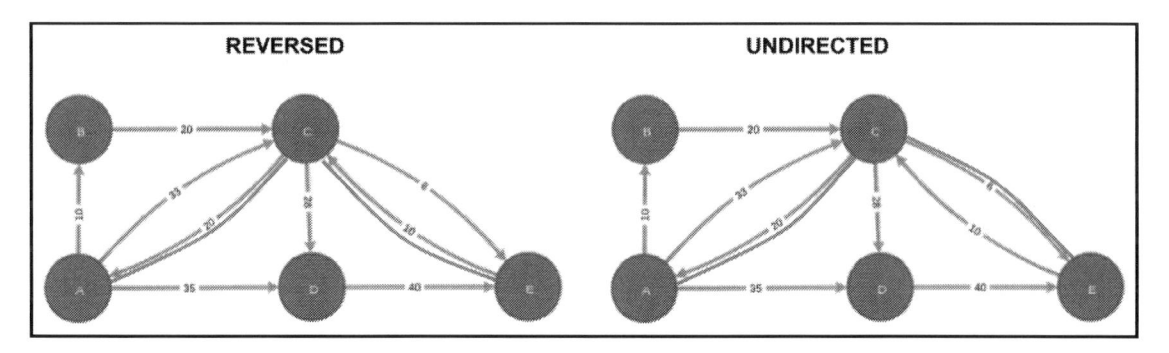

In the reversed case, the algorithm is only able to choose the relationships in the reverse direction, meaning its iteration ends at the start node. In the undirected scenario, it can choose either outgoing or incoming relationships. It will then choose the path that minimizes the total cost.

This concludes our discussion of Dijkstra's algorithm. After a review of the algorithm's functioning, we have been able to use it directly on a graph stored in a Neo4j database through the GDS plugin. Although this is probably the most famous pathfinding algorithm, Dijkstra's algorithm is not always the best performing. In the next section, we are going to discuss the A* algorithm, another pathfinding algorithm inspired by Dijkstra's algorithm.

Finding the shortest path with the A* algorithm and its heuristics

Developed in 1968 by P. Hart, N. Nilsson and B. Raphael, the A* algorithm (pronounced *A-star*) is an extension of Dijkstra's algorithm. It tries to optimize searches by guessing the traversal direction thanks to **heuristics**. Thanks to this approach, it is known to be faster than Dijkstra's algorithm, especially for large graphs.

Algorithm principles

In Dijkstra's algorithm, all possible paths are explored. This can be very time-consuming, especially on large graphs. The A* algorithm tries to overcome this problem, with the idea that it can guess which paths to follow and which path expansions are less likely to be the shortest ones. This is achieved by modifying the criterion for choosing the next start node at each iteration. Instead of using only the cost of the path from the start to the current node, the A* algorithm adds another component: the estimated cost of going from the current node to the end node. It can be expressed as follows:

$$estimatedTotalCost(endNode) = costSoFar(currentNode) + estimatedCost(currentNode, endNode)$$

While `costSoFar(currentNode)` is the same as the one computed in Dijkstra's algorithm, `estimatedCost(currentNode, endNode)` is a guess about the remaining cost of going from the current node to the end node. The guess function, often noted as h, is a heuristic function.

Defining the heuristics for A*

The choice of the heuristic function is important. If we set `h(n) = 0` for all nodes, the A* algorithm is equivalent to Dijkstra's algorithm and we will see no performance improvement. If `h(n)` is too far away from the real distance, the algorithm runs the risk of not finding the real shortest path. The choice of the heuristic is then a matter of balance between speed and accuracy.

> Since choosing `h(n)=0` is equivalent to Dijkstra's algorithm, the A* algorithm is a variant of Dijkstra. It means it suffers from the same constraints regarding the positivity of the weights.

Within the GDS plugin, the implemented heuristic uses the **haversine** equation. This is a formula to compute the distance between two points on the Earth's surface, given their latitude and longitude. It corresponds to the great circle distance, as illustrated in the following:

The guess function ignores the exact shape of the network but is able to say that, to go from A to B, you are more likely to find the shortest path by starting to move toward the right than toward the left, so you will arrive at the destination nodes in fewer iterations.

Using the haversine formula means that the A* algorithm with Neo4j can only be used if the nodes in the projected graph have spatial attributes (latitude and longitude).

Using A* within the Neo4j GDS plugin

The A* algorithm is accessible through the `gds.alpha.shortestPath.astar` procedure. The signature follows the same pattern as the other algorithms: the first parameter is the name of the projected graph the algorithm will use, while the second parameter is a map specific to each algorithm. In the A* algorithm configuration, we will find the same `startNode`, `endNode`, and `relationshipWeightProperty` we have already used for the `shortestPath` procedure. On top of that, two new properties are added to specify the name of the node property holding the latitude and longitude: `propertyKeyLat` and `propertyKeyLon`. Here is an example call to the A* algorithm on a projected graph:

```
MATCH (A:Node {name: "A"})
MATCH (B:Node {name: "B"})
CALL gds.alpha.shortestPath.astar.stream("graph", {
        startNode: A,
        endNode: B,
        relationshipWeightProperty: "weight",
        propertyKeyLat: "latitude",
        propertyKeyLon: "longitude",
    }
) YIELD nodeId, cost
RETURN gds.asNode(nodeId).name, cost
```

Warning: for the A* algorithm, only streamed results are available.

We will use this algorithm in the next chapter (Chapter 5, *Spatial Data*), where we will be able to build a real routing engine.

But before that, we will learn about other algorithms related to shortest pathfinding, such as the all-pairs shortest path or the spanning trees algorithms.

Discovering the other path-related algorithms in the GDS plugin

Being able to find the shortest path between two nodes is useful, but not always sufficient. Fortunately, shortest path algorithms can be extended to extract even more information about paths in a graph. The following subsections detail the parts of those algorithms that are implemented in the GDS plugin.

K-shortest path

Dijkstra's algorithm and the A* algorithm only return one possible shortest path between two nodes. If you are interested in the second shortest path, you will have to go for the k-shortest path or **Yen's algorithm**. Its usage within the GDS plugin is very similar to the previous algorithms we studied, except we have to specify the number of paths to return. In the following example, we specify k=2:

```
MATCH (A:Node {name: "A"})
MATCH (E:Node {name: "E"})
CALL gds.alpha.kShortestPaths.stream("graph_weighted", {
            startNode: A,
            endNode: E,
            k:2,
            relationshipWeightProperty: "weight"}
)
YIELD index, sourceNodeId, targetNodeId, nodeIds
RETURN index,
        gds.util.asNode(sourceNodeId).name as source,
        gds.util.asNode(targetNodeId).name as target,
        gds.util.asNodes(nodeIds) as path
```

The results are represented in the following table. The first shortest path is the one we already know: A, B, C, E. The second shortest path is A, C, E:

"index"	"source"	"target"	"path"
0	"A"	"E"	[{"name":"A"},{"name":"B"},{"name":"C"},{"name":"E"}]
1	"A"	"E"	[{"name":"A"},{"name":"C"},{"name":"E"}]

This algorithm can be very helpful when trying to define alternative routes.

The Graph Data Science Library and Path Finding

Single Source Shortest Path (SSSP)

The aim of the SSSP algorithm is to find the shortest path between a given node and all other nodes in the graph. It is also based on Dijkstra's algorithm, but enables parallel execution by packaging nodes into buckets and processing each bucket individually. Parallelism is governed by the bucket size, itself determined by the `delta` parameter. When setting `delta=1`, SSSP is exactly equivalent to using Dijkstra's algorithm, meaning no parallelism is used. A value of delta that is too high (greater than the sum of all edge weights) would place all nodes in the same bucket, hence canceling the effect of parallelism.

The procedure in the GDS library is called `deltaStepping`. Its signature is as expected:

```
CALL gds.shortestPath.deltaStepping.stream(graphName::STRING,
configuration::MAP)
```

Its configuration, however, is slightly different:

- `startNode`: The node from which all shortest paths will be computed
- `relationshipWeightProperty`: The usual relationship property carrying the weight
- `delta`: The delta parameter controlling the parallelism

> **TIP:** There is no `endNode` since we are interested in the shortest path between a start node and **all other nodes in the graph**.

With our simple graph, we can use this procedure with `delta=1` using this query:

```
MATCH (A:Node {name: "A"})
CALL gds.alpha.shortestPath.deltaStepping.stream("graph_weighted", {
        startNode: A,
        relationshipWeightProperty: "weight",
        delta: 1
    }
)
YIELD nodeId, distance
RETURN gds.util.asNode(nodeId).name, distance
```

The returned values are as follows:

"gds.util.asNode(nodeId).name"	"distance"
"A"	0.0
"B"	10.0
"C"	30.0
"D"	35.0
"E"	36.0

The first column contains each node in the graph, and the second column is the distance from the startNode, A, to each other node. We again encounter here the shortest distance from A to E of 36. We also find the results we found before when running Dijkstra's algorithm: the shortest distance between A and B is 10, and between A and C it's 30. On top of that, we have a new result: the shortest distance from A to D, which is 35.

All-pairs shortest path

The all-pairs shortest path algorithm goes even further: it returns the shortest path between each pair of nodes in the projected graph. It is equivalent to calling the SSSP for each node, but with performance optimizations to make it faster.

The GDS implementation procedure for this algorithm looks as follows:

```
CALL gds.alpha.allShortestPaths.stream(graphName::STRING,
configuration::MAP)
YIELD sourceNodeId, targetNodeId, distance
```

The configuration parameters include, as usual, relationshipWeightProperty, the relationship property in the projected graph to be used as the weight.

There are two additional parameters to set the number of concurrent threads: concurrency and readConcurrency.

The Graph Data Science Library and Path Finding

We can use it on our small test graph with the following:

```
CALL gds.alpha.allShortestPaths.stream("graph_weighted", {
  relationshipWeightProperty: "weight"
})
YIELD sourceNodeId, targetNodeId, distance
RETURN gds.util.asNode(sourceNodeId).name as start,
  gds.util.asNode(targetNodeId).name as end,
  distance
```

The result is the following matrix:

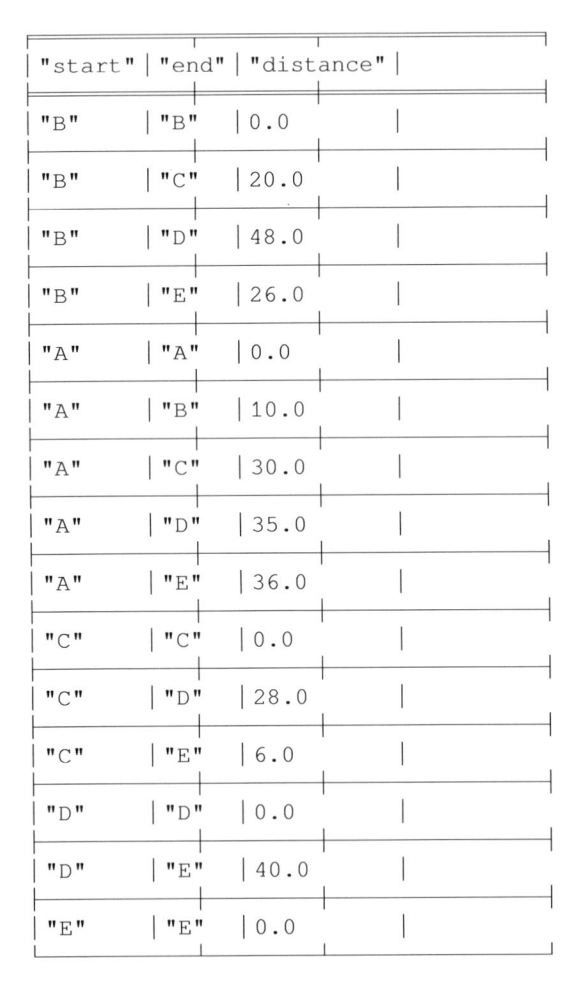

"start"	"end"	"distance"
"B"	"B"	0.0
"B"	"C"	20.0
"B"	"D"	48.0
"B"	"E"	26.0
"A"	"A"	0.0
"A"	"B"	10.0
"A"	"C"	30.0
"A"	"D"	35.0
"A"	"E"	36.0
"C"	"C"	0.0
"C"	"D"	28.0
"C"	"E"	6.0
"D"	"D"	0.0
"D"	"E"	40.0
"E"	"E"	0.0

You are now able to extract the following path-related information from your graph:

- One or several shortest paths between two nodes
- The shortest path between a node and all other nodes in the graph
- The shortest path between all pairs of nodes.

In the next section, we will talk about graph optimization problems. The traveling-salesman problem is the most famous graph optimization problem.

Optimizing processes using graphs

An optimization problem's objective is to find an **optimal solution** among a large set of candidates. The shape of your favorite soda can was derived from an optimization problem, trying to minimize the amount of material to use (the surface) for a given volume (33 cl). In this case, the surface, the quantity to minimize, is also called the **objective function**.

Optimization problems often come with some constraints on the variables. The fact that a length has to be positive is already a constraint, mathematically speaking. But constraints can be expressed in many different forms.

The simpler form of an optimization problem is so-called **linear optimization**, where both the objective function and the constraints are linear.

Graph optimization problems are also part of mathematical optimization problems. The most famous of them is the **traveling-salesman problem** (TSP). We are going to talk a bit more about this particular problem in the following section.

The Graph Data Science Library and Path Finding

The traveling-salesman problem

The TSP is a famous problem in computer science. Given a list of cities and the shortest distance between each of them, the goal is to find the shortest path visiting all cities once and only once, and returning to the starting point. The following map illustrates a solution to the traveling-salesman problem, visiting some cities in Germany:

Image credit: https://commons.wikimedia.org/wiki/File:TSP_Deutschland_3.png

So we have an optimization problem with the following:

- **An objective function**: The cost of the path. This cost can be the total distance, but if the driver is only paid hourly, it may be more useful to use the total travel time as the objective to minimize.
- **Constraints**:
    - Each city must be visited once and only once.
    - The path must start and end in the same city.

Despite the straightforward formulation, this is an NP-hard problem. The only way to reach the exact solution in all cases is the brute-force approach, where you compute the shortest path between each pair of nodes (an application of the `allPairsShortestPath` algorithm) and checks all possible permutations. The time complexity of this approach is `O(number of nodes!)`. You can imagine that with only a few nodes, this solution becomes impossible for a normal computer. Assuming each combination requires 1 ms processing time, a configuration with 15 nodes would require 15 ms, which would mean more than 41 years to test all possible combinations. With 20 nodes, this computation time increases to more than 77 million years.

Fortunately, some algorithms exist to find solutions that are not guaranteed to be 100% accurate, but close enough. Giving an exhaustive list of such solutions is out of the scope of this book, but we can quote two of the most common ones, both based on a science and nature analogy:

- **Ant colony optimization (ACO)**: This algorithm is based on the observation of how ants communicate with each other in an ant colony using pheromones (odorous molecules) to achieve perfect synchronization. In the algorithm, many explorer ants (agents) are sent into the graph and travel along its edges based on some local optimization.
- **Gene algorithms (GA)**: These are based on an analogy with genetics and how genes are propagated through generations via mutations in order to select the stronger individuals.

The TSP can be extended to even more complex use cases. For example, if a delivery company has more than one available vehicle, we can extend the TSP problem to determine the best course of action for more than one salesman. This is known as the **multiple traveling-salesman problem (MTSP)**. More constraints can also be added, for instance:

- **Capacity constraints**, where each vehicle has a capacity constraint and can only carry up to a certain volume of goods.
- **Time window constraints**: In some cases, the package can only be delivered during a certain time window.

These TSP algorithms are not (yet) implemented in the GDS plugin. However, we can find an upper bound for the optimal solution using the spanning tree algorithm.

The Graph Data Science Library and Path Finding

Spanning trees

A spanning tree is built from the original graph such that:

- The nodes in the spanning tree are the same as in the original graph.
- The spanning tree edges are chosen in the original graph such that all nodes in the spanning tree are connected, without creating loops.

The next figure illustrates some spanning trees for the graph we have studied in this chapter:

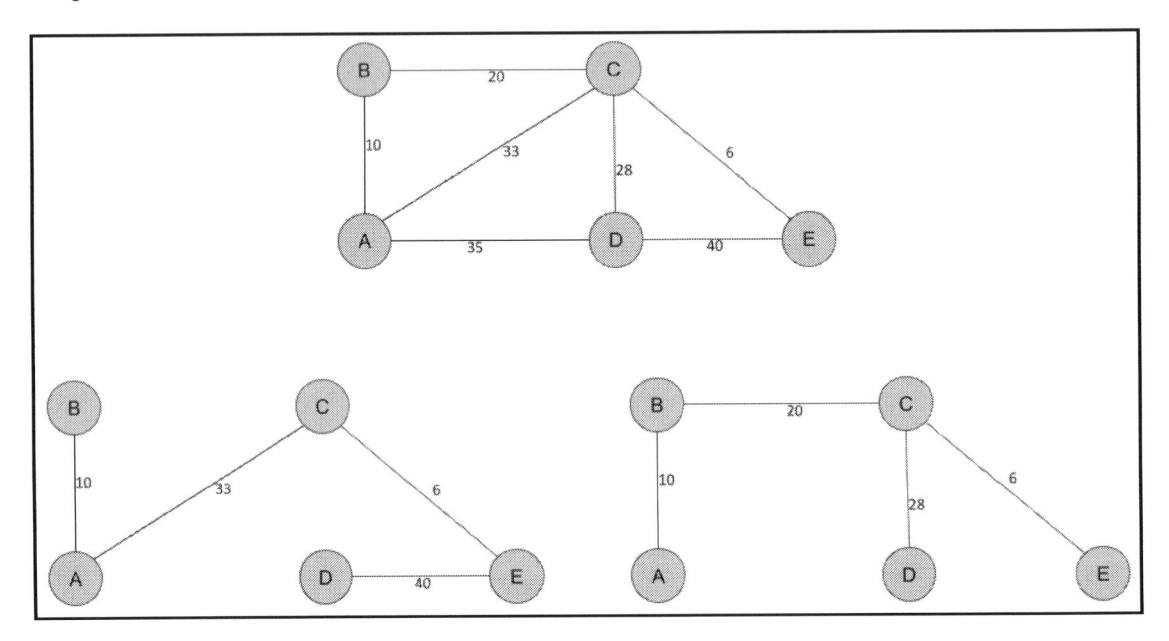

Among all possible spanning trees, the *minimal* spanning tree is the spanning tree with the lowest sum of weight for all edges. In the preceding diagram, the bottom-left spanning tree has a total sum of weights of 89 (10+33+6+40), while the bottom-right spanning tree has a total sum of weights of 64 (10+20+28+6). The bottom-right spanning tree is hence more likely to be the minimal spanning tree. To verify this, in the following section, we will discuss the algorithm implemented in the GDS plugin to find spanning trees, Prim's algorithm.

Prim's algorithm

This is how Prim's algorithm runs on our simple test graph:

1. It chooses a starting node – node *A* in the following diagram.
2. Iteration 1: It checks all edges connected to that node, and chooses the one with the lowest weight. Vertex *B* is selected and the edge between *A* and *B* is added to the tree.
3. Starting from *B*, it visits *C*. Among *C* and *D* are already visited nodes. The one with the lowest weight is *C*, so *C* is selected and the edge between *B* and *C* is added to the tree.
4. Starting from *C*, it can go to *A*, *D*, and *E*. *A* was already visited and the new edge (*C->A*) would add a higher weight than the already existing one, so this edge is skipped. However, you can see that the new edge reaching *D* (*C->D*) has a lower weight than the previously selected edge (*A->D*), meaning the previous edge is dropped from the tree and the new one is added.
5. The last step consists of checking the last node, *E*. Here, adding the edge between *D* and *E* would increase the total weight by 40 instead of 6 (the weight of the edge between *C* and *E*), so this last edge is skipped.

The following diagram summarizes these four iterations, with edge creation (green lines), edges not taken into account (dashed green lines), and edges removed (dashed red lines):

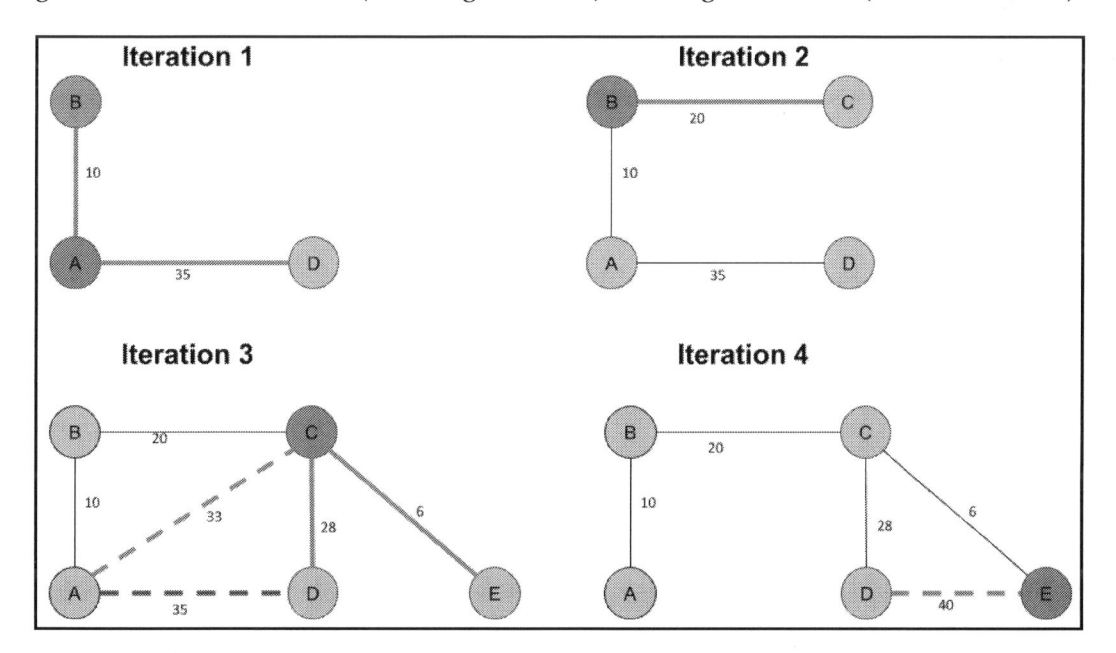

The minimum spanning tree of our graph is then composed of the following edges:

```
A-B (weight 10)
B-C (weight 20)
C-D (weight 28)
C-E (weight 6)
```

You can check that all nodes are connected (there is a path between each pair of nodes in the graph) and the total weight is 64.

Let's try and retrieve this information from Neo4j.

Finding the minimum spanning tree in a Neo4j graph

The procedure to find the minimum spanning tree in the GDS plugin is as follows:

```
MATCH (A:Node {name: "A"})
CALL gds.alpha.spanningTree.minimum.write("graph_weighted", {
    startNodeId: id(A),
    relationshipWeightProperty: 'weight',
    writeProperty: 'MINST',
    weightWriteProperty: 'writeCost'
})
YIELD createMillis, computeMillis, writeMillis, effectiveNodeCount
RETURN *
```

This will actually create new relationships for each edge in the minimum spanning tree. To retrieve these edges, you can use the following:

```
MATCH (n)-[r:MST]-(m)
RETURN n, r, m
```

This query produces the following output, consistent with the result we obtained earlier by running Prim's algorithm:

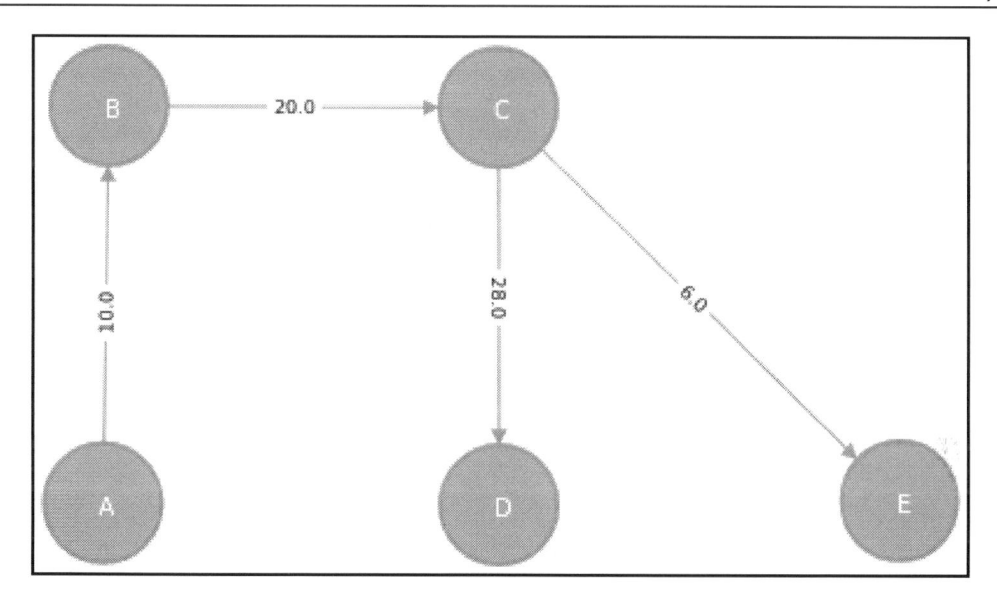

> **TIP:** Note that you can also find the maximum spanning tree and the k-spanning tree to find a spanning tree using only k nodes.

Summary

This chapter was a long one, as it was our introduction to the GDS plugin. It is important to understand how to define the projected graph and the different entities to be included in it. We will see more examples in the following chapters, as we are going to use this library in all remaining chapters of the book.

The following table summarizes the different algorithms we have studied in this chapter, with some important characteristics to keep in mind:

Algorithm	Description	Stream/Write	Negative weights
shortestPath	The shortest path between two nodes using Dijkstra's algorithm	Both	No
shortestPath.astar	The shortest path between two nodes using the A* algorithm and great circle heuristics (requires nodes with latitude and longitude properties)	Stream	No

`kShortestPath`	The k-shortest paths between two nodes using Yen's algorithm	Both	Yes
`shortestPath.deltaStepping`	Single source shortest path: the shortest path between a node and all other nodes in the graph	Both	No
`allShortestPaths`	The shortest path between each pair of nodes in the graph	Stream	No
`spanningTree.*`	The minimum, maximum, or k-spanning tree within a graph	Write	Yes

As you will discover in the following chapters, shortest paths can also be used to infer other metrics on a graph, such as node importance (Chapter 5, *Node Importance*). But before going into those algorithms, as we talked a lot in this chapter about routing and geographical data, the next chapter will be dedicated to geodata management within Neo4j, using built-in data types and another Neo4j plugin: `neo4j-spatial`.

Questions

In order to test your understanding, try to answer the following questions. The answers are provided in the *Assessment* part at the end of this book:

1. The GDS plugin and projected graphs:

    - Why does the GDS plugin use projected graphs?
    - Where are these projected graphs stored?
    - What are the differences between named and anonymous projected graphs?
    - Create a projected graph containing:
        - Nodes: label `Node`
        - Relationships: types `REL1` and `REL2`
    - Create a projected graph with:
        - Nodes: labels `Node1` and `Node2`
        - Relationships: type `REL1` and properties `prop1` and `prop2`
    - How do you consume the results of a graph algorithm from the GDS plugin?

2. Pathfinding:

    - Which algorithms are based on Dijkstra's algorithm?
    - What is the important restriction regarding an edge's weight for these algorithms?
    - What information is needed to use the A* algorithm?

Further reading

- Applications of graph algorithms in video games: *Graph Algorithms for AI in Games [Video]*, D. Jallov, Packt Publishing
- An example project with custom functions and procedures is available at `https://github.com/stellasia/neoplus` . It includes an implementation of Dijkstra's algorithm using the Neo4j Java API.
- A* and heuristics: `http://theory.stanford.edu/~amitp/GameProgramming/Heuristics.html`
- Routing optimization solver, including the traveling-salesman problem, provided by Google: `https://developers.google.com/optimization/routin`

5
Spatial Data

Spatial data refers to anything that needs to be localized on the Earth. From points to localize a person or a point of interest on the Earth surface, to lines to model a street or a river path, and to areas to delimit countries and buildings, all of these geometries are spatial data. They have been harmonized within **Geographic Information System (GIS)**, which provides a unified approach for representing these objects. In this chapter, we will discover the `shapefile` and `GeoJSON` formats. The full power of these systems is their ability to compute metrics based on these geometries with ease: getting a line length, a surface area, or computing the distance between objects.

While spatial data has always been important in the field of cartography, it has attracted more and more interest with the development of smartphones that are equipped with GPS sensors and are able to localize their carrier at any time. In this chapter, we are going to learn how to manage spatial data with Neo4j. Indeed, Neo4j provides both a built-in type for spatial points and another plugin to manage more complex types, such as lines and polygons. In the later sections of this chapter, we will be linking the GDS plugin that we covered in the previous chapter (Chapter 4, *The Graph Data Science Library and Path Finding*) with spatial data to build a routing engine for New York City.

The following topics will be covered in this chapter:

- Representing spatial attributes
- Creating a geometry layer in Neo4j with `neo4j-spatial`
- Performing spatial queries
- Finding the shortest path based on distance
- Visualizing spatial data with Neo4j

Technical requirements

The following tools will be used in this chapter:

- Neo4j graph database with the following plugins:
    - `neo4j-spatial`: https://github.com/neo4j-contrib/spatial
  - **Graph Data Science (GDS)** library
- Neo4j desktop application. On top of the usual Neo4j browser, we will also use neomap for visualization
- The code for this chapter is available on GitHub at the following link: https://github.com/PacktPublishing/Hands-On-Graph-Analytics-with-Neo4j/ch5

> `neo4j-spatial` **is not yet compatible with Neo4j 4.0 (lastest version at the time of writing: 0.26.2).**
> If you are using Neo4j < 4.0, then the latest compatible version of the GDS is 1.1.
> If you are using Neo4j ≥ 4.0, then the first compatible version of the GDS is 1.2.

Representing spatial attributes

In this section, we are going to use the point built-in data type from Neo4j. Before that, we need to understand a few concepts purely related to spatial data.

Understanding geographic coordinate systems

The spatial data we'll be talking about in this chapter are points on the Earth's surface. There is no unique way to assign coordinates to each point.

Coordinates of a point P on a fixed radius sphere rely on two angles: the **longitude**, the angle from a reference meridian (θ in the following diagram), and the **latitude**, the angle with respect to the equator (δ in the following diagram):

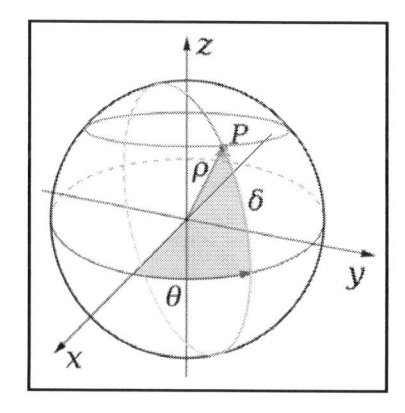

> **TIP** Changing the longitude involves moving in a north-south direction, which corresponds to the y-axis in other projection systems. This means in a general case that longitude is denoted with an x and latitude with a y, which is counter-intuitive.

But, as you may know, the Earth is not a perfect sphere. Indeed, the radius close to the equator is higher than the radius at the poles due to centripetal forces, as illustrated in the following image (with exaggerated flatness):

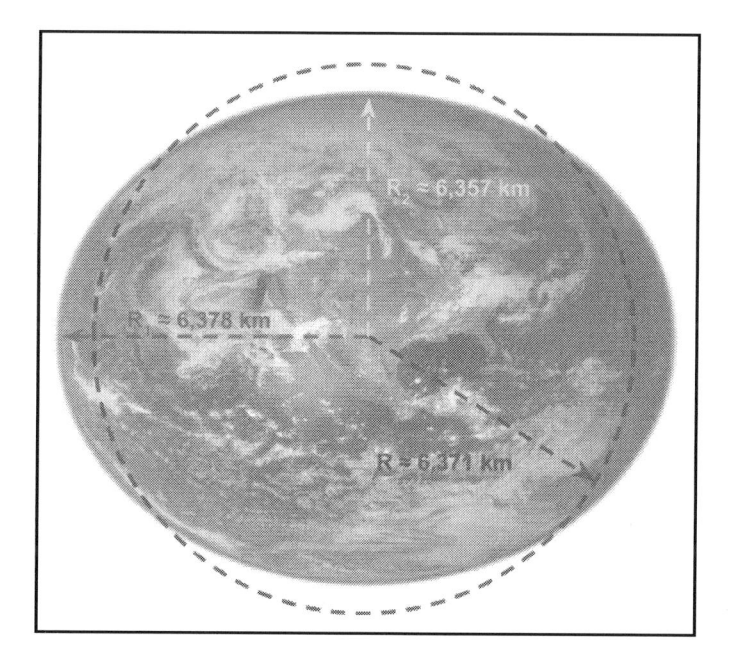

Spatial Data

To make things even more complex, the Earth's surface is not smooth, but has a distorted shape due to the effects of gravity. The following image shows the Earth's actual shape, with exaggerated distortion:

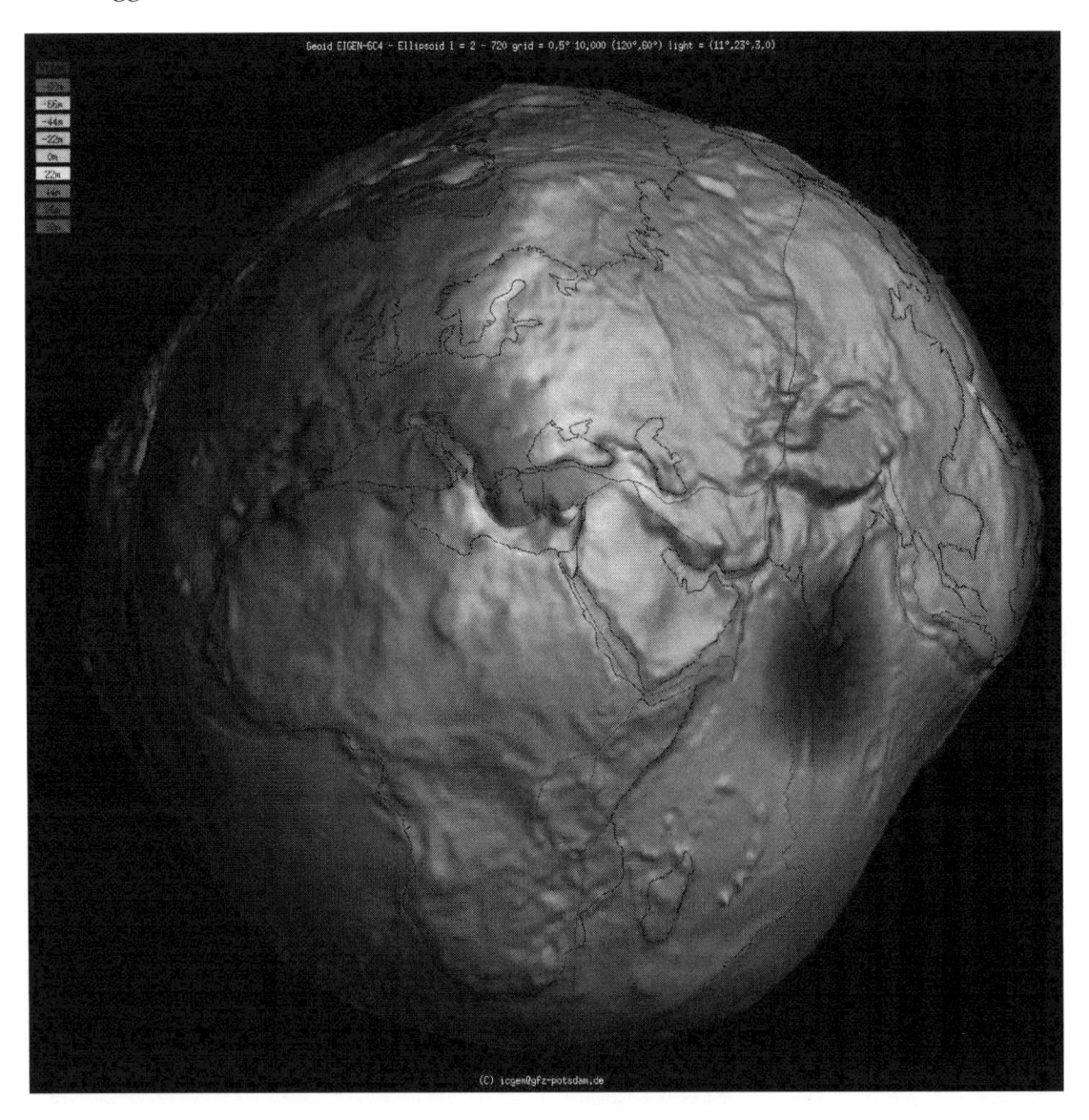

Image credits: https://en.wikipedia.org/wiki/File:Geoid_undulation_10k_scale.jpg

In order to assign a unique coordinate to a point on such a shape, we have to decide between two tradeoffs:

- **Global**: A global model of the Earth has the advantage of being universal, but its accuracy won't be constant in all places.
- **Local**: On the other hand, you can use a local model, a representation of the Earth surface valid for a small area (say, a country like the UK). Local models are required when accuracy is crucial.

In the rest of this chapter, we will work with the **World Geodetic System 1984 (WSG84)**, which is the most widely used system due to its adoption by all GPS systems. According to the preceding nomenclature, WSG84 is a global model, working everywhere on the Earth's surface.

After choosing a convenient shape, you will face the problem of drawing maps on a plane. Spheres have an annoying mathematical property: they cannot be mapped into a plane without any distortion. This means that, when projecting a sphere on a plane, you have to make choices about which properties will be conserved and which properties will be distorted.

Look at the following diagram, representing two different projections of the Earth on a map:

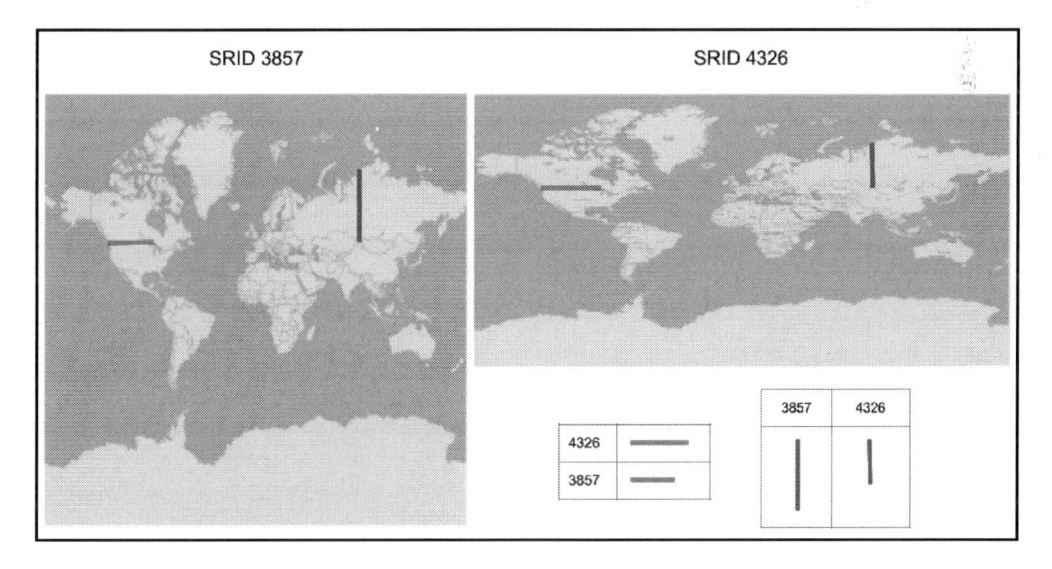

Spatial Data

You can see that the distances along the horizontal axis are much shorter in the left projection compared to the right one, while the distances along the vertical axis are much higher in the left image. Although we are mostly used to the left representation, the right image corresponds to the WSG84, so we will stick to this representation in this chapter.

Using the Neo4j built-in spatial types

If your application only deals with punctual coordinates, then the Neo4j built-in spatial type is perfect for you. It allows you to store locations as points and perform queries based on distance without adding any external dependency.

Creating points

To create a point, we need to provide its latitude and longitude:

```
RETURN point({latitude: 45, longitude: 3})
```

The point representation looks like this:

```
point({srid:4326, x:3, y:45}
```

You can recognize SRID 4326, meaning the coordinates are given in the GPS projection system. As I have already mentioned previously, the `y` coordinate holds the latitude, while the longitude is stored to the `x` coordinate.

We can also use the equivalent syntax by explicitly setting the `srid` and using the *xy* notation directly:

```
RETURN point({srid: 4326, y: 45, x: 3})
```

Be careful, however. If you omit the `srid` parameter in the preceding expression, the point will be interpreted as being in a Cartesian projection with SRID 7203. Creating a point in the Cartesian projection can be achieved with the following syntax:

```
RETURN point({y: 45, x: 3})
```

The previous query returns a totally different point:

```
point({srid:7203, x:3, y:45})
```

If you try to draw this point on a map, it will not be at latitude 45 and longitude 3, since it is not defined using the latitude/longitude coordinate system (srid=4326).

In the rest of this chapter, we will only work with latitude and longitude.

Of course, a point can be attached to a node as a property. We are going to import some data to help demonstrate this. The NYC_POI.csv dataset contains several points of interest in Manhattan (New York City). You can download the file from GitHub (https://github.com/PacktPublishing/Hands-On-Graph-Analytics-with-Neo4j/ch5/data/NYC_POI.csv) and check it has the following structure:

```
longitude,latitude,name
-73.9829219091849,40.76380762325644,ED SULLIVAN THTR
-73.98375310434135,40.76440130450186,STUDIO 54
-73.96566408280091,40.79823099029733,DOUGLASS II HOUSES BUILDING 13
```

Each row contains the information about a single point of interest: its name, its latitude, and its longitude. In total, there are 1,076 points of interest.

We can import this data into a new Neo4j graph by using the LOAD CSV statement:

```
LOAD CSV WITH HEADERS FROM "file:///NYC_POI.csv" AS row
CREATE (n:POI) SET  n.name=row.name,
                    n.latitude=toFloat(row.latitude),
                    n.longitude=toFloat(row.longitude),
                    n.point = point({latitude: toFloat(row.latitude),
                                     longitude: toFloat(row.longitude)})
```

You can check that each created node has a point attribute:

```
MATCH (n:POI) RETURN n LIMIT 1
```

The preceding query returns the following JSON result, which includes a point key:

```
{
  "name": "ST NICHOLAS HOUSES BUILDING 11",
  "point": point({srid:4326, x:-73.9476517312946, y:40.813276483717175}),
  "latitude": "40.813276483717175",
  "longitude": "-73.9476517312946"
}
```

Now, let's see what we can do with this information.

[173]

Querying by distance

The only built-in spatial operation as of Neo4j 4.0 is the `distance` function, which computes the distance between two points. It can be used in the following way:

```
RETURN distance(point({latitude: 45, longitude: 3}), point({latitude: 44, longitude: 2}))
```

According to this function, the distance between these two random points in France is 136,731 meters, that is to say, around 137 km (approximately 85 miles).

> The two points in the `distance` function need to be in the same CRS! The result is in meters if the two points were in the GPS projection, otherwise the unit depends on the unit of the projection.

Let's use this function in a more realistic example. We are going to use the `NYC_POI.csv` dataset we imported in the previous section to get the five closest points of interest from a given point, for instance, Times Square, whose GPS coordinates are (40.757961, -73.985553):

```
MATCH (n:POI)
WITH n, distance(n.point, point({latitude: 40.757961, longitude: -73.985553})) as distance_in_meters
RETURN n.name, round(distance_in_meters)
ORDER BY distance_in_meters
LIMIT 5
```

The result looks like the following table:

"n.name"	"round(distance_in_meters)"
"MINSKOFF THEATRE"	34.0
"BEST BUY THEATER"	58.0
"MARQUIS THEATRE"	83.0
"LYCEUM THEATRE"	86.0
"PALACE THEATRE"	132.0

In other words, we've found many theaters close to Times Square.

> **TIP**: This kind of distance-based query can be used to recommend activities close to the location of the user.

If we want to represent more complex spatial data, such as lines (streets) or polygons (area boundaries), we will have to use a plugin, `neo4j-spatial`, which we are going to look at in the following section.

Creating a geometry layer in Neo4j with neo4j-spatial

`neo4j-spatial` is an extension of Neo4j containing tools to represent and manipulate complex spatial data types. In this section, we are going to learn about this plugin by importing data on districts in Manhattan and finding points of interest located within each district.

Introducing the neo4j-spatial library

The `neo4j-spatial` plugin can be installed by downloading the latest release jar from https://github.com/neo4j-contrib/spatial/releases and copying this jar to the `plugins` directory of your active graph. You then need to restart the graph for the changes to be taken into account. Once this is done, you can check that the spatial plugin is enabled by calling the `spatial.procedures()` procedure, listing all available procedures within the plugin:

```
CALL spatial.procedures()
```

With this plugin, we will be able to do the following:

- Import from well-known geographic data formats such as `shapefile`
- Use topology operations such as *contains* or *intersects*
- Take advantage of spatial indexing for faster queries

Spatial Data

A note on spatial indexes

Spatial indexes, like any other indexes, are a way of running spatial queries much faster by avoiding having to perform the most complex operations on all the entities. For instance, let's consider the *intersection* query, where we're trying to find the points intersecting a complex polygon, similar to the one illustrated in the following diagram:

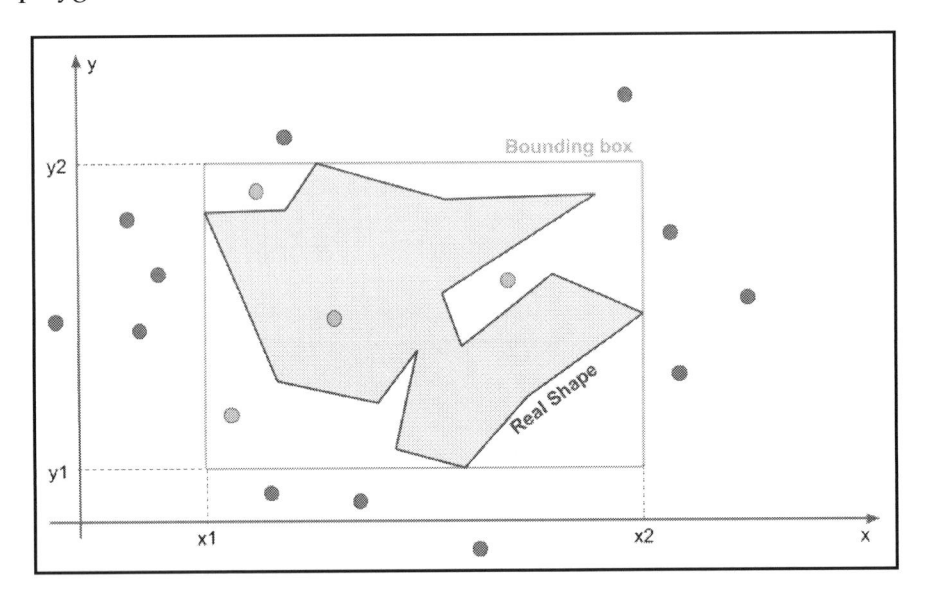

The rules of deciding whether points lie within the real shape are quite complex. However, it is straightforward to decide whether the same points are within the rectangle drawn around the complex area: we just have to perform four comparisons:

$$x1 < x < x2$$
$$\text{and } y1 < y < y2$$

Only the points fulfilling this condition will be tested in order to decide whether they belong to the real shape Doing this usually reduces the number of (complex) operations to be performed considerably.

The rectangle drawn around the real shape is called the **bounding box** of the real shape. It is the smaller rectangle containing the whole shape.

Let's now go back to `neo4j-spatial` and create our first spatial layer.

Creating a spatial layer of points

`neo4j-spatial` is able to represent complex geometries, but also points, so that we do not have to switch between using Neo4j built-in and `neo4j-spatial` for spatial data. In the first example we are going to study now, we will create a spatial layer of points, using the same dataset as the previous section, representing some points of interest within the Manhattan district of New York.

Defining the spatial layer

The first step to managing geometries within `neo4j-spatial` is to define a **layer**. A layer contains information about the type of data it stores. To create a simple point layer named `pointLayer`, we can use the `addPointLayer` procedure:

```
CALL spatial.addPointLayer('pointLayer');
```

You will notice that this procedure adds a new node to the graph. This node is the one containing the information about the layer. To check the existing layers within a graph, you can call the following:

```
CALL spatial.layers();
```

The result of the previous statement is copied here:

"name"	"signature"
"pointLayer"	"EditableLayer(name='pointLayer', encoder=SimplePointEncoder(x='longitude', y='latitude', bbox='bbox'))"

So far, we have only created a layer, or a container for our spatial data, but this container is empty. Let's now add some data to it.

Spatial Data

Adding points to a spatial layer

Once the spatial layer is created, we can add data to it, which will also update the spatial index. The following query adds all nodes with the POI label to the newly created spatial layer with the name 'pointLayer':

```
MATCH (n:POI)
CALL spatial.addNode('pointLayer', n) YIELD node
RETURN count(node)
```

This operation adds two more properties to the node:

- A point attribute, similar to the built-in Neo4j type
- A bbox attribute used for querying the data with a spatial index, as discussed earlier in this chapter

We will see how to use this data in the following sections. Before that, we are going to deal with other types of geometries, so as to take full advantage of neo4j-spatial compared to built-in Neo4j types.

Defining the type of spatial data

So far, we have only used points, defined as a single couple of x and y coordinates. But when dealing with geometries, we may have to deal with more complex data structures:

- **POINT** is a single location.
- **LINESTRING** represents lines, an ordered collection of points. It can be used to represent the shape of a street or a river, for instance.
- **POLYGON** represents closed areas, such as city and country boundaries, forests, or buildings.

There are standard representations for each of these types of geometries. The one we are going to use in the rest of this section is the **Well-Known Text (WKT)** representation, which is a human-readable list of coordinates. The following tables give examples of WKT representation for each of the aforementioned three types of geometries:

Type	WKT representation
POINT	POINT (x y)
LINESTRING	LINESTRING (x1 y1, x2 y2, x3 y3, ..., xn yn)
POLYGON	POLYGON (x1 y1, x2 y2, x3 y3, ..., xn yn, x1 y1)

In the following subsection, we are going to use some polygon geometries representing the districts of Manhattan. After that, we will use linestrings to represent the streets in this borough.

Creating layers with polygon geometries

We are now going to use some `Polygon` geometries with our Manhattan data. In this section, we will download and import the data into Neo4j.

Getting the data

The dataset we are going to use now was created from data published by the city of New York. You can download it from the GitHub repository associated with this book, under `ch5/data/mahattan_district.shp`. More information about how this file was created can also be found at the same location.

The data file is in a `shapefile` format, a format very common among spatial data professionals. It contains the boundaries and name of each community district within Manhattan in New York. The following image shows the districts we are going to work with:

Spatial Data

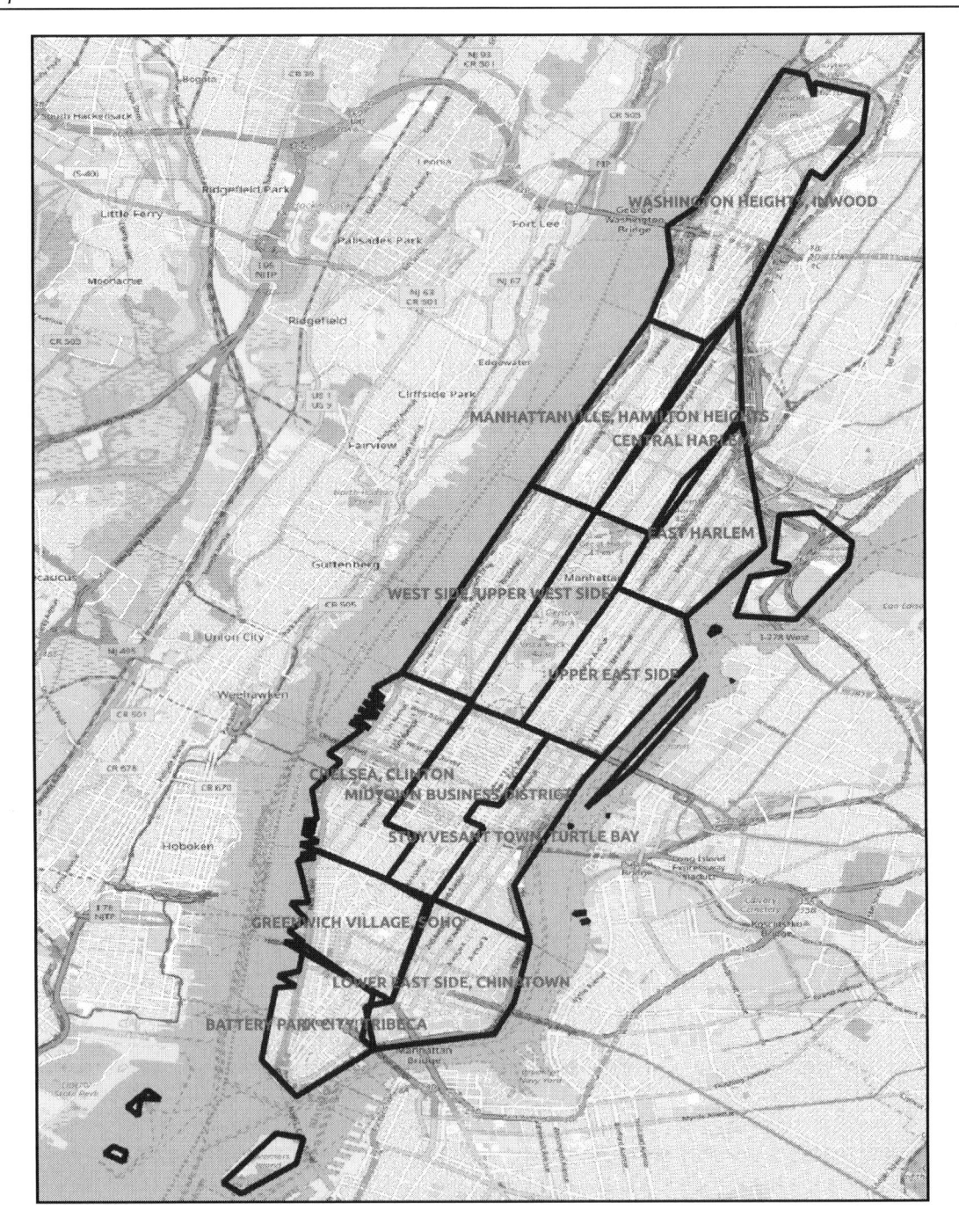

The 11 districts of the borough of Manhattan in New York. Image created using QGIS

Any GIS is able to decode the `shapefile` format, as is `neo4j-spatial`. The first step of our analysis with Neo4j is to import the data into our graph.

Creating the layer

With `neo4j-spatial`, we can load data directly from a `shapefile`. The procedure is called `spatial.importShapefile` and accepts a single parameter: the path to the data file. It will automatically create a new spatial layer to hold the data, with a name derived from the input file name, and create a node for each geometry.

The full syntax is as follows:

1. First, let's create the layer, with a given name and type:

```
CALL spatial.addLayer("manhattan_districts")
```

2. Import the shapefile data into this newly created layer:

```
CALL spatial.importShapefile("/<absolute_path_to>/manhattan_districts.shp")
```

After you run this procedure, your database contains twelve more nodes, one for each district contained in the `shapefile`. Each of these nodes contains the following information:

```
{
  "CD_ID": 4,
  "geometry": {....},
  "gtype": 6,
  "ID": 1,
  "bbox": [
      -74.01214813183593,
      40.7373608893982,
      -73.98142817921234,
      40.77317951096692
  ],
  "NAME": "Chelsea, Clinton"
}
```

I have cut the geometry representation because it is very long, but the `geometry` attribute is there and non-empty. It also contains a `NAME` node (taken from `shapefile`) and the `bbox` property (added by `neo4j-spatial` to serve the spatial index).

Spatial Data

To summarize, we now have two spatial layers in our graph:

1. The `pointLayer` class we created in the previous section to hold the point of interest.
2. Our newly created `manhattan_districts` layer, containing the boundaries of twelve partitions of Manhattan.

It is now time to learn how to use these geometries. The following section deals with spatial queries, in other words, how to take full advantage of the fact that we know the exact location and shape of our nodes.

Performing spatial queries

Now that we have data inside our graph, we are going to use it to extract geographical information. More precisely, we will learn how to select nodes that lie within a certain distance from a given point. We will also discover a new functionality: the ability to find nodes contained within a polygon.

Finding the distance between two spatial objects

With `neo4j-spatial`, we can get nodes within a certain distance from another node. The procedure to perform this operation is called `spatial.withinDistance` and its signature is the following:

```
spatial.withinDistance(layerName, coordinates, distanceInKm) => node, distance
```

This means it will search, within a given layer, all points that are less than `distanceInKm` away from `coordinates`. It returns those nodes and the computed distance between the returned node and `coordinates`.

The `coordinates` parameter can be an instance of a point or a map of latitude and longitude.

For instance, we can find the point of interest located less than 1 km away from Times Square with this query:

```
CALL spatial.withinDistance("ny_poi_point", {latitude: 40.757961,
longitude: -73.985553}, 1)
YIELD node, distance
RETURN node.name, distance
ORDER BY distance
```

We could also look for the points of interest that are close to the Marquis Theater. In this case, we would first find the node corresponding to the Marquis Theater, and then use the point property of this node for the spatial query:

```
MATCH (p:POI {name: "MARQUIS THEATRE"})
CALL spatial.withinDistance("ny_poi_point", p.point, 1)
YIELD node, distance
RETURN node.name, distance
ORDER BY distance
```

Last but not least, distance queries also work for non-point layers:

```
MATCH (p:POI {name: "MARQUIS THEATRE"})
CALL spatial.withinDistance("manhattan_districts", p.point, 1)
YIELD node, distance
RETURN node.NAME, round(distance*1000) as distance_in_meters
ORDER BY distance
```

The preceding query returns a list of districts whose closest distance to the Marquis Theater is less than 1 km:

"node.NAME"	"distance_in_meters"
"Midtown Business District"	0.0
"Chelsea, Clinton"	205.0
"Stuyvesant Town, Turtle Bay"	965.0

We are now experts in writing distance queries. Next, we are going to discover other kinds of queries that can be performed with spatial data.

Finding objects contained within other objects

From the last query we wrote, we can infer that the Marquis Theater is located within the Midtown Business District of Manhattan. But there is an easier way to find this information, thanks to the `intersects` procedure:

```
MATCH (p:POI {name: "MARQUIS THEATRE"})
CALL spatial.intersects("manhattan_districts", p) YIELD node as district
RETURN district.NAME
```

Now, we get only one result – Midtown Business District. We can even use the graph pattern to save this information by adding a relationship, `CONTAINED_IN`, between the point of interest and the matched district:

```
MATCH (p:POI {name: "MARQUIS THEATRE"})
CALL spatial.intersects("manhattan_districts", p) YIELD node as district
CREATE (p)-[:CONTAINED_IN]->(district)
```

In this way, we will have to perform the spatial query only once, when inserting the node or creating the data, and then rely on graph traversals and Cypher only to get the information we need, which may simplify the queries.

We now know how to import, store, and query spatial data within Neo4j. During the last few sections, we talked a lot about distance between points. This is related to the *shortest path* concept we studied in the previous chapter (Chapter 4, *The Graph Data Science Library and Path Finding*). In the next two sections, we will use both spatial data and shortest path algorithms to build a routing engine to guide us around New York.

Finding the shortest path based on distance

Spatial data and path finding algorithms are very much related. In this section, we are going to use a dataset representing the road network in New York, `neo4j-spatial`, and the GDS plugin (see Chapter 4, *The Graph Data Science Library and Path Finding*) to build a routing system.

The specifications for this routing application are the following:

- The user will input the start and end locations as (latitude, longitude) tuples.
- The system must return an ordered list of the streets the user needs to follow in order to go from his start to his end location by traveling the shortest distance.

Let's start by discovering and preparing the data.

Importing the data

In order to build a routing engine, we need a precise description of the road network in our area of interest. Luckily, the street network of New York is available as open data. You can find this file in the GitHub repository for this book, together with more information about its provenance (https://github.com/PacktPublishing/Hands-On-Graph-Analytics-with-Neo4j/ch5/data/manhattan_road_network.graphml.zip). The file format is called GraphML. It is an XML-like file format, with graph-specific entities. Here's a sample of this data file:

```xml
<?xml version='1.0' encoding='utf-8'?>
<graphml xmlns="http://graphml.graphdrawing.org/xmlns"
xmlns:xsi="http://www.w3.org/2001/XMLSchema-instance"
xsi:schemaLocation="http://grap
hml.graphdrawing.org/xmlns
http://graphml.graphdrawing.org/xmlns/1.0/graphml.xsd">
  <key attr.name="geometry" attr.type="string" for="edge" id="d16" />
  <key attr.name="maxspeed" attr.type="string" for="edge" id="d15" />
  <key attr.name="length" attr.type="string" for="edge" id="d9" />
  <key attr.name="name" attr.type="string" for="edge" id="d8" />
  <key attr.name="ref" attr.type="string" for="node" id="d7" />
  <key attr.name="osmid" attr.type="string" for="node" id="d5" />
  <key attr.name="longitude" attr.type="double" for="node" id="d4" />
  <key attr.name="latitude" attr.type="double" for="node" id="d3" />
  <key attr.name="streets_per_node" attr.type="string" for="graph" id="d2" />
  <key attr.name="name" attr.type="string" for="graph" id="d1" />
  <key attr.name="crs" attr.type="string" for="graph" id="d0" />
  <graph edgedefault="directed">
    <data key="d0">{'init': 'epsg:4326'}</data>
    <data key="d1">Manhattan, New York, USA</data>
    <node id="42459137">
      <data key="d3">40.7755735</data>
      <data key="d4">-73.9603796</data>
      <data key="d5">42459137</data>
    </node>
    <node id="1773060099">
      <data key="d3">40.7137811</data>
      <data key="d4">-73.9980743</data>
      <data key="d5">1773060099</data>
    </node>
    <edge source="42434559" target="1205714910">
      <data key="d8">Margaret Corbin Drive</data>
      <data key="d16">LINESTRING (-73.9326239 40.8632443, -73.93267090000001 40.8631814, -73.93273120000001 40.8630891, -73.9327701 40.863009, -73.9338518 40.8594721, -73.93399549999999 40.8594143)</data>
      <data key="d9">491.145731265</data>
```

Spatial Data

```
        </edge>
    </graph>
</graphml>
```

As you can infer, the first part defines the different keys or attributes that can be associated with the different entities. These attributes have a name, a type, are assigned to either nodes or edges, and have a key identifier. Only these identifiers is used in the rest of the document. For instance, the node with ID `42459137` (the first one in the preceding reproduced list) has `d3=40.7137811`, and checking the definition of keys, d3 means y or latitude.

In the previous snippet, I have highlighted the fields we are going to use for this section:

- For the nodes representing the intersections between streets, we are going to use `latitude` and `longitude` fields. `osmid` will also be used to uniquely identify nodes.
- For the edges representing the streets themselves, we are mainly going to use `name` and `length`. In the final section dedicated to visualization, we will also use the `geometry` attribute.

It is now time to import this data into our Neo4j graph. This section will not use the data from the beginning of this chapter, so you can import it into a new empty graph.

Preparing the data

Fortunately, someone has already implemented the import procedure to load this data into Neo4j. It is part of the APOC plugin. You can easily install it from Neo4j Desktop from the **Plugins** tab of the **Manage** view of your graph.

Importing data

So, after installing APOC and copying the data file into your `import` folder, you can simply call the `apoc.import.graphml` procedure in this way:

```
CALL apoc.import.graphml("manhattan_road_network.graphml",
{defaultRelationshipType:"LINKED_TO"})
```

After a couple of seconds, you will see a result similar to this one:

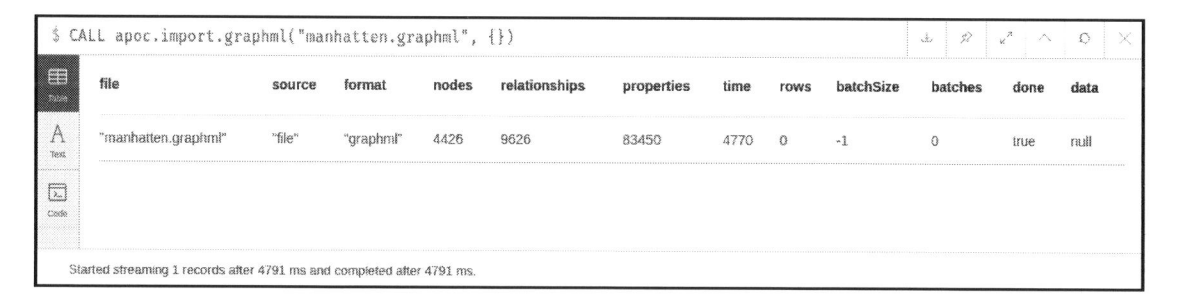

file	source	format	nodes	relationships	properties	time	rows	batchSize	batches	done	data
"manhatten.graphml"	"file"	"graphml"	4426	9626	83450	4770	0	-1	0	true	null

Started streaming 1 records after 4791 ms and completed after 4791 ms.

4,426 nodes (junctions) were inserted and 9,626 relationships of type `LINKED_TO` representing road segments were created between them.

In order to facilitate the queries in the rest of this chapter, we will assign a label, `Junction`, to the newly created nodes:

```
MATCH (n)
WHERE n.latitude IS NOT NULL AND n.longitude IS NOT NULL
SET n:Junction
```

Our graph is well imported. You can check a few nodes and relationships. For instance, those associated with Fifth Avenue look like the following diagram:

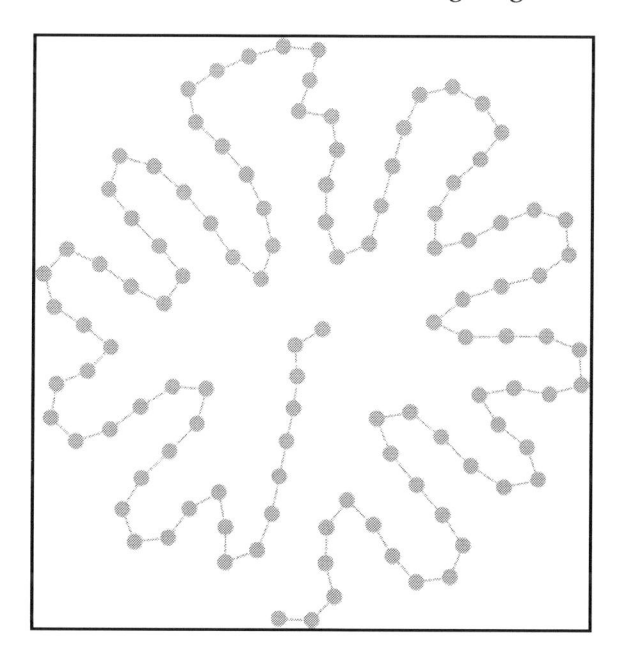

Spatial Data

In the final section of this chapter, we will learn how to represent this data on a map for a more realistic visualization. Before that, let's work on our routing engine.

Creating a spatial layer

Both junctions and streets have spatial attributes. Junctions have latitude and longitude properties and streets (relationships of the `LINKED_TO` type in our graph) have a geometry property containing the WKT representation of a `LINESTRING` object. We can create a spatial layer for each of these entities; however, remember that the GDS path finding algorithms work between nodes, not relationships. This means that, from the `(latitude, longitude)` user input, we will have to find the closest `Junction` node. So we need to create a spatial point layer to index our 4426 junctions. For now, there is no need to create a layer to hold the streets; we will create it later on if necessary.

Let's then create the point layer that will index the nodes with the `Junction` label:

```
CALL spatial.addPointLayer("junctions")
```

Now, add points to it:

```
MATCH (n:Junction)
CALL spatial.addNode("junctions", n) YIELD node
RETURN count(node)
```

After a few seconds, 4,426 nodes are added to the `junctions` spatial layer.

Let's now enter into the most important part of the exercise: the path finding algorithm itself.

Running the shortest path algorithm

Before running any algorithm from the GDS, we need to create a projected graph. At this stage, we need to be very careful about the entities to include in this graph. For shortest path applications, we need `Junction` nodes, `LINKED_TO` relationships, and the length of each road segment, stored in the `length` property of each relationship. However, this property is a `String` type, which is not compatible with the addition operation we need to do in shortest path algorithms. For this reason, we are going to create the projected graph using Cypher projection in order to cast the length property in the projected graph:

```
CALL gds.graph.create.cypher(
    "road_network",
    "MATCH (n:Junction) RETURN id(n) as id",
```

```
    "MATCH (n)-[r:LINKED_TO]->(m) RETURN id(n) as source, id(m) as
target, toInteger(r.length) as length"
)
```

Now, we can use the shortest path finding algorithm. Since our nodes do have latitude and longitude properties, we are able to use the A* implementation in Neo4j, which uses the Haversine formula as heuristics. Let's remind ourselves of the A* algorithm syntax:

```
CALL gds.alpha.shortestPath.astar.stream(
        graphName::STRING,
        {
            startNode::NODE,
            endNode::NODE,
            relationshipWeightProperty::STRING,
            propertyKeyLat::STRING,
            propertyKeyLon::STRING
        }
)
```

In this signature, we have the following:

- `graphName` is the name of the projected graph we want our algorithm to run on.
- `startNode` is the starting node in the path. We are going to use the closest `Junction` to a given pair of coordinates, (`latStart`, `lonStart`).
- `endNode` is the destination node. Again, we will use the closest `Junction` to a given pair of coordinates, (`latEnd`, `lonEnd`).
- `relationshipWeightProperty` is the relationship property containing the weight to be applied to each link, if any. In our case, we will use the length of the street as the weight.
- `propertyKeyLat` and `propertyKeyLon` are the names of the properties containing the latitude and longitude of each node. The A* algorithm uses them to infer which way it needs to go for the shortest path.

The first step is to identify the closest junctions. For the given location, let's say Times Square. This can be achieved with the following query:

```
WITH {latitude: 40.757961, longitude: -73.985553} as p
CALL spatial.withinDistance("junctions", p, 1) YIELD node, distance
RETURN node.osmid
ORDER BY distance LIMIT 1
```

With this query, we get that the closest junction to Times Square has `osmid = 42428297`.

Spatial Data

Let's set Times Square as our start location. Our destination for the rest of this section is Central Park (South), whose coordinates are (40.767098, -73.978869). Using a similar query to the previous one, we find out that the closest node to the end location has `osmid=42435825`. This information is summarized in the following table.

	Name	Latitude	Longitude	OSM ID Closest Node
Start location	Times Square	40.757961	-73.985553	"42428297"
End location	Central Park (South)	40.767098	-73.978869	"42423674"

With these identifiers (`osmid`), we can then execute the A* algorithm using the following query:

```
MATCH (startNode:Junction {osmid: "42428297"})
MATCH (endNode:Junction {osmid: "42423674"})
CALL gds.alpha.shortestPath.astar.stream(
    "road_network",
    {
        startNode: startNode,
        endNode: endNode,
        relationshipWeightProperty: "length",
        propertyKeyLat: "latitude",
        propertyKeyLon: "longitude"
    }
) YIELD nodeId, cost
WITH gds.util.asNode(nodeId) as node, cost
RETURN node.osmid as osmid, cost
```

This produces the following result:

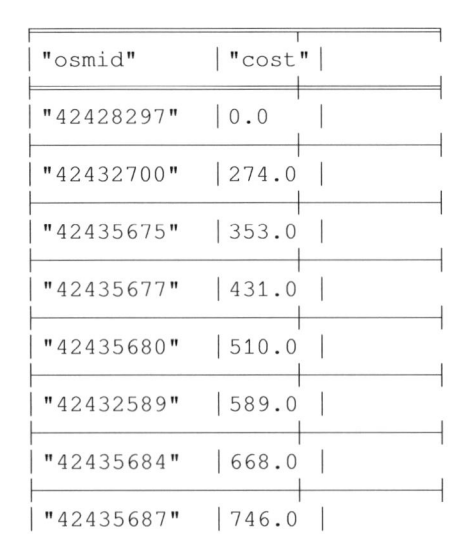

```
| "osmid"     | "cost" |
| "42428297"  | 0.0    |
| "42432700"  | 274.0  |
| "42435675"  | 353.0  |
| "42435677"  | 431.0  |
| "42435680"  | 510.0  |
| "42432589"  | 589.0  |
| "42435684"  | 668.0  |
| "42435687"  | 746.0  |
```

"42435702"	823.0
"42435705"	903.0
"42435707"	984.0
"42435710"	1062.0
"42431556"	1140.0
"42435714"	1226.0
"42435716"	1312.0
"1825841700"	1361.0
"1825841743"	1370.0
"4557482266"	1393.0
"4347550074"	1444.0
"42423674"	**1631.0**

The last row tells us that the shortest path between Times Square and South Central Park is around 1.6 km long.

We can extract more useful information by getting the name of the street and summing the length of all relationships belonging to the same street. The RETURN statement from our previous query is then replaced by the following code:

```
WITH gds.util.asNode(nodeId) as node, cost
WITH collect(node) as path, collect(cost) as costs
UNWIND range(0, size(path)-1) AS index
WITH path[index] AS currentNode, path[index+1] AS nextNode
MATCH (currentNode)-[r:LINKED_TO]->(nextNode)
RETURN r.name, sum(toFloat(r.length)) as length
```

The result of the full query is as follows:

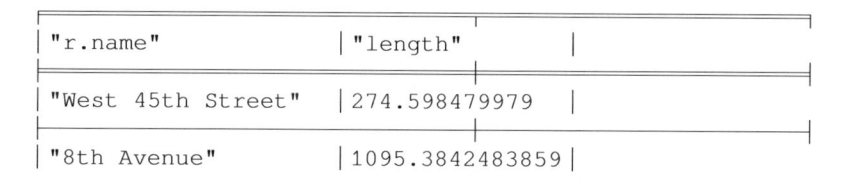

"r.name"	"length"
"West 45th Street"	274.598479979
"8th Avenue"	1095.3842483859

Spatial Data

```
| "Columbus Circle"    | 33.37408896743  |
| "Central Park South" | 238.7529348628  |
```

This means that, starting from Times Square, I will have to walk 275 meters along West 45th Street, then turn onto 8th Avenue and follow it for 1 km. Arriving at Columbus Circle, I will have to walk along Central Park South for 240 meters before reaching my destination. Let's check this result on a map:

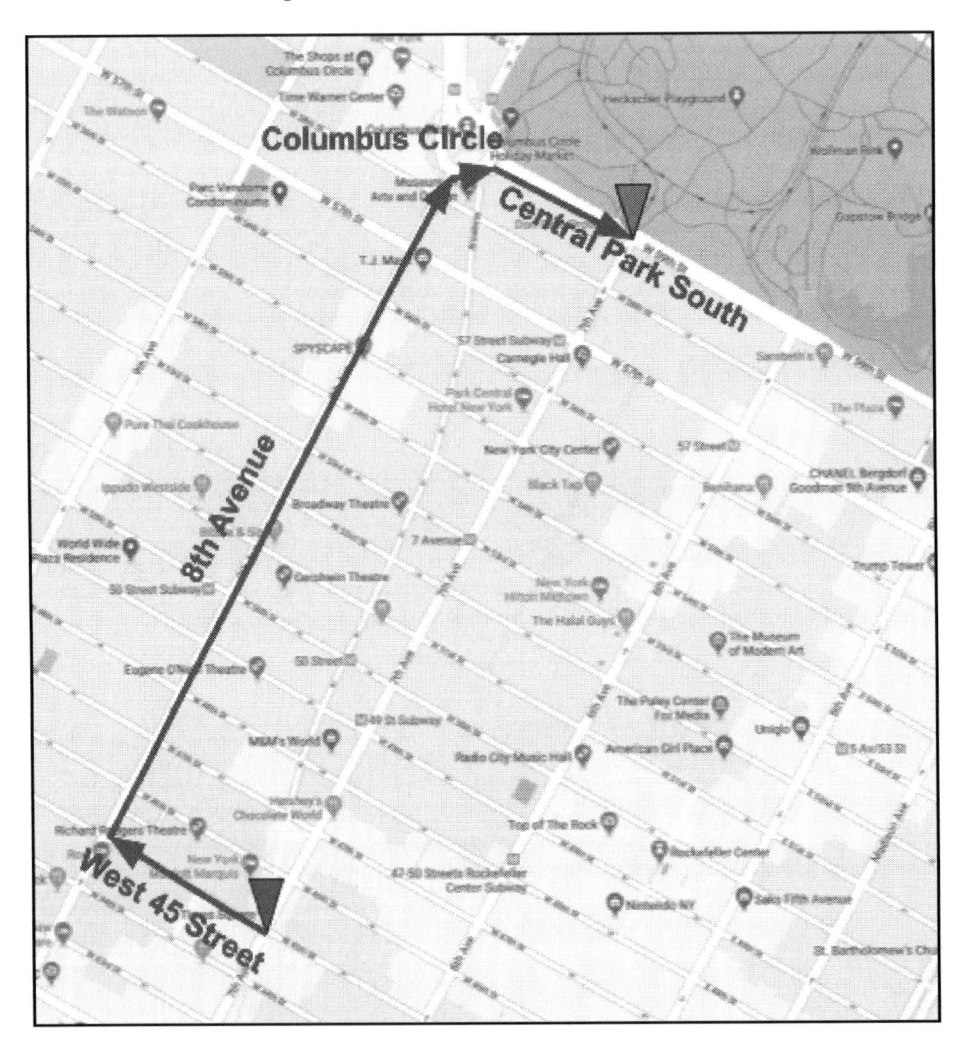

As you can see, the shortest path from the starting point (bottom triange) to the destination point (top triangle, close to Center Park), is using 7th Avenue. However, this is a one-way street, and cars are not allowed to use it in the south-north direction. If we were driving, the preceding route would be correct. But let's assume we are walking and we do not want to make such a detour. With the GDS plugin, this means we have to create another projected graph, `road_network_undirected`, where the relationships direction will be ignored. We can do this in the following way:

```
CALL gds.graph.create.cypher(
    "road_network_undirected",
    "MATCH (n:Junction) RETURN id(n) as id",
    "MATCH (n)-[r:LINKED_TO]-(m) RETURN id(n) as source, id(m) as target, toInteger(r.length) as length"
)
```

The difference compared to the `road_network` graph is the query used to define the relationships:

- In `road_network`, we used directed edges from `(n)` to `(m)`.

    ```
    MATCH (n)-[r:LINKED_TO]->(m)
    ```

- On the other hand, in `road_network_undirected`, we used undirected edges simply by removing the > symbol in Cypher:

    ```
    MATCH (n)-[r:LINKED_TO]-(m)
    ```

Running the same path finding algorithm on `road_network_undirected`, we get the following result:

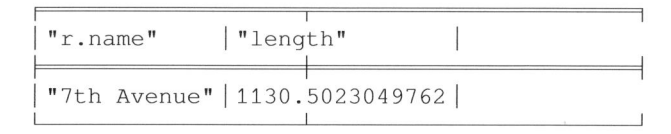

"r.name"	"length"
"7th Avenue"	1130.5023049762

> **TIP**: Remember to remove the > symbol in the query producing the result as well.

We reduced the route by 500 meters, which is a long way on foot!

Spatial Data

Thanks to spatial data and the A* path finding algorithm from the Neo4j GDS plugin, we have built a fully functional routing system. It even works for cars (with the directed projected graph) and pedestrians (with the undirected projected graph).

> For the routing system to be fully trusted by pedestrians, we'll need to exclude motorways and unsuitable roads for walkers.

In the following section, we are going to talk about spatial data visualization when it is stored inside a Neo4j graph.

Visualizing spatial data with Neo4j

Spatial data experts have developed several tools for visualizing and manually updating geometries. `ArgQIS` and `QGIS` desktop applications allow us to load data from various data sources, such as `shapefile`, create edit geometries, and perform operations such as distance calculations.

In this section, we are going to investigate two solutions compatible with Neo4j. The first one is an application that can be installed to Neo4j Desktop and that allows us to visualize nodes. The second one uses the Neo4j JavaScript driver and `leaflet`, a JavaScript library done especially to visualize maps in order to start creating a web application to visualize the shortest path between two points.

neomap – a Neo4j Desktop application for spatial data

`neomap` is an open source application available at https://github.com/stellasia/neomap/. It can be added to Neo4j Desktop and connected to the active graph when you start it. It allows you to visualize nodes with spatial attributes (latitude and longitude). We will see two applications in this section.

> *Disclaimer*: I am the author of this application, and as far as I know at the time of writing, there is no equivalent.

Visualizing nodes with simple layers

There are two ways to create a layer in `neomap`. The first and simplest one is to select the node **label(s)** you want to fetch and to set the name of the properties holding the latitude and longitude properties. The following screenshot shows the simple layer configuration needed to display the `Junctions` node from our Manhattan street network graph:

When needed, you can turn the markers into a heatmap by changing the map rendering configuration.

Visualizing paths with advanced layer

The advanced layer mode allows the user to more precisely select the nodes to be displayed. For instance, we may want to visualize only the nodes involved in the shortest path from Times Square to Central Park South. In that case, we will have to write the `Cypher` query to match the nodes, and return at least two elements: the latitude and longitude of the nodes.

[195]

Spatial Data

You can see the configuration used to display the nodes belonging to our shortest path in the following screenshot:

This application helps in visualizing data for data analysis and understanding. However, if we want to visualize spatial attributes in a more interactive way in web applications, we will have to investigate other methods. The following section will demonstrate how to use two `JavaScript` libraries, the Neo4j JavaSscript driver, and `leaflet`, to visualize the same path.

In the following section, we will go deeper into the Neo4j JavaScript driver to build stand-alone web pages able to interact with Neo4j.

Using the JavaScript Neo4j driver to visualize shortest paths

Neo4j officially provides a driver for JavaScript. We are going to use this driver to create a small web application to visualize the shortest paths between two junctions. The full code is available at https://github.com/PacktPublishing/Hands-On-Graph-Analytics-with-Neo4j/blob/master/ch5/shortest_path_visualization.html and you just have to open it with your favorite web browser to see the result (all dependencies are included in the file).

Neo4j JS driver

The first step is to set the connection parameters to Neo4j:

```
var driver = neo4j.driver(
    // update the next two lines depending on your configuration
    'bolt://127.0.0.1:7687',
    neo4j.auth.basic('user', 'password')
);
var session = driver.session();
```

You can find the bolt port in the active graph management window as illustrated in the following screenshot:

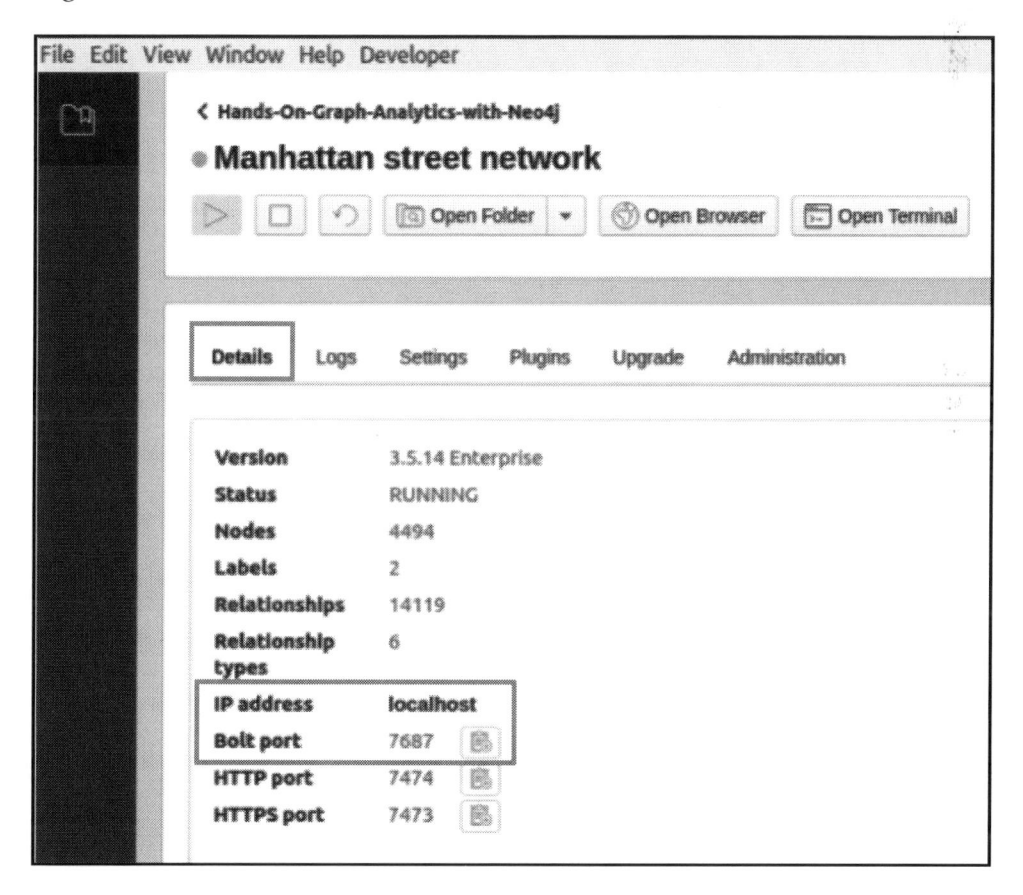

Spatial Data

Leaflet and GeoJSON

`Leaflet` is an open source JavaScript library used to visualize maps. Like many map visualization systems, it works with superimposed layers. Each layer can be a different type. In this section, we will only use two of them:

- The **Tile layer** displays square PNG images. Depending on the layer, it can contain streets, toponymy, or even points of interest. In our case, we will only use the default **Open Street Map** tile layer.
- The **GeoJSON layer** displays data with the `GeoJSON` format. So far, we have only seen geometries stored as `WKT`. `GeoJSON` is another human-readable representation of geometries. The following code shows the `WKT` and `GeoJSON` representations of the same shape:

```
WKT:
LINESTRING(-73.9879285 40.7597869,-73.9878847 40.759847)

GeoJSON:
{"type":"LineString","coordinates":[[-73.9879285,40.7597869],[-73.9
878847,40.759847]]}
```

Let's get started and build our map. Creating a `leaflet` map is as simple as executing the following command:

```
var map = L.map('mapid').setView([40.757965, -73.985561], 7);
```

The `mapid` parameter is the ID of the HTML element the map will be drawn in. This means that our **document object model** (**DOM**) needs to contain the following:

```
<div id="mapid"></div>
```

The parameters in `setView` are the coordinates of the map center and the initial zoom level, respectively. As we will see later, these are not really of any importance for us.

Once the map is created, we can start adding layers to it. The first layer we are going to add is the `OSM` tiles, in order to work out where we are:

```
L.tileLayer(
    'https://{s}.tile.openstreetmap.org/{z}/{x}/{y}.png', {
    maxZoom: 19,
    attribution: '&copy; <a href="https://openstreetmap.org/copyright">OpenStreetMap contributors</a>'
}).addTo(map);
```

[198]

Then, we can start querying Neo4j and adding the geometry to the map. To do so, we will use the same query we wrote earlier in this chapter to find the shortest path between two junctions. The `osmid` of the `junction` node will be a parameter of our query, so the beginning of the query has to be written as follows:

```
MATCH (startNode:Junction {osmid: { startNodeOsmId }})
MATCH (endNode:Junction {osmid: { endNodeOsmId }})
```

We are going to display the street geometries, which are contained in the `geometry` parameter of the relationships, as `WKT` format, so let's return this information at the end of our query like this:

```
RETURN r.name, r.geometry as wkt
```

We can define our `query` variable as follows:

```
var query = `
MATCH (startNode:Junction {osmid: { startNodeOsmId }})
MATCH (endNode:Junction {osmid: { endNodeOsmId }})
// [...] same query than in previous section
RETURN r.name, r.geometry as wkt
`;
```

The parameters of our query are as follows:

```
var params = {
    "startNodeOsmId": "42428297",
    "endNodeOsmId": "42423674"
};
```

Finally, we can query Neo4j and add the result to the map. This is done in two steps:

1. Send a query to Neo4j, read the result, and parse `WKT` to `GeoJSON` in a format understood by `leaflet`:

```
        session
            .run(query, params)
            .then(function(result){
                let results = [];
                result.records.forEach(function(record) {
                    let wkt = record.get("wkt");
                    // we need to filter out records
                    // for which we do not have any geometry information
                    if (wkt !== null) {
                        // parse result from WKT to GeoJSON
                        let geo = wellknown.parse(wkt);
                        results.push(geo);
```

Spatial Data

```
            }
        });
        return results;
    })
```

2. Once we have a list of `GeoJSON` objects, we can create the new layer:

```
.then(function(result) {
    var myLayer = L.geoJSON(
        result,
        {
            "weight": 5,
            "color": "red",
        }
    ).addTo(map);
    map.fitBounds(myLayer.getBounds());
});
```

We need to set some some styling properties for this new layer in order for it to be more visible. Finally, with the `fitBounds` operation, we tell `leaflet` to automatically find the correct viewport so that our path is fully visible.

If you open the full HTML file with your browser, after updating your connection parameters, you should see a map similar to the one reproduced in the preceding section. It looks pretty nice, except for the fact that some segments are missing from the path. The reason is that some edges in our graph do not have a `geometry` property. Since the streets in this area are quite straight, we just need the position of the first and last point of the segment to have the geometry displayed nicely. This means we can manually update the geometry of the road segment by using the position of its starting and ending nodes, like this:

```
MATCH (currentNode)-[r:LINKED_TO]->(nextNode)
WHERE r.geometry is null
SET r.geometry = 'LINESTRING (' + currentNode.longitude + ' ' +
currentNode.latitude + ', ' + nextNode.longitude + ' ' + nextNode.latitude
+ ')'
```

If you reload the `shortest_path_visualization.html` page once this update is complete, you will see a fully colored path, as illustrated on the following map:

Visualizing paths with Neo4j and JS

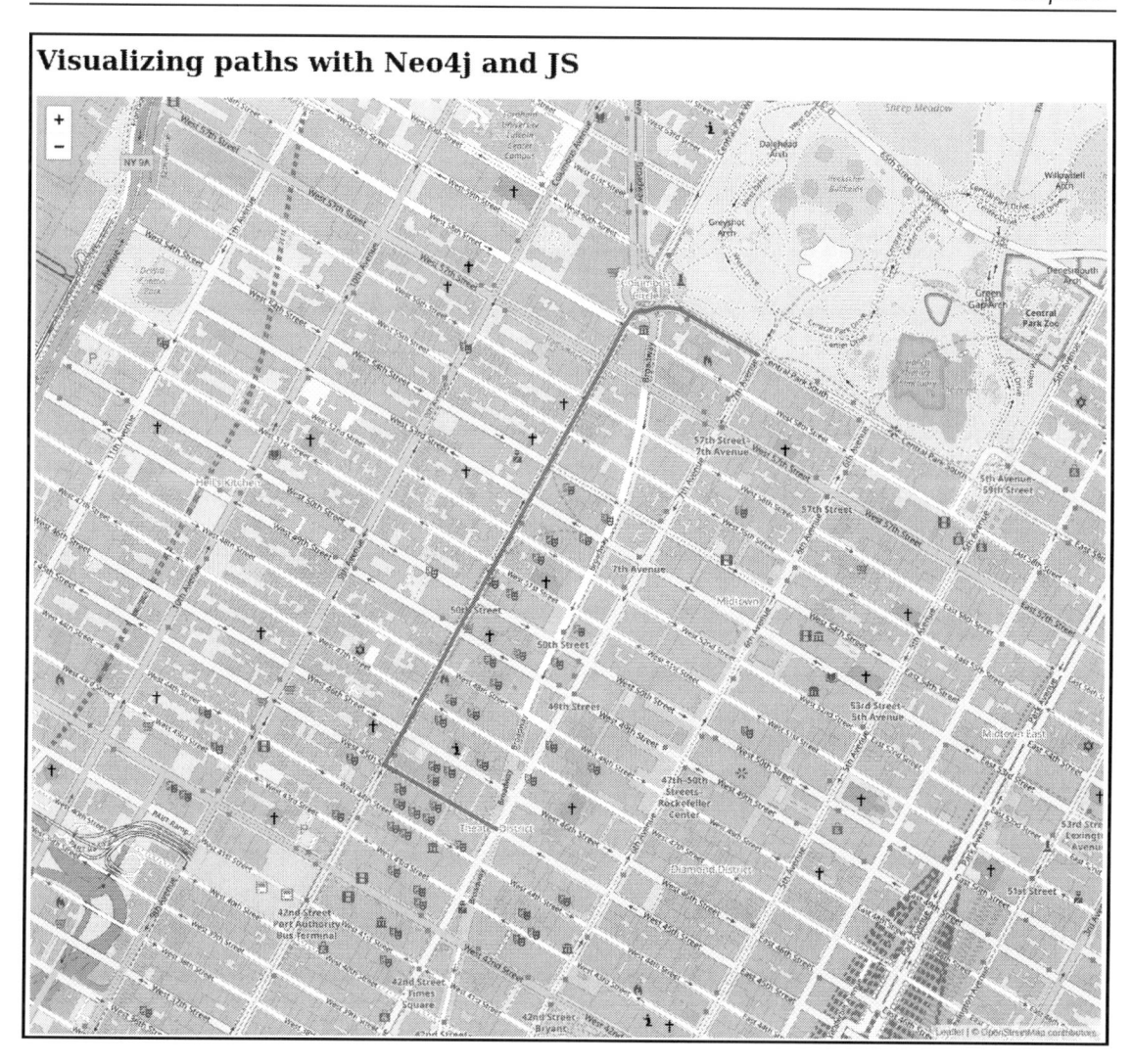

You can also check the result by running the algorithm on the undirected projected graph, or even choosing different start and end nodes.

This first visualization example can, of course, be improved. We'll touch on some ideas for improvement in the *Questions* section of this chapter, and we will learn more interesting techniques later in this book, especially *GraphQL*, to prevent exposing the query in the JavaScript code (see `Chapter 11`, *Using Neo4j in Your Web Application*).

Summary

In this chapter, you have learned how spatial data is stored in information systems, and how to use it with Neo4j. You now know how to use the Neo4j built-in `point` type and perform distance queries using it. You have also learned about the `neo4j-spatial` plugin, allowing more complex operations such as geometry intersection and *within distance* queries.

Finally, you have learned how to build a graph-based routing engine using spatial data and the shortest path algorithms implemented in the GDS library. With the help of some JavaScript code, you have even been able to nicely display the result of the path finding algorithm on a map.

In the next chapter, you will discover a new type of algorithm: centrality algorithms. They are used to quantify the node importance, depending on your definition of importance.

Questions

1. Spatial data:
    1. Add a new point of interest in New York and create a Neo4j relationship between it and the district it belongs to.
    2. Write the query to find the closest street to a given point (latitude, longitude).
2. Routing engine:
    1. Modify the shortest path algorithm to find the shortest path in terms of duration instead of distance.
    2. Improve the routing engine for pedestrians by excluding motorways from the possible streets.
    3. How would you find alternative paths?
3. Visualization:
    1. Modify the web page we created to let the user choose the start and end nodes.
    2. Modify the web page we created to let the user choose the start and end latitude and longitude. The script will have to find the OSM ID of the start and end nodes in order to display the shortest path between them.

Further reading

- To learn more about spatial data and especially projections, I recommend the following sources:
    - *PostGIS Essentials*, A. Marquez, Packt Publishing
    - *Intro to GIS and Spatial Analysis*, M. Gimond, `https://mgimond.github.io/Spatial/coordinate-systems.html`, especially Chapter 9.

6
Node Importance

In this chapter, we are going to talk about node importance, also known as **centrality algorithms**. As you will discover, several techniques have been developed, based on the definition of importance for a given graph and a given problem. We will learn about the most famous techniques, starting with degree centrality and the PageRank algorithm used by Google. For the latter, we will go through an example implementation and run it on a simple graph to fully understand how it works and when it can be used. After discovering the other types of centrality algorithms, such as betweenness centrality, we will conclude this chapter with explanations of how centrality algorithms can be used in the context of fraud detection. In this example, we will use, for the first time, the tools provided in the GDS to create a projected graph from Cypher in order to create fake relationships between nodes to meet analysis needs.

The following topics will be covered in this chapter:

- Defining importance
- Computing degree centrality
- Understanding the PageRank algorithm
- Path-based centrality metrics
- Applying centrality to fraud detection

Let's get started!

Technical requirements

In this chapter, we will use the following tools:

- The Neo4j graph database with the Graph Data Science Library
- The code files for this chapter, which are available at https://github.com/PacktPublishing/Hands-On-Graph-Analytics-with-Neo4j/tree/master/ch6

Node Importance

> ℹ️ If you are using **Neo4j < 4.0**, then the latest compatible version of the **GDS** plugin is **1.1**, whereas if you are using **Neo4j ≥ 4.0**, then the first compatible version of the **GDS** plugin is **1.2**.

Defining importance

Determining the most important node of a graph depends on your definition of importance. This definition itself depends on the goal you are trying to achieve. In this chapter, we will study two examples of importance:

- Information spread within a social network
- Critical nodes in a road or computer network

We will learn that each of these problems can be tackled with centrality algorithms. In this section, we will consider the following graph as an example to help us understand the different definitions of importance:

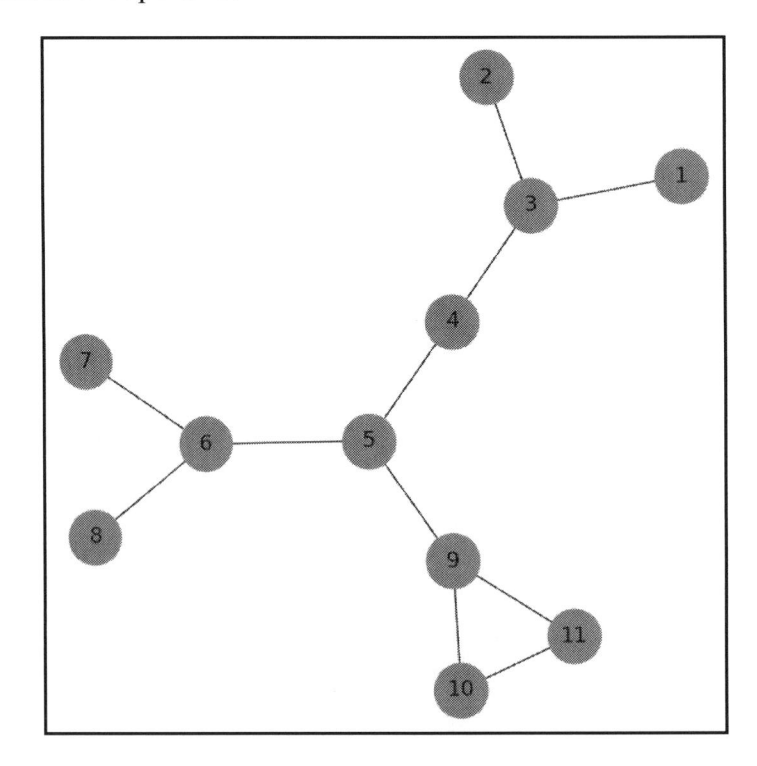

Which node is the most important in this network? The answer depends on what *important* means in a given context. Let's consider the different ways of defining importance.

Popularity and information spread

The most obvious way to define importance is with the **influencer** concept. Most influential nodes have many connections and, as such, are well placed to spread information. In the context of social networks, influencers often get offered advertising contracts with brands that want to harness their influencing power and let as many people as possible know about their products. With this in mind, nodes *3, 5, 6,* and *9* in the previous diagram all have three connections, making them the most important nodes.

To go further and try to disentangle these four nodes, other methods have been proposed. The most famous of them is the PageRank algorithm, used by Google to rank the results of its search engine. PageRank updates the importance of a given node, taking into account the importance of its neighbors. If a web page has backlinks from an important page, its importance will increase, compared to another page that is referenced by less important pages.

These methods, based on degrees, have many applications, from influencing to fraud detection. But if you are looking for a critical node in a road or computer network, for instance, they are not the most well-suited methods.

Critical or bridging nodes

Degree-based centrality algorithms identify important nodes in terms of their connections. But what happens to our graph if node *5* disappears? We end up with three disconnected components:

- Nodes *1, 2, 3,* and *4*
- Nodes *6, 7,* and *8*
- Nodes *9, 10,* and *11*

Node Importance

This new layout is illustrated in the following diagram:

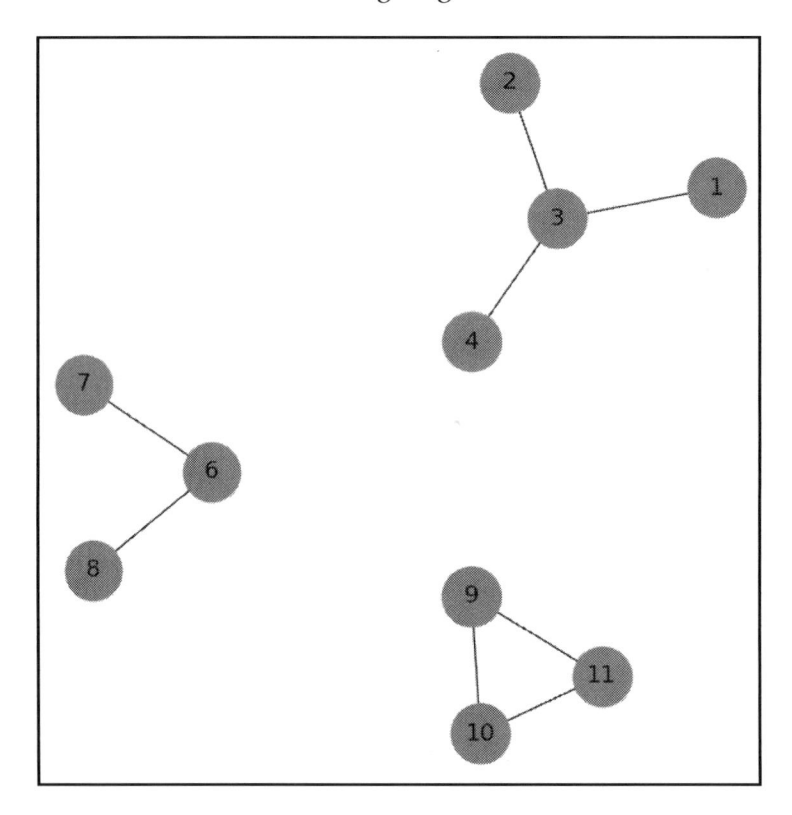

As you can see, communication from one component to another will be completely impossible. Consider, for instance, nodes *1* and *10*. There is no possible path between them anymore. In a telecommunication or road network, this situation can have serious consequences, from huge traffic jams to the impossibility of calling emergency services. It needs to be avoided at any cost, meaning that nodes such as node 5 in our test graph need to be identified in order to be better protected. For this reason, node 5 is called a **critical** (or **bridging**) **node**.

Fortunately, we have centrality algorithms to measure this kind of importance. We will group them together under the path-based category. The closeness and betweenness centrality algorithms, which we will look at later in this chapter, are part of this category.

In the next two sections, we are going to detail degree centrality and the PageRank algorithm. The following section will be more focused on two examples of path-based centrality: closeness and betweenness.

Computing degree centrality

Computing degree centrality involves sorting nodes based on how many relationships they have. This can be computed with base Cypher or invoked via the GDS plugin and a projected graph.

Formula

Degree centrality C_n is defined as follows:

$$C_n = deg(n)$$

Here, $deg(n)$ denotes the number of edges connected to the node n.

If your graph is directed, then you can define the incoming and outgoing degree as the number of relationships starting from node n and the number of relationships ending in n, respectively.

For instance, let's consider the following graph:

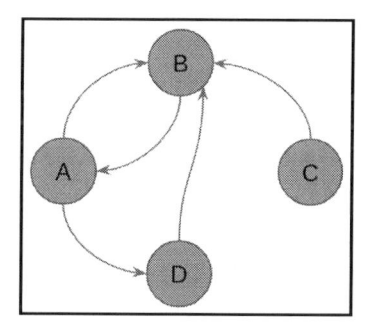

Node A has one incoming relationship (coming from B) and two outgoing relationships (to B and D), so its incoming degree is 1 and its outgoing degree is 2. The degrees of each node are summarized in the following table:

Node	Outgoing degree	Incoming degree	Degree (undirected)
A	2	1	3
B	1	3	4
C	1	0	1
D	1	1	2

Node Importance

Let's now see how to get these results in Neo4j. You can create this small graph using the following Cypher statement:

```
CREATE (A:Node {name: "A"})
CREATE (B:Node {name: "B"})
CREATE (C:Node {name: "C"})
CREATE (D:Node {name: "D"})

CREATE (A)-[:LINKED_TO {weight: 1}]->(B)
CREATE (B)-[:LINKED_TO]->(A)
CREATE (A)-[:LINKED_TO]->(D)
CREATE (C)-[:LINKED_TO]->(B)
CREATE (D)-[:LINKED_TO]->(B)
```

Computing degree centrality in Neo4j

Counting the number of edges connected to a node with Neo4j is possible using only Cypher and aggregation functions. For instance, the following query counts the number of outgoing relationships from each node:

```
MATCH (n:Node)-[r:LINKED_TO]->()
RETURN n.name, count(r) as outgoingDegree
ORDER BY outgoingDegree DESC
```

Running this query on the small graph we studied in the previous section gives us the following result:

"nodeName"	"outgoingDegree"
"A"	2
"B"	1
"C"	1
"D"	1

The incoming degree can also be computed using a slightly modified Cypher query, where the direction of the relationship is reversed thanks to the use of the <-[]- notation (instead of -[]->):

```
MATCH (n:Node)<-[r:LINKED_TO]-()
RETURN n.name as nodeName, count(r) as incomingDegree
ORDER BY incomingDegree DESC
```

The results of this query are reported in the following table:

"nodeName"	"incomingDegree"
"B"	3
"A"	1
"D"	1

As you can see, the centrality result is missing from node C, which is not connected to any other node. This can be fixed using OPTIONAL MATCH, like this:

```
MATCH (n:Node)
OPTIONAL MATCH (n)<-[r:LINKED_TO]-()
RETURN n.name as nodeName, count(r) as incomingDegree
ORDER BY incomingDegree DESC
```

This time, the result contains node C:

"nodeName"	"incomingDegree"
"B"	3
"A"	1
"D"	1
"C"	0

However, it is much more convenient to use the GDS implementation, which already takes care of these components.

Computing the outgoing degree using GDS

When using GDS, we need to define the projected graph. In this case, we can use the simplest syntax since we want to add all the nodes and all their relationships in their natural direction:

```
CALL gds.graph.create("projected_graph", "Node", "LINKED_TO")
```

Node Importance

Then, we can use this projected graph to run the degree centrality algorithm:

```
CALL gds.alpha.degree.stream("projected_graph")
YIELD nodeId, score
RETURN gds.util.asNode(nodeId).name as nodeName, score
ORDER BY score DESC
```

The result of this query is reproduced here:

"nodeName"	"score"
"A"	2.0
"B"	1.0
"C"	1.0
"D"	1.0

If you want to compute the incoming degree instead, you have to change the definition of the projected graph.

Computing the incoming degree using GDS

In GDS, we need to define a projected graph, which we can name (and save for future use in the same session) or keep unnamed.

Using a named projected graph

Creating a projected graph that will have all the relationships in the reverse direction requires a detailed configuration for the relationship's *orientation*:

```
CALL gds.graph.create(
    "projected_graph_incoming",
    "Node",
    {
        LINKED_TO: {
            relationship: "LINKED_TO",
            orientation: "REVERSE"
        }
    }
)
```

This new projected graph (`projected_graph_incoming`) contains the nodes with the Node label. It will also have relationships that are of the LINKED_TO type, which will be copies of the LINKED_TO relationships from the original graph but in the REVERSE direction. In other words, if the original graph contains the (A)-[:LINKED_TO]->(B) relationship, then the projected graph will only contain the (B)-[:LINKED_TO]->(A) pattern. You can run the degree centrality algorithm on this new projected graph with the following query:

```
CALL gds.alpha.degree.stream("projected_graph_incoming")
YIELD nodeId, score
RETURN gds.util.asNode(nodeId).name as name, score
ORDER BY score DESC
```

Here are the results:

"nodeName"	"score"
"B"	3.0
"A"	1.0
"D"	1.0
"C"	0.0

If your graph is undirected, you will have to use the `orientation: "UNDIRECTED"` parameter in the projected graph definition, as we did in the chapters dedicated to the shortest path (Chapter 4, *The Graph Data Science Library and Path Finding*) and spatial data (Chapter 5, *Spatial Data*).

Using an anonymous projected graph

GDS also gives us the option to run an algorithm without a named projected graph. In this case, the projected graph will be generated on the fly when calling the GDS procedure. For instance, in order to get the node degree for an undirected graph, you can use the following code:

```
CALL gds.alpha.degree.stream(
    {
        nodeProjection: "Node",
        relationshipProjection: {
            LINKED_TO: {
                type: "LINKED_TO",
```

Node Importance

```
                orientation: "UNDIRECTED"
            }
        }
    }
) YIELD nodeId, score
RETURN gds.util.asNode(nodeId).name as nodeName, score
ORDER BY score DESC
```

This query returns the following results:

"nodeName"	"score"
"B"	4.0
"A"	3.0
"D"	2.0
"C"	1.0

This closes this section on degree centrality calculations with Neo4j. However, as we discussed in the first section of this chapter, degree centrality can be improved to take into account the quality of each connection. This is what the PageRank algorithm is trying to achieve, as we will discover now.

Understanding the PageRank algorithm

The PageRank algorithm is named after Larry Page, one of the co-founders of Google. The algorithm was developed back in 1996 in order to rank the results of a search engine. In this section, we will understand the formula by building it step by step. We will then run the algorithm on a single graph to see how it converges. We will also implement a version of the algorithm using Python. Finally, we will learn how to use GDS to get this information from a graph stored in Neo4j.

Building the formula

Let's consider PageRank in the context of the internet. The PageRank algorithm relies on the idea that not all incoming links have the same weight. As an example, consider a backlink from a New York Times article to an article in your blog. It is more important than a link from a website that gets 10 visits a month since it will redirect more users to your blog. So, we would like the New York Times to have more *weight* than the low-traffic website. The challenge here is to assess the weight of an incoming connection. In the PageRank algorithm, this weight is the importance of the page or the rank of the page. So, we end up with a recursive formula where each page's importance is measured compared to the other pages:

$$PR(A) = PR(N_1) + ... + PR(N_n)$$

Here, N_i ($i=1...n$) is the pages pointing to page *A* (the incoming relationships).

> The PageRank of node *A* tends to be higher if the sum of the PageRank of the nodes pointing to *A* is high.

This is not the final formula for PageRank. Two other aspects need to be taken into account. First, we will balance the importance of an incoming link for pages that have many outgoing links. It is as if each page has an equal number of votes to distribute to others. It can give all its votes to one single page, in which case the link is very strong, or share them among many pages, giving many links less importance.

So, we can update the PageRank formula like this:

$$PR(A) = PR(N_1)/C(N_1) + ... + PR(N_n)/C(N_n)$$

Here, $C(N_i)$ is the number of outgoing links from N_i.

The second aspect to integrate to finally get to the PageRank formula is the *damping factor*. It requires some more explanation and will be covered in the following subsection.

The damping factor

Last but not least, the PageRank algorithm introduces a **damping factor** to mitigate the effect of the neighbors. The idea is that, when navigating from one page to another, the internet user usually clicks on links. But in some cases, the user might become bored or, for whatever reason, go to another page. The probability of this happening is modeled by the damping factor. The final PageRank formula from the initial paper is as follows:

$$PR(A) = (1 - d) + d * (PR(N_1)/C(N_1) + ... + PR(N_n)/C(N_n))$$

Usually, the damping factor d is set to be around 0.85, meaning the probability of a user randomly navigating to a page without following a link is $1 - d = 15\%$.

Another important effect of the damping factor is visible for nodes with no outgoing links, also called **sinks**. Without the damping factor, these nodes will have the tendency to take the rank given by their neighbors without giving it back, breaking the principle of the algorithm.

Normalization

Although the previous formula is the one from the original paper, which introduced the PageRank algorithm in 1996, be aware that another one is sometimes used instead. In the original formula, the sum of ranks for all nodes adds up to N, which is the number of nodes. The updated formula is normalized to 1 instead of N and is written as follows:

$$PR(A) = (1 - d) / N + d * (PR(N_1)/C(N_1) + ... + PR(N_n)/C(N_n))$$

You can understand this easily by assuming that the ranks for all the nodes are initialized to $1/N$. Then, at each iteration, each node will equally distribute this rank to all its neighbors so that the sum remains constant.

This formula was chosen for the PageRank implementation in `networkx`, the Python package for graph manipulation. However, Neo4j GDS uses the original formula. For this reason, in the following subsections, we are going to use the original version of the PageRank equation.

> The PageRank algorithm was designed for **directed graphs**.

Running the algorithm on an example graph

The PageRank algorithm can be implemented with an iterative process where, at each iteration, the rank of a given node is updated based on the rank of its neighbors in the previous iteration. This process is repeated until the algorithm converges, meaning that the PageRank difference between two iterations is lower than a certain threshold. In order to understand how it works, we are first going to run it manually on the simple graph we studied in the *Degree centrality* section.

In order to compute PageRank, we need an outgoing degree for each node, which is simply the number of arrows *starting* from the node. In the graph illustrated in the preceding diagram, these degrees are as follows:

```
A => 2
B => 1
C => 1
D => 1
```

In order to run the PageRank algorithm (in its iterative form), we need to give an initial value to the rank of each node. Since we do not have any *a priori* preference for a given node, we can initialize these values with the uniform value of 1. Note that this initialization preserves the PageRank algorithm's normalization: the sum of PageRank in its initial state is still equal to N, which is the number of nodes.

Then, during iteration 1, the page rank values are updated as follows:

- **Node A**: Receives one incoming connection from node B, so its updated PageRank is as follows:

    - new_pr_A = (1 - d) + d * (old_pr_B / out_deg_B)
               = 0.15 + 0.85 * (1 / 1)
               = 1.0

- **Node B**: Has three incoming connections:
    - One coming from *A*
    - One coming from *C*
    - And a final one coming from *D*

So, its page rank is updated with the following:

```
new_pr_B = (1 - d)
         + d * (old_pr_A / out_deg_A
              + old_pr_C / out_deg_C
              + old_pr_D / out_deg_D)
         = 0.15 + 0.85 * (1 / 2 + 1 / 1 + 1 / 1)
         = 2.275
```

- **Node C**: Has no incoming connection, so its rank is updated with the following:

  - ```
    new_pr_C = (1 - d)
             = 0.15
    ```

- **Node D**: Receives one connection from *A*:

  - ```
    new_pr_D = (1 - d) + d * (old_pr_A / out_deg_A)
             = 0.15 + 0.85 * (1 /2)
             = 0.575
    ```

Iteration 2 consists of repeating the same operation but changing the `old_pr` values. For instance, the updated PageRank of node *B* after iteration 2 would be as follows:

```
new_pr_B = (1 - d) + d * (old_pr_A / out_deg_A + old_pr_C / out_deg_C + old_pr_D / out_deg_D)
         = 0.15 + 0.85 * (1.0 / 2 + 0.15 / 1 + 0.575 / 1)
         = 1.191
```

The rank of *B* in the second iteration decreases a lot, while the rank of *A* increases from 0.575 to 1.117.

The first three iterations are summarized in the following table:

Iteration/Node	A	B	C	D
Initialization	1	1	1	1
0	1.0	2.275	0.15	0.575
1	2.084	1.191	0.15	0.575
2	1.163	1.652	0.15	1.036

> The PageRank of node *C* is 0.15 and will not evolve since this node does not receive any connection from other nodes. So, for all iterations, its rank will always be `new_pr_C = (1-d) = 0.15`.

The question of when to stop iterating will be answered in the following subsection, where we are going to implement a version of PageRank using Python.

Implementing the PageRank algorithm using Python

In order to implement the PageRank algorithm, we need to agree on a graphical representation. In order to avoid introducing other dependencies, we will use a simple representation via dictionaries. Each node in the graph will have a key in the dictionary. The associated value contains another dictionary whose keys are the linked nodes from the key. The graph we are studying in this section is written as follows:

```
G = {
    'A': {'B': 1, 'D': 1},
    'B': {'A': 1},
    'C': {'B': 1},
    'D': {'B': 1},
}
```

The `page_rank` function we are going to write has the following parameters:

- G, the graph for which the algorithm will compute the PageRank.
- d, the damping factor whose default value is 0.85.
- tolerance, the tolerance to stop the iteration when the algorithm has converged. We will set a default value of 0.01.
- max_iterations, a sanity check to make sure we do not loop infinitely in case the algorithm fails to converge. As an order of magnitude, in the initial PageRank publication, the authors reported that the convergence was reached after around 50 iterations, for a graph containing more than 300 million edges.

Here is the function definition:

```
def page_rank(G, d=0.85, tolerance=0.01, max_iterations=50):
```

Then, we need to initialize the PageRank. Similar to the previous section, we assign a value of 1 to all nodes, since we do not have any *a priori* belief about the final result:

```
pr = dict.fromkeys(G, 1.0)
```

Node Importance

We also compute the number of outgoing links for each node, since this will be used later on. With our definition of the graph G, the number of outgoing links is just the length of the dictionary associated with each key:

```
outgoing_degree = {k: len(v) for k, v in G.items()}
```

Now that we have initialized all the variables we need, we can start the iterative process, where we will have `max_iter` iterations at most. At each iteration, we will save the `pr` dictionary from the previous iteration into the `old_pr` dictionary and create a new `pr` dictionary, initialized to 0, that will be updated each time we find an incoming relationship to the node so that `old_pr` finally contains the updated `pr` for each node:

```
for it in range(max_itererations):
    print("======= Iteration", it)
    old_pr = dict(pr)
    pr = dict.fromkeys(pr.keys(), 0)
```

The next step is to iterate over each node of the graph and update its rank with the fixed `(1-d)/N` term and one of its neighbors:

```
for node in G:
    for neighbor in G[node]:
        pr[neighbor] += d * old_pr[node] / outgoing_degree[node]
    pr[node] += (1 - d)
print("New PR:", pr)
```

Finally, after this iteration on each node, we can compare the `pr` dictionary from the previous iteration (`old_pr`) and the new one (`pr`). If the mean of the differences is below the `tolerance` threshold, the algorithm has converged and we can return the current `pr` values:

```
# check convergence
    mean_diff_to_prev_pr = sum([abs(pr[n] - old_pr[n]) for n in G]) / len(G)
        if mean_diff_to_prev_pr < tolerance:
            return pr
```

Finally, we can call this newly created function on the graph we defined earlier:

```
pr = page_rank(G)
```

This gives us the following output after the ninth iteration:

```
{'A': 1.50, 'B': 1.57, 'C': 0.15, 'D': 0.78}
```

This implementation is useful for understanding the algorithm, but that's its only purpose. When using the PageRank algorithm in a real-life application, you will have to rely on optimized and tested solutions, such as the one implemented in the GDS plugin for Neo4j.

Using GDS to assess PageRank centrality in Neo4j

As usual, when using GDS, we need to define the projected graph that will be used to run the algorithm. In this example, we will run the PageRank algorithm on the *directed* graph, which is the default behavior of projected graphs. If you didn't do so in the previous section, you can use the following query to create the named projected graph out of the nodes with a `Node` label and relationships with the `LINKED_TO` type:

```
CALL gds.graph.create("projected_graph", "Node", "LINKED_TO")
```

We can then run the PageRank algorithm on this projected graph. The signature of the PageRank procedure in Neo4j is as follows:

```
CALL gds.pageRank(<projected_graph_name>, <configuration>)
```

The configuration map accepts the following parameters:

- `dampingFactor`: A float between 0 and 1 corresponding to the damping factor (d, in our Python implementation). The default value is 0.85.
- `maxIterations`: The maximum number of iterations (the default is 20).
- `tolerance`: The tolerance to measure convergence (the default is 1E-7).

When using default values for all parameters, we can run the PageRank algorithm and stream the results with the following Cypher statement:

```
CALL gds.pageRank.stream("projected_graph", {}) YIELD nodeId, score
RETURN gds.util.asNode(nodeId).name as nodeName, score
ORDER BY score DESC
```

The streamed results are comparable to the ones we obtained earlier in this chapter with a custom implementation, even if they're not strictly identical.

> It is important to note that the PageRank algorithm is part of the **production-quality algorithms** in GDS. As of version 1.0, this is the only centrality algorithm in that state.

Comparing degree centrality and the PageRank results

In order to understand what PageRank is doing, let's compare the results of degree centrality and the PageRank algorithms on our small directed graph. This comparison is shown in the following table:

Node	Degree centrality	PageRank centrality
A	2	1.44
B	1	**1.52**
C	1	0.15
D	1	0.76

While node *A* has the highest outgoing degree (2), it receives only one link, meaning only one other page in the graph trusts it. On the other hand, node *B* has an outgoing degree of 1, but three other pages of the network are pointing to it, giving it more credibility. That's the reason why, with PageRank centrality, the most important node is now node *B*.

Variants

Depending on the desired goal, PageRank has several variants. These are also implemented in GDS.

ArticleRank

ArticleRank is a variant of PageRank whereby the chance of assuming that a link coming from a page with a few outgoing links is more important than others is smaller. This is achieved by introducing the *average degree* in the formula:

$$AR(A) = (1 - d) + d * (AR(N_1)/(C(N_1) + AVG(C)) + ... + AR(N_n)/(C(N_n) + AVG(C)))$$

Here, *AVG(C)* is the average number of outgoing connections for all pages in the network.

Usage within GDS is similar to that of PageRank:

```
CALL gds.alpha.articleRank.stream("projected_graph", {})
YIELD nodeId, score
RETURN gds.util.asNode(nodeId).name as name, score
ORDER BY score DESC
```

However, the results, as shown here, are much closer to each other:

"nodeName"	"score"
"B"	0.37
"A"	0.29
"D"	0.23
"C"	0.15

> **TIP**: To round the results with Cypher, you can use the RETURN round(score*100)/100 as score command.

Personalized PageRank

In personalized PageRank, more weight is given to some user-defined nodes. For instance, giving a higher importance to node C can be achieved with this query:

```
MATCH (A:Node {name: "A"})
CALL gds.pageRank.stream("projected_graph", {
    sourceNodes: [A]
})
YIELD nodeId, score
RETURN gds.util.asNode(nodeId).name AS nodeName, round(score*100)/100 as score
ORDER BY score DESC
```

[223]

Node Importance

The results are listed in the following table. You can see that node A has gained more importance than it did in the traditional PageRank:

"nodeName"	"score"
"A"	0.44
"B"	0.34
"D"	0.19
"C"	0.0

Applications of personalized PageRank include recommendations, where we already have some prior knowledge about the products a given customer might like based on their previous purchases.

Eigenvector centrality

PageRank is actually a variant of another centrality metric called **eigenvector centrality**. Let me introduce some math here by rebuilding the PageRank formula using matrices.

The adjacency matrix

To work on a graph and simulate information spread within it, we need a way to model the complex relationship pattern. The simplest way of doing so is to build the **adjacency matrix** of the graph. It is a 2D array where the element on line i and column j is equal to 1 if there is an edge going from node i to node j and 0 otherwise.

The adjacency matrix of the graph we studied during the implementation of the PageRank algorithm is as follows:

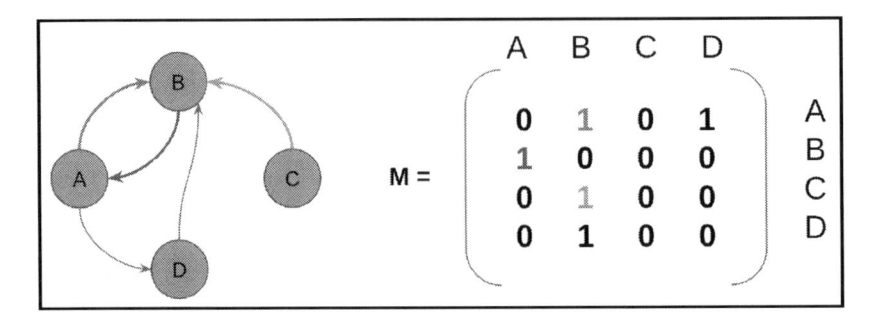

$$M = \begin{pmatrix} & A & B & C & D \\ A & 0 & 1 & 0 & 1 \\ B & 1 & 0 & 0 & 0 \\ C & 0 & 1 & 0 & 0 \\ D & 0 & 1 & 0 & 0 \end{pmatrix}$$

[224]

The first element of the first row corresponds to the edge between A and A. Since A is not connected to itself, this element is 0. The second element of the first row holds information about the edge between A and B. Since there is a relationship between these two nodes, this element is equal to 1. Similarly, the second row of the adjacency matrix contains information about the outgoing edges from node B. This node has a single outgoing edge going to A. A corresponds to the first column of the matrix, so only the first element of the second row is 1.

> This definition can be extended to the weighted graphs, where the value of the m_{ij} element becomes the weight of the edge between nodes i and j.

Lots of information can be extracted from this matrix. For instance, we can find the outgoing degree of each node by summing the values in a given row and the incoming degree by summing the values in a given column.

The adjacency matrix with normalized rows is as follows:

$$M_n = \begin{pmatrix} & A & B & C & D \\ A & 0 & 1/2 & 0 & 1/2 \\ B & 1 & 0 & 0 & 0 \\ C & 0 & 1 & 0 & 0 \\ D & 0 & 1 & 0 & 0 \end{pmatrix}$$

PageRank with matrix notation

Now, let's consider that node A contains a value that we want to propagate to its neighbors. We can find how the value will be propagated through the graph with a simple dot product:

$$X' = M_n \cdot X = \begin{pmatrix} 0 & 1/2 & 0 & 1/2 \\ 1 & 0 & 0 & 0 \\ 0 & 1 & 0 & 0 \\ 0 & 1 & 0 & 0 \end{pmatrix} \cdot \begin{pmatrix} 1 \\ 0 \\ 0 \\ 0 \end{pmatrix} = \begin{pmatrix} 0 & 1/2 & 0 & 1/2 \end{pmatrix}$$

Node Importance

This is what happens if all the initial values are initialized to 1:

$$X' = M_n \cdot X = \begin{pmatrix} 0 & 1/2 & 0 & 1/2 \\ 1 & 0 & 0 & 0 \\ 0 & 1 & 0 & 0 \\ 0 & 1 & 0 & 0 \end{pmatrix} \cdot \begin{pmatrix} 1 \\ 1 \\ 1 \\ 1 \end{pmatrix} = \begin{pmatrix} 1 & 2.5 & 0 & 1/2 \end{pmatrix}$$

We are almost there. The only missing part to retrieving the PageRank formula is the damping factor d:

$$\begin{aligned} X' &= (1-d) + d \times M_n \cdot X \\ &= (1-d) + d \times \begin{pmatrix} 0 & 1/2 & 0 & 1/2 \\ 1 & 0 & 0 & 0 \\ 0 & 1 & 0 & 0 \\ 0 & 1 & 0 & 0 \end{pmatrix} \cdot \begin{pmatrix} 1 \\ 1 \\ 1 \\ 1 \end{pmatrix} \\ &= (1-d) + d \times \begin{pmatrix} 1 & 2.5 & 0 & 1/2 \end{pmatrix} \\ &= \begin{pmatrix} 1 & 2.3 & 0.15 & 0.58 \end{pmatrix} \end{aligned}$$

As you can see, we are getting the same values that we found in the previous sections. With this formalism, finding the rank of each node is equivalent to solving the following equation:

$$X' = (1-d) + d * M\_n * X = X$$

In this equation, the values of the X vector are the PageRank centralities for each node.

Now, let's go back to eigenvector centrality.

Eigenvector centrality

Finding eigenvector centrality involves solving a similar but simpler equation:

$$M.X = \lambda.X$$

Here, M is the adjacency matrix. In mathematical terms, this means finding the eigenvectors of this adjacency matrix. There might be several possible solutions with different values for λ (the eigenvalues), but the constraint that the centrality for each node must be positive only leaves one single solution – eigenvector centrality.

Due to its similarity with PageRank, its use cases are also similar: use eigenvector centrality when you want a node's importance to be influenced by the importance of its neighbors.

Computing eigenvector centrality in GDS

Eigenvector centrality is implemented in GDS. You can compute it on your favorite projected graph using the following code:

```
CALL gds.alpha.eigenvector.stream("projected_graph", {}) YIELD nodeId,
score as score
RETURN gds.util.asNode(nodeId).name as nodeName, score
ORDER BY score DESC
```

This closes a long section about the PageRank algorithm and its variants. However, as we discussed earlier, node importance is not necessarily related to popularity. In the next section, we are going to talk about other centrality algorithms, such as betweenness centrality, which can be used to identify the critical nodes in a network.

Path-based centrality metrics

As we discussed in the first section of this chapter (*Defining importance*), the neighborhood approach is not the only way to measure importance. Another approach is to use a path within the graph. In this section, we will discover two new centrality metrics: closeness and betweenness centrality.

Closeness centrality

Closeness centrality measures how close a node is, on average, to all the other nodes in the graph. It can be seen as centrality from a geometrical point of view.

Normalization

The corresponding formula is as follows:

$$C_n = 1 / \sum d(n, m)$$

Here, m denotes all the nodes in the graph that are different from n, and $d(n, m)$ is the distance of the shortest path between n and m.

A node that is, on average, closer to all other nodes will have a low $\sum d(n, m)$, resulting in high centrality.

Closeness centrality prevents us from comparing values across graphs with different numbers of nodes since graphs with more nodes will have more terms in the sum and hence lower centrality by construction. To overcome this issue, normalized closeness centrality is used instead:

$$C_n = (N-1) / \sum d(n, m)$$

This is the formula that's selected for GDS.

Computing closeness from the shortest path algorithms

In order to understand how closeness is computed, let's compute it manually using the shortest path procedures of GDS. In Chapter 4, *The Graph Data Science Plugin and Path Finding*, we discovered the Single Source Shortest Path algorithm (`deltastepping`), which can compute the shortest path between a given start node and all the other nodes in the graph. We are going to use this procedure to find the sum of distances from one node to all others, and then infer centrality.

To do so, we are going to use the undirected version of the test graph we used in the *Understanding the PageRank algorithm* section. To create the projected graph, use the following query:

```
CALL gds.graph.create("projected_graph_undirected_weight", "Node", {
        LINKED_TO: {
            type: "LINKED_TO",
            orientation: "UNDIRECTED",
            properties: {
                weight: {
                    property: "weight",
                    defaultValue: 1.0
                }
            }
        }
    }
)
```

On top of using the undirected version of our graph, we also add a *weight* property to each relationship, with a default value of 1.

> **TIP**
> When adding a property to the projected graph, the property name has to exist in the original (Neo4j) graph. That's the reason why we added a `weight` property to one of the relationships when creating our test graph earlier in this chapter.

We can then call the SSSP algorithm with a query like this:

```
MATCH (startNode:Node {name: "A"})
CALL gds.alpha.shortestPath.deltaStepping.stream(
    "projected_graph_undirected_weight",
    {
        startNode: startNode,
        delta: 1,
        relationshipWeightProperty: 'weight'
    }
) YIELD nodeId, distance
RETURN gds.util.asNode(nodeId).name as nodeName, distance
```

Node Importance

Now, you can check that the distances are correct. Starting from here, we can apply the closeness centrality formula:

```
MATCH (startNode:Node)
CALL gds.alpha.shortestPath.deltaStepping.stream(
    "projected_graph_undirected_weight",
    {
        startNode: startNode,
        delta: 1,
        relationshipWeightProperty: 'weight'
    }
) YIELD nodeId, distance
RETURN startNode.name as node, (COUNT(nodeId) - 1)/SUM(distance) as d
ORDER BY d DESC
```

Here are the results:

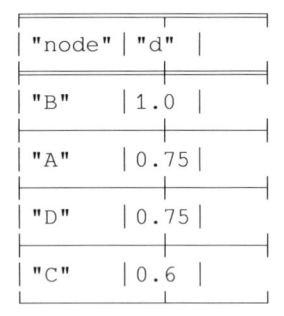

"node"	"d"
"B"	1.0
"A"	0.75
"D"	0.75
"C"	0.6

In terms of closeness, B is the most important node, which is expected since it is linked to all the other nodes in the graph.

We managed to get the closeness centralities using the SSSP procedure, but there is a much simpler way to get the closeness centrality results from GDS.

The closeness centrality algorithm

Fortunately, closeness centrality is implemented as a standalone algorithm within GDS. We can directly get closeness centralities for each node with the following query:

```
CALL gds.alpha.closeness.stream("projected_graph_undirected_weight", {})
YIELD nodeId, centrality as score
RETURN gds.util.asNode(nodeId).name as nodeName, score
ORDER BY score DESC
```

> **TIP:** Contrary to the other centrality algorithms we studied in this chapter, the return value of the closeness and betweenness centrality algorithms is called `centrality` (and not `score`).

Closeness centrality in multiple-component graphs

Some graphs are made of several **components**, meaning some nodes are totally disconnected from others. This was the case for the US states graph we built in `Chapter 2`, *The Cypher Query Language*, because some states do not share borders with any other state. In such cases, the distance between nodes in two disconnected components is infinite and the centrality of all the nodes drops to 0. Because of that, the centrality algorithm in GDS implements a slightly modified version of the closeness centrality formula, where the sum of distances is performed over all the nodes in the same component. In the next chapter, `Chapter 7`, *Community Detection and Similarity Measures*, we will discover how to find nodes belonging to the same component.

In the next section, we are going to learn about another way to measure centrality using a path-based technique: betweenness centrality.

Betweenness centrality

Betweenness is another way to measure centrality. Instead of summing the distances, we are now counting the number of shortest paths traversing a given node:

$$C_n = \sum \sigma(u, v \mid n) / \sum \sigma(u, v)$$

Here, $\sigma(u, v)$ is the number of shortest paths between u and v, and $\sigma(u, v \mid n)$ is the number of such paths passing through n.

This measure is particularly useful for identifying critical nodes in a network, such as bridges in a road network.

It is used in the following way with GDS:

```
CALL gds.alpha.betweenness.stream("projected_graph", {})
YIELD nodeId, centrality as score
RETURN gds.util.asNode(nodeId).name, score
ORDER BY score DESC
```

Node Importance

> If you are using GDS ≥ 1.3, then the betweenness centrality procedures have been moved to the production tier and are hence named `gds.betweenness.stream` and `gds.betweenness.write`.

> **TIP**: You can check which version of GDS you are using with the `RETURN gds.version()` Cypher code.

Here are the sorted betweenness centralities for our test graph:

"nodeName"	"score"
"B"	3.0
"A"	2.0
"C"	0.0
"D"	0.0

As you can see, B is still the most important node. But the importance of node D has decreased because none of the shortest paths between two pairs of nodes go through D.

We have now studied many different types of centrality metrics. Let's try and compare them on the same graph to make sure we understand how they work and which metric to use in which context.

Comparing centrality metrics

Let's go back to the graph we started analyzing in the first section. The following diagram shows a comparison of several of the centrality algorithms we studied in this chapter:

Chapter 6

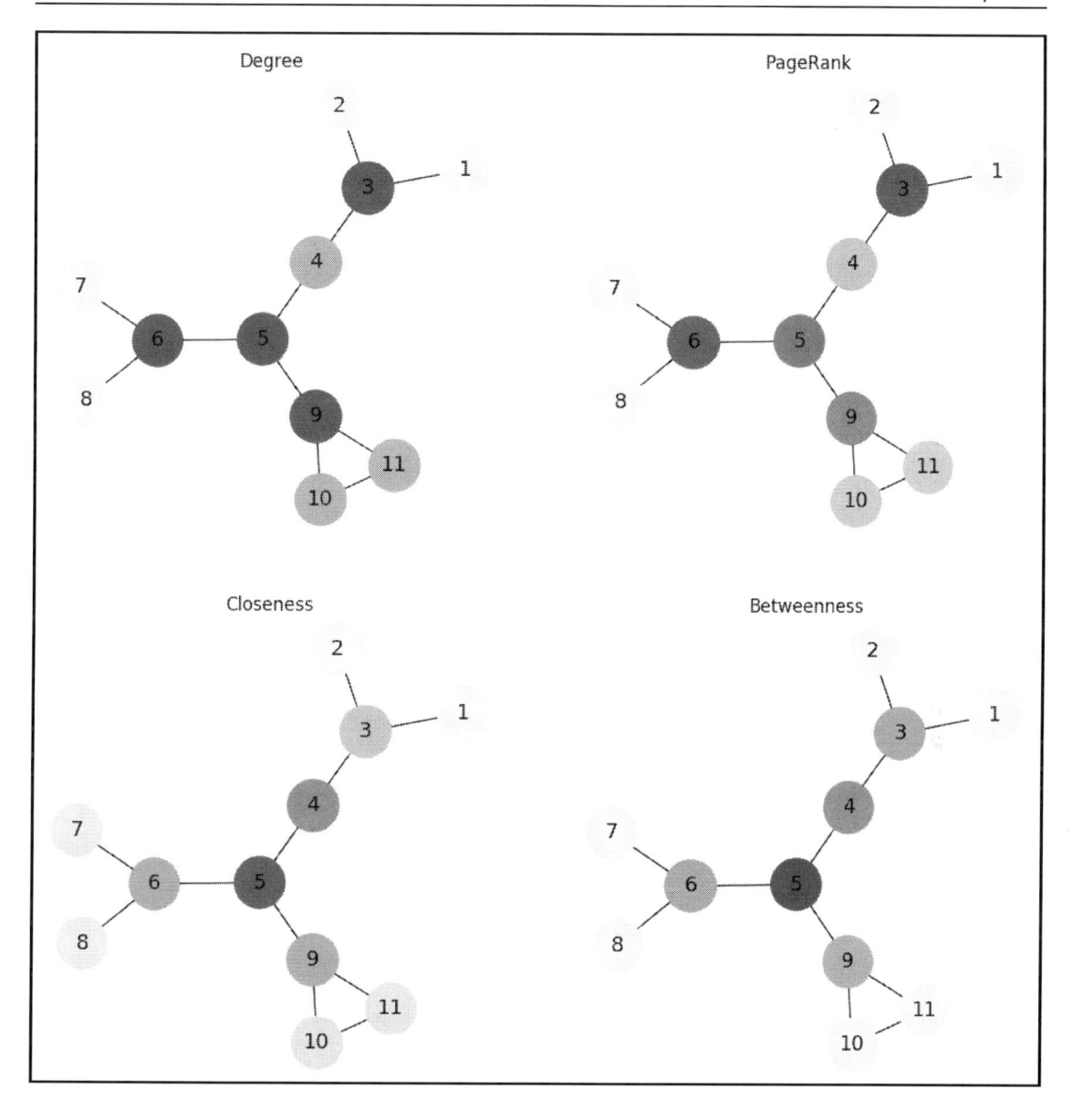

If degree centrality can't differentiate between four nodes that all have three connections (nodes 3, 5, 6, and 9), PageRank is able to make some nodes stand out from the crowd by giving more importance to nodes 3 and 6. Closeness and betweenness both clearly identify node 5 as the most critical: if this node disappears, the paths within the graph will be completely changed or even impossible, as we discussed in the first section of this chapter.

[233]

Node Importance

Centrality algorithms have many types of applications. In the next section, we will review some of them, starting from the fraud detection use case.

Applying centrality to fraud detection

Fraud is one of the major sources of loss for private companies, as well as public institutions. It takes many different forms, from duplicating user accounts to insurance or credit card fraud. Of course, depending on the type of fraud you are interested in, solutions for identifying fraudsters will vary. In this section, we are going to review the different types of fraud and how a graph database such as Neo4j can help in identifying fraud. After that, we will learn how centrality measures (the main topic of this chapter) are able to provide interesting insights regarding fraud detection in some specific cases.

Detecting fraud using Neo4j

Fraudulent behavior can have multiple forms and is constantly evolving. Someone with bad intentions might steal a credit card and transfer a large amount of money to another account. This kind of transaction can be identified with traditional statistical methods and/or machine learning. The goal of these algorithms is to spot *anomalies*, rare events that do not correspond to the normal expected pattern; for instance, if your credit card starts to be used from another country than your usual place of living, it would be highly suspicious and likely to be flagged as fraudulent. This is the reason why some banks will ask you to let them know when you are traveling abroad so that your credit card does not get blocked.

Imagine a criminal that withdraws $1 from one billion credit cards, for a total theft of $1 billion, instead of one single person transferring $1 billion from one card at once. While the latter case can be identified easily with the traditional methods outlined previously, the former is much more difficult to flag. And things become even more complex when criminals start acting together.

Another trick used by fraudsters consists of creating alliances, referred to as **criminal rings**. They can then operate together in what seems to be a normal way. Imagine two people cooperating to create false claims regarding their car insurance. In these situations, a more global analysis is required, and that's where graphs bring a lot of value. By the way, if you've ever watched a detective movie, you'll have seen walls filled with sticky notes connected by strings (usually red): this is a lot like a graph, which illustrates how useful graphs can be in criminal activity detection.

Now, let' go back to the topic of fraud and investigate an example.

Using centrality to assess fraud

During auction sales, sellers propose objects at a minimal price and interested buyers have to outbid each other, hence making the price increase. Fraud can occur here when a seller asks fake buyers to outbid on some products, just to make the final price higher.

Have a look at the simple graph schema reproduced in the following diagram:

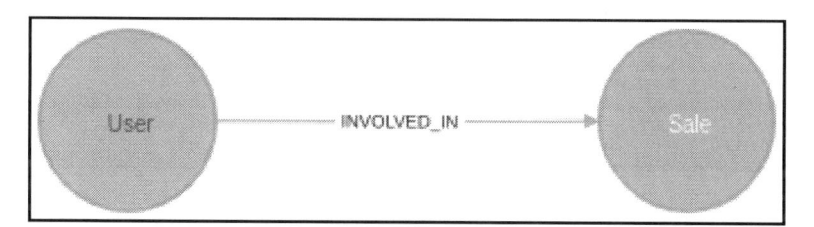

Users are only allowed to interact with a given sale. Let's build a simple test graph with this schema:

```
CREATE (U1:User {id: "U1"})
CREATE (U2:User {id: "U2"})
CREATE (U3:User {id: "U3"})
CREATE (U4:User {id: "U4"})
CREATE (U5:User {id: "U5"})

CREATE (S1:Sale {id: "S1"})
CREATE (S2:Sale {id: "S2"})
CREATE (S3:Sale {id: "S3"})

CREATE (U1)-[:INVOLVED_IN]->(S1)
CREATE (U1)-[:INVOLVED_IN]->(S2)
CREATE (U2)-[:INVOLVED_IN]->(S3)
CREATE (U3)-[:INVOLVED_IN]->(S3)
CREATE (U4)-[:INVOLVED_IN]->(S3)
CREATE (U4)-[:INVOLVED_IN]->(S2)
CREATE (U5)-[:INVOLVED_IN]->(S2)
CREATE (U5)-[:INVOLVED_IN]->(S1)
```

Node Importance

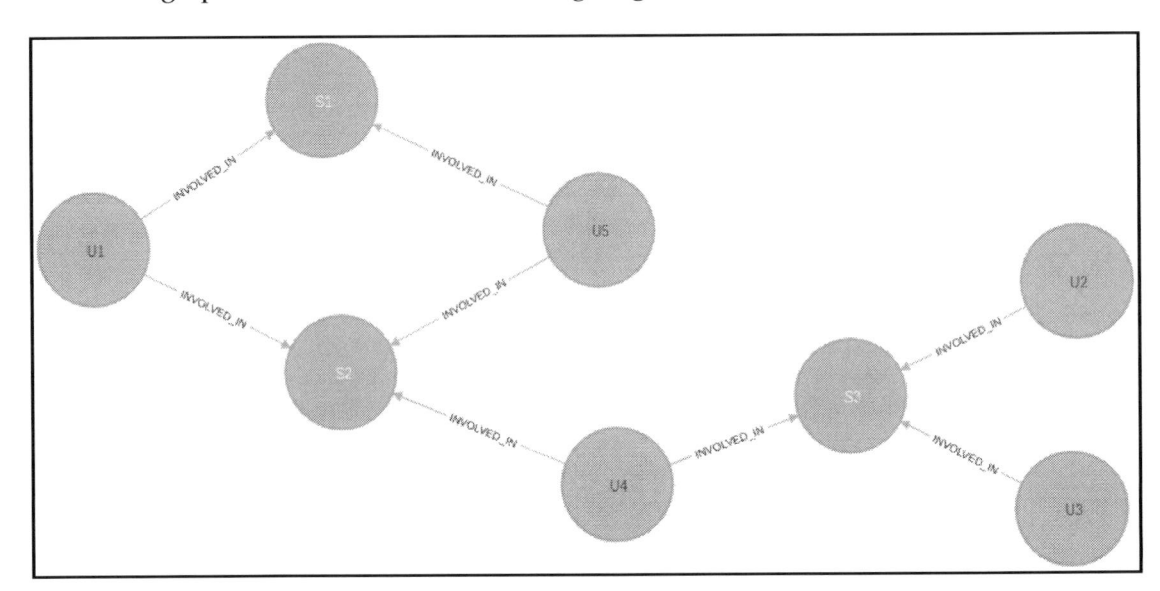

This small graph is illustrated in the following diagram:

[Figure: Graph showing users U1, U2, U3, U4, U5 connected via INVOLVED_IN relationships to sales S1, S2, S3]

The idea behind the use of centrality algorithms such as PageRank in this context is as follows: given that I know that user 1 (U1) is a fraudster, can I identify their partner(s) in crime? To solve this issue, personalized PageRank with user 1 as the source node is a good solution to identify the users that interact more often with user 1.

Creating a projected graph with Cypher projection

In our auction fraud case, there is no direct relationship between users, but we still need to create a graph to run a centrality algorithm on. GDS offers a solution whereby we can create a projected graph for such cases using Cypher projection for nodes and/or relationships.

To create fake relationships between users, we consider them connected if they have joined at least one sale together. The following Cypher query returns these users:

```
MATCH (u:User)-[]->(p:Product)<-[]-(v:User)
RETURN u.id as source, v.id as target, count(p) as weight
```

The count aggregate will be used to assign a weight to each relationship: the more common sales they have, the stronger the relationship between two users.

The syntax to create a projected graph using Cypher is as follows:

```
CALL gds.graph.create.cypher(
    "projected_graph_cypher",
    "MATCH (u:User)
        RETURN id(u) as id",
    "MATCH (u:User)-[]->(p:Product)<-[]-(v:User)
        RETURN id(u) as source, id(v) as target, count(p) as weight"
)
```

The important points here are as follows:

- Use the `gds.graph.create.cypher` procedure.
- The node's projection needs to return the Neo4j internal node identifier, which can be accessed with the `id()` function.
- The relationship projection has to return the following:
    - `source`: The Neo4j internal identifier for the source node
    - `target`: The Neo4j internal identifier for the target node
    - Other parameters that will be stored as relationship properties

Our projected graph is as follows:

- Undirected.
- Weighted: We also want our edges to have higher weights if users interact with each other more often.

We can now use personalized PageRank with this projected graph:

```
MATCH (U1:User {id: "U1"})
CALL gds.pageRank.stream(
    "projected_graph_cypher", {
        relationshipWeightProperty: "weight",
        sourceNodes: [U1]
    }
) YIELD nodeId, score
RETURN gds.util.asNode(nodeId).id as userId, round(score * 100) / 100 as score
ORDER BY score DESC
```

Node Importance

Here are the results:

"userId"	"score"
"U1"	0.33
"U5"	0.24
"U4"	0.23
"U2"	0.08
"U3"	0.08

Thanks to personalized PageRank, we are able to say that user 5 is suspicious, closely followed by user 4, while users 2 and 3 display less fraudulent behavior.

> Cypher projections are known to be slower than native projections. In the case of large graphs, a better solution is to add extra relationships to your graph so that they aren't recreated each time you have to create the projected graph.

Using PageRank, in this case, is associated with the concept of **guilt by association**. The results still have to be taken with caution and double-checked with other data sources. Indeed, users sharing the same interests are more likely to interact more often, without any bad intention.

This is, of course, an oversimplified example. Since the suspicious behavior of user 5 can be identified just by looking at the graph, using PageRank is certainly overkill. But imagine the same situation on a larger graph; for instance, the graph of eBay users and auctions containing millions of transactions each day. In the latter case, algorithms such as the ones studied in this chapter are really useful.

PageRank even has other improvements, such as TrustRank, which are dedicated to identifying other kinds of fraudsters. Web spam is pages that are built to mislead search engines and redirect traffic to them, even if the content is not relevant to the user. TrustRank helps with the identification of such pages by labeling trusted sites.

Other applications of centrality algorithms

Beyond fraud detection, centrality algorithms can also be used in many contexts. We have already talked about influencer detection in a social network. By now, you may understand why PageRank is a good choice in that case since it not only takes into account a given person's connections, but also the connections of those connections... In this case, overall, the information spread will be faster if it starts from a node with a higher PageRank.

Biology and genetics are two other important fields of application of centrality. For instance, when building a network of protein interactions inside some yeast, researchers can determine which of these proteins are more essential to the yeast and which are not vital. Many other applications of centrality, especially PageRank, have been explored in the domain of genetics to determine gene importance in some given disease, for instance. See the article *PageRank beyond the web* (link in the *Further reading* section) for a broader list of applications in bioinformatics but also chemistry and sports.

Path-related centrality metrics can be used in any network, such as a road or computer network, to identify nodes whose breakdown could be fatal to the whole system, thus breaking (or slowing down) the communication between two parts of the network.

This is not an exhaustive list of applications and, depending on your domain of expertise, you will probably find other use cases for these algorithms.

Summary

In this chapter, we studied different ways of defining and measuring node importance, also known as centrality, either using the number of connections for each node (degree centrality, PageRank, and its derivatives) or path-related metrics (closeness and betweenness centrality).

In order to use these algorithms from GDS, we also studied different ways to define the projected graph, which is the graph that's used by GDS to run the algorithm. We learned how to create this projected graph using both *native* and *Cypher* projection.

In the last section of this chapter, we saw how centrality algorithms can help in the practical application of fraud detection, assuming fraudsters are more likely to interact with each other.

A related topic is the concept of communities or patterns within a graph. We will investigate this in the next chapter. We'll use different types of algorithms to find communities or clusters within a graph in an unsupervised or semi-supervised way and identify groups of nodes that are highly connected to each other.

Exercises

Here a few exercises to test your understanding of this chapter:

1. Modify the Python implementation of PageRank to take weighted edges into account.
2. Rework this implementation using `networkx`, especially using a `networkx.Graph` object (instead of a dictionary) as input.
3. Store the PageRank results in a new node property.

    Hint: Use the `gds.pagerank.write` procedure.

In a more general way, I encourage you to modify the test graph whose centrality results are shown in the *Comparing centrality metrics* section by adding/removing nodes and/or relationships. This will help you see how the different centralities evolve and make sure you understand this evolution.

Further reading

- The initial PageRank idea is detailed in this paper: *S. Brin & L. Page, The anatomy of a large-scale hypertextual Web search engine*, Computer Networks and ISDN Systems 30 (1-7); 107-117.
- For more information about algorithms in Python, you can refer to the following:
    - *Hands-On Data Structures and Algorithms with Python*, Dr. B. Agarwal and B. Baka, Packt Publishing.
    - The following GitHub repository contains implementations for many algorithms in Python: https://github.com/TheAlgorithms/Python. If Python is not your favorite language, you can probably find yours at https://github.com/TheAlgorithms/.
- An example of fraud detection in time series in the context of cybersecurity can be found in *Machine Learning for Cybersecurity Cookbook*, E. Tsukerman, Packt Publishing.
- The following Neo4j whitepaper gives some examples of fraud detection using Neo4j: *Fraud Detection: Discovering Connections with Graph Databases*, white paper, G. Sadowksi & P. Rathle, Neo4j. It's available for free (after providing your contact information) at https://neo4j.com/whitepapers/fraud-detection-graph-databases/.

- Check the freely available graph gists related to fraud on the Neo4j website: https://neo4j.com/graphgists/?category=fraud-detection.
- The paper *Centralities in Large Networks: Algorithms and Observations* by U. Kang et al. shows some interesting approaches to computing centrality on large graphs (https://doi.org/10.1137/1.9781611972818.11).
- The paper *PageRank beyond the web* by D. F. Gleich (https://arxiv.org/abs/1407.5107) lists some applications of PageRank beyond Google and search engines.

7
Community Detection and Similarity Measures

Real-world graphs are neither regular nor fully random grids. Their edge densities are not homogeneous, so we end up finding some interesting patterns. The fact that some nodes can have more connections than others is exploited in centrality algorithms to assess node importance (see `Chapter 6`, *Node Importance*). In this chapter, we will discover a new type of algorithm whose goal is to identify groups of nodes highly connected to each other and form a community or cluster. Several of these community detection algorithms are already implemented in the GDS: components algorithms, Label Propagation algorithms, and Louvain algorithms. This chapter is our opportunity to build a graph representation of communities with JavaScript and to discover NEuler, the Graph Algorithms Playground application developed by Neo4j. Finally, we will also learn about the different metrics implemented in the GDS to measure the similarity between two nodes locally.

The following topics will be covered in this chapter:

- Introducing community detection and its applications
- Detecting graph components and visualizing communities
- Running the Label Propagation algorithm
- Understanding the Louvain algorithm
- Going beyond Louvain for overlapping community detection
- Measuring the similarity between nodes

Technical requirements

In this chapter, we will use the following tools:

- The Neo4j graph database with the following indent extensions listed:
    - Plugins: The Graph Data Science Library
    - The Neo4j Desktop Application
    - NEuler for graph visualization
- You will also need a browser to open HTML and the JavaScript file that we will build for graph visualization.
- Python (recommended ≥ 3.6) to run the example implementation of some algorithms.
- The code used in this chapter is available in the GitHub repository for this book at https://github.com/PacktPublishing/Hands-On-Graph-Analytics-with-Neo4j/ch7

> - If you are using **Neo4j < 4.0**, then the last compatible version of the **GDS** is **1.1**.
> - If you are using **Neo4j ≥ 4.0**, then the first compatible version of the **GDS** is **1.2**.

Introducing community detection and its applications

Community detection gathers techniques that have been developed to understand the structure of a graph and extract information from it. This structure can then be used in many applications, such as recommendation engines, fraud detection, property prediction, and link prediction.

> Throughout this chapter, I will use the words *community*, *cluster*, or *partition* to refer to a group of nodes sharing common properties.

Chapter 7

Identifying clusters of nodes

The following image shows the graph of Neo4j GitHub users we built in `Chapter 2`, *The Cypher Query Language*. Community detection algorithms were able to identify several communities:

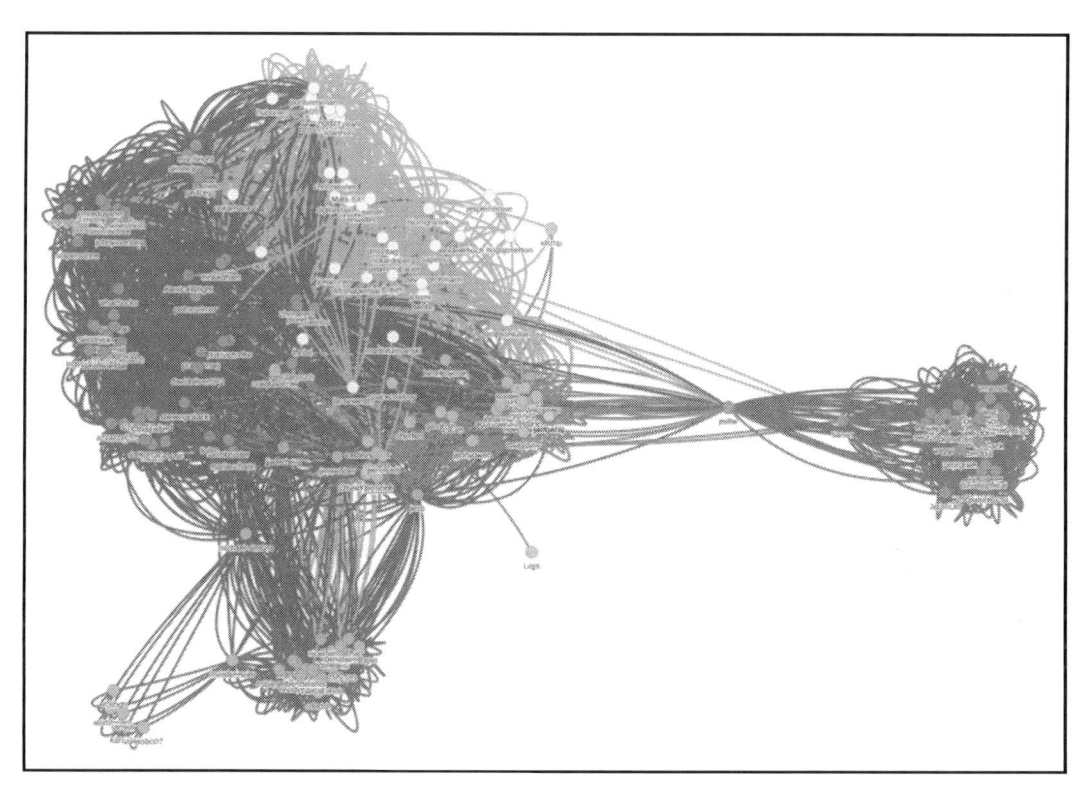

Image generated using the Louvain algorithm and neoviz.js

By the end of this chapter, you will be able to reproduce this image. Further analysis will be needed to understand the common properties of the users belonging to the violet community. A deeper analysis of this graph teaches us that the users in the violet community clearly stand out from the crowd and have mostly contributed to a unique repository.

Before going into the technical details of each algorithm, we are first going to talk more about the advantages of knowing which community a node belongs to. Although we are talking about communities made of users here, this can be applied to many other fields. We will present some of them in the rest of this section.

Applications of the community detection method

There are many applications of community detection and clustering with graphs. They can be used, for instance, in the following fields:

- **Biology:** Protein-protein interaction networks model the protein interactions within a cell. Proteins belonging to the same community are more likely to be involved in the same function.
- **Neuroscience**: Researchers model the human brain as a graph, where each node is a small number of cells. Understanding the community structure of this graph has proven particularly useful for understanding how different parts of the brain coordinate with each other.
- **Public health**: We can use the community structure of the population to try and predict the evolution and spread of a disease.

The next sections will focus on some applications that are more likely to be directly useful to you.

Recommendation engines and targeted marketing

We have already explored recommendations using Neo4j and Cypher, in `Chapter 3`, *Empowering Your Business with Pure Cypher*. But at that time, we only used graph traversal to find products bought together or products bought by a user that the current customer is connected to via social relationships. Community detection brings a new kind of information into the game, which can be used to provide even more relevant recommendations.

Clusters of products

For instance, being able to group similar products together can help in identifying similar products that would not normally be classified in the same category. It can also be used to find identical products sold by different retailers in market places like eBay. With that information, you can prevent recommending a product that has already been bought by a given customer, from another provider.

Clusters of users

Another way to use community detection to improve a recommendation engine is to try and create groups of customers. In that way, you can create groups of customers with similar habits, which can reflect similar interests. On an e-commerce website proposing sport-related articles, you can create a community of fishermen and a community of football players, without any prior knowledge about your users except their purchases: if the purchased products are mostly about fishing, you know this customer is likely a fisherman. This knowledge can be used to extend the list of relevant recommendations. For instance, some new football socks that have not been bought by anyone yet can probably be recommended to the users identified as being football players.

Fraud detection

Fraud detection was addressed in the preceding chapter (Chapter 6, *Node Importance*). We talked about the way fraudsters create crime rings and collaborate with each other to avoid detection. This kind of organization is hard to detect by traditional methods, but graphs, thanks to their native structure based on relationships, are a very helpful tool to fight against all types of fraud. Assuming that fraudsters will interact more with each other, like in the case of fake users sharing the same phone number or address, graphs can form a community and be more easily identified.

Predicting properties or links

One of the underlying ideas in community detection and most of the applications outlined above is that nodes belonging to the same community share some properties. This can be used to make predictions, based on the community structure of the graph. Let's start with the subgraph illustrated in the following figure:

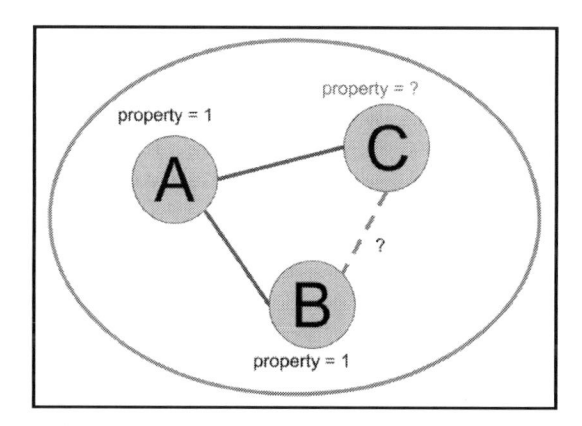

It contains three nodes, *A*, *B* and *C*, and two edges ((*A*, *B*) and (*A*, *C*)). This could be a part of a larger graph with more outgoing edges. Nodes *A* and *B* have a property whose value is 1. That could be the age category of some users, which is not always available. Users *A* and *B* have filled that field, indicating they are between 21 and 30. On top of that, some community detection algorithms have managed to cluster all three nodes into the same community. Intuitively, we can say that the probability of node *C* also falling into the 21-30 age category increases with this new knowledge about the graph structure.

Similarly, if we try to measure the probability of the edge between *B* and *C* existing without us knowing it or appearing in the future, it's higher for nodes in the same community.

A brief overview of community detection techniques

One of the first graph structure studies was performed by Weiss and Jacobson and published in 1955. Since then, several types of algorithms have been studied and implemented, using different types of rules.

As for the node importance problem, the first thing to think of in the case of a community detection problem is the definition of the metric or objective function that will quantify how good the graph partitions are. The most common definition of community states that a community is a set of nodes with more infra-community connections (more edges between nodes in the same community) than inter-community connections (edges between nodes in two different communities). But even with that definition, there are several possible ways to achieve a satisfactory partitioning.

Many algorithms have been proposed, using different metrics. For instance, hierarchical clustering uses some rules to create a dendrogram, creating a hierarchy of clusters. The Girvan-Newman algorithm is an example of hierarchical clustering using an extension of the betweenness centrality usually used for nodes to edges: edges with the highest betweenness centrality are the edges involved most often in the shortest path between two pairs of nodes in the graph. Other hierarchical clustering algorithms use similarity measures instead of topological ones. At the end of this chapter (in the *Measuring the similarity between nodes* section), we will learn how to measure the similarity between nodes.

In this book, we will focus on some of the algorithms implemented in Neo4j:

- Connected components, which allows us to detect disconnected sub-graphs.
- Label Propagation, as the name suggests, propagates community labels through the graph base on the majority-vote rule to assign each node to its new community.
- The Louvain algorithm optimizes the modularity, defined as the difference between the number of infra-community connections versus the number of inter-community connections.

Even if not yet implemented in the GDS, we will also talk about some proposed improvements of these algorithms, especially the Leiden algorithm, which was proposed to fix some issues with the Louvain algorithm. We will also briefly address the problem of overlapping communities, which isn't covered by the aforementioned algorithms.

Let's now start our community detection journey with the connected components algorithms. In the following section, we will learn about components algorithms. We will also discover tools to visualize detected communities in a graph format, which is crucial to understand the structure of medium graphs.

Detecting graph components and visualizing communities

Graph components have a clear mathematical definition. In a given component, two nodes are always connected to each other through a path but are not connected to any other nodes out of the component. There are two versions of connected components:

- **Strongly connected components**: These make sure that the path between two nodes in the same component exists in both directions.
- **Weakly connected components**: A single direction is enough for weakly connected components.

Let's see an example of this in Neo4j. In this section, we are also going to use, for the first time in this book, the write procedure to store the algorithm results in Neo4j. We will also introduce a new JavaScript library to customize the visualization of large graphs.

Community Detection and Similarity Measures

Let's start with the following **directed** graph:

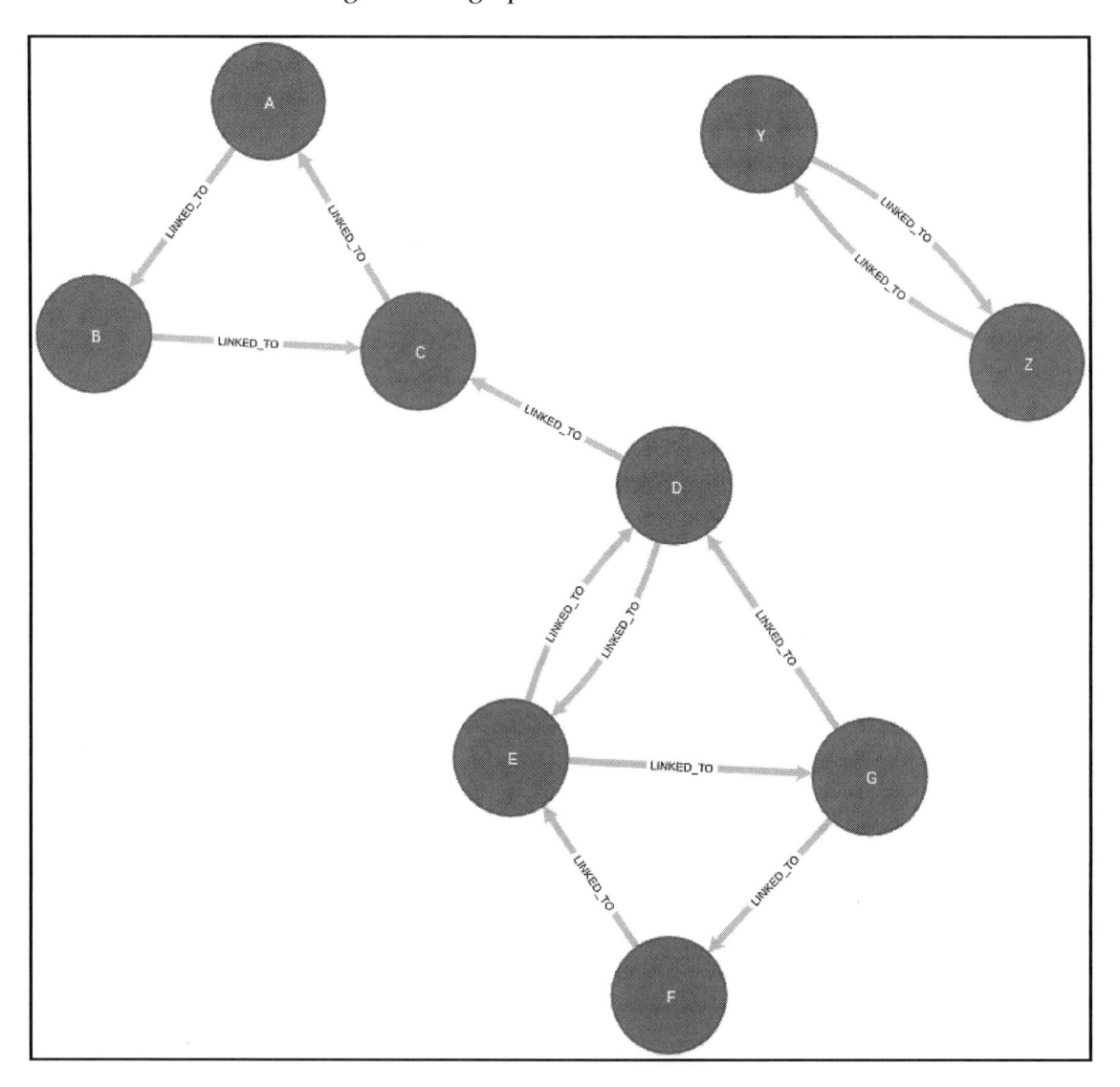

The Cypher code used to create the graph is available on GitHub (https://github.com/PacktPublishing/Hands-On-Graph-Analytics-with-Neo4j/blob/master/ch7/test_graph.cql).

Visually, we can say that there are at least two components in this graph. Nodes Y and Z are totally disconnected from any other node in the graph, so there isn't any path from these two nodes to any other node in the graph. Let's see how we can learn this information from the algorithms implemented in the GDS.

We will use the following projected graph:

```
CALL gds.graph.create("simple_projected_graph", "Node", "LINKED_TO")
```

This projected graph contains all nodes with the Node label and all relationships with the LINKED_TO type in their natural orientation (as defined when creating them with Cypher and as illustrated in the preceding figure), without any properties attached to them.

Weakly connected components

The first algorithm we are going to study here is weakly connected components or union-find.

> Weakly connected components, together with the Louvain and Label Propagation algorithms we are going to cover later on in this chapter, are production-ready algorithms in the GDS as of version 1.0.

To see the results of graph partitioning using weakly connected components, use the following query:

```
CALL gds.wcc.stream("simple_projected_graph")
YIELD nodeId, componentId
RETURN gds.util.asNode(nodeId).name as nodeName, componentId
ORDER BY componentId
```

Here are our results:

"nodeName"	"componentId"
"A"	0
"B"	0
"C"	0
"D"	0
"E"	0

Community Detection and Similarity Measures

"F"	0
"G"	0
"Y"	7
"Z"	7

As you can see, the algorithm successfully identified two components:

- The component labeled 7 in this example, containing nodes Y and Z
- Another component labeled 0, containing all the other nodes

> The exact number used to label communities is not relevant; it depends on the internal functioning of the GDS. Depending on how your graph was created, the numbers you get might be different, but the same communities should be detected.

Weakly connected components tell us that we have two disconnected partitions in our graph, considering that the graph is undirected. If relationship direction is important, for instance in a road network, then we will have to use the strongly connected component algorithm.

Strongly connected components

In strongly connected components, the direction of relationships matters. Each node in a component must be able to join any other node in the same component in both directions. Focusing on the nodes A to G, which were grouped in the same community by the weakly connected component algorithm, you can see that it is not always possible to go from one node to another in both directions. For instance, going from D to A is possible (through C), but going from A to D is impossible.

To see the components identified with this stronger rule, we can use the gds.alpha.scc procedure in the following way:

```
CALL gds.alpha.scc.stream("simple_projected_graph")
YIELD nodeId, partition as componentId
RETURN gds.util.asNode(nodeId).name as nodeName, componentId
ORDER BY componentId
```

Here are the results of the preceding code:

"nodeName"	"componentId"
"A"	0
"B"	0
"C"	0
"D"	3
"E"	3
"F"	3
"G"	3
"Y"	7
"Z"	7

This time, three components are identified: while nodes Y and Z are still in their own component, nodes A, B, and C are now disconnected from D, E, F, and G.

> **TIP**
> Connected components are very useful algorithms for understanding our graph structure. Some algorithms like PageRank (see Chapter 6, *Node Importance*) can lead to unexpected results on graphs with multiple components. Running connected components algorithms is good practice in the data exploration part of your graph data analysis.

Before moving on to the study of the other community detection algorithms, we will talk about some tools that allow us to visualize the communities in a better format. Some of them will require the community number (componentID) to be a node attribute. That's why we'll now address a functionality of the GDS we have not exploited so far: the possibility to write the results of an algorithm in the Neo4j graph, instead of streaming them back to the user and letting them decide what do to with them.

Writing the GDS results in the graph

In `Chapter 4`, *The Graph Data Science Library and Path Finding*, we introduced the write feature of the GDS, allowing us to store the results of an algorithm in Neo4j. This feature is available for almost all algorithms implemented in the GDS. Basically, the algorithms that do not offer this option are the algorithms returning matrices, such as the *All Pairs shortest path* algorithms or the *some similarity* algorithms we are going to cover at the end of this chapter.

Let's see an application of the write procedure with the connected components algorithms.

The syntax of the write procedure is pretty similar to the stream one. The main difference is that it accepts another configuration parameter, `writeProperty`, which allows us to configure the name of the property that will be added to each node.

The following query will write the result of the weakly connected component algorithm into a `wcc` property for each node:

```
CALL gds.wcc.write(
    "simple_projected_graph", {
        writeProperty: "wcc"
    }
)
```

Here, the returned result contains information about the algorithm running time and graph structure:

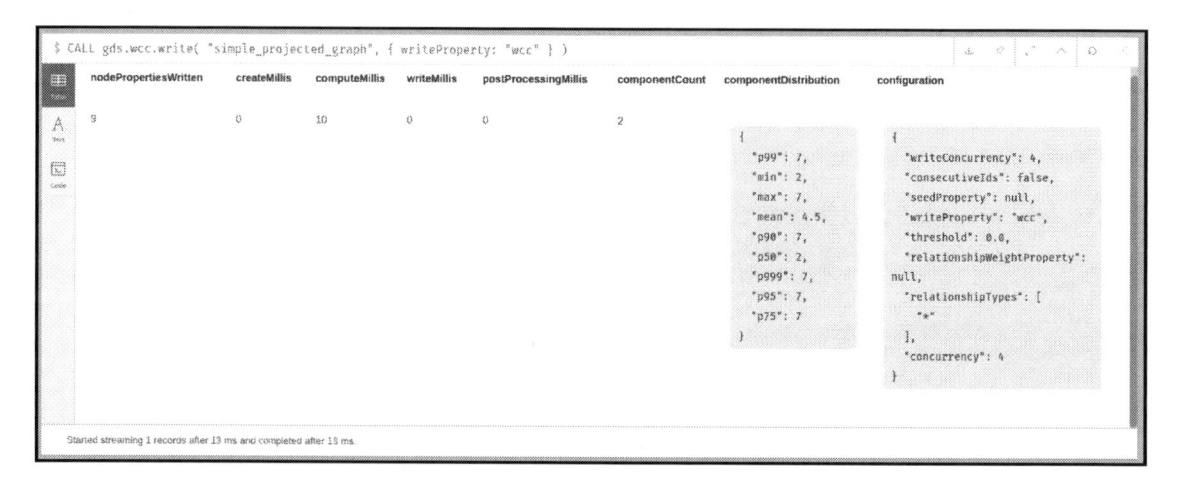

nodePropertiesWritten	createMillis	computeMillis	writeMillis	postProcessingMillis	componentCount	componentDistribution	configuration
9	0	10	0	0	2	{ "p99": 7, "min": 2, "max": 7, "mean": 4.5, "p90": 7, "p50": 2, "p999": 7, "p95": 7, "p75": 7 }	{ "writeConcurrency": 4, "consecutiveIds": false, "seedProperty": null, "writeProperty": "wcc", "threshold": 0.0, "relationshipWeightProperty": null, "relationshipTypes": ["*"], "concurrency": 4 }

But to see the partition each node belongs to, we will have to use another Cypher query:

```
MATCH (n:Node)
RETURN n.name as nodeName, n.wcc
```

The same thing can be achieved with strongly connected components:

```
CALL gds.alpha.scc.write(
    "simple_projected_graph", {
        writeProperty: "scc"
    }
)
```

On top of its `name`, each node now contains two more properties called `wcc` and `scc`, containing the ID of the component the node belongs to according to both weakly and strongly connected component algorithms. Here, you can see the content of node D:

```
{
  "name": "D",
  "scc": 3,
  "wcc": 0
}
```

Writing results to the graph is sometimes the only solution when the graph is very big (we'll discuss the case of big data more in Chapter 12, *Neo4j at Scale*). But it can also be useful in other cases. We'll discuss one of those now.

So far, we have only used very small graphs, and by reading the results from a table it was easy enough to understand them. But this is not the most common use case for graph algorithms, which are mostly useful for medium- and large-scale graphs. In these situations, visualizing the result of community detection algorithms in a graph format can be much more important for understanding the structure of the graph. In the following section, we are going to discover two ways of drawing nodes with different sizes or colors depending on their attributes: the first is the `neovis.js` JavaScript library used to embed the graph visualization into an HTML page, and the second is NEuler, the Graph Algorithms Playground, a Neo4j Desktop application based on this package.

Visualizing a graph with neovis.js

When it comes to communities, it is always useful to have a way to visualize both the node classification and the relationships between them. Graph visualization is a research field in itself and many packages exist out there for good visualizations. For instance, one of the most complete JavaScript libraries for data visualization, d3.js, also has features to draw graphs. However, when using d3.js, one has to manage the connection to Neo4j, data retrieval, and formatting. That's the reason why, in this section and the rest of this chapter, we are going to use the open source neovis.js JavaScript library. It is very easy to use because the connection to Neo4j is managed internally and we don't need to have any knowledge about the Neo4j JavaScript driver to make it work. neovis.js also creates pretty nice visualizations, like the one shown on the first figure of this chapter illustrating the Neo4j GitHub community, and it has a lot of customizable parameters.

A full working example is available in the graph_viz.html file available at https://github.com/PacktPublishing/Hands-On-Graph-Analytics-with-Neo4j/ch7/connected_components/graph_viz.html.

Import the library from the GitHub repository with the following:

```
<script src="https://rawgit.com/neo4j-contrib/neovis.js/master/dist/neovis.js"></script>
```

The minimal HTML code is as follows:

```
<body onload="draw()">
    <div id="graph"></div>
</body>
```

It will call the preceding draw function after loading the body, and draw the graph into the div function with id="graph". The main function is the draw function, which contains the configuration parameters and the rendering methods:

```
function draw() {
    let config = {
        // the ID of the "div" the graph will be drawn into
        container_id: "graph",
        // connection parameters to your Neo4j Graph
        // default is "bolt://localhost:7687"
        server_url: "bolt://localhost:7687",
        server_user: "neo4j",
        server_password: "*****",
        // Node labels to be fetched
        // and properties used to customize each node rendering
```

```
              labels: {
                  "Node": {
                      "caption": "name",  // label drawn next to each node
                      "community": "scc",  // defines the node color
                  }
              },
              relationships: {
                  "LINKED_TO": {
                      // disable caption for relationships
                      // since they do not carry any relevant information in
    our case
                      "caption": false,
                  }
              },
              arrows: true, // display the relationships direction
              initial_cypher: "MATCH (n:Node)-[r:LINKED_TO]->(m) RETURN *"
          };

      let viz = new NeoVis.default(config);
      viz.render();
  }
```

> **TIP**
>
> You need to update the connection parameters to your graph: `server_url`, `server_user`, and `server_password`. `server_password` corresponds to the password you are asked to create when adding a new graph in Neo4j Desktop.

The file `graph_viz.html` can be opened with your favorite browser to see the different communities in our graph, as identified by the strongly connected component algorithm (the `scc` property). The resulting image should look like the one displayed in the following figure:

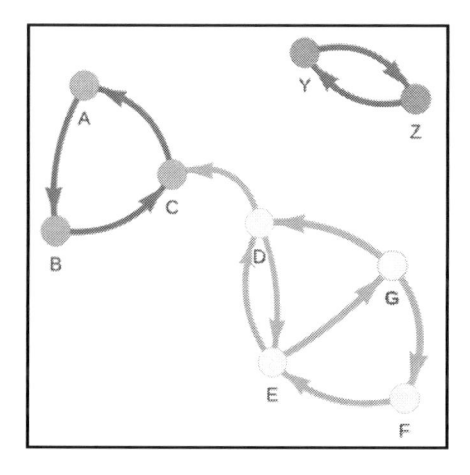

You can also, if needed, visualize the node importance by indicating the size parameter of the node configuration in the `draw` function and the property of the node containing its importance; for instance:

```
labels: {
    "Node": {
        "caption": "name",     // label drawn next to each node
        "community": "scc",    // defines the node color
        "size": "pagerank"
    }
},
```

> For this code to work, you need to run the PageRank algorithm with the write procedure on your projected graph:
> `CALL gds.pageRank("simple_projected_graph", {writeProperty: "pagerank"})`
> But remember that PageRank may produce unexpected results in the case of disconnected graphs.

`neoviz.js` is a powerful and interesting tool if you want to embed the graph into an HTML page. However, if you just need to test the results of an algorithm, a simpler solution exists: NEuler.

Using NEuler, the Graph Data Science Playground

NEuler is an open source application integrated within Neo4j Desktop, whose code is available on GitHub at https://github.com/neo4j-apps/neuler.

It is a very powerful tool allowing us to test all the algorithms implemented in the GDS, from path finding (Chapter 4, *The Graph Data Science Library and Path Finding*) and centrality (Chapter 5, *Node Importance*) to community detection and similarity. It also enables visualizing the results with a graph visualization feature based upon `neoviz.js`.

Installation instructions are available in the GitHub repository of this book.

Usage for community detection visualization

The home screen, illustrated in the following screenshot, is where you can choose the type of algorithm you are going to run:

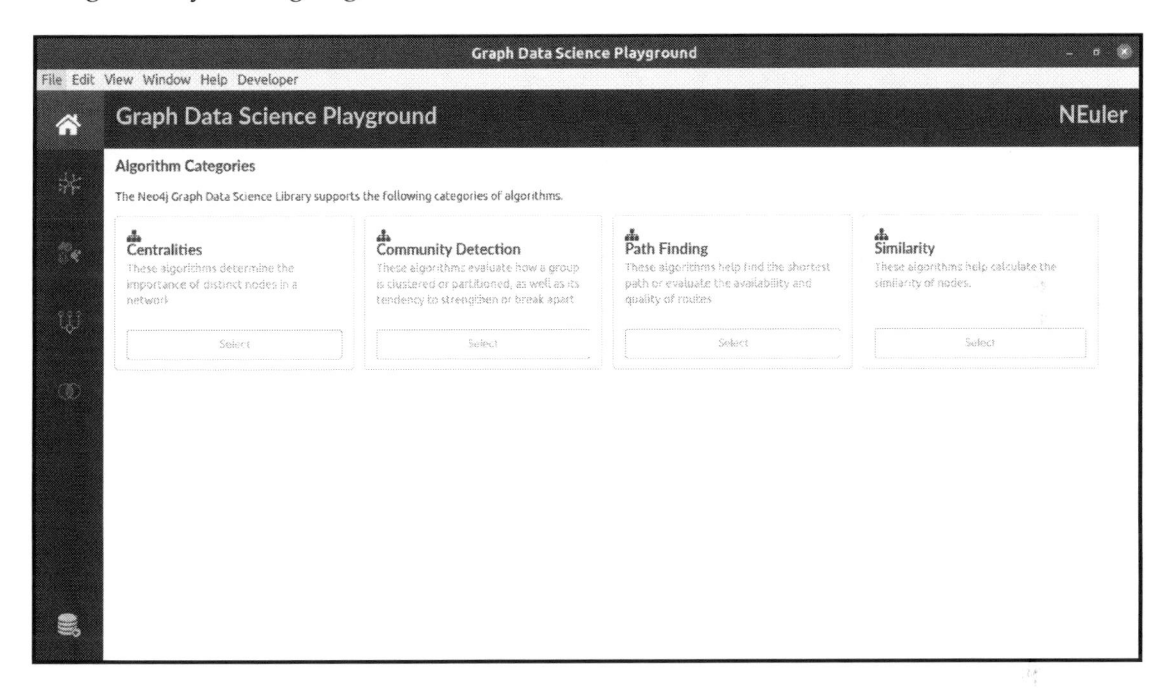

Once you have selected the community detection algorithms, you can choose the algorithm you want to try from the upper menu. For this example, we are going to use the *Strongly Connected Components* algorithm. After clicking on its name, you can configure the projected graph and the algorithm parameters from the right bar. The configuration illustrated in the following screenshot will do the following:

- Run the algorithm on the projected graph containing the node labels `Node` and relationship types `LINKED_TO` with `orientation=UNDIRECTED`.

- Store the results in a property called `scc`.

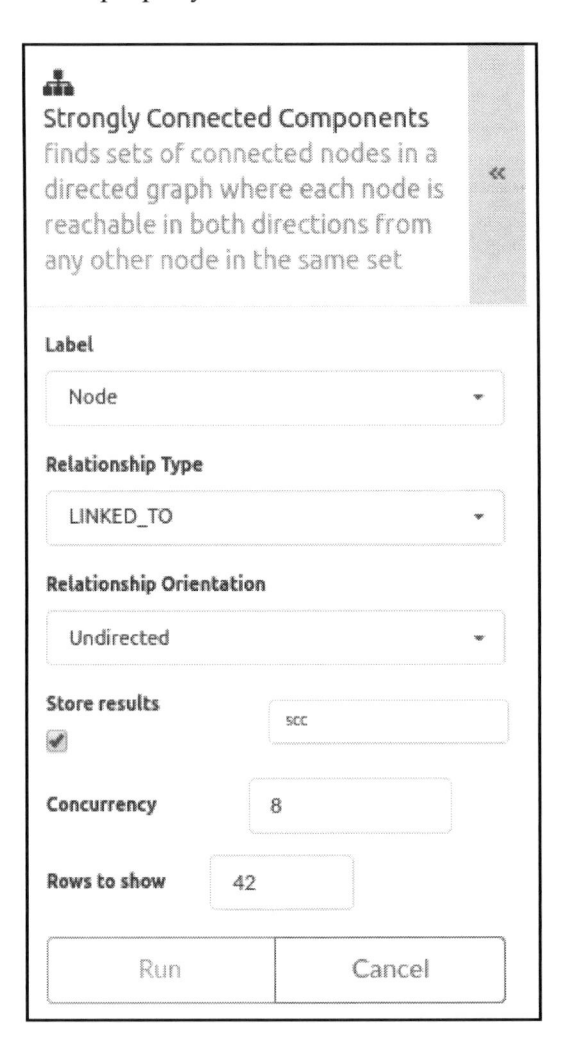

Strongly Connected Components finds sets of connected nodes in a directed graph where each node is reachable in both directions from any other node in the same set

Label

Node

Relationship Type

LINKED_TO

Relationship Orientation

Undirected

Store results ☑   scc

Concurrency   8

Rows to show   42

Run   Cancel

Clicking on the **Run** button will call the proper Cypher procedure, which you can check via the **Code** tab:

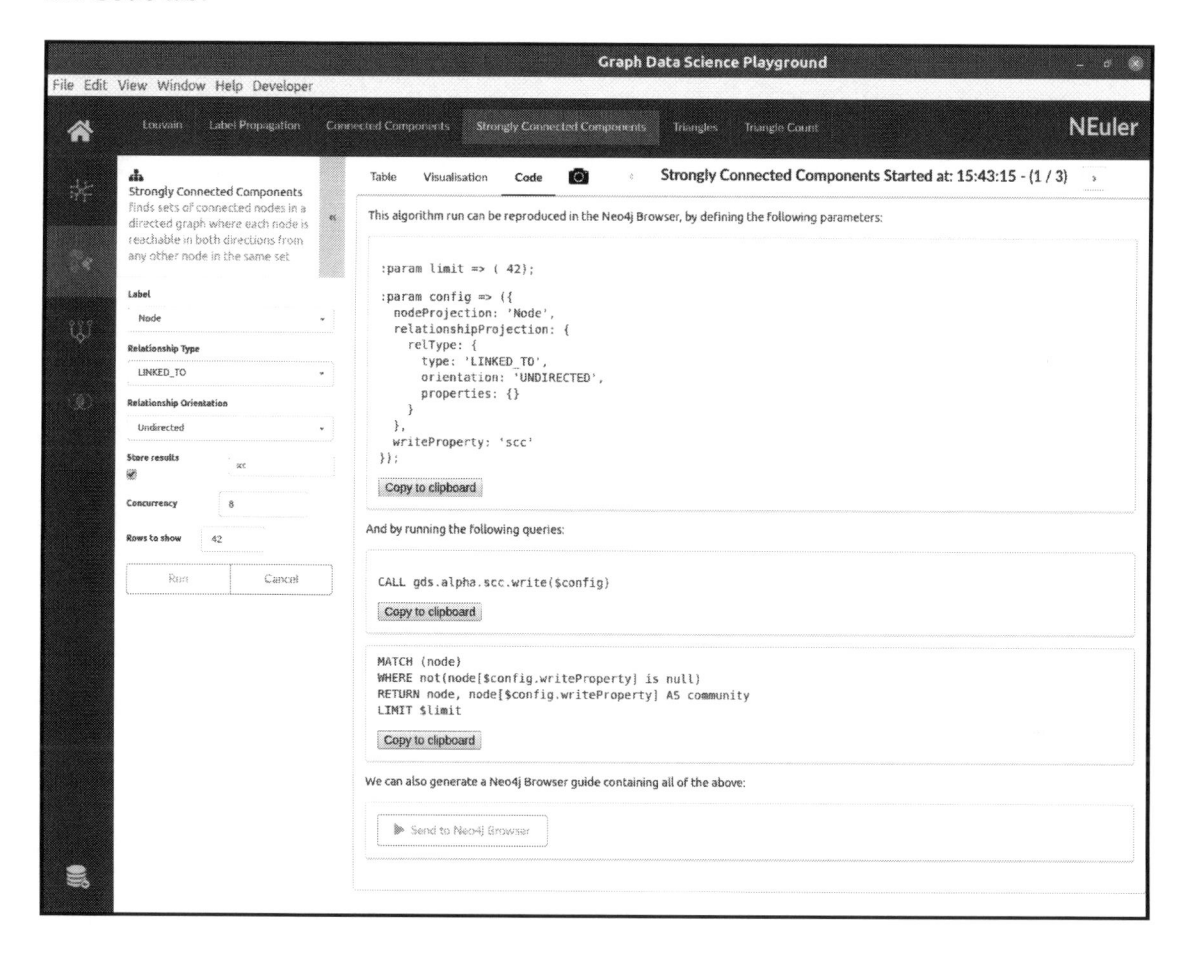

Finally, you can visualize the results inside the **Visualization** tab. There, you can customize the node property that will be used to color them, as we did in the previous section with `neovis.js`:

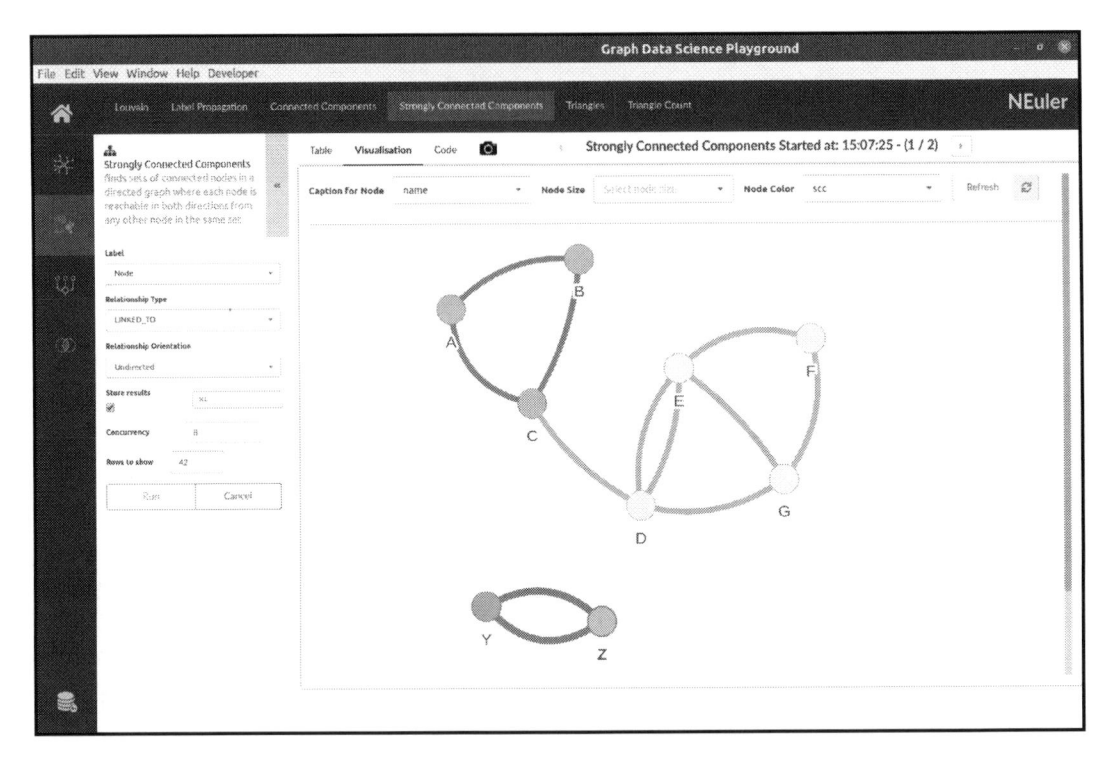

This closes our section about connected components. We have learned how weakly and strongly connected components algorithms can help us identify disconnected communities in our graph. We have also discovered two different ways of visualizing the results of community detection algorithms. We will continue using them in the following sections, where we are going to discover new types of community detection algorithms: the Label Propagation and Louvain algorithms, both part of the production-quality tier of the GDS.

Running the Label Propagation algorithm

Label Propagation is another example of a community detection algorithm. Proposed in 2017, its strength is in its possibility to set some labels for known nodes and derive the unknown labels from them in a **semi-supervised way**. It can also take into account both relationships and node weights. In this section, we are going to detail the algorithm with a simple implementation in Python.

Defining Label Propagation

Several variants of Label Propagation exist. The main idea is the following:

1. Labels are initialized such that each node lies in its own community.
2. Labels are iteratively updated based on the **majority vote rule**: each nodes receives the label of its neighbors and the most common label within them is assigned to the node. Conflicts appear when the most common label is not unique. In that case, a rule needs to be defined, which can be random or **deterministic** (like in the GDS).
3. The iterative process is repeated until all nodes have fixed labels.

The optimal solution is a partition with the minimum number of edges connecting two nodes with different labels. Let's consider the following graph:

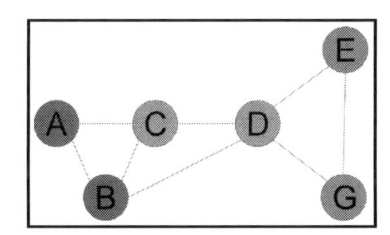

After some iterations, the algorithm assigned nodes A and B to one community (let's call it CR), and nodes E and G to another one (CG). According to the majority vote rule, in the next iteration, node C will be assigned to the CR community since two nodes connected to C already belong to this partition, while only one node (D) belongs to another cluster. Similarly, node D will be assigned to the CG community. The resulting graph is illustrated in the following figure:

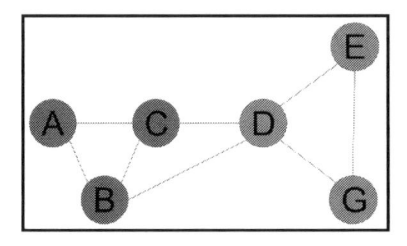

Weighted nodes and relationships

In order to take into account the weight of a node or relationship, we can update the majority vote rule so that it does not only count the number of nodes with a given label but sums their weight. The selected label will then be the one with the highest *sum of weights*.

Let's consider the weighted version of the preceding graph illustrated in the following figure:

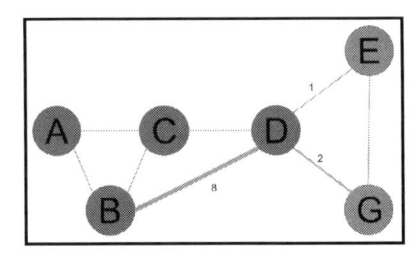

This time, in order to choose the label for node D, we have to take into account the weights of each edge connected to D:

- Weight for the CR community = 1 (C) + 8 (D) = 9
- Weight for the CG community = 1 (E) + 2 (G) = 3

Hence, in this weighted version of the graph, node D would belong to the CR community.

Semi-supervised learning

Another interesting aspect of Label Propagation is its ability to take into account prior knowledge. If you already know the community of some of the nodes, this information can be used in the initialization phase instead of setting random initial values. This technique is known as **semi-supervised** learning since only some nodes are labeled with their community.

Implementing Label Propagation in Python

In this section, we are going to implement a simplified version of Label Propagation, considering seed labels can only take two different values: 0 or 1.

We will use the same graph representation as in the previous chapters, based on a Python dictionary. The graph we will use is represented by the following object:

```
G = {
    'A': {'B': 1, 'C': 1},
    'B': {'A': 1, 'C': 1},
    'C': {'A': 1, 'B': 1, 'D': 1},
    'D': {'C': 1, 'E': 1, 'G': 1},
    'E': {'D': 1, 'F': 1, 'G': 1},
    'F': {'E': 1, 'G': 1},
    'G': {'D': 1, 'E': 1, 'F': 1},
}
```

It tells us that node A is connected to nodes B and C, both edges having a weight equal to 1.

Let's now start the algorithm. In the initialization phase, we initialize all labels with unique values. One way to find unique values is to use their index in the loop over the keys of G, which can be achieved in Python with the following:

```
labels = {node:k  for k, node in enumerate(G)}
```

> **TIP**
> The enumerate(iterable) function returns a tuple containing a count (from 0) and the value obtained by iterating over iterable. Here, iterable is our dictionary G, and iterating over G is equivalent to iterating over its keys in Python.

We then enter into the main loop. At each iteration, we perform a loop on all nodes in the graph and for each of them count the number of votes it receives:

```
for it in range(max_iterations):
    print("======= Iteration", it)
    # create a copy of the labels computed in previous iteration
    old_labels = dict(labels)
    for node, neighbors in G.items():
        # counting the number of votes from each neighbors:
        votes = Counter([old_labels[n] for n in neighbors])
```

To find the majority vote, we can use the following piece of code, which will iterate over the received votes and update the value of the new label each time a value above the current max value is found:

```
max_vote = -9999
new_label = old_labels[node]
for label, vote  in votes.items():
    if vote > max_vote:
        max_vote = vote
        new_label = label
```

```
                elif vote == max_vote:
                    # deterministic rule to disentangle equality votes
(arbitrary)
                    if label > new_label:
                        new_label = label
            labels[node] = new_label
```

In order to disentangle cases where two labels have the same number of votes, we use a totally arbitrary rule to select the label with the highest value.

Once all labels have been updated, we can check the algorithm's convergence by checking that no label has changed since the previous iteration:

```
        end = True
        for node in G:
            if old_labels[node] != labels[node]:
                # if at least one node's label has changed, go to next
iteration
                end = False
                break
        if end:
            return labels
```

Running this code on graph G defined at the beginning of this section, we get the following results:

```
{'A': 3, 'B': 3, 'C': 3, 'D': 6, 'E': 6, 'F': 6, 'G': 6}
```

Two communities are identified: the first one is labeled 3 and contains nodes A, B, and C, while the second one is labeled 6 and contains nodes D to G. Remember that the labels themselves are meaningless since they just come from the node position in the graph definition. Different implementations will return different values for the labels, but the community structure will be preserved.

> Convergence is not guaranteed with Label Propagation and we can end up with an *oscillation* where the label of a given node is unstable and oscillates between two values at each iteration, making the convergence fail.

The full code is available on GitHub at https://github.com/PacktPublishing/Hands-On-Graph-Analytics-with-Neo4j/ch7/label_propagation/label_propagation.py. You are encouraged to copy and modify it to help you understand how it works. For instance, update the code to take into account nodes and relationship weights. Note that the implementation is kept as simple as possible to allow you to leverage your prior knowledge about Python. If you already know about networkx and numpy, for instance, you can try and modify this code to make it work with a netwokx graph or by using matrix formulation (see the previous chapter, Chapter 6, *Node Importance*).

Using the Label Propagation algorithm from the GDS

The Label Propagation algorithm is part of the production-quality algorithm, which means it is well tested and optimized for large graphs. We are going to test run the Label Propagation algorithm on the graph we studied in the *Weakly connected components* section. The Cypher code to create it is available at https://github.com/PacktPublishing/Hands-On-Graph-Analytics-with-Neo4j/ch7/test_graph.cql.

Let's create an undirected projected graph:

```
CALL gds.graph.create(
    "projected_graph",
    "Node",
    {
        LINKED_TO: {
            type: "LINKED_TO",
            orientation: "UNDIRECTED"
        }
    }
)
```

To execute the Label Propagation algorithm on this graph, we can use the following query:

```
CALL gds.labelPropagation.stream("projected_graph")
YIELD nodeId, communityId
RETURN gds.util.asNode(nodeId).name AS nodeName, communityId
ORDER BY communityId
```

Community Detection and Similarity Measures

Here are the results:

"nodeName"	"communityId"
"A"	39
"B"	39
"C"	39
"D"	42
"E"	42
"F"	42
"G"	42
"Y"	46
"Z"	46

Three communities have been identified: two are similar to the ones we identified in the previous section plus an extra community containing the nodes Y and Z, which were not included in our previous study.

> Here again, the exact value of communityId may vary; it is related to the nodeId property. But all nodes in the same community will always have the same communityId.

Using seeds

In order to test our algorithm, we first need to add a new property to the graph that will hold our prior belief about the node community membership – knownCommunity:

```
MATCH (A:Node {name: "A"}) SET A.knownCommunity = 0;
MATCH (B:Node {name: "B"}) SET B.knownCommunity = 0;
MATCH (F:Node {name: "F"}) SET F.knownCommunity = 1;
MATCH (G:Node {name: "G"}) SET G.knownCommunity = 1;
```

To some nodes, we have added a property called knownCommunity, which stores our prior knowledge (or belief) about the community each node belong to.

Then, we can create the named projected graph. This graph will contain all nodes with the Node label and all relationships with the LINKED_TO type. In order to use the algorithm in a semi-supervised way, we also need to explicitly tell the GDS to store the knownCommunity node property in the projected graph. Finally, we will consider our graph as undirected, which is achieved by specifying the orientation: "UNDIRECTED" parameter in the relationship projection:

```
CALL gds.graph.create("projected_graph_with_properties", {
    // node projection:
    Node: {
        label: "Node",
        properties: "knownCommunity"
    }}, {
    // relationship projection:
    LINKED_TO: {
        type: "LINKED_TO",
        orientation: "UNDIRECTED"
    }
})
```

Now we can run the Label Propagation algorithm on this named projected graph and stream the results with the following:

```
CALL gds.labelPropagation.stream("projected_graph_with_properties", {
    seedProperty: "knownCommunity"
})
YIELD nodeId, communityId
RETURN gds.util.asNode(nodeId).name AS nodeName, communityId
ORDER BY communityId
```

You can see from the results that the identified communities are similar, however, communityId now reflects the values given via seedProperty.

Writing results to the graph

To visualize the results in the browser with the code we wrote in the previous section, we need to store the results in the graph, which can be achieved with the gds.labelPropagation.write procedure:

```
CALL gds.labelPropagation.write(
    "projected_graph_with_properties", {
        seedProperty: "knownCommunity",
        writeProperty: "lp"
    }
)
```

Community Detection and Similarity Measures

Algorithms such as Label Propagation are a good example of how graph algorithms have already been used in more *classical* machine learning models. Indeed, Label Propagation is used both for classification and regression in machine learning, where the *propagation* is performed through a *similarity* matrix (instead of the adjacency matrix discussed in the previous chapter).

For now, we will focus on another important algorithm for community detection: the Louvain algorithm.

Understanding the Louvain algorithm

The Louvain algorithm was proposed in 2008 by researchers from the university of Louvain in Belgium, giving the algorithm its name. It relies on a measure of the density of connections within a community compared to the connections toward other nodes. This metric is called **modularity**, and it is the variable we are going to understand first.

Defining modularity

Modularity is a metric quantifying the density of links within nodes in the same community, compared to links between nodes in different communities.

Mathematically speaking, its definition is as follows:

$$Q = 1/(2m) * \Sigma_{ij} [A_{ij} - k_i k_j / (2m)] \delta(c_i, c_j)$$

Where:

- A_{ij} is 1 if nodes i and j are connected, 0 otherwise.
- k_i is the degree of node i.
- m is the sum of all weights carried by the edges. We also have the relation $\Sigma_i k_i = 2m$, since the sum over all nodes will count each edge twice.
- c_i is the community the node i is assigned to by the algorithm.
- $\delta(x, y)$ is the Kronecker delta function, which is equal to 1 if $x=y$ and 0 otherwise.

To understand the meaning of this equation, let's focus on each of the terms separately. A node i with k_i edges has k_i chances of being connected to any other node in the graph. So two nodes i and j have $k_i \times k_j$ chances of being connected to each other. Hence, the term $k_i k_j / (2m)$ corresponds to the *probability* of nodes i and j being connected to each other.

On the other side of the equation, A_{ij} is the real connection status between i and j. So the term under the sigma sign quantifies the difference between the real and expected number of edges between two nodes of the same community (in a random graph).

Two nodes in the same community should be connected more often than the average, hence having $A_{ij} > k_i k_j / (2m)$. The Louvain algorithm is based on this property and tries to maximize the modularity Q.

> This definition of modularity also works for weighted graphs. In that case, A_{ij} is the weight of the relationship between i and j.

Before moving on to the algorithm itself, let's investigate special graph partitions and what the value of the modularity is for them. The results can be challenged using the simple Python implementation for the modularity found at `https://github.com/PacktPublishing/Hands-On-Graph-Analytics-with-Neo4j/ch7/louvain/modularity.py`.

In the rest of this section, we will use a graph similar to in one of the previous sections, excluding nodes Y and Z in order to work on a single component, for simplicity's sake.

All nodes are in their own community

If all nodes are in their own community, then $\delta(c_i, c_j)$ is always 0 since c_i is always different from c_j, except in the cases where $i=j$. Since our graph does not have a self-loop (a node connected to itself), A_{ii} is always equal to zero and only the negative term in the sum remains. So in that particular case, the modularity Q is negative. In the following, we will write it as Q_{diag} and its value for our graph is $Q_{diag} = -0.148$.

All nodes are in the same community

In the other extreme case, where all nodes are in the same community, $\delta(c_i, c_j)$ is always 1. So the modularity is as follows:

$$Q = 1/(2m) * \Sigma_{ij} [A_{ij} - k_i k_j / (2m)]$$

The sum over all pairs of nodes of the Aij term corresponds to the sum of the weights of all edges, counted twice (for ij and ji pairs). So, we have the following:

$$\Sigma_{ij} A_{ij} = 2m$$

Let's rewrite the second term of the equation:

$$\Sigma_{ij} k_i k_j / (2m) = \Sigma_i (k_i (\Sigma_j k_j)) / 2m = \Sigma_i (k_i (2m)) / 2m = \Sigma_i k_i = 2m$$

So, in the special case where all nodes are in the same community, then the modularity $Q=0$.

Optimal partition

The optimal partition for the simple graph we are using in this section is similar to the one obtained with connected components or Label Propagation algorithms: nodes A, B, and C are in their own partition while nodes D to G are in another community.

With m = 9, the modularity in that case is as follows:

$Q = 1/18$ (
  $2 * (A_{AB} - k_A k_B / 18 + A_{AC} - k_A k_C / 18 + A_{BC} - k_B k_C / 18)$
  $+ 2 * (A_{DE} - k_D k_E / 18 + A_{DG} - k_D k_G / 18 + A_{DF} - k_D k_F / 18 + A_{EF} - k_E k_F / 18 + A_{EG} - k_E k_G / 18 + A_{GF} - k_G k_F / 18)$
) $+ Q_{diag}$
$= 1 / 18 * 2 * ($
  $1 - 2 * 2 / 18 + 1 - 2 * 3 / 18 + 1 - 2 * 3 / 18$
  $+ 1 - 3 * 3 / 18 + 1 - 3 * 3 / 18 + 0 - 3 * 2 / 18 + 1 - 3 * 2 / 18 + 1 - 3 * 3 / 18 + 1 - 3 * 2 / 18$
) $- 0.148$
$= 0.364 > 0$

> **TIP**
> Since our graph is undirected, we can afford to double the term corresponding to the relationship between A and B (A – B), instead of summing the terms A -> B and B -> A.

> Modularity can also be used to measure the quality of the partitioning detected by another algorithm.

Now that we have a better understanding of modularity, we will look at how to reproduce the Louvain algorithm, before showing some examples with Neo4j and the GDS.

Steps to reproduce the Louvain algorithm

The Louvain algorithm aims at maximizing the modularity, which acts as the **loss function**. Starting from a graph where each node is assigned to its own community ($Q=0$), the algorithm will try to move nodes to the community of their neighbors, and keep this configuration only if it makes the modularity increase.

The algorithm performs two steps at each iteration. During the first one, an iteration over all nodes is performed. For each node n and each of its neighbors k, the algorithm tries to move the node n to the same community as k. The node n is moved to the community that leads to the highest increase in modularity. If it is not possible to increase the modularity with such an operation, the community of node n is left unchanged for this iteration.

In the second step, the algorithm will group together nodes belonging to the same community in order to create new nodes, and sum the weights of the inter-community edges in order to create the new weighted edge between them.

> **TIP**
> The change of modularity induced by moving a single node from one community to another can be computed without looping over the whole graph again.

The Louvain algorithm in the GDS

The Louvain algorithm is part of the production quality implementation from the Graph Data Science library as of version 1.0.

Syntax

The Louvian algorithm's usage is similar to the other algorithms. To stream the results, use the `gds.louvain.stream` procedure with a named projected graph as a parameter:

```
CALL gds.louvain.stream(<projectedGraphName>)
```

We can also save the results in the graph with the equivalent `write` procedure:

```
CALL gds.louvain.write(<projectedGraphName>, {writeProperty: <newNodeProperty>})
```

Community Detection and Similarity Measures

Using the Louvain algorithm on our graph leads the two usual partitions, with nodes A, B, and C on one side and nodes D to G on the other side. To see the differences between these algorithms, we will have to move to slightly larger graphs. We will see an example of this with Zachary's karate club in a later section.

The aggregation method in relationship projection

If you use the `write` procedure instead, you'll notice it returns, among other information, the final modularity. If you run this procedure on our previously created projected graph, `projected_graph`, you will notice a slightly different modularity value compared to the one we obtained in the previous section. The explanation comes from our projected graph. The initial graph, stored in Neo4j, contains two relationships between D and E (one from D to E and one from E to D). When the GDS creates the projected graph, the default behavior is to store both relationships, which is equivalent to increasing the weight of this edge (the A_{ij} term). Our projected graph is hence equivalent to the following:

```
G = {
    'A': {'B': 1, 'C': 1},
    'B': {'A': 1, 'C': 1},
    'C': {'A': 1, 'B': 1, 'D': 1},
    'D': {'C': 1, 'E': 2, 'G': 1},
    'E': {'D': 2, 'F': 1, 'G': 1},
    'F': {'E': 1, 'G': 1},
    'G': {'D': 1, 'E': 1, 'F': 1},
}
```

The edge between D and E has a weight of 2 instead of 1.

If we want the projected graph to contain only one relationship between two nodes, we have to add another property to the relationship projection: `aggregation: "SINGLE"`, which will enforce each pair of nodes to be connected by one single relationship **of a given type**. The following query will create a new projected graph with that property enabled:

```
CALL gds.graph.create(
    "projected_graph_single",
    "Node",
    {
        LINKED_TO: {
            type: "LINKED_TO",
            orientation: "UNDIRECTED",
            aggregation: "SINGLE"
        }
    }
)
```

Chapter 7

Run the Louvain algorithm on this new projected graph with the following statement:

```
CALL gds.louvain.write("projected_graph_single", {writeProperty:
"louvain"})
YIELD nodePropertiesWritten, modularity
RETURN nodePropertiesWritten, modularity
```

You will again find the same value for modularity, around 0.36, as shown in the following screenshot:

nodePropertiesWritten	modularity
7	0.3641975308641975

If you look at the full result of the `gds.louvain` procedures, you will find another field called `modularities`. It corresponds to the modularity computed at each stage of the algorithm.

Intermediate steps

An interesting feature of the GDS is its ability to store the communities at intermediate steps of the algorithm. This option needs to be enabled by setting the configuration parameter `includeIntermediateCommunities` to `true`. For instance, the following query will stream the results of the Louvain algorithm for our projected graph, returning an extra column containing the list of communities each node was assigned to at each iteration:

```
CALL gds.louvain.stream(
    "projected_graph_single",
    {
```

[275]

Community Detection and Similarity Measures

```
            includeIntermediateCommunities: true
    }
)
YIELD nodeId, communityId, intermediateCommunityIds
RETURN gds.util.asNode(nodeId).name as name, communityId,
intermediateCommunityIds
ORDER BY name
```

In the case of our simple graph, the `intermediateCommunityIds` column contains a list with a single element corresponding to the final community. This means that one single iteration was sufficient to converge, which is not surprising given the very small size of the graph. When using this algorithm on larger graphs, you will be able to see the state of the graph at each step.

> If you use `intermediateCommuntiyIds` with the write procedure, the written property will contain a list of IDs corresponding to the intermediate community IDs, instead of a single integer encoding only the final community.

A comparison between Label Propagation and Louvain on the Zachary's karate club graph

With the small test graph we've used so far, the Label Propagation and Louvain algorithms yield the same communities, but this is not the case in general. The Zachary's karate club graph is a slightly larger graph and one of the most famous ones among graph experts. It was collected by Wayne W. Zachary, a teacher at the University of Chicago. He observed the different connections between the members of the karate club of this university in the 1970s.

The following image shows the result of Label Propagation (left) and the Louvain algorithm (right) on this graph, containing 34 nodes (students). While Label Propagation only captures two communities, the Louvain algorithm is able to detect four clusters:

Chapter 7

Communities in Zachary's Karate Club

Label propagation   **Louvain**

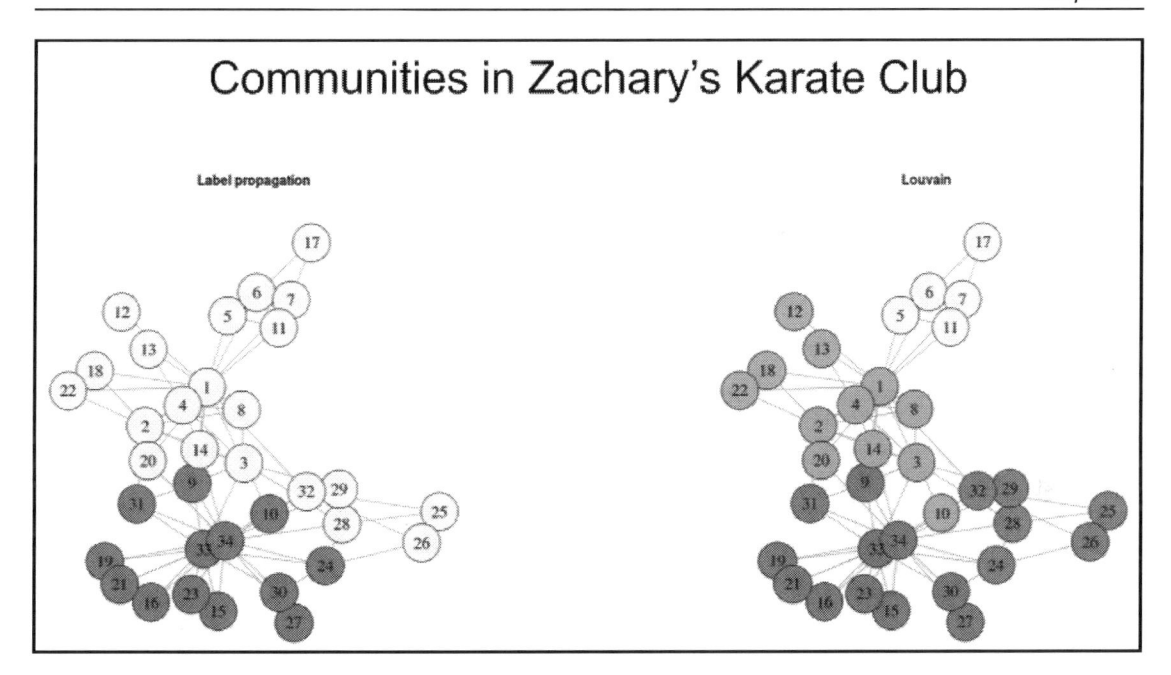

Let me give you more context to understand this result better. In the karate club of the University of Chicago in around 1970, a conflict started between two instructors, which led to the club being split into two entities. At that time, both parties tried to attract students, and interactions between each instructor and the students were important. Zachary modeled these interactions with a graph, where each node is a student and edges between them indicate whether they interacted during that period. So this graph has the big advantage of having ground-truth information: Zachary recorded which part of the club each member chose to go to after the split.

Going back to the community partition detected by the two algorithms, Label Propagation gets it right, detecting two communities consistent with the real student partition. Looking at the results of the Louvain algorithm, it seems to have detected one more partition. However, if we merge the partition containing node 17 (top) and the one containing node 2 (middle), then the results are pretty similar. The only difference is node 10 will be in the *top* community whereas in the Label Propagation, it is in the *bottom* one.

> **TIP:** Like some famous data science datasets shipped with `scikit-learn`, Zachary's karate club is included in the main Python package for dealing with graphs, `networkx`:
> `import networkx as nx G = nx.karate_club_graph()`

We now know a lot about modularity and the Louvain algorithm. In the following section, we will learn about some limitations of this algorithm, and some alternatives that have been proposed to improve it, even if they are not (yet) implemented in the GDS.

Going beyond Louvain for overlapping community detection

As all algorithms do, the Louvain algorithm has its limitations. Understanding them is very important, so we'll try to do that in this section. We will also tackle possible alternatives. Finally, we are also going to talk about some algorithms that allow a node to belong to more than one community.

A caveat of the Louvain algorithm

Like any other algorithm, the Louvain algorithm has some known drawbacks. The main one is the resolution limit.

Chapter 7

Resolution limit

Consider the following graph, consisting of strongly connected blobs of seven nodes each, weakly connected to each other with a single edge:

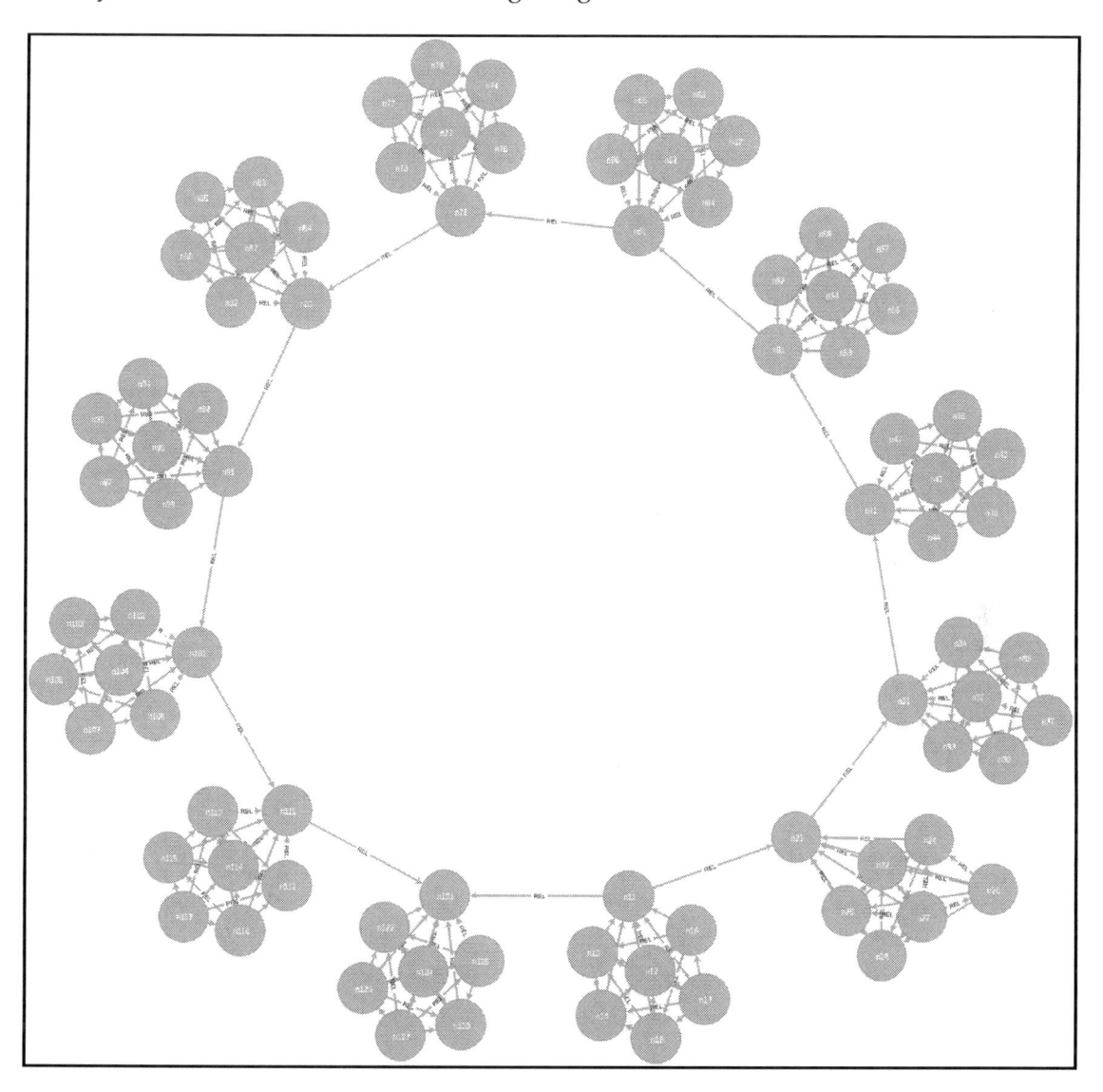

Running community detection on this graph, you would expect each of the blobs to form a community. While this works well for the Louvain algorithm on small graphs, it is known to fail on larger graphs. For instance, when run on a graph with a structure similar to the one depicted in the preceding figure but with 100 blobs, the Louvain algorithm will only identify 50 communities. This problem is known as the **resolution limit problem**: for a graph with edges of a fixed size (number of nodes) and density, the communities detected by the Louvain algorithm cannot be larger (or smaller) than a given number of nodes. This means that the algorithm will fail at discovering small communities in large networks (the 100 blobs case). It will also fail at detecting large communities in small networks. A special case for this last example is the *no community* case in small networks.

> TIP: You can try to identify the large network issues by checking the intermediate steps that can be returned by the GDS implementation of the Louvain algorithm, as discussed in the previous section.

Another limitation is the fact that the modularity is a global measure. As a consequence, an update in one part of the graph can have consequences far away from it. For instance, if you iteratively add blobs to the ring in the preceding diagram, at some point the communities will suddenly become very different, even if only a small part of the graph has been changed.

Alternatives to Louvain

Many alternatives to the Louvain algorithm have been proposed. Among them are the following:

- Algorithms involving a resolution parameter γ in order to tackle the resolution limit of the Louvain algorithm.
- The Leiden algorithm is a variant of the Louvain algorithm, which is also able to split clusters instead of just merging them. By doing so, the Leiden algorithm is able to guarantee that communities will be well-connected, which is not the case with the Louvain algorithm (see the *Further reading* section for links to resources going deeper into this topic).

These algorithms have been proven to perform better than Louvain in the cases listed in the preceding section. However, there are two other cases that are covered by none of the algorithms addressed so far:

- **Overlapping communities**: Cases where a given node can belong to several communities

- **Dynamic networks**: How do communities change when the network evolves with time (new edges and/or new nodes)

Those two topics will be covered separately in the next two subsections.

Overlapping community detection

All the algorithms we have studied so far have one point in common: each node is assigned to one and only one community. But this is not always representative of reality: a friend can also be a colleague, a colleague can also be a family member. Being able to detect the nodes belonging to several communities also brings up interesting information about the graph structure and community borders, as suggested by the following illustration.

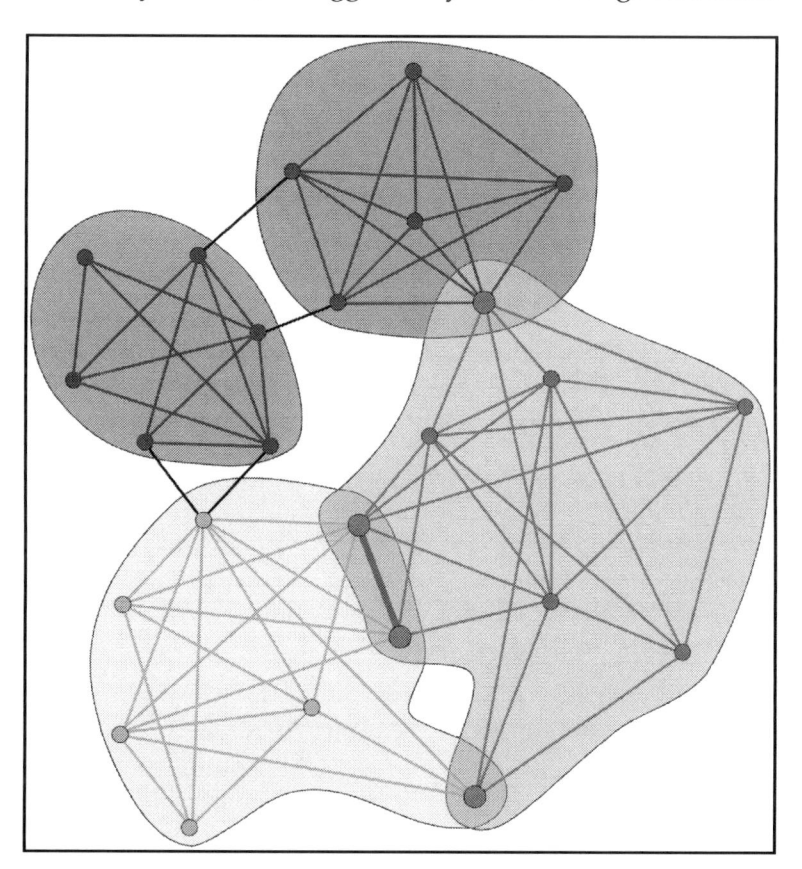

One of the most famous algorithms for overlapping community detection is the **Clique Percolation Method** (**CPM**). A clique in graph theory is a subset of nodes where each node is connected to all other nodes. A *k-clique* is a clique containing *k* nodes. The simplest example of a clique is the *3-clique*, which is a triangle made of three fully connected nodes. The CPM algorithm defines a community based on an adjacent *k-clique*, where two *k*-cliques are considered adjacent if they share *k-1* nodes, which makes it possible for the kth node to be assigned to several communities.

Dynamic networks

A dynamic network is a graph evolving in time, where nodes and edges can be added, modified, or even deleted. The problem of community detection becomes much more complex because communities can do the following:

- Appear
- Grow
- Be reduced
- Fuse with another community
- Be split
- Disappear

A community can also stay unchanged or even temporarily vanish only to appear again sometime later. One technique to solve such problems consists of using snapshots of the graph at different times. A **static** algorithm such as the ones studied in this book can then be used on each of the snapshots. However, when comparing the communities discovered in two consecutive snapshots, it will be hard to decide whether the differences are due to the real community evolution or to the algorithm instability (think about the resolution limit of the Louvain algorithm). Many solutions have been proposed to solve this issue by using smoothing techniques. For instance, you can build an algorithm that will require the communities at time *t* to be somehow similar to the communities at time *t-1*. More details about this topic can be found in the references (see the *Further reading* section).

We have now covered community detection algorithms, understanding how they work, when to use them, and how to use them from the GDS in Neo4j. We have even gone beyond the GDS and described some techniques for overlapping community detection. Communities are about grouping together nodes with similarities: similar neighborhood (Label Propagation) and similar edge density compared to the rest of the graph (Louvain). If you want to quantify the similarity between two nodes, you can start by checking whether they belong, or not, to the same community. But more precise metrics exist, which we are going to introduce in the following section.

Measuring the similarity between nodes

There are several techniques used to quantify the similarity between nodes. They can be divided into two categories:

- **Set-based measures**: Compare the content of two sets globally. For instance, sets (A, B, C) and (C, D, B) have two common elements.
- **Vector-based measures**: Compare vectors element-wise, meaning that the position of each element is important. Euclidean distance is an example of such measures.

Let's go into more detail about these metrics, starting from the set-based similarities.

Set-based similarities

The GDS 1.0 implements two variants of set-based similarities we'll cover here.

Overlapping

The overlapping similarity is a measure of the number of common elements between two sets, relative to the size of the smallest set.

Definition

This measure's mathematical definition is as follows:

$$O(A, B) = |A \cap B| / min(|A|, |B|)$$

$A \cap B$ is the intersection between sets A and B (common elements) and $|A|$ denotes the size of set A.

The GDS contains, in its alpha tier, a function that will allow us to test and understand this similarity measure. We use it in the following way:

    RETURN gds.alpha.similarity.overlap(<set1>, <set2>) AS similarity

The following statement returns the result of $O([1, 2, 3], [1, 2, 3, 4])$:

    RETURN gds.alpha.similarity.overlap([1,2,3], [1,2,3,4]) AS similarity

The intersection between sets [1, 2, 3] and [1, 2, 3, 4] contains the elements that are in both sets: 1, 2, and 3. It contains three elements, so its size is | A ∩ B | = 3. On the denominator, we need to find the size of the smallest set. In our case, the smallest set is [1, 2, 3] containing three elements. So the expected value for the overlapping similarity is 1, which is the value returned by the GDS function. The following table contains a few more examples:

A	B	A ∩ B	|A ∩ B|	min(|A|, |B|)	O(A, B)
[1, 2, 3]	[1, 2, 3, 4]	[1, 2, 3]	3	3	1
[1, 2, 3]	[1, 2, 4]	[1, 2]	2	3	2/3≈0.67
[1, 2]	[3, 4]	[]	0	2	0

> **TIP**
> Note that the overlap similarity is symmetric; exchanging A and B does not change the result.

Quantifying user similarity in the GitHub graph

We are going to use the Neo4j community GitHub graph, containing GitHub users characterized by a login, the repositories owned by Neo4j, and relationships of type CONTRIBUTED_TO between users and the repositories they contributed to. If you have not yet built the graph from previous parts of this book, data and loading instructions are available in this book's repository on GitHub.

The first step to use similarity algorithms is to build a set of data associated with each user:

```
MATCH (user:User)-[:CONTRIBUTED_TO]->(repo:Repository)
WITH {item: user.login, categories: collect(repo.name)} as userData
RETURN userData
```

`userData` contains the following content, for a given user with login j:

```
{
  "item": "j",
  "categories": [
    "cypher-shell",
    "neo4j-ogm",
    "docker-neo4j",
    "doctools"
  ]
}
```

Computing the similarity between two users in that case means comparing the repositories they contributed to (stored in the `categories` key). In order to be usable by the GDS, we just need to replace our user login and repository name with the Neo4j internal IDs:

```
MATCH (user:User)-[:CONTRIBUTED_TO]->(repo:Repository)
WITH {item: id(user), categories: collect(id(repo))} as userData
RETURN userData
```

`userData` can then be used to feed the `gds.alpha.overlap.stream` procedure:

```
MATCH (user:User)-[:CONTRIBUTED_TO]->(repo:Repository)
WITH {item:id(user), categories: collect(id(repo))} as userData
WITH collect(userData) as data
CALL gds.alpha.similarity.overlap.stream(
    {
        nodeProjection: '*',
        relationshipProjection: 'CONTRIBUTED_TO',
        data: data
    }
)
YIELD item1, item2, count1, count2, intersection, similarity
RETURN *
```

The procedure returns the similarity, but also intermediate results such as the number of items in both categories' set and the size of the intersection.

> **TIP**
> `item1` and `item2` are node IDs. To retrieve the node object, you can use the `gds.util.asNode` function. For instance, to get the user login corresponding to `item1`, you can write `gds.util.asNode(item1).login`.

Here are some chosen rows from our result:

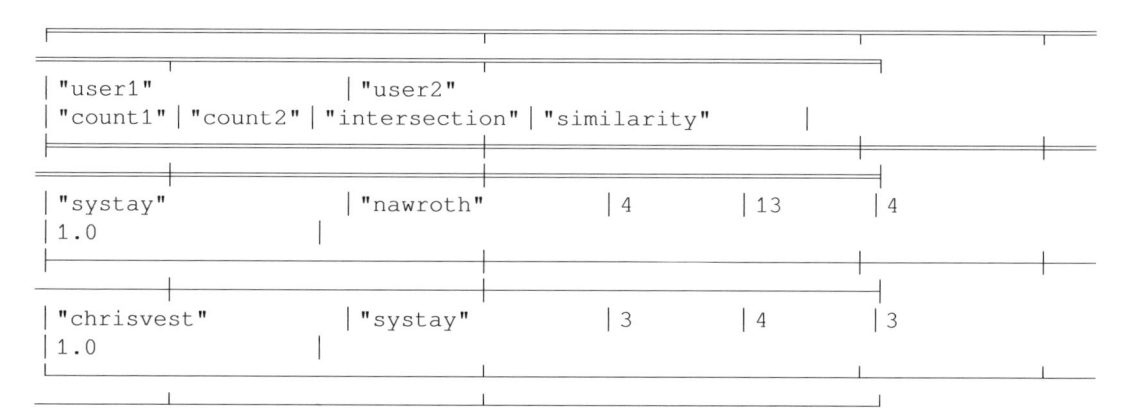

"user1"	"user2"	"count1"	"count2"	"intersection"	"similarity"
"systay"	"nawroth"	4	13	4	1.0
"chrisvest"	"systay"	3	4	3	1.0

[285]

As you can see, even for pairs of nodes with a similarity equal to 1. There are large differences between the size of the intersection: we would maybe expect `systay` to be more similar to `chrisvest` than `nawroth` since `navroth` contributed to nine more repositories than `systay`, while the difference in the number of repositories is only one between `systay` and `chrisvest`. This is solved by the Jaccard similarity we are going to look at in the following paragraph.

Jaccard similarity

The Jaccard similarity definition is similar to the overlap similarity, except that the denominator contains the size of the union of sets A and B:

$$J(A, B) = | A \cap B | / | A \cup B |$$

Using the union of both sets in the denominator is useful for identifying the cases where a user would have contributed to a single repository, with many different contributors. With the overlap similarity, this user would have a similarity of 1 to all other contributors. With the Jaccard formula, the similarity will depend on the number of repositories each of the other users contributed to and will be equal to 1 only for the contributors that have contributed to that single repository as well.

Running the Jaccard similarity algorithm on this projected graph is as simple as this:

```
MATCH (u:User)
MATCH (v:User)
RETURN u, v, gds.alpha.similarity.jaccard(u, v) as score
```

You can check the similarity between `systay` and the other users in this graph and notice that, now, the similarity with `chrisvest` is much higher than the one with `navroth`.

These kinds of similarities are based on a comparison between the elements nodes are connected to. In the following section, we will discover how to use vector-based similarity metrics such as the Euclidean distance or cosine similarity within the GDS. Even if they are not specific to graphs, they offer useful information when it comes to data analysis.

Vector-based similarities

Vector-based similarities are similar to the ones encountered in classical machine learning pipelines. They compare two vectors containing an ordered list of numbers.

Euclidean distance

The Euclidean distance is a measure of the distance between two points. It is an extension of the distance metrics in a Cartesian plane, and is computed using the following formula:

$$d(u, v) = \sqrt{(u_1 - v_1)^2 + (u_2 - v_2)^2 + \ldots + (u_n - v_n)^2}$$

Instead of simply counting the number of repositories each pair of users has in common, we can try to quantify the *distance* between their vectors of contribution. Let's make it clearer with an example. We will add a new property to some relationships, to count how often users contributed to a given repository:

```
MATCH (u1:User {login: "systay"})-[ct1]->(repo)
SET ct1.nContributions = round(rand() * 10)
```

I'm using random numbers here for simplicity, but it means your result may differ. If we do the same thing for another user, for instance, chrisvest, we can then create the vector of contributions of each user to each of the repositories:

```
MATCH (u1:User {login: 'chrisvest'})-[ct1]->(repo)
MATCH (u2:User {login: 'systay'})-[ct2]->(repo)
WITH collect(ct1.nContributions) as contrib1, collect(ct2.nContributions) as contrib2
RETURN contrib1, contrib2
```

The `collect` statement creates two lists, one for each user, containing the contribution of this user to each of the repositories. To compute the Euclidean distance between these two vectors, we just need to call the `gds.alpha.similarity.euclideanDistance` function:

```
MATCH (u1:User {login: 'chrisvest'})-[ct1]->(repo)
MATCH (u2:User {login: 'systay'})-[ct2]->(repo)
WITH collect(ct1.nContributions) as contrib1, collect(ct2.nContributions) as contrib2
RETURN gds.alpha.similarity.euclideanDistance(contrib1, contrib2) AS similarity
```

This leads to a similarity close to 38 in my case.

Similar to the overlap similarity, the GDS also contains procedures to run on a projected graph and computes similarities between all pairs of nodes.

Remember that you can find the full name and signature of the functions and procedures available in your version of the GDS with the following:

```
CALL gds.list() YIELD name, signature
WHERE name =~ '.*euclidean.*'
RETURN *
```

Cosine similarity

Cosine similarity is well-known, especially within the NLP community, since it is widely used to measure the similarity between two texts. Instead of computing the distance between two points like in Euclidean similarity, cosine similarity is based on the angle between two vectors. Consider the following scenario:

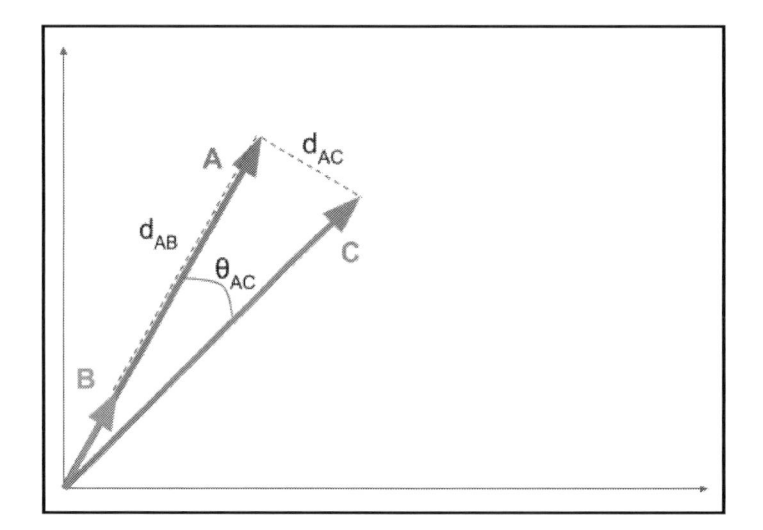

The Euclidean distance between vectors A and C is d_{AC}, while θ_{AC} represents the cosine similarity.

Similarly, the Euclidean distance between A and B is represented by the d_{AB} line, but the angle between them is 0, and since $cos(0)=1$, the cosine similarity between A and B is 1 – much higher than the cosine similarity between A and C.

To replace this example in the context of the GitHub contributors, we could have the following:

- A contributes to two repositories *R1* and *R2*, with 5 contributions to *R1* (*x* axis) and 10 contributions to *R2* (*y* axis).
- *B*'s contributions to the same repositories are: 1 contribution to *R1* and 2 contributions to *R2*, so that the vectors are aligned.
- *C* has more contributions to *R1*, let's say 8, but fewer contributions to *R2* (let's say 8).

Looking only at the total number of contributions, users *A* and *C* are more similar than *A* and *B*. However, the distribution of contributions of users *A* and *B* is more similar: each of them contributed twice as often to *R1* as to *R2*. This last fact is encoded in the cosine similarity, which is higher between *A* and *B* than between *A* and *C* (see the following table).

Cosine similarity usage with the GDS is identical to the one of Euclidean distance, using the following names:

- A function, `gds.alpha.similarity.cosine`
- Two procedures, `gds.alpha.similarity.cosine.stream` and `gds.alpha.similarity.cosine.write`

The following table shows a comparison of the Euclidean and cosine similarity between users *A*, *B*, and *C* with the values given previously:

	Euclidean	Cosine
A/B	RETURN gds.alpha.similarity.euclidean([5, 10], [1, 2]) ~ 0.10	RETURN gds.alpha.similarity.cosine([5, 10], [1, 2]) 1.0
A/C	RETURN gds.alpha.similarity.euclidean([5, 10], [8, 8]) ~ 0.22	RETURN gds.alpha.similarity.cosine([5, 10], [8, 8]) ~ 0.95

That's the end of our section dedicated to node similarity. We will come back to it in the following chapters, when we will use some of the metrics we discovered in this chapter and the preceding ones as features in a machine learning model.

Summary

In this chapter, we talked a lot about ways to measure the similarity between nodes, either on a global scale by grouping nodes into communities or with a more local similarity assessment, for example, using the Jaccard similarity metric. Several algorithms were studied – the weakly and strongly connected components, the Label Propagation algorithm, and the Louvain algorithms. We also used a feature offered by the GDS that allows us to write the results of an algorithm into Neo4j for future use. We also used two new tools to visualize a graph and the results of the graph algorithms implemented in the GDS: `neovis.js`, which is used to embed a Neo4j graph visualization into an HTML page, and NEuler, which is the Graph Algorithms Playground, from which you can run a graph algorithm without writing code.

Our exploration of the algorithms implemented in the GDS (1.0) is now finished. In the next chapters, we will learn how to use graphs and these algorithms in a machine learning pipeline to make predictions. To start with, in the following chapter, we will build a machine learning pipeline and introduce a graph-based feature to enhance performance.

Questions

- Connected components:
    - What do you think would happen if you ran the strongly connected component algorithm on an undirected projected graph?
    - How will the community structure of the test graph change if we add a relationship from D to C? Or if we remove the relationship from D to E?
- Label propagation:
    - Update our algorithm implementation to take into account seeds, that is, prior knowledge about the node community.

Further reading

- *Applications of community detection techniques to brain graphs: Algorithmic considerations and implications for neural function*, J. O. Garcia et al., Proceedings of the IEEE doi: `10.1109/JPROC.2017.278671`
- *A Method for the Analysis of the Structure of Complex Organizations*, R. S. Weiss and E. Jacobson, American Sociological Review, Vol. 20, No. 6, 1955, pp. 661-668. doi:10.2307/2088670
- The Louvain algorithm: original paper: `https://arxiv.org/abs/0803.0476`
- *Community detection in dynamic networks, a survey*, G. Rossetti & R. Cazabet, ACM Journal (Full text available at `https://hal.archives-ouvertes.fr/hal-01658399/`)

Section 3: Machine Learning on Graphs

Now that we have all the tools to describe our graph, we will focus on how to use this new knowledge to make predictions out of our data. We'll start from a low graph dependency where we just add some graph-based features to our dataset. We will be upskilling to graph embedding, where the graph structure is at the core of machine learning techniques.

This section consists of the following chapters:

- Chapter 8, *Using Graph-Based Features in Machine Learning*
- Chapter 9, *Predicting Relationships*
- Chapter 10, *Graph Embedding -from Graphs to Matrices*

8
Using Graph-based Features in Machine Learning

In this chapter, we will take what you have learned about graphs, graph databases, and the different types of information that can be extracted from graph structures (node importance, communities, and node similarity) and learn how to integrate this knowledge into a machine learning pipeline to make predictions out of data. We will start by using a classical CSV file, containing information from a questionnaire, and recap the different steps of a data science project using this data as the central theme. We will then explore how to transform this data into a graph and how to characterize this graph using graph algorithms. Finally, we will learn how to automate graph processing using Python and the Neo4j Python driver.

The following topics will be covered in this chapter:

- Building a data science pipeline
- The steps toward graph machine learning
- Using graph-based features with `pandas` and `scikit-learn`
- Automating graph-based feature creation with the Neo4j Python driver

Technical requirements

The following tools will be used throughout this chapter:

- Neo4j with the Graph Data Science plugin
- Python (recommended ≥ 3.6) with the following requirements:
  - `neo4j`, the official Neo4j Python driver (≥ 4.0.2)
  - `networkx` for graph management in Python (optional)
  - `matplotlib` and `seaborn` for data visualization
  - `pandas`
  - `scikit-learn`
- Jupyter to run notebooks (optional)

> If you are using **Neo4j < 4.0**, then the latest compatible version of the **GDS** plugin is **1.1**, whereas if you are using **Neo4j ≥ 4.0**, then the first compatible version of the **GDS** plugin is **1.2**.

Building a data science project

Machine learning can be defined as the process from which an algorithm *learns* from data in order to be able to extract information that is useful for some business or research interest.

Even though all data science projects are different, a certain number of common steps can still be identified:

1. Problem definition
2. Data collection and cleaning
3. Feature engineering
4. Model building and evaluation
5. Deployment

Even if these steps follow a logical order, the process is never linear and consists of back and forth operations between these different steps. It can be useful to go back to the problem definition after the data collection phase, for example, as well as returning to the feature engineering and model evaluation phases as many times as required to reach the desired outcomes. The following diagram illustrates this idea of moving back and forth between the different steps of a project:

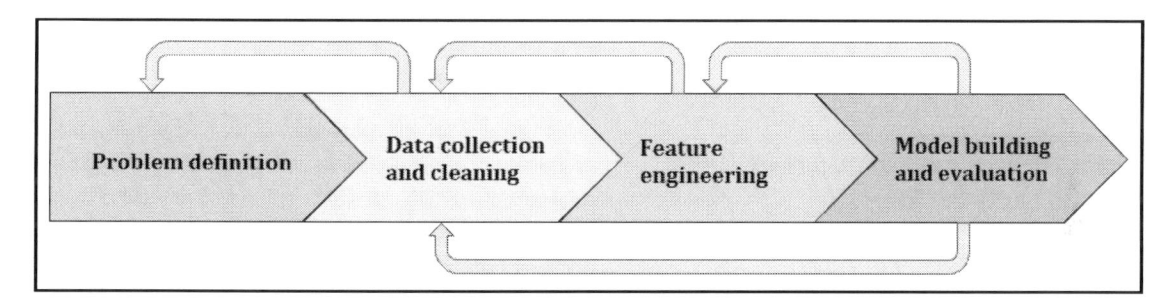

Problem definition > Data collection and cleaning > Feature engineering > Model building and evaluation

This project structure also applies when analyzing graph data, which is why we are going to go through these steps in detail in this chapter.

Problem definition – asking the right question

A project's success depends on many factors. Whatever the kind of project, it is vital that the project leader has a good idea of the goal and scope from the very beginning. Even the famous physicist Albert Einstein spoke about the importance of having a clear goal:

> *"If I had an hour to solve a problem and my life depended on it, I would use the first 55 minutes determining the proper question to ask, for once I know the proper question, I could solve the problem in less than five minutes."* - Einstein

Even if the proportion here is exaggerated, it reflects the importance of the problem definition: what exactly is the problem that needs to be solved? If you don't know what you are looking for, you won't find it! That sounds like an obvious statement, but people tend to forget or neglect this step too often when starting a project. This mistake can easily lead to a data science project failure.

As a data analyst or data scientist, you are the bridge between the field expert and the mathematical world of algorithms. While field experts have knowledge about the data and good intuition about the processes, as a technical expert you can judge the feasibility of a project and decide whether the goal can be met given the inputs (data), the foreseen length of the project, and the available tools (the team, CPU, and so on). As such, you have a crucial role from the very beginning of the project planning process; it is your job to make sure all the stakeholders understand the project limits. For example, you may need to explain that you can work with pictures that are already in your database but that working with videos would require significantly more time and money (for data collection, storage, learning how to use the tools, and so on).

When a data science project starts, it is also important to define the success criterion in order to later decide whether the project was a success or not. For this, we need to define an indicator, or **Key Performance Indicator** (KPI) - a quantitative variable that will serve as a benchmark. Usually, this KPI would have already been computed by the managers as the *pain point* that led to the project idea. It is important to make sure everybody understands how it was computed and that it can be reproduced. Even if you have to help define this indicator, its initial value must be known in order to measure the improvements provided by the use of machine learning. From there, you can decide on a threshold value or a minimum percentage improvement that will both make the project a real success for everyone and be feasible using state-of-the-art techniques.

Don't forget that, as a technical expert, you also have a teaching role, to explain what can be achieved and what cannot be achieved and why. You will realize that taking the time to explain to all the people involved in the project – from the person collecting the data to the final user – how everything works in simple terms will save you hours of difficulty, in the long run, trying to solve problems that occur just because of misunderstandings by others.

In this phase of the project, you should already be able to get an idea of the type of machine learning algorithm you will need to use:

- Supervised or unsupervised
- Regression or classification

Supervised versus unsupervised learning

It might be tempting to define machine learning as the process by which computers learn known observations to be able to make *predictions* about unseen data. However, this definition only reflects a subset of machine learning called **supervised learning**, which is only possible when we have access to some *labeled data* that the algorithm can learn from. If this is not the case, we have to rely on **unsupervised learning**.

When labeled data exists, it means we have some observations with a known output. From there, we can *train* an algorithm to recognize this output based on other characteristics of the observations – that is, the **features**. After this training phase, the algorithm will have adjusted its parameters in order to have the best possible predictions on the training data. These tuned parameters can then be used to make predictions about unseen observations – that is, data that does not have a label. This is how you can predict the price of a house given the sale prices of other houses in the same neighborhood or hand-written digits on postal envelopes.

Unsupervised learning is completely different. It is used when we do not have access to the **ground truth** or the real labels of some data. Clustering is the most famous example of unsupervised learning. In a clustering algorithm, you try to find similarities between observations and create groups of observations sharing some common **pattern**, but nothing, *a priori*, can tell the algorithm whether it is right or not.

The algorithms we studied in the last two chapters – centrality and the community detection algorithm on graphs – are actually unsupervised algorithms, since we did not have any prior knowledge about the result before running the algorithm. Remember that in our PageRank implementation, the score was initialized equally for all nodes. Similarly, the labels for the nodes in the label propagation algorithm are initialized such that each node belongs to its own community. Only after a few iterations can we see ranking and communities appear.

Label propagation is a special kind of algorithm since it can be used in a **semi-supervised** way when a small subset of nodes already has known labels. This knowledge can be used to infer the labels of the other nodes.

Regression versus classification

Depending on the nature of the variable we are trying to predict – that is, the target variable – we may be facing a regression or a classification problem. If the target is categorical, meaning it can only take a small number of values, then we have a classification problem. Examples of classification problems include the following:

- **Cancer detection**: A practitioner looking at medical imagery and deciding whether a tumor is cancerous or benign is actually performing classification with two classes (cancer or not cancer).
- **Spam detection**: This is another example of a two-class classification problem (an email is either spam or it is not).

- **Sentiment analysis**: When trying to determine whether a comment was positive, negative, or neutral, we are performing classification into three classes.
- **Hand-written digit classification**: Here, the target value is between 0 and 9, and we have 10 possible classes.

A regression problem is different by nature because the target variable is a real number and can take an infinite amount of values. House price prediction is an example of regression.

Introducing the problem for this chapter

In this chapter, we will start by using a classical CSV file that we will use to review the different steps of a machine learning project, before enriching it to go forward with graph analysis.

The context is the following: during a conference centered around graphs, you submit a questionnaire to the attendees in order to learn more about them. Among the different questions, one of them is whether the user contributed directly to Neo4j. Unfortunately, not all of the participants answered that question but you would like to infer from the ones who gave an answer the status of the other ones. So, we have a situation with a supervised classification problem whose target categories are *contributed to Neo4j* or *didn't contribute to Neo4j*.

> The data is available in the `data_ch8.csv` file; you can find it in the code bundle of this book.

Whether this problem can be solved with data and statistical models depends on the availability and quality of the data, which we are going to quantify now.

Getting and cleaning data

If you work in an organization, you probably already have access to some datasets used by the IT systems. However, acquiring them and formatting them is not all that simple. Some clear requirements need to be specified regarding the valid data range – that is, the list of characteristics available and/or needed. Getting a usable dataset can require several iterations with the data provider. At each iteration, some data quality checks need to be performed. These checks, of course, depend on the problem to be solved, but some of them are mandatory. For example, you always need to ask whether it's good quality data and whether you need more.

Data characterization

When first looking at a dataset, there are a certain number of checks that can be performed. The following is a non-exhaustive list of the preliminary information that we need to extract from a given dataset in order to understand it.

Quantifying the dataset size

Probably the easiest information and the first thing to extract from a dataset is the number of rows, or observations, it contains. Very small datasets may prevent some kind of analyses. As you can see in the diagram at the following link, created by the `scikit-learn` development team, the number of observations in the dataset is a key factor for choosing the machine learning algorithm that can be used to solve the problem. According to the `scikit-learn` algorithm cheat-sheet, for instance, the recommended algorithm to start an analysis varies depending on the number of observations in your dataset (see: https://scikit-learn.org/stable/tutorial/machine_learning_map/index.html).

So, let's start analyzing the data by importing the CSV file into a DataFrame using `pandas`:

```
import pandas as pd
data = pd.read_csv("data_ch8.csv")
```

The length of the DataFrame can be found using the following function:

```
len(data)
```

The result of the preceding function shows that our dataset contains 596 observations. This is not a particularly large dataset and we will try to be cautious in the rest of the processing not to drop observations.

> The import needed to run the code block will only be written out the first time we need it in this chapter. All the code that you will see in this section is available in the `Data_Analyais_CSV.ipynb` Jupyter notebook.

Labels

Once the dataset size is known, the next most important information to gather is whether the dataset contains labels for each observation. The label is the value the algorithm should target in your problem. It can be a text or integer class in the context of a classification task, and a real number for regression problems. If the dataset contains labels, we are in the context of supervised learning. Otherwise, we have two choices: either rely on unsupervised techniques or try and fetch data labels from other sources.

Using Graph-based Features in Machine Learning

Remember, our problem consists of determining whether a user contributed to Neo4j or not. So, our dataset does have labels via the column named `contributed_to_neo4j`, thus we are in a supervised classification problem. We can check the distribution of this variable with the `seaborn` Python package, a wrapper around the historical `matplotlib` package that was built for data analysis. As an example, a single line of code (apart from the import!) is required to draw a bar chart showing the number of elements in each class:

```
import seaborn as sns
sns.countplot(x="contributed_to_neo4j", data=data);
```

> **TIP**
> Adding a semi-colon (;) at the end of a statement in a notebook prevents Jupyter from displaying it (default behavior). If you omit it in the previous code, you will see the following displayed before the figure:

> **TIP**
> `<matplotlib.axes._subplots.AxesSubplot at 0x7f67c047e950>`

The resulting distribution is shown on the following plot:

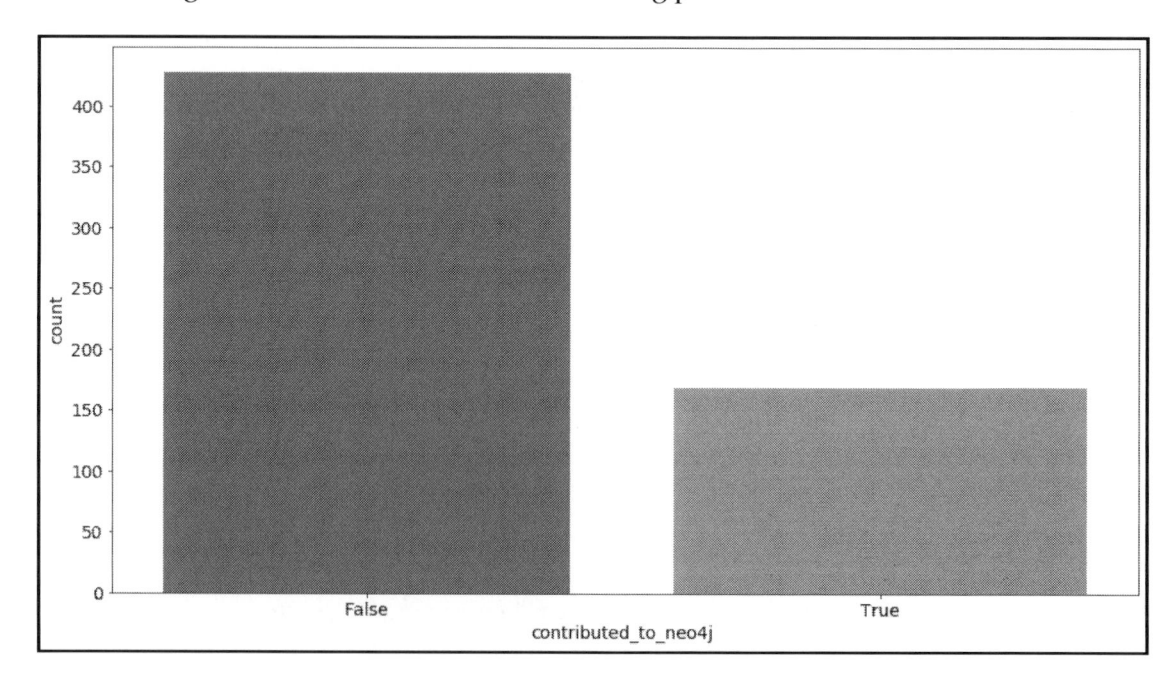

Out of the 596 people who filled in the questionnaire, 169 contributed to Neo4j and 427 did not. The number of users who didn't contribute to Neo4j is equal to more than twice the number of users who did contribute to Neo4j. This means we have a non-uniform distribution of the observations between each of the target classes. This dataset is said to be **imbalanced**: it has more observations in the `False` category than observations with the `True` label. This is important information that we need to keep in mind moving forward since it will influence the analysis of the results.

Columns

The columns in a dataset contain the "natural" features. This refers to the data characteristics that are present in the initial dataset, before any *feature engineering*.

At this point, it is important to make sure the feature definition is clear. For instance, if the dataset contains a column reporting a product price, is this price including the VAT? If the price is set to 0, does it really mean it was free, or is it the default value in case the person or system filling out the data doesn't know the real value? All these questions need to be answered, and involve a lot of communication with the dataset owner.

The column definition is not the only information that needs to be described well. Before going further, you also have to characterize each feature. Two definitions are possible:

- **Numerical feature**: A feature whose value is an integer (number of floors in a house) or a floating-point number (its surface area). If the feature represents a physical quantity, such as the surface, the unit must be included (for example, feet or meters).
- **Categorical feature**: A feature representing a discrete attribute, such as a person's gender. It will be represented by full text, `Male/Female`, or `M/F`, or encoded as numbers, such as `1` for male and `2` for female. This is why it is really important to get a description of the features. Categorical features can be created from numerical ones – for instance, defining a shirt size as `Small`, `Medium`, and so on, from its length, and/or from its width. This is part of feature engineering work.

Using Graph-based Features in Machine Learning

`pandas` provides two useful methods that can be used to get a first idea of the content of a DataFrame. The first one is the `info` method:

```
data.info()
```

It displays the following result for our DataFrame:

```
<class 'pandas.core.frame.DataFrame'>
RangeIndex: 596 entries, 0 to 595
Data columns (total 4 columns):
 #   Column                Non-Null Count  Dtype
---  ------                --------------  -----
 0   user_id               596 non-null    int64
 1   followers             594 non-null    float64
 2   publicRepos           594 non-null    float64
 3   contributed_to_neo4j  596 non-null    bool
dtypes: bool(1), float64(2), int64(1)
memory usage: 14.7 KB
```

The `info` method tells us many things:

- The DataFrame contains 596 rows (entries).
- It has four columns:
    - `user_id` is of type integer, and is never null.
    - `followers` has been interpreted as a float by `pandas` and contains only 594 non-null entries, meaning two observations do not have this information.
    - `publicRepos` has also been interpreted as a float and also has two missing values.
    - `contributed_to_neo4j`, our target variable, is a Boolean and is never null.

To get more information about each column, we can use the `describe` method:

```
data.describe()
```

The result of this method is reproduced as follows:

```
            user_id       followers     publicRepos
count    596.000000     594.000000     594.000000
mean    3025.988255      93.457912      90.321549
std     5333.331601     525.309949     547.851252
min        1.000000       0.000000       0.000000
25%      188.750000       5.000000      11.000000
50%      337.500000      21.000000      28.000000
75%      486.250000      61.750000      63.750000
max    14599.000000   11644.000000   12670.000000
```

For all numeric columns (`int` or `float`), `pandas` is showing us some statistics about the variable distribution:

- `count` (the number of non-null entries)
- `mean` and standard deviation (`std`)
- The `min` and `max` values
- The median (`50%`)
- The first and third quartiles (`25%` and `75%`)

These numbers can give us an idea about the range of possible values of the variables. We can, for instance, already see that some of our users do not have any followers or public repositories (`min=0`).

Another important piece of information to extract from this result is the presence of abnormal values or outliers. While 75% of the users have fewer than 34 public repositories, one of them has 12,670! We will deal with this kind of data during the data cleaning stage.

`followers` and `publicRepos` seem to have a similar distribution with very close values for all of the indicators reported by the `describe` method. But these indicators alone are not sufficient; in order to fully understand the data, we will have to produce some more charts.

Using Graph-based Features in Machine Learning

Data visualization

On top of the mean, standard deviation, and quartiles that we can see from the DataFrame description, we also need to look at the real data distribution. The following figure illustrates the importance of data visualization:

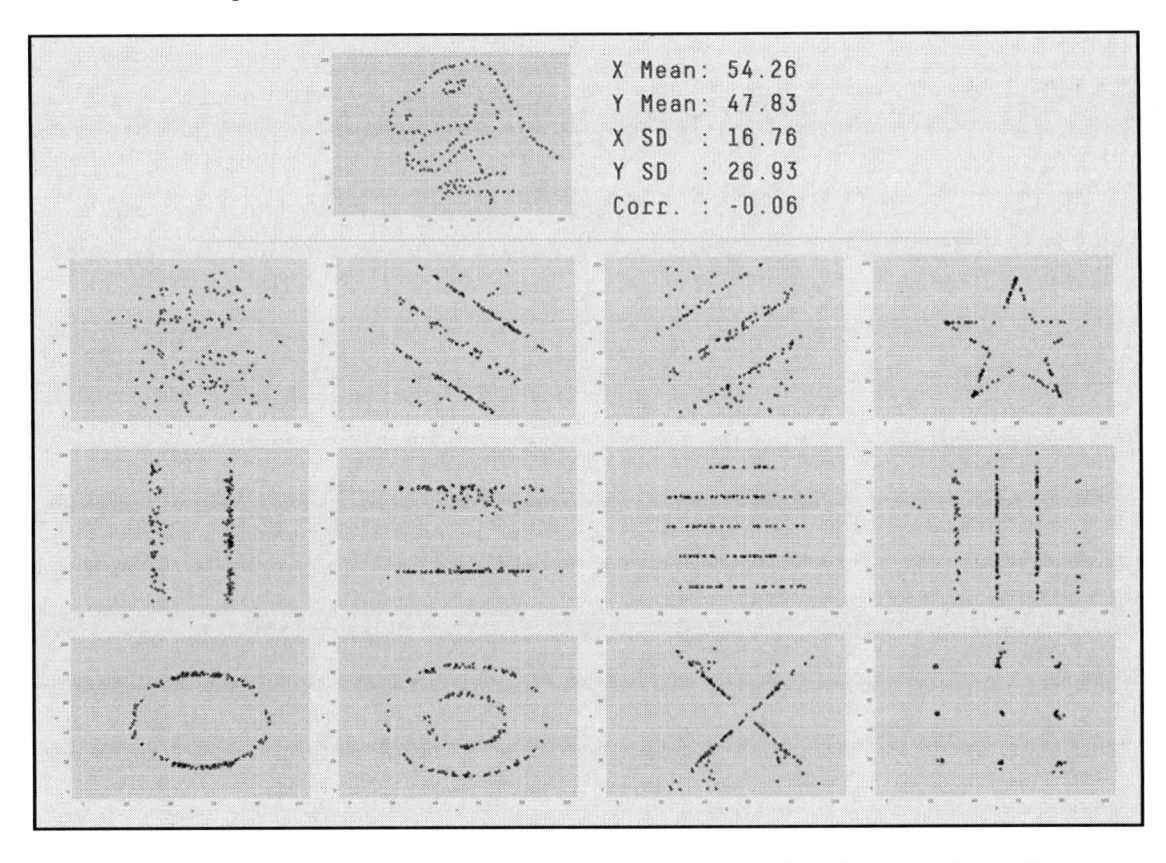

Image from *Same Stats, Different Graphs: Generating Datasets with Varied Appearance and Identical Statistics through Simulated Annealing* by *J. Matejka* and *G. Fitzmaurice*, available at https://www.autodeskresearch.com/publications/samestats

This figure shows 13 datasets of two variables: x and y. In each of these datasets, the mean value of the x variable is 54.26 and the mean value for y is 47.83. They also share the exact same standard deviation (up to two-digit precision) and the same correlation between x and y. However, the shape is totally different and if you were to select an algorithm to predict y from x, you probably wouldn't pick the same method for the lower-left dataset (the circle) as for the cross.

We will continue our visualization using the `seaborn` Python package. We can, for instance, visualize the distribution of each of the features and the correlation between them in a single plot with the following line of code:

```
sns.pairplot(data, vars=("followers", "publicRepos"),
    hue="contributed_to_neo4j");
```

The preceding line of code will return the following output:

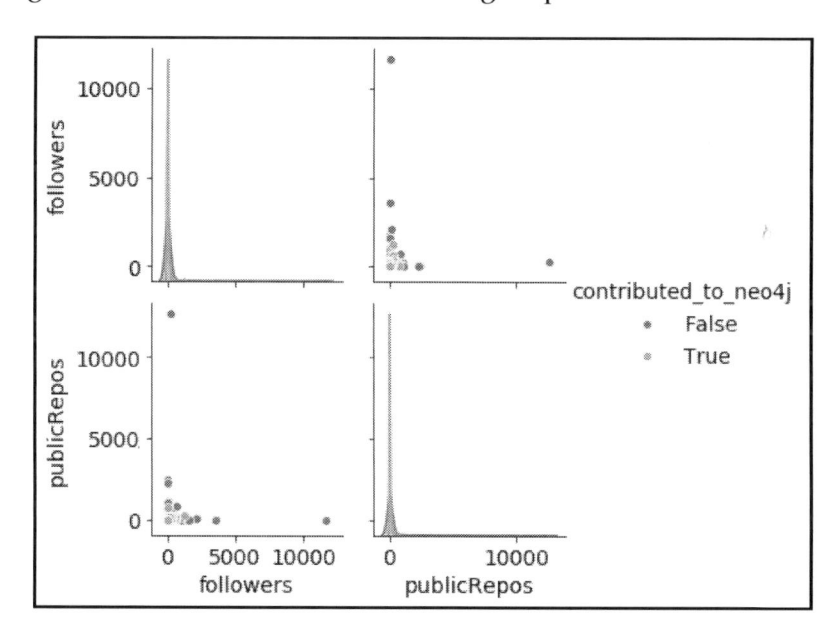

However, due to the outliers we have already identified in the previous section, this plot is not particularly helpful yet. So, let's proceed to the next step, which consists of checking the data quality and doing some cleaning when necessary.

Data cleaning

Real-life data is never perfect. It can contain unintentional mistakes and even missing data where information could not be collected for some reason.

Outliers detection

Outliers appear in a dataset for two main reasons:

- **Human error**: If the values are typed by a human being, it is likely that this person will make mistakes from time to time. They might type an extra zero at the end of a number, or invert two numbers so that we end up with a price of $91 instead of $19 for some products.
- **Rare observation**: Although almost all of your products cost less than $100, you may have some more expensive ones, up to $1,000 or maybe more. Trying to model both usual and rare events is often complicated. Therefore, if it is not of particular importance to you; it is better to leave rare events out of the model.

Sometimes, the outliers are actually the anomalies you are trying to identify – for example, for fraud or intrusion detection in a network. Several methods exist to identify outliers and deal with them; some are very simple and some more sophisticated.

In our example, we will use an oversimplified method consisting of replacing values higher than 100 with the value `100`:

```
data["publicRepos"] = data.publicRepos.clip(upper=100)
data["followers"] = data.followers.clip(upper=100)
```

We can now reproduce the pair plot we created earlier, which is now much more readable:

Chapter 8

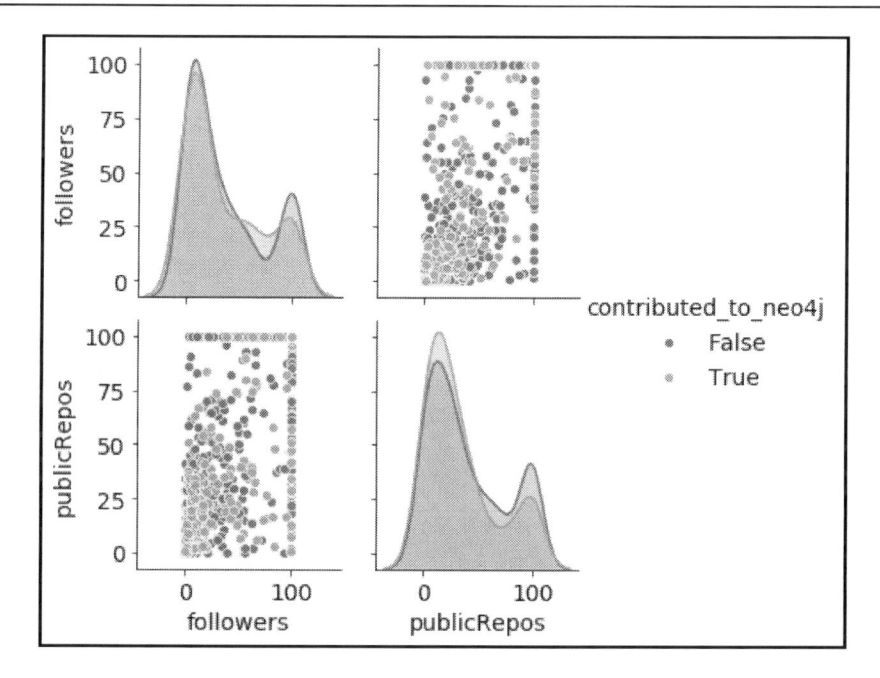

From the preceding plot, we can see that the person contributing to Neo4j has slightly fewer public repositories than the others. This is confirmed by the boxplots shown in the following plot:

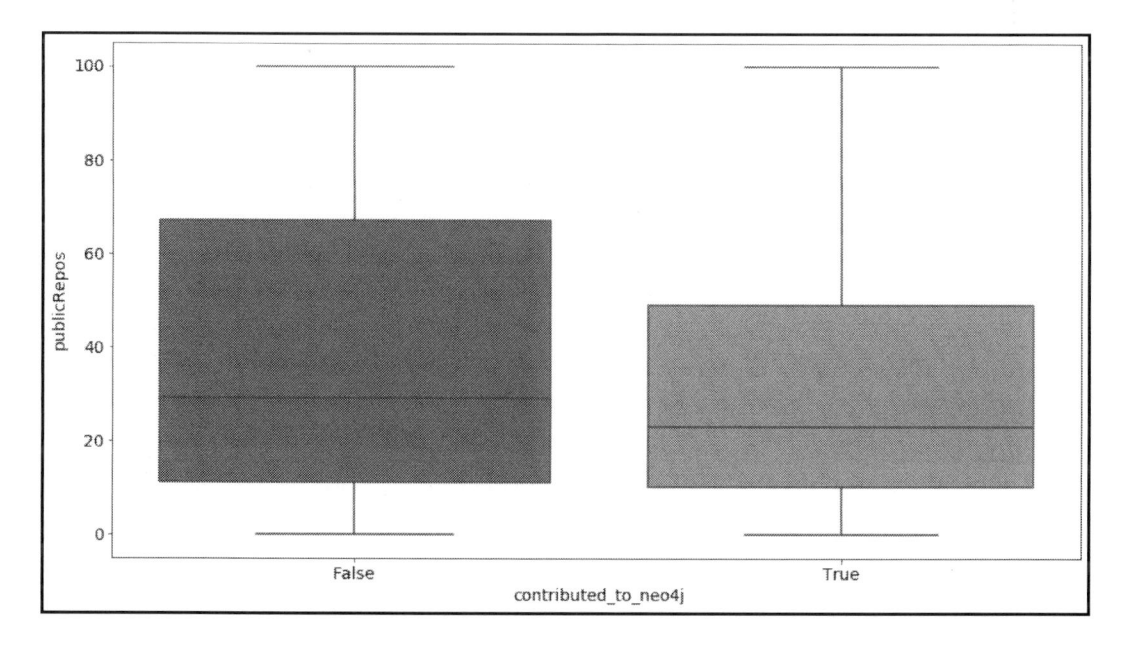

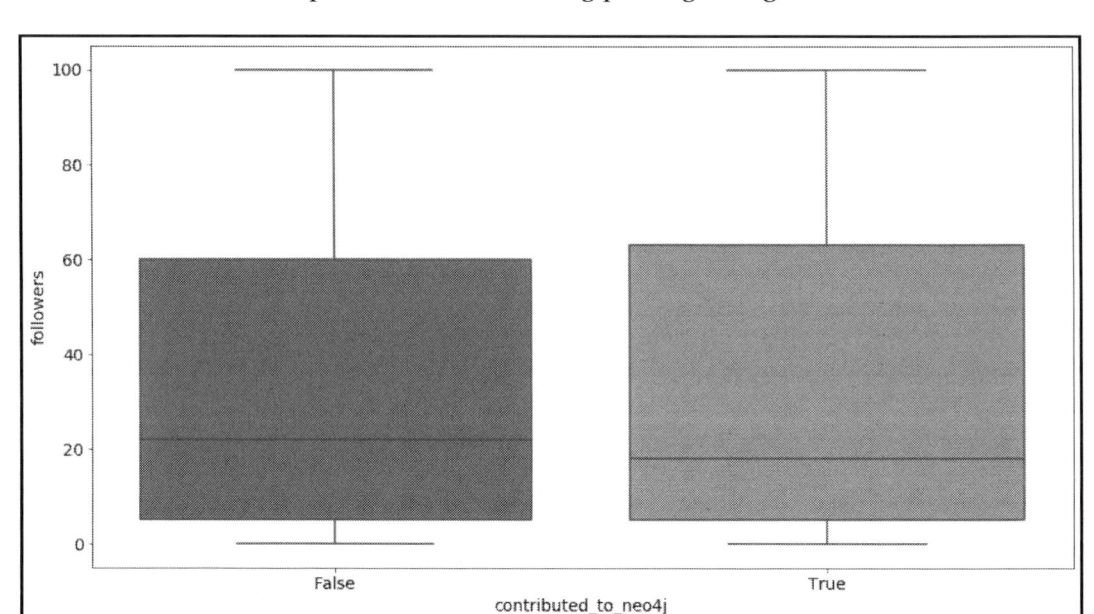

You can also see a similar pattern in the following plot regarding the number of followers:

After dealing with the outliers, we need to stop for a moment and look at the missing data.

Missing data

Missing data is another topic data scientists have to deal with in real life. Some fields may not be filled due to oversight, lack of information, or just because the information is not relevant.

While some machine learning algorithms are able to deal with missing data, most of them will not be able to process the data properly and raise errors if your dataset contains such values. It is safer, therefore, to find a way to remove them. If your dataset is large and the amount of missing data represents only a small proportion of it, you could simply drop the observations containing incomplete information. However, in most cases, it is good practice to keep all of the information and instead try to compensate for what is missing. One way of doing this is to use the mean value of all the known observations as a default value for the observations with missing data. In this way, the observations are retained and, in most cases, the *fake* data that we integrate into the model will not have a large effect on the model prediction.

Correlation between variables

These checks will enable us to understand the data, and so checks are the second most important step after the problem definition. Doing this will rule out some algorithms that won't perform well on some types of data:

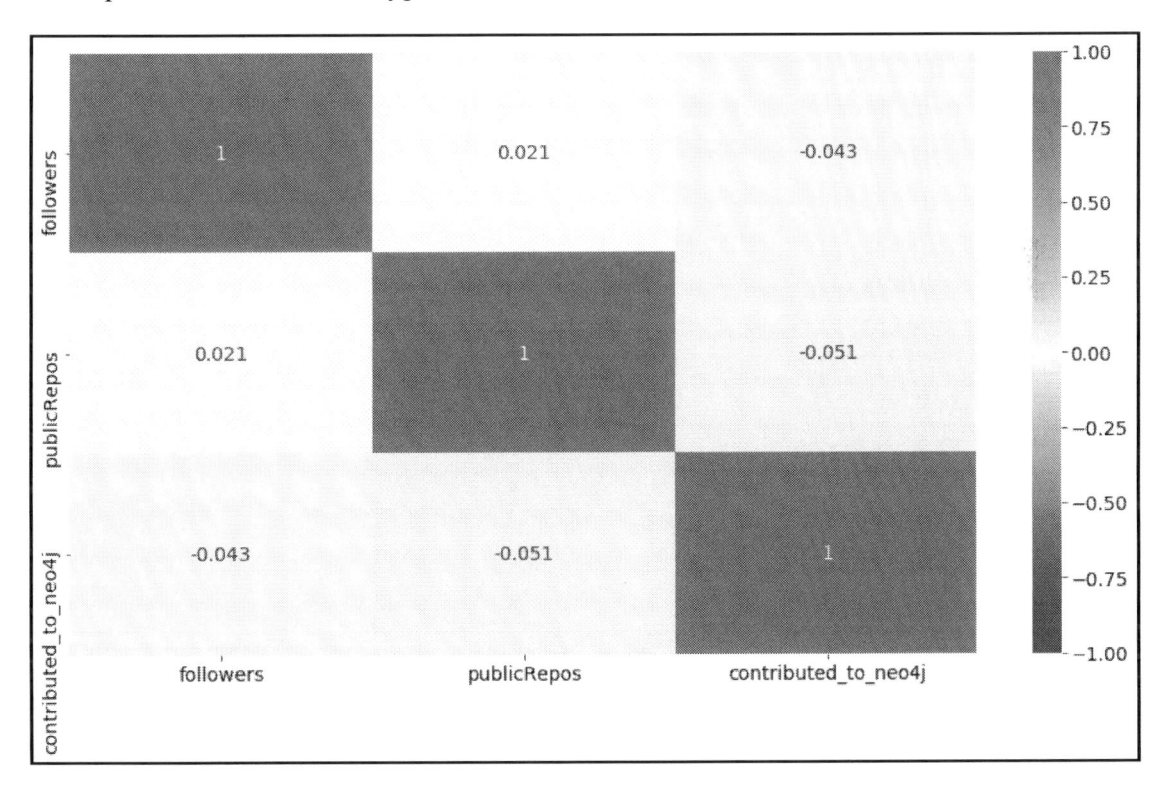

As the preceding matrix suggests, the correlation between our target variable, `contributed_to_neo4j`, and the two remaining features, `publicRepos` and `followers`, is quite low. This is also the case for the two features that weakly correlate to each other (0.021); this tells us that we can keep both of them and proceed to the next step.

Data enrichment

At this point, the main question we must address is *is this data enough to answer the problem?* We might ask, *are there important features missing?* And *can we take into account another dataset to add more information to this data?*

For instance, if your problem is about predicting house prices and your data contains the house address as typed by the user, the address could be written as `5th Avenue`, `Fifth avenue`, or even `Av. 5`. In this case, a step of normalization might be necessary so that all addresses have the same format and common addresses can be identified. In addition, it is likely that the location of the address, written in terms of latitude and longitude, is important in order to compute the distance, for example. This would mean that a geocoding step would be necessary.

At this point, you can also check the open data pages that are relevant to your problem. Consider the following:

- States and countries maintain websites to list all publicly available datasets issued by official government agencies. For instance, you can find all open data from the UK at `https://data.gov.uk/` and US open data at `https://www.data.gov`. You can find a lot of information on these websites, from the number of inhabitants per geographical area to the location of schools or other public services.

- Google provides a service to search for public datasets at `https://datasetsearch.research.google.com/`.

Feature engineering

Feature engineering is the process of creating new input variables for a machine learning algorithm based on the existing "natural" features. After carefully studying the observation characteristics and discussing with the field experts, you may want to create new features. For example, a real estate agent can tell you that, for a given surface area, a house with three bedrooms will cost more than a house with two bedrooms. Does your data already contain a feature that takes into account this information? If not, can you build it from the square footage and the number of bedrooms? These are the kinds of questions that can be answered in this phase of the project.

It is also important to be aware that some algorithms will only perform well on standardized features, meaning the feature distribution must be normal. Before running these algorithms, you need to transform your data so that the distributions match the expected one.

Building the model

Once you have a clear idea of the goal of the project and the data has been collected and cleaned, it is time to start the modeling phase.

Train/test split and cross-validation

When we have a dataset, it is preferred to use all of the observations available to train the model since, typically, more data results in better performances. By doing so, however, we take the risk of falling into a scenario where the model is perfectly able to model the data it has already seen, but will perform very badly with unseen data – this is referred to as the over-fitting scenario.

Take a look at the following plot:

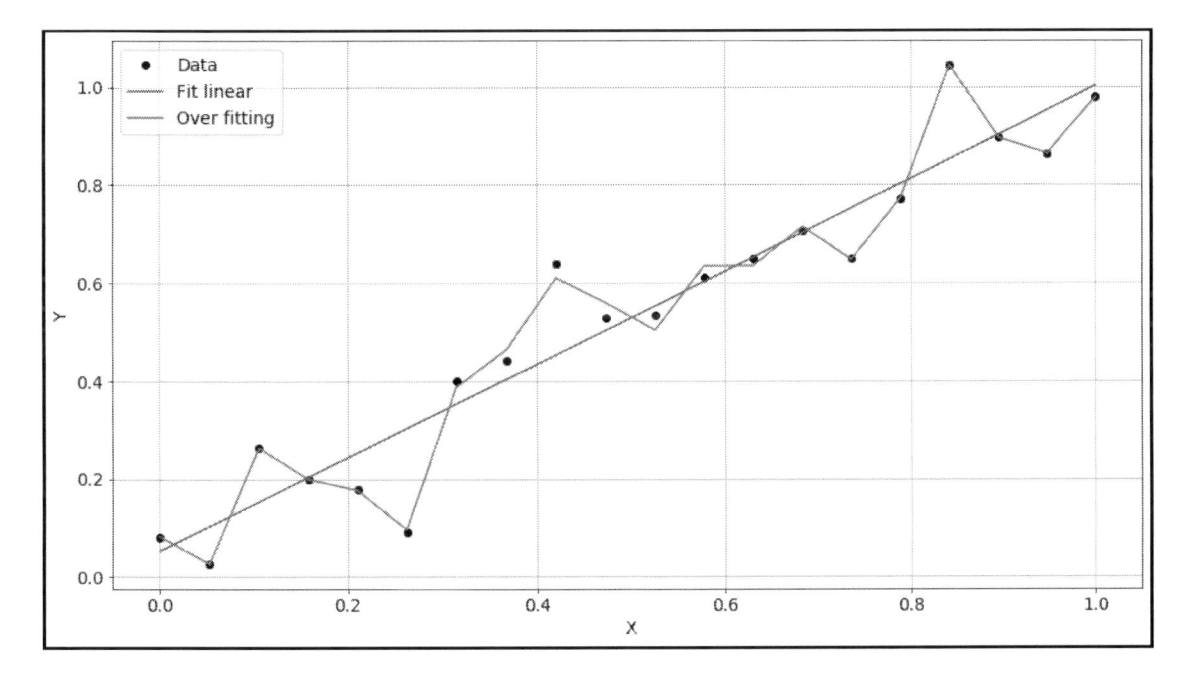

The observations are plotted with black dots and the green line represents the ground truth – that is, the real underlying model. The model whose results are displayed with the red line performs very well at predicting the values for the observed data but it will be poor at describing unseen data. In other words, it is over-fitted on the training set. To avoid this situation, we need to keep some observations apart that the model won't see at all during the training phase. Once the training is done, we will then be able to test the model performances on this test sample. If the model performs poorly on this sample compared to the training phase, it can be an indication of over-fitting.

Creating the train and test samples with scikit-learn

Splitting the data into a training and a testing set is not simple. Both the training and the testing sets have to be *representative* of the full dataset. If your dataset contains apartment sizes ranging from 15 to 200 square meters, it is probably *not* a good idea to use the observations that have an area lower than 50 square meters as the training set and use the rest as the testing set. This would not work because both the train and the test samples must contain areas from the whole range. Randomly splitting the data is often sufficient and results in a good representation of the features in both sets.

However, some situations do require a different approach and we should take these into consideration – for example, when the target variable (or any of the categorical features) is unbalanced, meaning some classes are predominant. In this case, we need to make sure both the train and the test samples respect the same class repartitions and contain all the possible values. This is called **stratification** and can be achieved using the `scikit-learn` tools.

To do so, we first need to create the target variable, y, and the X array containing the features we are interested in. So far, we only have two features: the number of followers and the number of public repositories for a user. We can create these variables with the following:

```
features = ["followers", "publicRepos"]
y = data.contributed_to_neo4j
X = data[features]
```

Both y and X need to be split into a training and a testing sample. This is achieved with the following piece of code:

```
from sklearn.model_selection import train_test_split
X_train, X_test, y_train, y_test = train_test_split(
    X, y, test_size=0.3,
    random_state=123,
    stratify=y
)
```

You can see that the `stratify` parameter makes sure the train and the test sample both respect the proportions of the target variable, `contributed_to_neo4j`.

Training a model

In this chapter, we will use a simple **decision tree classifier**. It can be trained with scikit-learn using the following:

```
from sklearn.tree import DecisionTreeClassifier
clf = DecisionTreeClassifier(random_state=123, min_samples_leaf=10)
clf.fit(X_train, y_train)
```

However, if you run this code on our current dataset, you will receive some errors because a decision tree does not know how to handle `NaN` or missing data, and we have a couple of rows with missing information.

In order to fill these `NaN` values, we will use a `SimpleImputer` model, which will replace the `NaN` values with the mean value of each feature. Following the scikit-learn API, we need to train the transformer on our train sample:

```
from sklearn.impute import SimpleImputer
imp = SimpleImputer(strategy='mean')
imp.fit(X_train)
```

We then need to actually perform the transformation, on both our training and test samples:

```
X_train = imp.transform(X_train)
X_test = imp.transform(X_test)
```

Once the data has been transformed, the decision tree training can be performed. With a trained model, we can make predictions with the following:

```
clf.predict(X)
```

However, before using this model in a production environment, it is time to test the quality of the training by evaluating the model performances using the test sample we reserved especially for this.

Evaluating model performances

Depending on your goal, different metrics can be used to measure the performance of a model. When dealing with regression, a commonly used metric is the **Mean Squared Error** (**MSE**), which quantifies the average distance between the true and predicted values. The lower the MSE, the better the model.

However, in a classification problem, it doesn't make sense to use this metric, especially for multi-class problems.

The first indicator we may want to check when running a classifier is the accuracy, A, which is defined by the number of observations classified correctly, divided by the total *number of observations*.

We can compute the accuracy with `scikit-learn` using the following:

```
from sklearn.metrics import accuracy_score
accuracy_score(y_test, y_pred)
```

Here, `y_pred` was computed for the test sample using our fitted classifier:

```
y_pred = clf.predict(X_test)
```

This function will tell us we have an overall accuracy of 66%, which is not a terrific score for a machine learning model – let's explore the details.

As we discussed earlier, our dataset contains a class imbalance between the two target classes, with around twice the amount of users not having contributed to Neo4j than having contributed to it. It would be interesting to get more precise information about the observations that were classified incorrectly by the decision tree. To do so, let's take a look at the confusion matrix of our classifier:

```
from sklearn.metrics import plot_confusion_matrix
plot_confusion_matrix(
    clf, X_test, y_test,
    cmap=plt.cm.Blues,
    values_format="d"
);
```

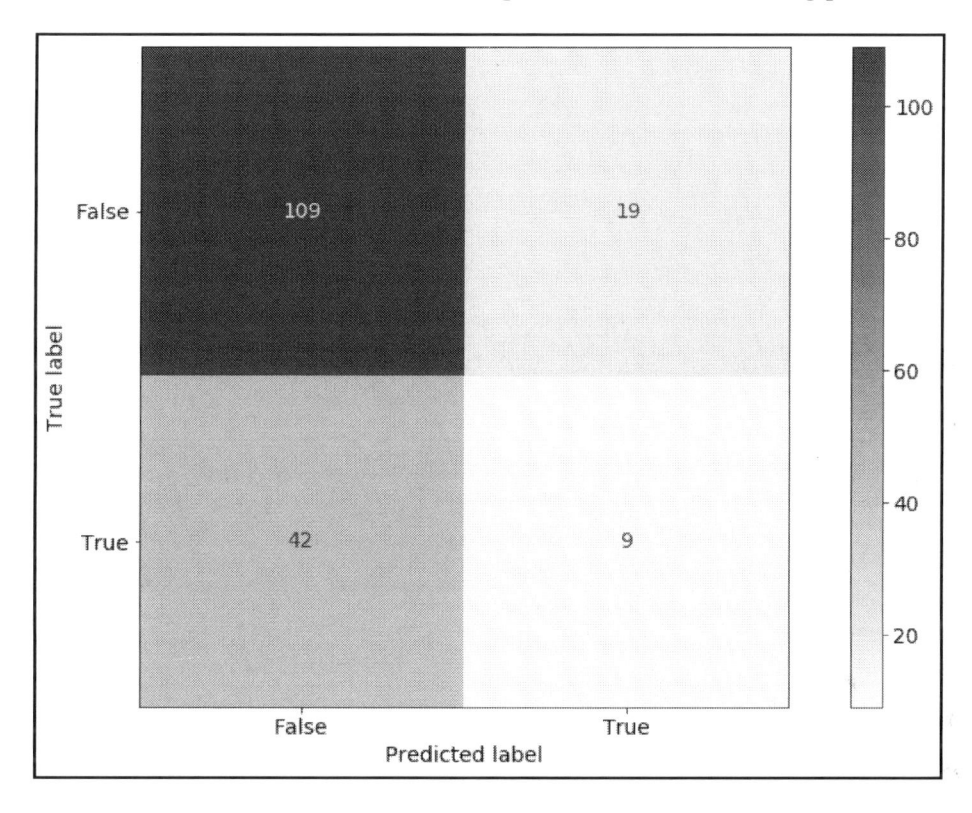

The confusion matrix for our decision tree is reproduced in the following plot:

As you can see, the classification for users not contributing to Neo4j is fairly good. For the True label equal to False (users not contributing to Neo4j), only 19 were wrongly classified into the True category, as the top row indicates. Out of 128 (109 + 19) users with the label False in the test sample, 109 were correctly classified; this means the success rate for this class is 85% (this metric is called **recall**). On the other hand, our model totally fails at identifying users having contributed to Neo4j; only 9 are identified out of 51.

scikit-learn provides another useful function that will display even more precise metrics, called classification_report. It can be used in the following way:

```
from sklearn.metrics import classification_report
print(classification_report(y_test, y_pred))
```

Using Graph-based Features in Machine Learning

A snapshot of this report is reproduced here:

```
              precision    recall  f1-score   support
       False       0.72      0.85      0.78       128
        True       0.32      0.18      0.23        51

    accuracy                           0.66       179
```

We can recognize the accuracy score of 66% we computed earlier and the 85% recall for the `False` label having 128 observations in the test sample.

While the recall is a measure of the model efficiency (how many of the real `True` labels have been predicted as true), the precision is a measure of the *purity* of the results. Measuring the purity addresses the question *out of all the observations labeled* `True` *by the algorithm, how many actually do have a* `True` *label?*

> Given the class distribution, a model classifying everyone as a noncontributor would have an accuracy of
> `number_of_users_not_contributing_to_neo4j` / `number_of_users` = *427 / 596 = 72%*.
>
> So, we can say that our model is even worse than a dummy model – there's a lot of room for improvement!

Now it's time to return to the data collection and/or feature engineering steps. Since this book is about graphs, we will investigate in the next section how graphs can help us achieve better accuracy in our classification tasks.

This section has been a very quick summary of the different steps of a data science project. If you are new to the topic, please refer to the *Further reading* section at the end of this chapter.

The pipeline described in this section is generic, and does not explicitly involve graphs. Without changing the overall strategy, let's now focus on how graphs can be progressively integrated into this process.

The steps toward graph machine learning

Neo4j is primarily a database and can be used as such to fetch data. However, a change of perspective is needed to express the data as a graph, as well as to exploit this graph structure by using graph algorithms and formulating the problem as a graph problem.

Building a (knowledge) graph

When beginning to build a graph out of a dataset, the main question to ask is *what are the relationships that exist in this data?* If we consider the CSV file we studied in the previous section alone, it does not contain a lot of information about relationships since it only has aggregated data, such as the number of followers per user.

To learn more about relationships in the data, we will have to enrich this dataset. This can be done in two ways. Either we can use an external data source as we did in Chapter 3, *Empowering Your Business with Pure Cypher,* or we can transform the way we see our relational data.

Creating relationships from existing data

Data can come from different types of databases. In an ideal scenario (for graph analytics), it will already be stored in a Neo4j graph, but most of the time, you will start from data in a more classical format, such as SQL. In the latter case, you can still create a graph structure and import this data into Neo4j in a simple way.

Creating relationships from relational data

Relationships can be created from existing (relational) data. For example, customers who have purchased the same product or watched the same movie have a form of relationship, even if it is not a real social relationship. With this information, we can find a link between these people. This link can even be weighted, depending on the number of products they have bought.

Let's consider a case where we have the following simplified SQL schema with three tables:

- Users with a column ID
- Products with a column ID
- Orders with `columns user_id` and `product_id`

Using Graph-based Features in Machine Learning

To find relationships between users who have purchased the same products, we could use the following query:

```
SELECT
    u1.id,
    u2.id,
    count(*) as weight
FROM users u1
JOIN users u2 ON u1.id <> u2.id
JOIN orders o1 ON o1.user_id = u1.id
JOIN orders o2 ON o2.user_id = u2.id AND o1.product_id = o2.product_id
```

The result of this query can be saved into a CSV file and then imported into Neo4j using the CSV import facilities (either Cypher `LOAD CSV` or the Neo4j import tool).

Creating relationships from Neo4j

The same data can also already be stored in a Neo4j graph, in cases where some relationships between observations already exist. However, we are interested in user interactions and, unless your website has a social component that would allow users to *follow* each other, for instance, we will have to create links between users in a different way.

Let's assume your graph contains information about users and products. The simplified graph schema could look like this:

```
(u:User)-[:BOUGHT]->(p:Product)
```

Creating a relationship between users having bought the same product(s) is then as simple as a single Cypher query:

```
MATCH (u1:User)-[:BOUGHT]->(p:Product)<-[:BOUGHT]-(u2:User)
WITH u1, u2, count(p) as weight
CREATE (u1)-[:LINKED_TO {weight: weight}]->(u2)
```

Your graph now contains an additional relationship type, `LINKED_TO`, which contains some kind of virtual interaction between users and can help you to extract more relevant information.

> **TIP**
> Here, we have created the relationship in the Neo4j graph, but this is not always necessary, especially in the prototyping phase. With the GDS library, we can create a projected graph using Cypher queries so that the projected graph contains the needed relationships without polluting the initial Neo4j database.

[320]

Using an external data source

In Chapter 2, *The Cypher Query Language,* and Chapter 3, *Empowering Your Business with Pure Cypher,* we studied ways to enrich a knowledge graph from different data sources, such as external APIs (GitHub) or Wikidata, in order to add more context to the data.

We are going to utilize that knowledge in this chapter. Thanks to the GitHub API, we can retrieve the list of followers for each user. This exercise was performed in Chapter 2, *The Cypher Query Language,* and won't be repeated here. The result is available in the data_ch8.edgelist file, which we are going to import into Neo4j now.

Importing the data into Neo4j

In order to import this data into Neo4j and create a graph, we first have to import the user's data (the nodes) and then create the relationships between them from the edgelist file. After copying both files into the import folder of your Neo4j graph, you can use the following two queries to import the data:

1. Run the following to import nodes:

    ```
    LOAD CSV WITH HEADERS FROM "file:///data_ch8.csv" AS row
    CREATE (u:User) SET u=row
    ```

2. Run the following to import the relationships:

    ```
    LOAD CSV FROM "file:///data_ch8.edgelist" AS row
    FIELDTERMINATOR " "
    MATCH (u:User {user_id: row[0]})
    MATCH (v:User {user_id: row[1]})
    CREATE (u)-[:FOLLOWS]->(v)
    ```

Once the data is imported into Neo4j, as we did with the CSV file in the previous section, we are going to characterize this data.

Graph characterization

As we have done before with our tabular data, we will now take the time to collect some generic information about our graph data in order to understand it better.

The number of nodes and edges

We can count the number of nodes with the `User` label with a simple Cypher query:

```
MATCH (u:User) RETURN count(u)
```

However, if your graph is more complex and contains multiple node labels and relationship types, it would be more efficient to use an APOC procedure:

```
CALL apoc.meta.stats()
```

The result you will get will be something like this:

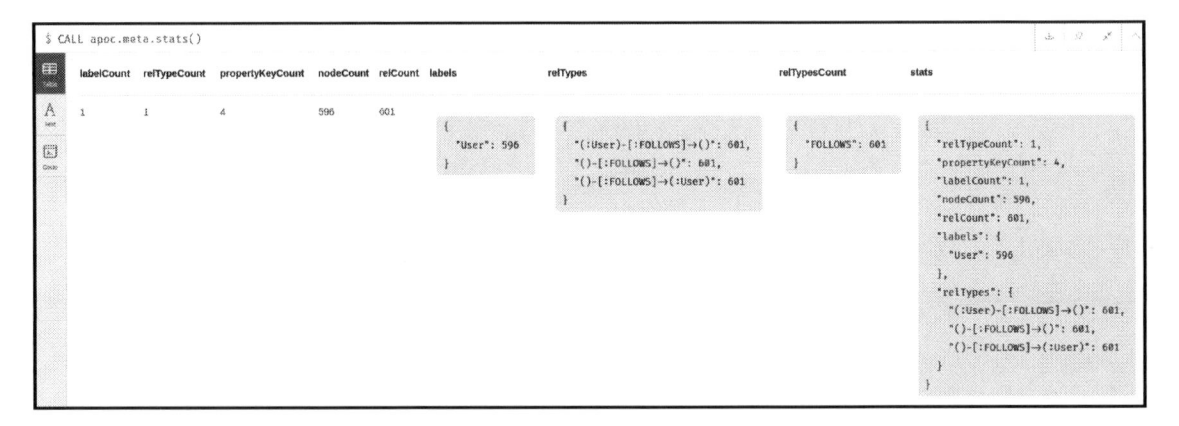

The sixth column contains the number of nodes for each label, while the eighth column shows the number of relationships per type.

Another interesting procedure from the same plugin is as follows:

```
CALL apoc.meta.data()
```

The result of this procedure for our graph is reproduced in the following screenshot:

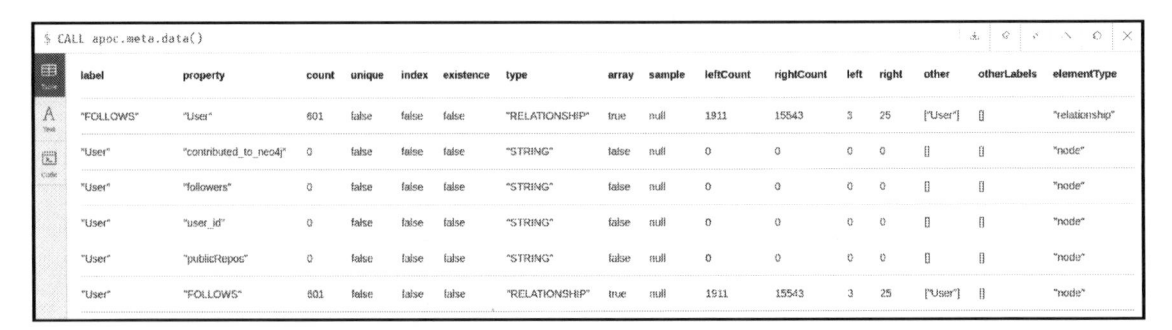

[322]

You can see that we have, in the preceding screenshot, a list of properties for each node label. In our graph, the nodes with the User label have four properties (contributed_to_neo4j, followers, user_id, and publicRepos).

With these functions, we can get an idea of the volume of data. To get a more precise idea about the graph structure, we will have to rely on graph algorithms, such as the **Weakly Connected Component** (WCC) community-detection algorithm we studied in the previous chapter (Chapter 7, *Community Detection and Similarity Measures*).

The number of components

In order to learn about the graph structure, a first common step is to identify graph components, or independent sub-graphs. To do so, we are going to use the WCC algorithm from the GDS.

In this example, we will use an anonymous projected graph:

```
CALL gds.wcc.write({
  nodeProjection: "User",
  relationshipProjection: {
  FOLLOWS: {
  type: "FOLLOWS",
  orientation: "UNDIRECTED",
  aggregation: "SINGLE"
  }
  },
  writeProperty: "wcc"
})
```

This procedure does all of the following:

- Runs the WCC algorithm.
- Writes the results back to the graph by adding a property called wcc to each node.
- Uses all nodes with the User label and all relationships with the FOLLOWS type, ignoring the relationship direction and taking into account one single edge between two identical nodes – if A follows B and B follows A and the graph is undirected, we would have two edges between A and B, adding the aggregation. The SINGLE parameter forces the GDS to use only one of them.

Let's analyze the results of this algorithm. The following query will return the components with the highest number of nodes:

```
MATCH (u:User)
    RETURN u.wcc, count(u) as c
    ORDER BY c DESC
    LIMIT 5
```

The first rows of the result are reproduced as follows:

"u.wcc"	"c"
1	438
30	31
470	1
471	1
0	1

> The value of the `wcc` property may differ on your local installation – it depends on the GDS internal behavior. However, the number of components and the nodes belonging to them should be identical.

As you can see, the graph is made up of one big component containing 438 nodes out of 596. It also contains another smaller component, made of 31 nodes. All the other users (127) are not connected to any other users as far as we know.

To get a deeper understanding of the graph structure, we can try and identify finer communities using, for instance, the Louvain algorithm. The result of this algorithm is represented in the following figure, using `neoviz.js`, as discussed in the previous chapter:

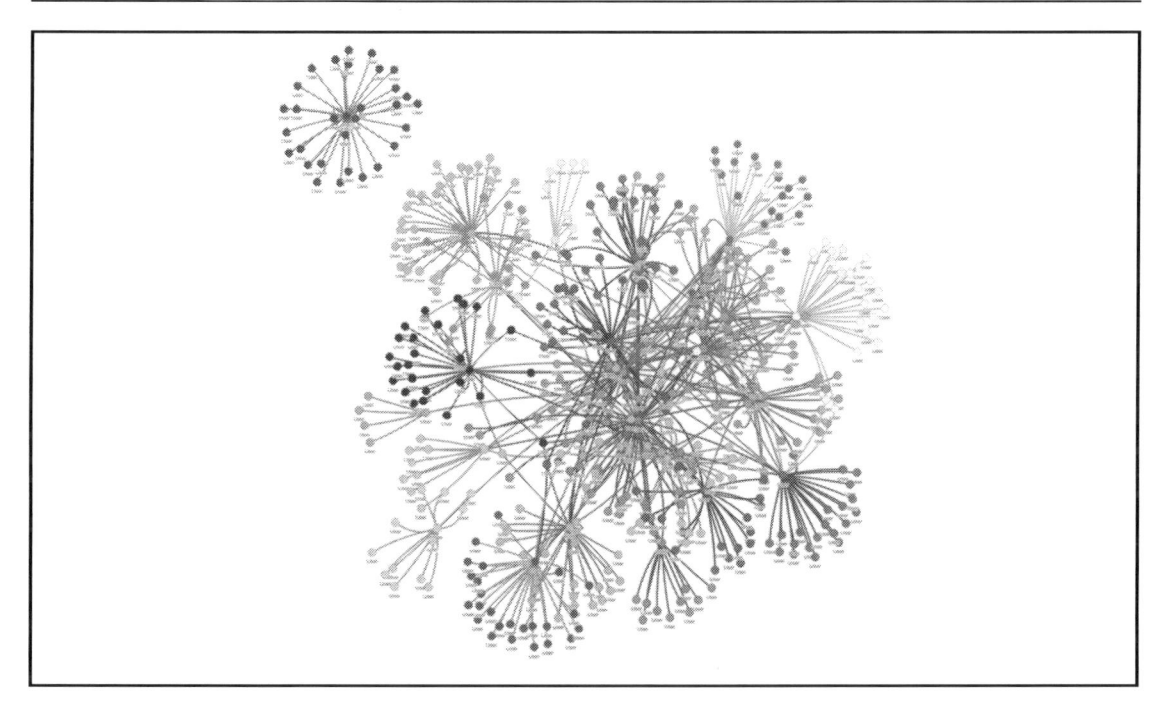

Community structure of our graph, ignoring components with less than 30 nodes

Extracting graph-based features

Now that we have imported our data into Neo4j and we have a better idea of the graph structure, we can start thinking about the type of graph-based features we can create to improve our classification model. In this section, we are going to create them through the browser. We will then study how this step can be automated using the Neo4j Python driver.

As the previous figure shows, it seems the graph has a clear community structure and it makes sense to assume that users contributing to the same repositories are more connected to each other. It follows that using the result of a community-detection algorithm as a feature for our classifier may improve the classification performances.

Another piece of information that can be extracted from the graph is the node importance. Since our graph of users is very Neo4j-centric, it would be a weak hypothesis to consider that the Neo4j contributors are the most important nodes in terms of PageRank, for instance.

So, in the following, we are going to run and save the results of two algorithms:

- PageRank for the centrality score
- Louvain for narrower community detection

In order to use algorithms from the GDS in production, these three steps are recommended:

1. **Define and create the projected graph**: The projected graph only contains a subset of nodes, relationships, and properties from the full Neo4j graph and it is optimized for graph algorithms.
2. **Run one or several algorithms on this projected graph**.
3. **Remove the projected graph**: The projected graph is saved into your computer's live memory, so it is good practice to delete the projected graph once you are done with it.

If you have read the preceding chapters, you should already be familiar with these steps. However, we will now review them one more time in the next section before checking how these new features can improve our classification model.

Using graph-based features with pandas and scikit-learn

In the previous section, we created a graph model connecting our users. We have also run some graph algorithms to understand the graph structure. We are now going to take full advantage of the GDS to extract graph-based features.

Extracting graph-based features from Neo4j Browser

In a prototyping phase, it is always good to be able to run single queries manually and extract the data from there. In the following subsections, we are going to review how to run graph algorithms from the GDS in Neo4j Browser and how to extract the data into a format usable by our data science tools – namely, CSV.

Creating the projected graph

We could create a named projected graph using the same parameters as in the previous section:

```
nodeProjection: "User",
relationshipProjection: {
FOLLOWS: {
type: "FOLLOWS",
orientation: "UNDIRECTED",
aggregation: "SINGLE"
}
}
```

However, we know that our graph contains several disconnected components and that running the PageRank algorithm on such a graph may lead to surprising results. In order to avoid that, we will run our two algorithms only on the biggest component identified with the WCC algorithm. This selection has to be achieved through a Cypher query. After you have identified the value of the `wcc` property for the community with the highest number of users, you can use the following:

```
CALL gds.graph.create.cypher(
    "graph",
    "MATCH (u:User) WHERE u.wcc = 1 AND v.wcc = 1 RETURN id(u) as id",
    "MATCH (u:User)-[:FOLLOWS]-(v:User) RETURN id(u) as source, id(v) as target"
)
```

Running one or several algorithms

Once the projected graph is created, we can run the PageRank algorithm using the following:

```
CALL gds.pageRank.write("graph", {writeProperty: "pr"})
```

We can also use the Louvain algorithm:

```
CALL gds.louvain.write("graph", {writeProperty: "lv"})
```

The results for the Louvain algorithm were shown in the figures at the end of the last section. We will analyze the results of the PageRank algorithm in the following sections.

Dropping the projected graph

Once the algorithms are done and the feature is written into the Neo4j graph, the projected graph is not needed anymore and can be deleted:

```
CALL gds.graph.drop("graph")
```

This will free up the required memory on your laptop/server.

Extracting the data

Our nodes now have three more properties – wcc, pr, and lv – which we want to extract on top of the pre-existing properties. We can do so with the following Cypher code:

```
MATCH (u:User)
RETURN
u.contributed_to_neo4j as contributed_to_neo4j,
u.followers as followers,
u.publicRepos as publicRepos,
u.wcc as wcc,
u.pr as pr,
u.lv as lv
```

The result of this query can be downloaded as CSV directly from the browser.

This is useful when trying to build a model; however, this is not viable in a production environment. That's why the following section is dedicated to the automation of these steps, using the Neo4j Python driver.

Automating graph-based feature creation with the Neo4j Python driver

Using Cypher to create our features is good for testing, but once we are in the production phase, it is not manageable to manually perform such operations. Fortunately, Neo4j officially provides drivers for several languages, including Java, .NET, and Go. In this book, we use Python, so we will learn about the Python driver in the following section.

Discovering the Neo4j Python driver

Python is officially supported by Neo4j, who provides a driver to connect to a Neo4j graph from Python at `https://github.com/neo4j/neo4j-python-driver`.

It can be installed through the `pip` Python package manager:

```
pip install neo4j
# or
conda install -c conda-forge neo4j
```

> The code for this section is available in a Jupyter notebook: `Neo4j_Python_Driver.ipynb`.

In order to use this database, the first step is the connection definition, which requires the active graph URI and the authentication parameters. `bolt` is a client-server communication protocol designed by Neo4j. The port used by the `bolt` protocol for your active database can be found in the **Management** area of your graph in Neo4j Desktop, in the **Details** tab:

```
from neo4j import GraphDatabase
driver = GraphDatabase.driver("bolt://localhost:7687", auth=("neo4j", "<YOUR_PASSWORD>"))
```

> In the case of misconfiguration, you will get the following:
> - A `ServiceUnavailable` error if the database is not reachable at the given URI
> - `AuthError` if the provided authentication credentials are not valid

With the driver created, we can now start sending Cypher queries and analyzing the results.

Basic usage

Once the connection is created, we need to create a session object from this connection. This can be achieved in a simple way:

```
session = driver.session()
```

All the created sessions need to be closed after we are done with them. This can be done by calling `session.close()` after our code, but we are going to use a more *Pythonic* method using the context manager and the `with` statement:

```
with driver.session() as session:
    # code using the session object goes here
    pass
```

Using this syntax, the session will be automatically closed when exiting the `with` block, and trying to use the `session` object out of this block will raise an exception.

Let's now actually use the session to send some Cypher queries to the graph and get the result back. The simplest way to do this is to use auto-commit transactions:

```
result = session.run("MATCH (n:Node) RETURN n")
```

To get a record from the result, several methods are possible. In order to take a look at an example, we can use the `.peek()` method:

```
record = result.peek()
```

From a record, we can then get each of the values returned by our Cypher query. In our case, we returned a single value called `n`:

```
node = record.get("n")
```

`node` is an instance of the `Node` class. In order to access its attributes, we can use the `get` method again:

```
node.get("user_id")
```

In order to get all the records of a result, we can loop over them:

```
for record in result.records():
    print(record.get("n").get("user_id"))
```

> The results can be consumed only once, meaning if you try to loop twice over the same result set, the second loop will find no elements in the result (Python generator behavior).

Transactions

Neo4j also supports transactions, meaning blocks of operations that will only alter the graph if all of them succeed.

Imagine the following situation, where you have to execute two statements:

```
with driver.session() as session:
  session.run(statement_1)
  session.run(statement_2)
```

If everything goes well, no problem. But what if the execution of `statement_2` fails? In some cases, you would end up with inconsistent data in your graph, which is something you need to avoid. Say you are saving a new order from an existing customer. `statement_1` creates the new `Order` node, while `statement_2` creates the relationship between the `Customer` node and the `Order` node. If the execution of `statement_2` fails, you will end up with an `Order` node, which you will not be able to link to any `Customer` node. In order to avoid these frustrating cases, we can use transactions instead. In a transaction, if `statement_2` fails, then the whole transaction block, including `statement_1`, will not be persisted in the graph. This ensures that the data is always consistent. It also makes it easier to retry a failed transaction, in case of connection loss due to network error, for instance, without having to worry about which operations were successfully performed – you would just need to restart all of them.

Creating a transaction with the Neo4j Python driver is quite simple:

```
with driver.session() as session:
  # start a new transaction
  tx = session.begin_transaction()
  # run cypher...
  tx.run(statement_1)
  tx.run(statement_2)
  # push changes to the graph
  tx.commit()
```

With this syntax, if `statement_1` is correct but `statement_2` fails, both `statement_1` and `statement_2` won't be persisted in the graph.

Now that we know more about the Python driver for Neo4j, let's return to our initial task – programmatically adding graph-based features in our pipeline.

Automating graph-based feature creation with Python

The code for this section is available in the `Python_GDS.ipynb` Jupyter notebook.

Creating the projected graph

Remember that we can create named projected graphs using both native and Cypher projections. Here, we will focus only on the native projections. A very simple projection can be written as follows:

```
CALL gds.graph.create("my_simple_projected_graph", "User", "FOLLOWS")
```

`my_simple_projected_graph` contains all the nodes with the `User` label and all the relationships with the `FOLLOWS` type, without modifications being made to the Neo4j graph (in particular, the relationship direction is preserved). But remember that such a projected graph does not contain any nodes or relationship properties. To include them in the projected graph, we will have to use a more complex format to define the projected graph, as follows:

```
CALL gds.graph.create(
  "my_complex_projected_graph",
  // node projection:
  {
  User: {
  label: "User",
  properties: [
  ]
  }
  },
  // relationship projection
  {
  FOLLOWS: {
  type: "FOLLOWS",
  orientation: "UNDIRECTED",
  aggregation: "SINGLE",
  properties: [
  ]
  }
  }
)
```

Even the more complex example has the advantage of using key-value and list structures to define the projections, which can be reproduced in Python with lists and dictionaries. The node projection defined in the preceding code block can be expressed in Python as follows:

```
nodeProj = {
  "User": {
  "label": "User",
  "properties": [],
  }
  }
```

The relationship projection will be defined by the following dictionary:

```
relProj = {
 "FOLLOWS": {
 "type": "LINKED_TO",
 "orientation": "FOLLOWS",
 "aggregation": "SINGLE",
 }
 }
```

In order to use these variables in a Cypher query, we are going to use parameters. Three parameters will be necessary:

- The graph name (string)
- The node projection definition (`dict`)
- The relationship projection definition (`dict`)

Our Cypher query can then be written like this:

```
cypher = "CALL gds.graph.create($graphName, $nodeProj, $relProj)"
```

In order to execute this query with the parameters defined in the preceding code, we need to run the following:

```
with driver.session() as session:
  result = session.run(
  cypher,
  graphName="my_complex_projected_graph",
  nodeProj=nodeProj,
  relProj=relProj
  )
```

After this code is executed, checking the result of `result.data()`, we can see the same information as what is displayed in the Neo4j browser, which is evidence that the query was successfully executed:

```
[{'graphName': 'my_complex_projected_graph', 'nodeProjection': {'User':
{'properties': {}, 'label': 'Node'}}, 'relationshipProjection': {'FOLLOWS':
{'orientation': 'UNDIRECTED', 'aggregation': 'SINGLE', 'type': 'FOLLOWS',
'properties': {}}},
 'nodeCount': 596,
 'relationshipCount': 1192,
 'createMillis': 8}]
```

Now that our projected graph is created, try to run an algorithm from the GDS.

Calling the GDS procedures

We are going to use the PageRank procedure as an example, which assigns an importance score to each node based on the importance of its neighbors. For further explanation about the PageRank algorithm, refer to Chapter 5, *Node Importance*.

The signature of the PageRank procedure in the GDS is as follows:

```
gds.pageRank.stream(<graphName>, <algoConfiguratioMap>)
```

So, let's first define the configuration map. If we want to use a damping factor different from the default value of 0.85, we need to specify it in this way:

```
algoConfig = {
  "dampingFactor": 0.8,
}
```

Similar to the graph creation query, we will build a query with parameters:

```
"CALL gds.pageRank.stream($graphName, $algoConfig)"
```

It can be executed in the following way:

```
with driver.session() as session:
  result = session.run(
  "CALL gds.pageRank.stream($graphName, $algoConfig)",
  graphName=graphName,
  algoConfig=algoConfig,
  )
```

We can check the results with a loop on the `result` object:

```
for record in result:
    print(record.data())
```

The printed results will look like this:

```
{'nodeId': 0, 'score': 0.15}
{'nodeId': 1, 'score': 1.21}
{'nodeId': 2, 'score': 0.94}
{'nodeId': 3, 'score': 0.40}
{'nodeId': 4, 'score': 0.65}
```

To get more meaningful results, we can get the node from `nodeId` returned by the GDS procedures, using the `gds.util.asNode` helper procedure. The Cypher query is slightly more complex, but the exact same Python code can be used to get results from it:

```
with driver.session() as session:
  result = session.run(
  """CALL gds.pageRank.stream($graphName, $algoConfig)
  YIELD nodeId, score
  RETURN gds.util.asNode(nodeId) as node, score
  """,
  graphName=graphName,
  algoConfig=algoConfig,
  )

  for record in result:
    print(record.get("node").get("user_id"), record.get("score"))
```

Thanks to the Neo4j Python driver, we are now able to create named projected graphs and call GDS procedures such as PageRank.

Writing results back to the graph

When writing the result back to the graph, we will have to use the `.write` procedure instead of `.stream`. In addition, an extra mandatory parameter is required – the name of the property that will be added to each node and hold the result of the algorithm (here, that is the PageRank score). This property is configured through the `writeProperty` configuration, so let's add it to our `algoConfig` dictionary:

```
algoConfig["writeProperty"] = "pr"
```

We can then use the same code to run this procedure, replacing `gds.pageRank.stream` with `gds.pageRank.write`:

```
with driver.session() as session:
  result = session.run(
  "CALL gds.pageRank.write($graphName, $algoConfig)",
  graphName=graphName,
  algoConfig=algoConfig,
  )
```

Using Graph-based Features in Machine Learning

If we check the content of the result this time, it only contains some statistics about the algorithm execution:

```
>>> result.single().data()

{'nodePropertiesWritten': 596,
'createMillis': 0,
'computeMillis': 132,
'writeMillis': 6,
'ranIterations': 20,
'didConverge': False,
'configuration': {'maxIterations': 20,
'writeConcurrency': 4,
'sourceNodes': [],
'writeProperty': 'pr',
'relationshipWeightProperty': None,
'dampingFactor': 0.85,
'relationshipTypes': ['*'],
'cacheWeights': False,
'tolerance': 1e-07,
'concurrency': 4}}
```

To see the results of the PageRank scoring, we will have to run another Cypher query. For example, we can get the node with the highest PageRank score with the following query:

```
MATCH (n:User)
RETURN n.user_id, n.pr
ORDER BY n.pr DESC
LIMIT 1
```

We can also check that, as expected, the users contributing to Neo4j have a higher PageRank. This is illustrated in the following figure, where the yellow nodes represent users contributing to Neo4j and have a PageRank score of around 10, while the green nodes are the other users and have a PageRank score that is below 1:

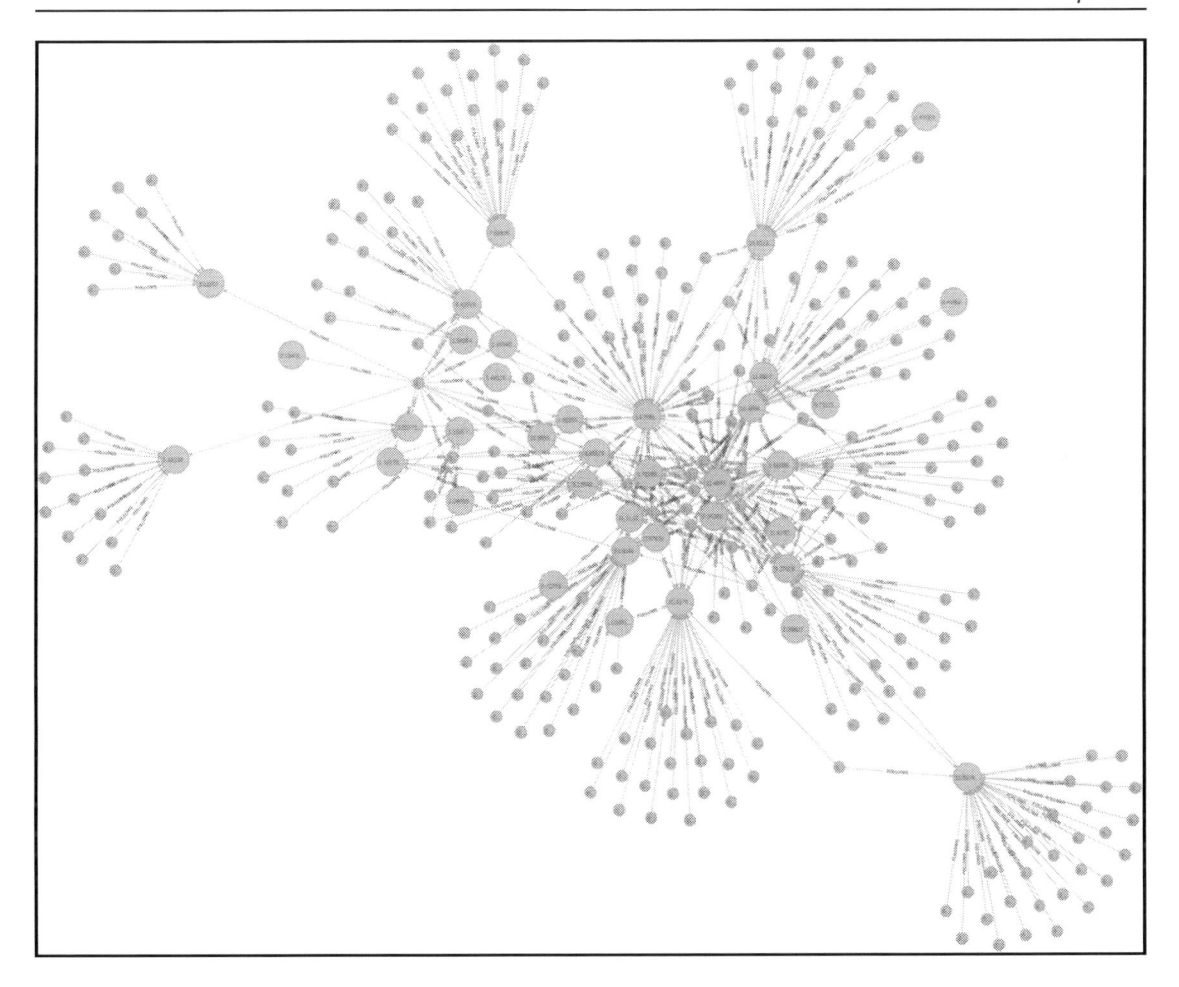

To create this image from Neo4j Browser, you can add a specific label to the nodes having `contributed_to_neo4j=true`, and change the size and color for this new node label in the graph rendering cell:

```
MATCH (u:User {contributed_to_neo4j: true})
  SET u:Contributor
```

We will see, in the *Exporting the data from Neo4j to pandas* section, how this result can be used to feed a `pandas` DataFrame for further analysis.

Before we get to that, however, let's talk about the important step of dropping the projected graph.

Dropping the projected graph

Named projected graphs are stored in memory and can be quite big, with lots of nodes, relationships, and properties. It is, therefore, important to delete them once all our operations have been performed.

This can be achieved with the following code, which should now be familiar to you:

```
with driver.session() as session:
    result = session.run(
    "CALL gds.graph.drop($graphName)",
    graphName=graphName,
    )
```

> **TIP**: `result.data()` contains the necessary information to recreate the projected graph when needed.

Getting back to our data analysis pipeline, we are now able to add graph-based features to our graph directly from Python. In the next section, we are going to continue in this direction and learn how to create a `pandas` DataFrame by reading data from Neo4j.

Exporting the data from Neo4j to pandas

`pandas` supports several data types, from CSV to JSON to HTML. Here, we will use the export capabilities of Neo4j in CSV files.

We learned, in a previous section, how to run a Cypher query from Python and get the results. The most interesting function for us now is the `result.data()` function, which returns a list of records, where each record is a dictionary. It is interesting because `pandas` does have a simple method to create a DataFrame from this structure – using the `pd.DataFrame.from_records` function.

First, let's check an example and define a list of records, as follows:

```
list_of_records = [
    {"a": 1, "b": 11},
    {"a": 2, "b": 22},
    {"a": 3, "b": 33},
]
```

Creating a DataFrame from this list is as simple as the following:

`pd.DataFrame.from_records(list_of_records)`

It creates a DataFrame with two columns, named a and b, and three rows indexed from 0 to 2:

```
  a b
0 1 11
1 2 22
2 3 33
```

Each row corresponds to a node or an observation, and each column to a characteristic or feature.

The same method can be used to create a DataFrame from the result of a Cypher query executed via the Neo4j Python driver using the following piece of code:

```
with driver.session() as session:
    result = session.run("MATCH (n:Node) RETURN n.name as name, n.pr as pr")
    record_data = result.data()
    data = pd.DataFrame.from_records(record_data)
```

In this case, `data` has two columns, `name` and `pr`, and a number of rows equal to the number of nodes with the `Node` label in our graph.

Using Graph-based Features in Machine Learning

We can then again perform the different steps of our data analysis pipeline. For example, the pair plot showing the distribution of each feature per class is reproduced in the following figure:

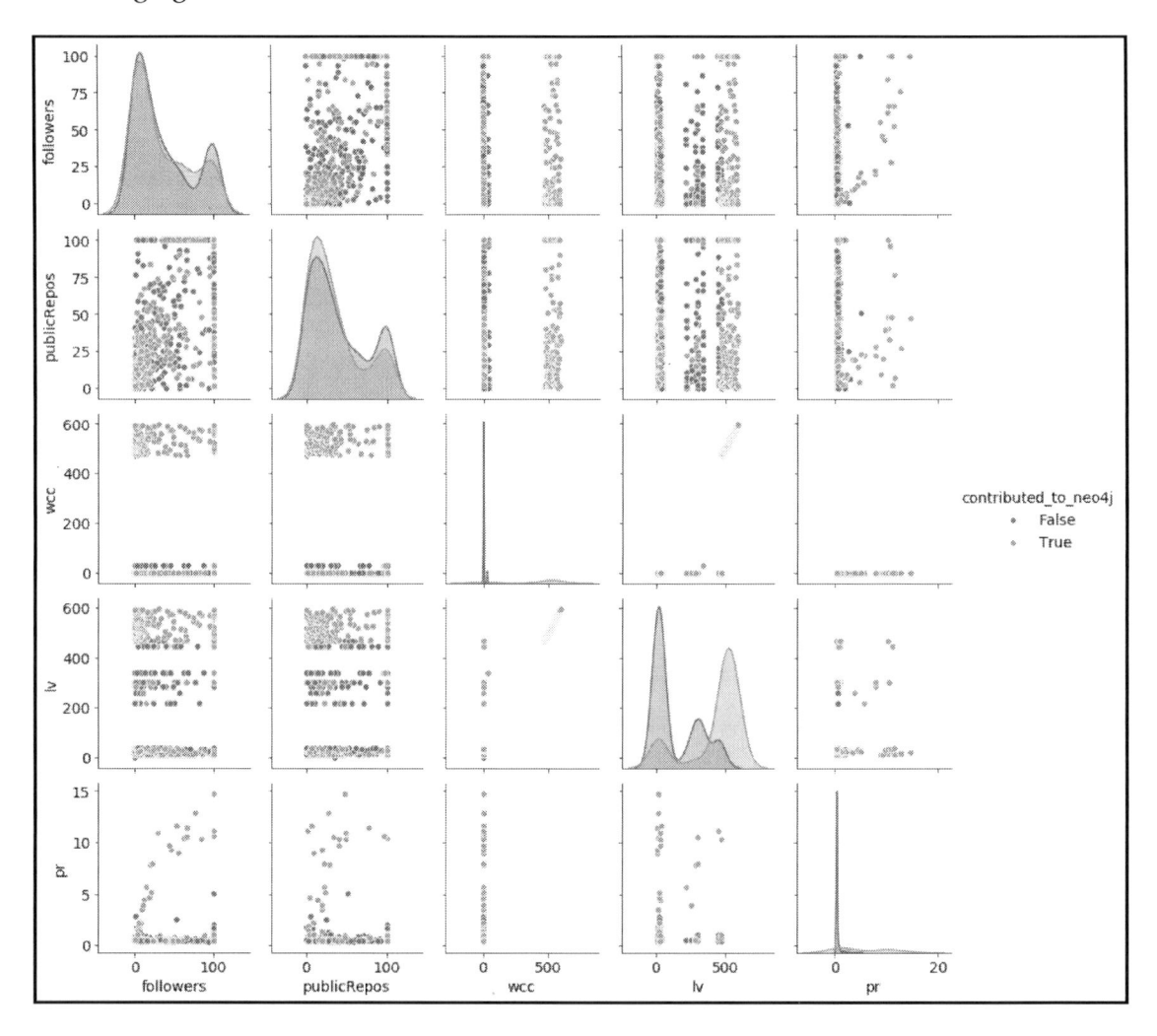

As you can see, the newly introduced variables, `wcc`, `lv` (for the Louvain community), and `pr` (the PageRank score), have very different shapes depending on the target class. This will very likely make the classifier results much more accurate.

Training a scikit-learn model

Finally, let's bring together what we have learned and try to run a classifier on this last dataset.

The code for this section is available in the `Data_Analysis_Graph.ipynb` Jupyter notebook.

Introducing community features

Community features, either `wcc` or `lv`, are categorical features. Let's imagine that node A belongs to community 1, node B to community 2, and node C to community 35. We cannot assume that nodes A and B are more similar than nodes A and C because their community number is closer. We just know that nodes A and B do not belong to the same community, exactly like A and C or B and C.

One way of handling categorical features in machine learning is to transform them through a one-hot encoder. Its role is to transform a vector feature with *N* categories into *N* vectors, having values of either 0 or 1:

```
[ [
1,   [1 0 0]
2,   [0 1 0]
3,   [0 0 1]
1, = [1 0 0]
1,   [1 0 0]
3    [0 0 1]
] ]
```

However, since our `wcc` feature contains 129 unique values, this would add 129 features to our model. This is too many, especially considering that we only have a few hundred observations! To avoid trouble with dimensionality, we will only consider communities with at least two observations to start with, but this number can be adapted later on. To create a list of values in the `wcc` vector that will be used to create one-hot encoded features, we can use the following code:

```
wcc_community_distribution =
data.wcc.value_counts().sort_values(ascending=False)
 wcc_keep = sorted(wcc_community_distribution [ wcc_community_distribution
> 1].index)
```

We can then build the pipeline:

```
from sklearn.impute import SimpleImputer
from sklearn.preprocessing import OneHotEncoder
from sklearn.tree import DecisionTreeClassifier
from sklearn.pipeline import make_pipeline
from sklearn.compose import make_column_transformer

pipeline = make_pipeline(
make_column_transformer(
(OneHotEncoder(categories=[wcc_keep], handle_unknown="ignore"), ["wcc",]),
(SimpleImputer(strategy="mean"), ["publicRepos", "followers"]),
# remainder='passthrough'
),
DecisionTreeClassifier(random_state=123, min_samples_leaf=10)
)
```

The pipeline contains two steps:

1. The data transformation:
    1. `OneHotEncoder` for the `wcc` feature, using only `wcc_keep` categories
    2. `SimpleImputer` to remove `NaN` numbers from the `publicRepos` and `followers` features
2. The classifier itself, `DecisionTreeClassifier`

The pipeline can be used as a normal `scikit-learn` model to fit the transformers and the model in one pass:

```
pipeline.fit(X_train, y_train)
```

Then, predictions are carried out by transforming the data using the fitted transformers, and calling the `predict` method of the model again in one pass:

```
y_pred = pipeline.predict(X_test)
```

The confusion matrix we obtain with this new model, by adding the community information, is represented here:

```
array([[128, 0], [ 22, 29]])
```

Unlike in the initial model, the users with no contributions to Neo4j are all properly classified (128) and out of the 51 users that have contributed to Neo4j, 29 are correctly identified (against 9 in our first model, which didn't use graph-based features).

Let's see whether we can improve this model even more with the following:

- Finer community information with the Louvain algorithm
- Node importance data – thanks to the PageRank algorithm

Using both community and centrality features

Following the exact same steps as in the previous section, using the most crowded Louvain communities and the PageRank score, we end up with the following final results for the decision tree classifier:

```
precision recall f1-score support False 0.91 0.99 0.95 128 True 0.97 0.75
0.84 51 accuracy 0.92 179 macro avg 0.94 0.87 0.90 179 weighted avg 0.93
0.92 0.92 179
```

The confusion matrix is reproduced here:

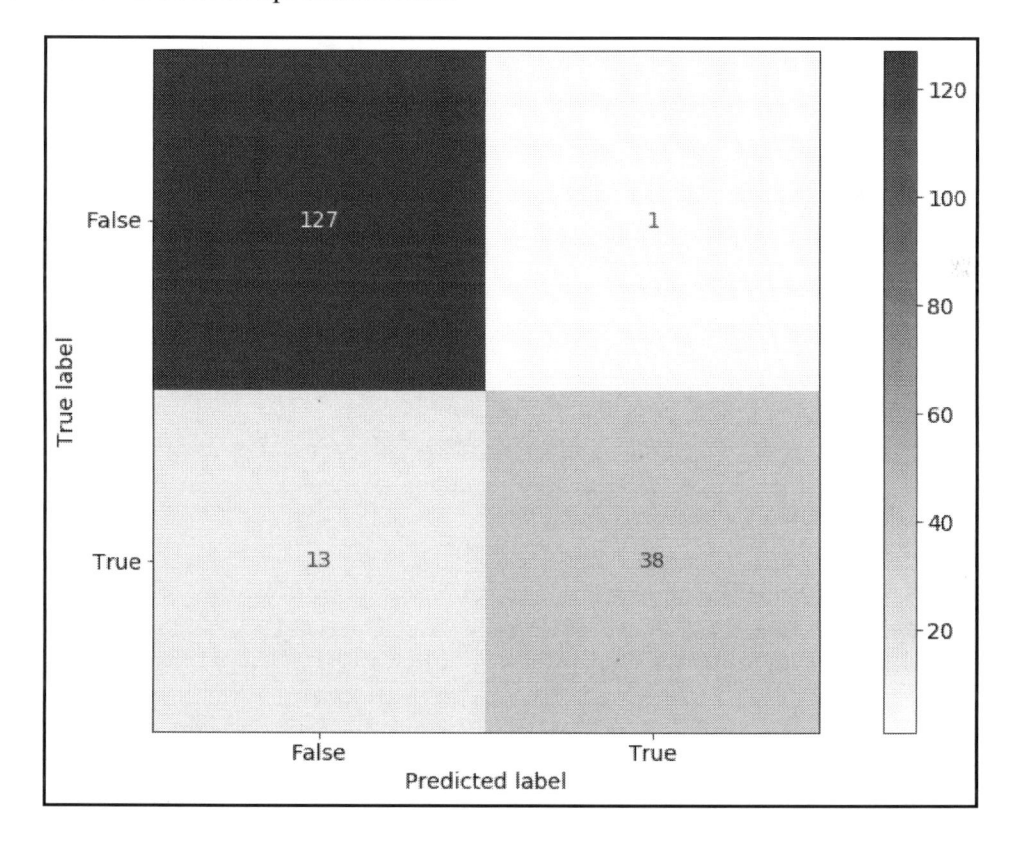

Our overall accuracy has jumped from 66% to 92%. Even more importantly, the algorithm is now able to correctly identify 38 users as having contributed to Neo4j, compared to only 9 with the non-graph features and 29 when using only the WCC information.

A feature importance study shows us that the most impactful feature in this model is the PageRank score, as shown in the following bar chart:

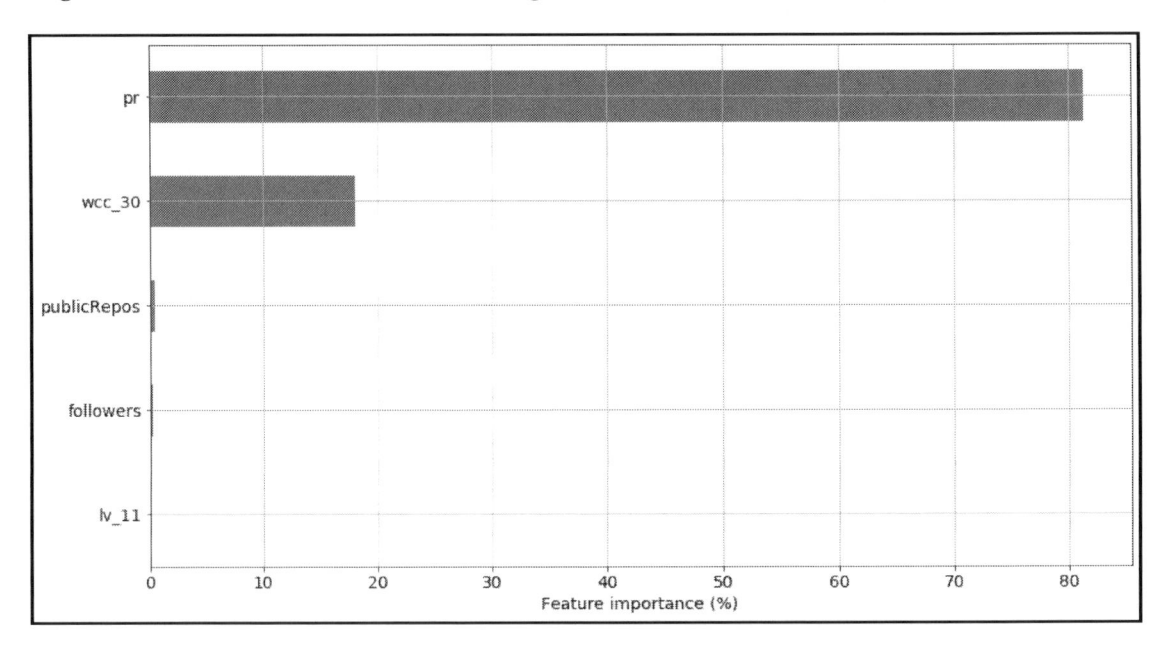

This means that our assumption about Neo4j contributors forming communities is not really reproduced by our graph. However, these users are clearly the most important in terms of connections and PageRank.

Summary

This chapter gave an overview of classical data science pipelines and how to integrate graph data into them. Thanks to the Neo4j Python driver, you are now able to import Neo4j data into a `pandas` DataFrame, which can then be used as usual in any other applications, such as model training with `scikit-learn`. You have also learned how to programmatically run a graph algorithm from the GDS and use the result as a new type of feature for your model.

In the following chapters, we will continue our journey through graph analytics. In this chapter, we stuck to classical machine learning methods such as decision trees. We will now go on to learn how the graph structure can be used to answer different kinds of questions, starting with the link prediction problem, which we are going to tackle in the next chapter.

Questions

Here are a couple of exercises that you can try on your own to get more confident with the concepts covered in this chapter:

- **Projected graph creation with Python**: Modify the code studied in this chapter to create a Cypher projected graph.
- **PageRank score distribution**: Can you explain the shape of the PageRank score distribution for users not contributing to Neo4j (label = `False`)?

You are also encouraged to try and create a graph out of your data and try to include graph-based features in your own pipeline.

Further reading

- *The business understanding stage of the Team Data Science Process lifecycle* by Microsoft: `https://docs.microsoft.com/en-us/azure/machine-learning/team-data-science-process/lifecycle-business-understanding`

9
Predicting Relationships

Graphs are a specific form of data representation. Over the course of the previous chapters, we learned how to extract information from graphs in an unsupervised or semi-supervised way. We explored how to use this information as features for a classical machine learning model, where nodes were the observations. In this chapter, we will deal with a completely new type of problem only possible with graphs: link prediction. After gaining an understanding of exactly what the link prediction problem is and how it can be applied to different cases, we will learn about the functions implemented in the Graph Data Science library, which can help us to find solutions for the problem. Finally, we will study a real-world example application problem using Python and its data science toolbox.

The following topics will be covered in this chapter:

- Why use link prediction?
- Creating link prediction metrics with Neo4j
- Building a link prediction model using an ROC curve

Technical requirements

The following tools will be used in this chapter:

- We rely on the Neo4j graph database, version ≥ 3.5, and the following plugin:
    - The Graph Data Science library (version ≥ 1.0)

- Code examples will be given using Python (≥ 3.6) and we will use the following packages for data modeling and data visualization:
    - To store data and create the DataFrame, we will rely on `pandas`.
    - To build the model, we will use `scikit-learn`.
    - Data visualization will be done using `matplotlib`.
- The code for this chapter can be found on GitHub at the following link: https://github.com/PacktPublishing/Hands-On-Graph-Analytics-with-Neo4j/ch9

> If you are using **Neo4j** < **4.0**, then the last compatible version of the **GDS** plugin is **1.1** whereas, if you are using **Neo4j** ≥ **4.0**, then the first compatible version of the **GDS** plugin is **1.2**.

Why use link prediction?

Link prediction consists of guessing which unknown connections between existing nodes in the graph are more likely to be real, now or in the future. With a proper formulation, this can be turned into a machine learning problem. But before trying to build a model for link prediction, as for any data science task, we must start with a deep understanding of the problem. That will be our goal in this section. First, by using the context of dynamic graphs, we will define what exactly is hidden behind *link prediction*. We will also review some applications, from marketing to science.

Dynamic graphs

So far in this book, we have studied graphs in a static manner; in other words, we imported graphs from an external data source and the graph content (nodes or relationships) was never changed. Studying the graph structure in this way gives us some information about the data it is representing. However, in a real-life scenario, whether your graph models a road network or an e-commerce website, it will change over time. In a dynamic graph, all parts of the graph can change. Here are some examples of the ways in which a graph can change:

- **Node addition**: New users subscribing to a service, new products added to the catalog, or new intersections created.

- **Node removal**: Products no longer manufactured or customers leaving.
- **Link addition**: An existing customer buys another product, or a road is added between two intersections.
- **Link removal**: A closed road or a customer unsubscribing from some services, but maintaining a subscription for other products.

Predicting all of these changes can be very challenging. Therefore, we will focus on links in the chapter, assuming the nodes are not changing. With this assumption, the state of graph G at time t_2 is given by the following formula:

$$G(t_1) + added\_links - removed\_links = G(t_2)$$

The following diagram is an illustration of the preceding formula:

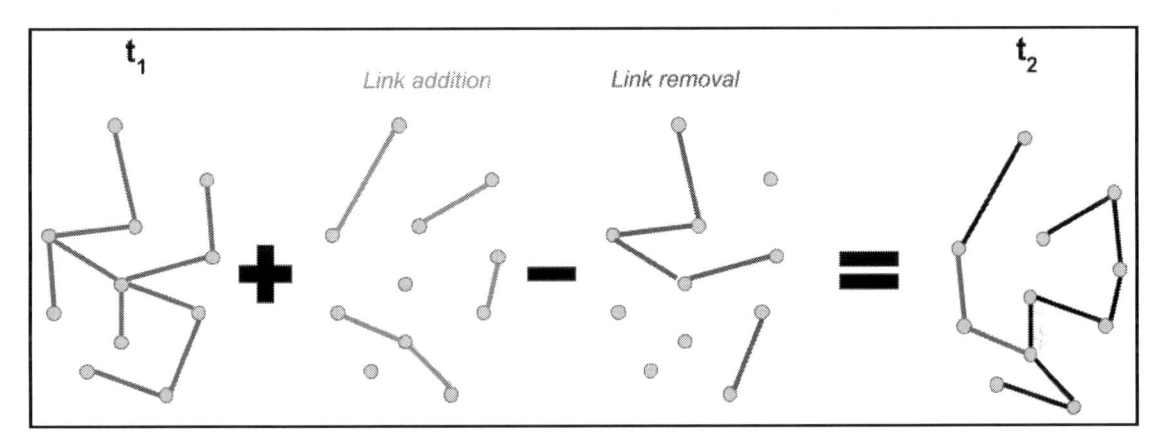

Since we are focusing only on *link addition*, our goal is to predict whether two existing but non-connected nodes in our graph are likely to be connected in the future. Many different types of applications can be considered for this.

Applications

Predicting future links is one of the goals of link prediction. But other applications can be found, especially in cases when the information at our disposal is incomplete.

Recovering missing data

Sometimes our graph data won't represent the full picture. Our knowledge will be incomplete and some links between entities in the graph might be missing. There are at least two cases where this frequently happens.

Fighting crime

In terms of criminal behavior, the police are not aware of all nodes or relationships within and between criminal organizations. Link prediction methods have been used to infer the missing links and find the criminals most likely to collaborate to commit a crime in the future.

Research

Research, by its very nature, is always developing and changing. When a graph is used to model knowledge about a certain topic, this knowledge is often partial because research is ongoing and we do not have a full understanding of the interactions between all the elements of the graph yet.

Link prediction techniques have been used a lot in biology, for example, to try to identify the genes involved in some diseases based on the current knowledge about genetic diseases.

Making recommendations

In day-to-day life, link prediction can be used to make recommendations to the user both in social networking and e-commerce contexts.

Social links (Facebook friends, LinkedIn contacts...)

Sites such as Facebook, Twitter, and LinkedIn, can all be represented using a connection graph:

- Facebook is an undirected graph modeling friendship.
- LinkedIn is also an undirected graph representing professional contacts.
- Twitter is a directed graph (you may follow someone who is not following you, and vice versa).

All of these social media sites include something like a *People you may know* section. These recommendations can be based on different factors. For instance, they can use the following facts:

- You attended the same university lecture, so you may know each other even if this relationship is not made official on social media.
- You have friends in common, so you are likely either to know each other or to be introduced in the future, at a party, wedding, or other event involving your common friend.

As well as connection recommendations, link prediction can also be used for product recommendations.

Product recommendations

Imagine a graph schema similar to this one:

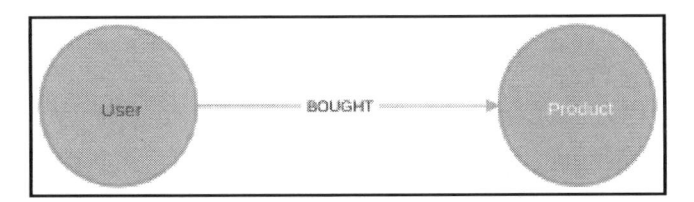

User —— BOUGHT ——▶ Product

Users are *linked* to products they bought. Recommending products for each user is therefore a link prediction problem where we try to predict the new link between users and products.

However, there is a fundamental difference between this kind of link prediction and the link prediction used in social networking. This difference comes from the graph's nature; in a social network, the graph is said to be **monopartite**, while the user-product graph is **bipartite**. The difference is illustrated in the following diagram:

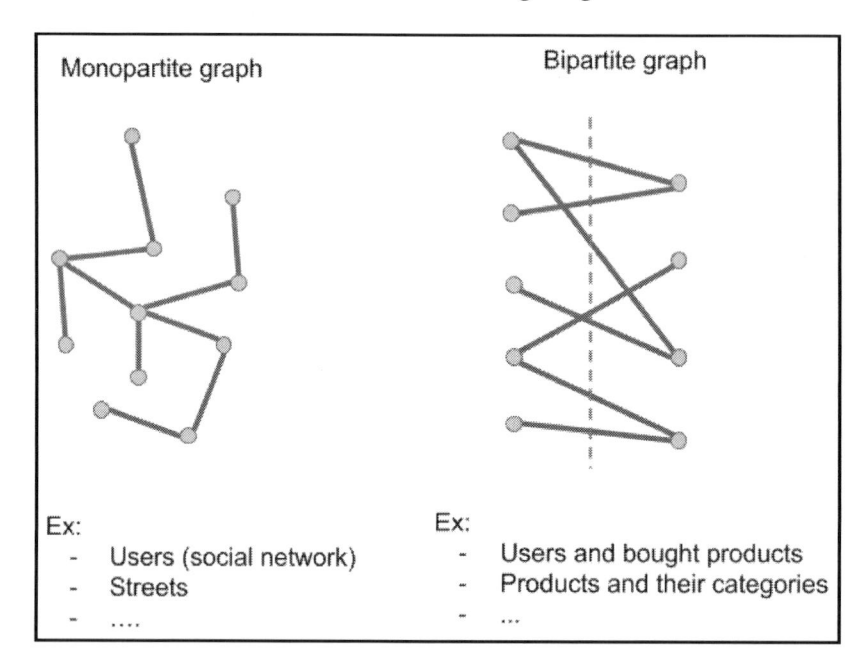

In a bipartite graph, the graph is made up of two sets of nodes, N and M, and the edges necessarily connect a node N to a node M. In the previous graph schema showing users and products, relationships only connect users and products; we never see user-user or product-product relationships. This is what makes the graph bipartite – users on one side and products on the other side.

The techniques we are going to study in this chapter have mainly been designed for monopartite graphs. We will see in the last section of this chapter how they can be adapted to bipartite graphs.

Making recommendations using a link prediction algorithm

In `Chapter 8`, *Using Graph-Based Features in Machine Learning*, we studied a dataset with the following columns:

	user_id	followers	publicRepos	contributed_to_neo4j
0	1	0.0	34.0	False
1	31	148.0	27.0	False
2	32	594.0	217.0	True
3	33	29.0	66.0	False
4	34	17.0	22.0	False

If you followed Chapter 2, *The Cypher Query Language*, you have probably noticed the similarity between this dataset and the graph we studied in this chapter. Built from the GitHub public API, it contains data related to the Neo4j organization on GitHub:

- Its contributors
- The repositories those contributors contributed to
- The contributors to those new repositories

The graph schema is as follows:

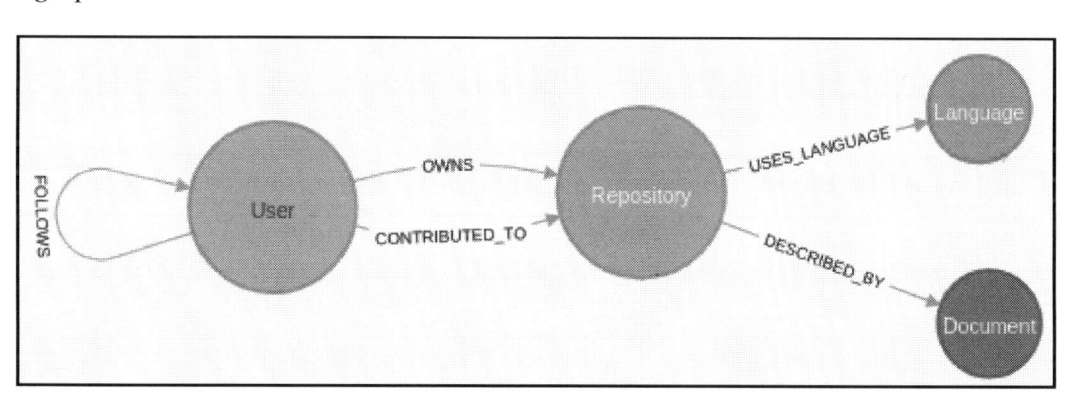

Language and Document are some special nodes added by an NLP-based analysis of the repository's README. We will focus here on the User and Repository labels.

From this graph, we can build the data used in the preceding chapter using the following Cypher query:

```
MATCH (u:User)
OPTIONAL MATCH (u)-[:CONTRIBUTED_TO]->(r:Repository)<-[:OWNS]-(:User
{login: "neo4j"})
WITH u, COLLECT(r) as rs
RETURN   id(u) as user_id,
```

```
            u.followers as followers,
            u.publicRepos as publicRepos,
            size(rs) > 0 as contributed_to_neo4j
ORDER BY user_id
```

The `OPTIONAL MATCH` statement allows us to retrieve all users, even those who did not contribute to Neo4j. Using a `COLLECT` statement is necessary so that we do not count a user twice who would have contributed to several repositories owned by Neo4j.

However, looking at the graph schema again, we can see that the question we tried to answer in the preceding chapter, "Has this user contributed to a repository owned by Neo4j?". can also be translated into a link prediction problem:

Is there a link between a user and a repository owned by Neo4j?

Several techniques have been developed over the years to find a way to address this problem. In the following section, we will explore the main algorithms that have been implemented in the GDS plugin.

Creating link prediction metrics with Neo4j

There are many metrics that can be used in a link prediction problem. We have already studied some of these in this book but we will review them with a new focus on link prediction in this section. Some other metrics have been introduced especially for this kind of application and come under the `linkprediction` namespace in the GDS.

The idea of link prediction algorithms is to be able to create a matrix $N \times N$, where N is the number of nodes in the graph. Each ij element of the matrix must give an indication of the probability of the existence of a link between nodes i and j.

Different kinds of metrics can be used to achieve this goal. One of these is node similarity metrics, such as the Jaccard similarity we studied in Chapter 7, *Community Detection and Similarity Measures*. In this method, by comparing the set of node neighbors, we can get an idea about the nodes' similarities and how likely they are to be connected in the future.

Similarity is one example of a metric that can be used in a link prediction context, but many more have been developed. The following paragraphs introduce the most famous of them.

Community-based metrics

Community metrics contain information about graph structure. Different kinds of such algorithms were covered in Chapter 7, *Community Detection and Similarity Measures*. These included the strongly and weakly connected components to spot isolated groups of nodes and the label propagation and Louvain algorithm for more subtle community identification.

In many cases, we can safely assume that two nodes in the same community are more likely to be connected. This concept is illustrated in the following diagram:

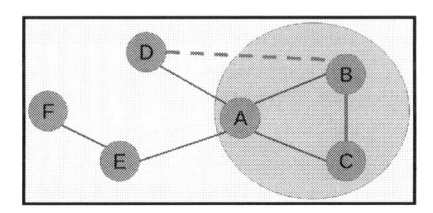

The link between *B* and *C* is more likely to be created next, since *B* and *C* are in the same community, unlike nodes *B* and *D*. In this case, the scoring function would be the following:

score(u, v) = 1 if u and v are in the same community, 0 otherwise

In these situations, we can use the `sameCommunity` function of the GDS plugin. This will simply check whether two nodes are in the same community, assuming the community is stored as a node property for each node:

```
MATCH (u:User {user_id: 32})
MATCH (v:User {user_id: 12464})
RETURN gds.alpha.linkprediction.sameCommunity(u, v, "louvain") as sameCommunity
```

This is exactly equivalent to using the following:

```
MATCH (u:User {user_id: 32})
MATCH (v:User {user_id: 12464})
RETURN u.louvain = v.louvain as sameCommunity
```

Path-related metrics

The distance between two nodes can be another indicator of their closeness and possible future connection.

Distance between nodes

Let's look again at the following graph:

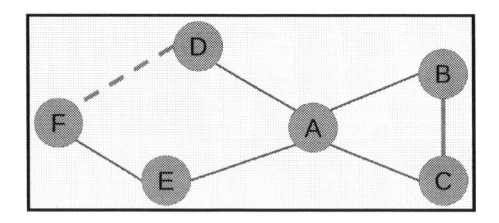

In the preceding graph, we can see that the relationship between B and C is more likely to be true than the one between D and F, because the shortest path between B and C is only 2 (unweighted graph), while the shortest path between D and F is 3.

So we can envisage a scoring function as follows:

$$score(u, v) = 1/d(u, v),$$

where $d(u, v)$ is the shortest path between nodes u and v

In Chapter 4, *The Graph Data Science Library and Path Finding*, we studied the all pairs shortest path algorithm, which can be useful here if link prediction metrics based on distance are relevant for your problem. Remember that the algorithm can be run on a previously created, named projected graph, `graph`, using the following query:

```
CALL gds.alpha.allShortestPaths.stream("projected_graph", {})
YIELD sourceNodeId, targetNodeId, distance
WITH gds.util.asNode(sourceNodeId) as startNode,
     gds.util.asNode(targetNodeId) as endNode,
     distance
RETURN startNode.name as start,
       endNode.name as end,
       distance
```

In order to transform this distance into a link prediction score, we will take the inverse of the distance and sort the results into ascending order based on this new metric. This causes the closest nodes to appear first. If we want to display only the non-existing links, we have to add an extra filter to remove the pairs of nodes already connected to each other by a direct link. Both operations are performed in the following Cypher query:

```
CALL gds.alpha.allShortestPaths.stream("projected_graph", {})
YIELD sourceNodeId, targetNodeId, distance
WITH gds.util.asNode(sourceNodeId) as startNode,
```

```
        gds.util.asNode(targetNodeId) as endNode,
        1.0 / distance as score
WHERE NOT ((startNode)-[:LINKED_TO]->(endNode))
RETURN startNode.name, endNode.name, score
LIMIT 10
```

The highest possible score in an unweighted graph would be 0.5 since disconnected nodes are at least two hops away from each other. Creating the edge between the two nodes B and C, having a score of 0.5, consists of closing the triangle made of the three nodes B, C, and their common neighbor, A. The following diagram illustrates this concept; nodes C and B are two hops away from each other since the shortest path between them goes through node A. Connecting them would close the triangle whose vertices are A, B, and C:

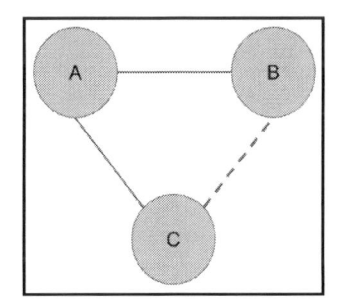

However, on a large graph, we might have many nodes, and in that situation, closing all the triangles is almost not feasible. Fortunately, more refined techniques exist, based on local neighborhoods.

The Katz index

Computing the shortest distance between nodes is a very basic approach and it does not take into account possible connections between nodes. An elaborated version, known as **the Katz index**, consists of summing all paths between two nodes, with increasing lengths. It is computed using the following formula:

$$score(u, v) = \sum_l \beta^l p(u, v; l)$$

Let's look at each of the components in detail:

- l is the path length, from 1 to ∞.
- $p(u, v; l)$ is the number of paths of length l between nodes u and v.
- β is a weight parameter whose value is chosen between 0 and 1 in order to give more weights to the shortest distances.

In practice, the adjacency matrix is used to compute this score, since it can be shown that the number of paths of length l between u and v is equal to the uv element of the adjacency matrix to the power l:

$$score(u, v) = \sum_l \beta^l A(u, v)^l$$

The Katz index has been shown to be among the best-performing, path-based link prediction algorithms. Take a look at, for instance, the paper entitled *Link Prediction in Complex Networks: A Survey*, from the *Further reading* section.

Using local neighborhood information

In order to understand the mathematics behind the following formulas, let's first introduce some notations, similar to the ones used in Chapter 7, *Community Detection and Similarity Measures*:

- u, v, and i are nodes of the graph.
- $N(u)$ denotes the set of neighbors of node u.
- $|N(u)|$ is the size of the set, meaning the number of neighbors of node u.

Common neighbors

The common neighbors approach supports the following hypothesis:

Two people who have a friend in common are more likely to be introduced than those who don't have any friends in common.

The common neighbors metric measures the size of the set of common friends between u and v:

$$score(u, v) = |N(u) \cap N(v)|$$

In the GDS plugin, link prediction metrics are *functions* and can be computed using the following:

```
MATCH (u) MATCH (v)
RETURN id(u), id(v), gds.alpha.linkprediction.commonNeighbors(u, v)
```

Adamic-Adar

The **Adamic-Adar** score is an improvement on the common neighbors approach. Adamic-Adar assumes that rare connections give more information than common ones. In the Adamic-Adar formula, each relationship with a neighbor is weighted by the inverse of the neighbor's degree according to the following formula:

$$score(u, v) = \Sigma_i \, 1/\log|N(i)|, \, i \in N(u) \cap N(v)$$

This idea is illustrated in the following diagram.

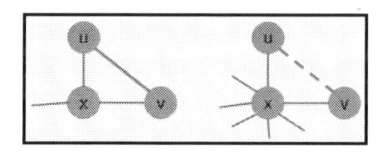

While nodes u and v are connected through x on both sides, since x has a lower degree on the left graph, its relationship to u and v is more important and the edge between u and v is more probable:

Total neighbors

The total neighbors metric has to be used when the following hypothesis is reasonable:

> *The more connected a node is, the more social it is, the more likely it is to receive new links.*

When quantifying the likelihood of nodes u and v being connected, we can use the number of nodes belonging to the neighboring set of both nodes:

$$score(u, v) = |\, N(u) \cup N(v)\, |$$

Let's understand this formula by considering the following two graphs:

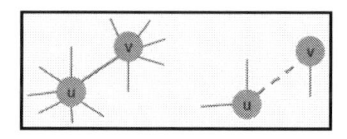

Nodes u and v on the left-hand side of the following diagrams have a lot of connections compared to nodes u and v on the right-hand side. Therefore, nodes u and v on the left-hand side are more likely to accept new connections:

Preferential attachment

In some cases, it is legitimate to assume the following:

> *More popular people are more likely to be linked to other popular people.*

In these cases, the preferential attachment method has to be used. The preferential attachment score of nodes *u* and *v* is equal to the product of the degrees of nodes *u* and *v*:

$$score(u, v) = |N(u)| \times |N(v)|$$

This score is also implemented in the GDS plugin under the `gds.alpha.preferentialAttachment` function:

```
MATCH (u), MATCH (v)
RETURN   id(u), id(v),
         gds.alpha.linkprediction.preferentialAttachment(u, v, {
                  relationshipType: "REL",
                  direction: "BOTH"
})
```

Note that we can optionally specify the type and direction of the relationships we use to find the neighborhood. We will look at an example application in the following section.

Other metrics

Not all the preceding metrics can be used at the same time. Which one is best to use in which situation depends on the underlying process governing the graph growth and, in many situations, it is necessary to test several metrics to find the most appropriate one. We can even imagine more metrics, such as the following:

- **Reciprocity**: The presence of a link makes the addition of a link in the opposite direction more likely and the removal of a reciprocal link less likely.
- **Newness weakness**: Newly formed links are less likely to persist than older links and hence hold less weight.
- **Instability**: If the properties or links attached to nodes *u* and *v* change very often, the edge between *u* and *v* is also more likely not to survive and has a less weight.

Following this review about link prediction scoring methods, we are now going to build a link prediction model using Neo4j and `scikit-learn`.

Building a link prediction model using an ROC curve

In all the graph analytics problems we have studied so far, our observations were the nodes of the graph. Now, however, we are moving on to a different concept where the *observations* are the **edges**. Each row of the dataset should contain information about one edge of the graph. Since our goal is to predict whether a link will appear in the future or is missing from our current knowledge, we can turn the problem into a *binary classification* one, that is, the edge can either have:

- the class `True`, the link exists or is likely to be created, or
- the class `False`, the link is very unlikely to appear.

Since we are about to build a classification model, our dataset must include both existing and non-existing edges (the two classes of the binary classifier).

Importing the data into Neo4j

The data we are going to use in the rest of this chapter is a randomly generated geometric graph. This kind of graph has many interesting features, one of them being its ability to reproduce the behavior of some real-life graphs such as social graphs.

After downloading the data and placing it in the `import` folder of our graph, we can use the following Cypher statement to import it into Neo4j:

```
LOAD CSV FROM "file:///graph_T2.edgelist" AS row
FIELDTERMINATOR " "
MERGE (u:Node {id: toInteger(row[0])})
MERGE (v:Node {id: toInteger(row[1])})
MERGE (u)-[:KNOWS_T2]->(v)
```

> The graph contains only 500 nodes and 3,565 relationships, which is the reason why we can ignore the warning regarding the `Eager` operator in the preceding query.

The training set contains edges that were already present in the graph at time t_2. So let's also import the graph at a prior time, t_1. At that moment, the nodes are the same as the already existing ones, so we can afford to use a `MATCH` clause instead of `MERGE`:

```
LOAD CSV FROM "file:///graph_T1.edgelist" AS row
FIELDTERMINATOR " "
```

Predicting Relationships

```
MATCH (u:Node {id: toInteger(row[0])})
MATCH (v:Node {id: toInteger(row[1])})
MERGE (u)-[:KNOWS_T1]->(v)
```

So we now have a graph with two types of relationships:

- `KNOWS_T1` links two nodes if they knew each other at time *t1*.
- `KNOWS_T2` links two nodes if they knew each other at time *t2*. The set of relationships of type `KNOWS_T1` is a subset of the set of relationships of type `KNOWS_T2` since two nodes that knew each other at time *t1* still know each other at time *t2*.

We will now learn how to compute the link prediction score for this graph.

Splitting the graph and computing the score for each edge

In order to make predictions using a link prediction score, we need to follow these steps:

1. Define the state of the graph at a given time, t_1
2. At time t_1, compute the link prediction score for each pair of nodes in the graph
3. Compare these predictions to the links created between t_1 and t_2
4. Determine a score threshold such that pairs with a score above this threshold are more likely to appear at time $t_2 > t_1$

In this example, the state of the graph at t_1 is already provided through the `KNOWS_T1` relationships.

We can now compute the link prediction score for each pair of nodes in the graph, considering only the knowledge at time t_1 by using the newly created relationship. Here, we choose to use the Adamic-Adar score:

```
MATCH (u) MATCH (v) WHERE u <> v
RETURN  u.id as u_id,
        v.id as v_id,
        gds.alpha.linkprediction.adamicAdar(u, v, {
            relationshipQuery: "KNOWS_T1",
            direction: "BOTH"
        }) as score
LIMIT 10
```

The most important parts of the preceding query are highlighted here:

- The link prediction function will use only one type of relationship, KNOWS_T1, ignoring the information about posterior relationships we are trying to predict.
- The graph is considered undirected; if A knows B (at whatever time), then we consider that B knows A.

Some of the most probable pairs of nodes identified by the Adamic-Adar algorithm are the following:

"u_id"	"v_id"	"score"
41	33	7.3
33	41	7.3
171	42	7.1
162	178	6.9
3	124	6.7
75	16	6.6

To use this score in a model, we need to quantify its discrimination power, which can be achieved with a **Receiver Operation Characteristics** (**ROC**) curve. We also need to find an optimal cutoff for the score to decide whether or not a link will appear in the future; for example, should we stop at score=5, score=4.5, or even less? We will discuss both of these topics now.

Measuring binary classification model performance

This problem is a binary classification task. Our observations are links and we have to decide which of the following two classes they belong to:

- The link will be created between time t_1 and t_2.
- The link will not be created between time t_1 and t_2.

In order to measure the performance of a given model, we can use the ROC curve.

Predicting Relationships

Understanding ROC curves

What information do we have so far? For the *test* sample, our graph at time t_2, we know the following for each pair of nodes:

- Whether there actually is a link between them at time t_2 (the ground truth)
- The score computed from the link prediction metric

From this information, we can draw the distribution of scores for each label. Let's consider the following plot:

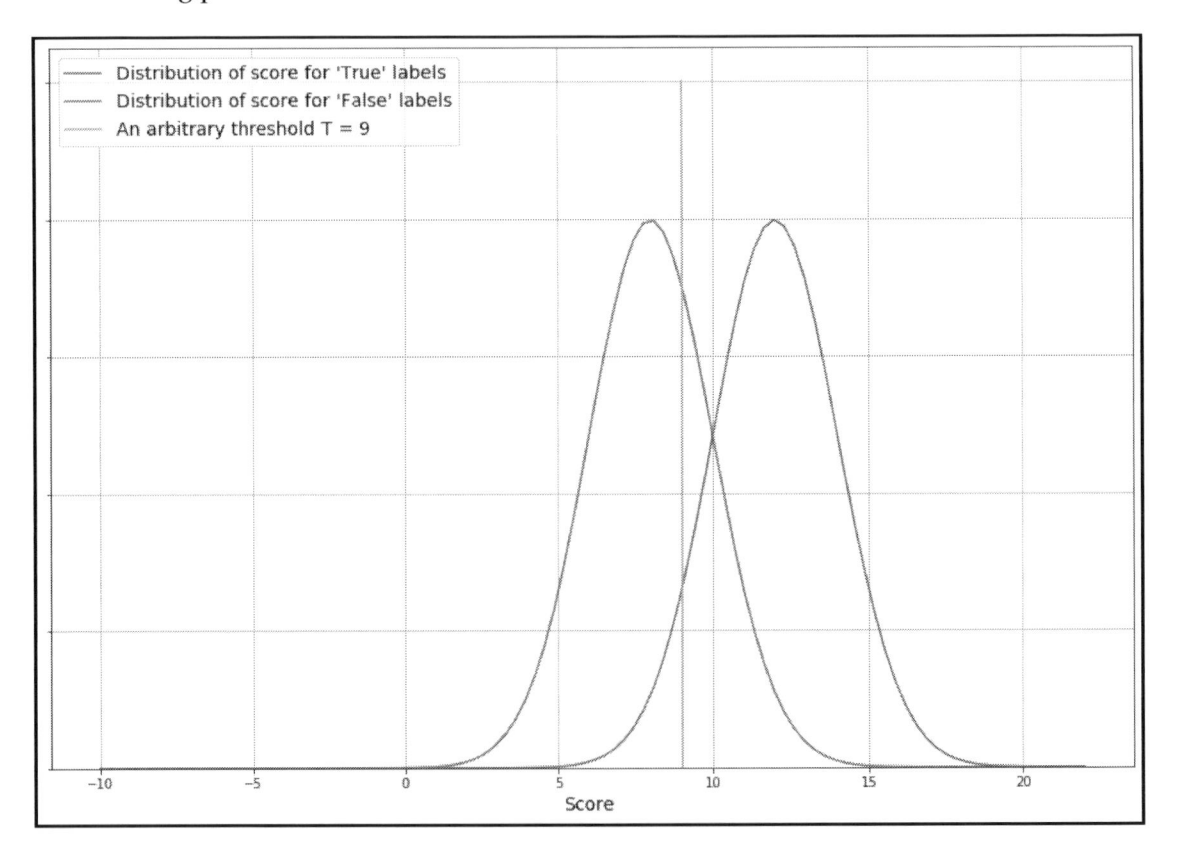

The left-most curve represents the distribution of scores for all observations that have the label False, while the right-most curve corresponds to the distribution of scores for all observations that have the label True. To assess the quality of the metric, we can use an ROC curve.

To make predictions out of this information, we need to define a score threshold. To define a score threshold, we need to set a vertical line so that all observations on the left of this line will be classified as `False` and all observations on the right (that is, the observations having a score higher than the threshold) will be classified as `True`. The following diagram illustrates two possible threshold choices; the top row has a threshold $T=11$, while the two plots on the bottom row have a threshold $T=7$:

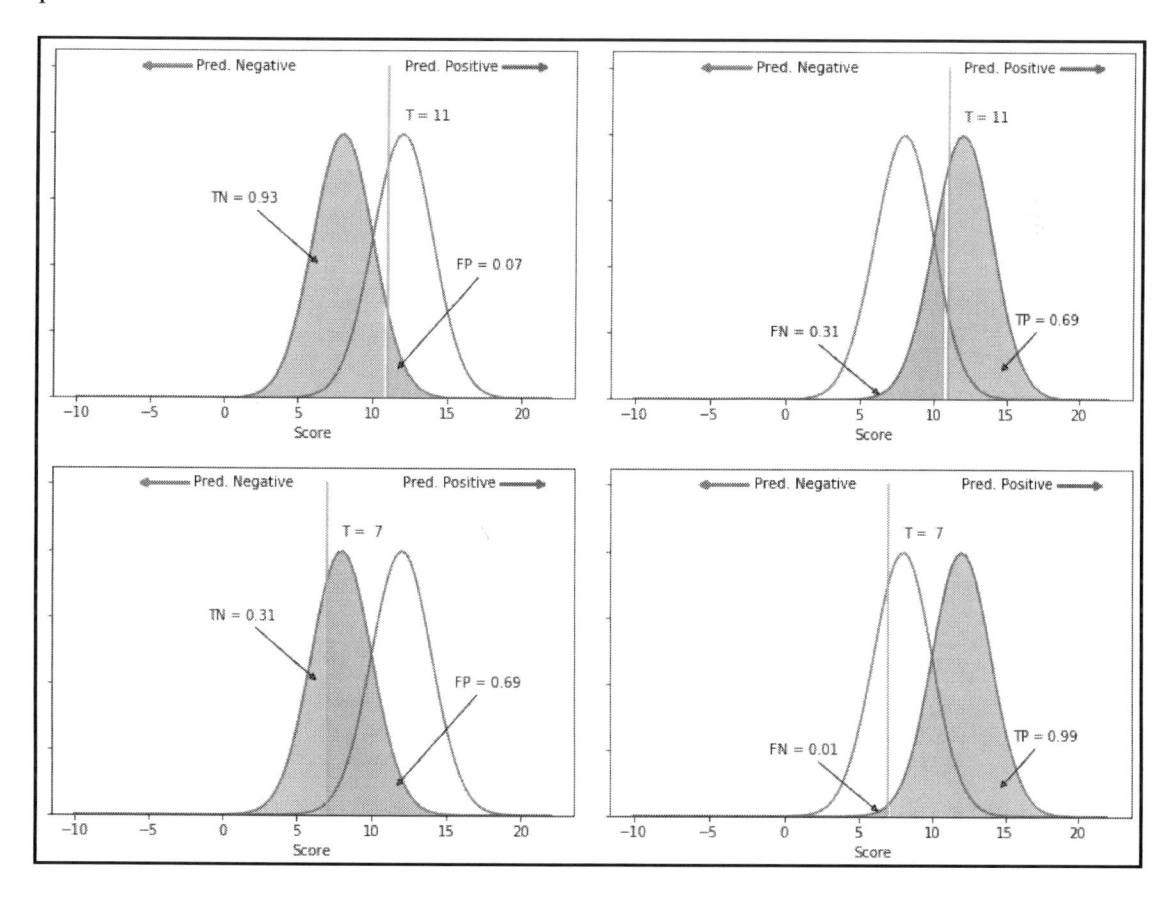

From these curves, we can define a few variables:

- **The True Positive (TP)**: The number of observations correctly classified as positive. This corresponds to the green area under the green curve and on the right of the chosen threshold.
- **The False Negative (FN)**: This is the counterpart of the TP, corresponding to the proportion of positive observations classified as negative. On the plot, this is the red area under the green curve.

- **The True Negative (TN)**: The number of negative observations correctly classified as negative. This is the green area under the red curve on the left.
- **The False Positive (FP)**: The number of negative observations wrongly classified as positive. This corresponds to the red area under the red curve.

These four variables are combined to define the **True Positive Rate (TPR)** and the **False Positive Rate (FPR)**:

$$TPR = TP / (TP + FN)$$
$$FPR = FP / (FP + TN)$$

The *TPR* measures the proportion of correctly classified `True` observations compared to the whole set of positive observations. The *FPR* quantifies the proportion of wrongly classified negative observations. The trade-off between these two quantities is represented by the ROC curve:

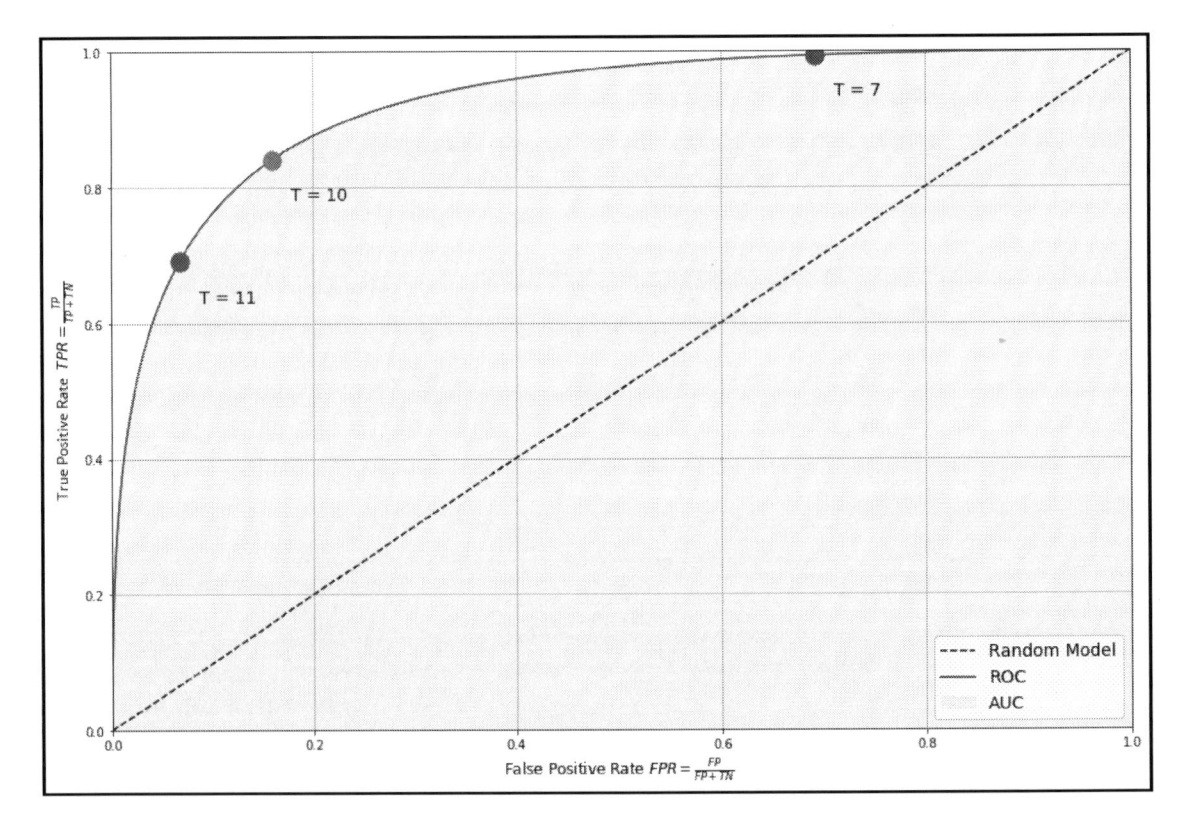

The dots each correspond to a given threshold. The dot at *T=10* is close to the *optimal* partition, that is, the one with the best compromise between the FPR and the TPR.

The following diagram illustrates some configurations to help us better understand what the ROC looks like in different scenarios:

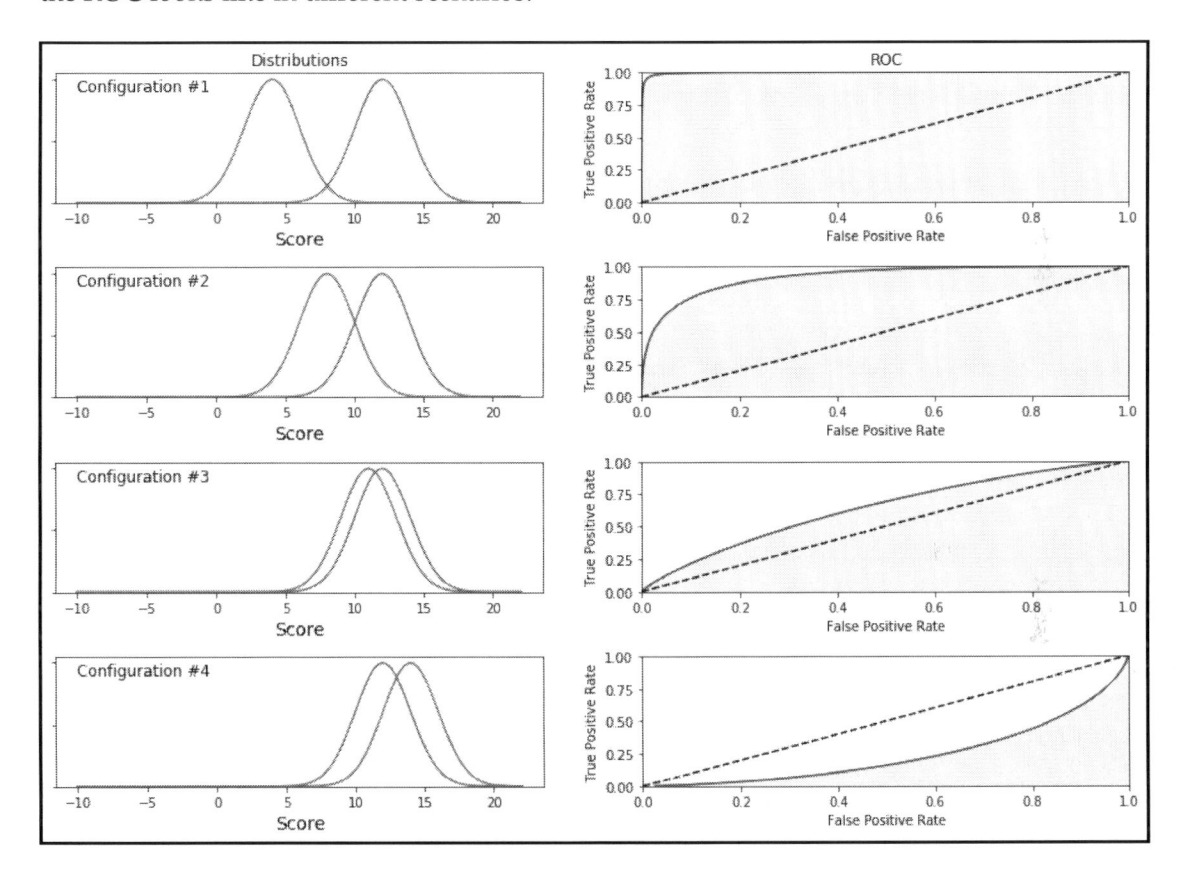

Predicting Relationships

Let's go through each of these configurations:

- In configuration 1, the score distribution for False (leftmost curve) and True (rightmost curve) labels is well separated. You can easily guess which threshold should be used to create a model that will successfully assign observations to the correct class. In this case, the AUC is close to 1, which is a sign of an almost perfect model.
- In configuration 2, the two distributions get closer, but are still distinguishable. The AUC is lower, around 0.8, but we can still achieve good performance.
- In configuration 3, the two distributions are almost identical and the model is barely better than the random choice.
- Finally, in configuration 4, the model seems to have reversed the two classes, since the False labels are now represented by the rightmost curve and hence have a higher score than the True labels. If we stick to the expected rule that higher scores are classified as positive, then the performance is worse than the random model.

Now let's return to our initial link prediction problem and draw the ROC curve.

Extracting features and labels

In order to create a dataset for a link prediction task, we need to do the following:

1. Compute the score for each pair of nodes in the graph, using the KNOWS_T1 relationships only.
2. Discard the pairs of nodes already linked to each other at t_1.
3. Extract the label for each of the remaining pairs; the label is True if a relationship between the two nodes exists at time t_2, otherwise False.

The following query performs these three operations:

```
MATCH (u)
MATCH (v)
// take only one link from undirected graph
WHERE u.id < v.id   // exclude u = v
// exclude edges that were already there at T1:
AND NOT ( (u)-[:KNOWS_T1]-(v) )
// compute score
WITH u, v,  gds.alpha.linkprediction.adamicAdar(
                u, v, {
                        relationshipQuery: "KNOWS_T1",
                        direction: "BOTH"
```

```
                } 
            ) as score
RETURN    u.id as u_id,
          v.id as v_id,
          score,
          // get the label: does the edge exist at time t2?
          EXISTS( (u)-[:KNOWS_T2]-(v) ) as label
```

> Be careful: the link prediction algorithms are still in the alpha tier of the GDS plugin (as of version 1.2.0). This means they are not yet optimized and the previous query can be quite long!
>
> The dataset created from this query is also available in the file `adamic_adar_scores_labelled.csv`.

Drawing the ROC curve

After using Neo4j to compute graph-based information, let's use some more classical data science tools to quantify the quality of the score. We will use functions implemented in `pandas` and `scikit-learn`.

Creating the DataFrame

First of all, let's export the data from Neo4j to a pandas DataFrame using the Neo4j Python driver (similar to the method used in Chapter 8, *Using Graph-Based Features in Machine Learning*):

```
import pandas as pd
from neo4j import GraphDatabase

driver = GraphDatabase.driver("bolt://localhost:7687", auth=("neo4j", "<YOUR_PASSWORD>"))

cypher = """
MATCH (u)
MATCH (v)
WHERE u.id < v.id   // exclude u = v
AND NOT ( (u)-[:KNOWS_T2]-(v) )
WITH u, v, gds.alpha.linkprediction.adamicAdar(
                u, v, {
                        relationshipQuery: "KNOWS_T1",
                        direction: "BOTH"
                }
            ) as score
RETURN    u.id as u_id,
```

```
                v.id as v_id,
                score,
                EXISTS( (u)-[:KNOWS_T1]-(v) ) as label
    """

    with driver.session() as session:
        rec = session.run(cypher)

    df = pd.DataFrame.from_records(rec.data())
```

> **TIP** Remember to update the preceding code to use your own credentials to connect to Neo4j.

We can check the class repartitions in the DataFrame:

```
False      105555
True         3839
```

We have roughly 30 times more non-existing links than existing links. Our dataset is unbalanced. For this phase of the analysis, this won't be a problem as long as we use indicators that are not biased by this unbalance.

The normalized score distribution per class is reproduced in the following plot:

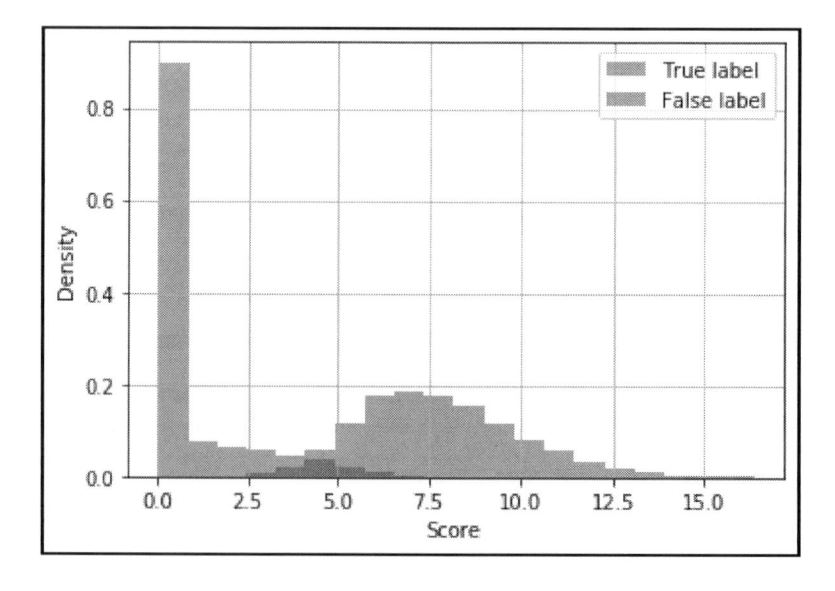

As you can see from the plot, the Adamic-Adar score seems to be quite a good metric to infer future links. Let's now quantify this using the ROC curve.

Plotting the ROC curve

First of all, we should split our dataset into train and test samples, respecting the class repartitions in both samples:

```
from sklearn.model_selection import train_test_split

X = df[["score"]]
y = df.label
X_train, X_test, y_train, y_test = train_test_split(
        X, y,
        test_size=0.2,
        random_state=42,
        # make sure both the train and test samples are representative
        # of the whole dataset in terms of class unbalance
        stratify=y
)
```

As we noticed earlier, our dataset is unbalanced. We can use some sampling techniques to restore class balance in the training set:

```
from imblearn.under_sampling import RandomUnderSampler

rus = RandomUnderSampler(random_state=SEED)
X_train, y_train = rus.fit_resample(X_train, y_train)
```

In order to compute FPR and TPR at different thresholds, we will use a scikit-learn function that will do so for us:

```
from sklearn.metrics import roc_curve

fpr, tpr, thresholds = roc_curve(y_train, X_train.score)
```

To plot the ROC curve with matplotlib, use the following code:

```
import matplotlib.pyplot as plt

plt.plot(fpr, tpr, color='blue', linewidth=2)
```

Predicting Relationships

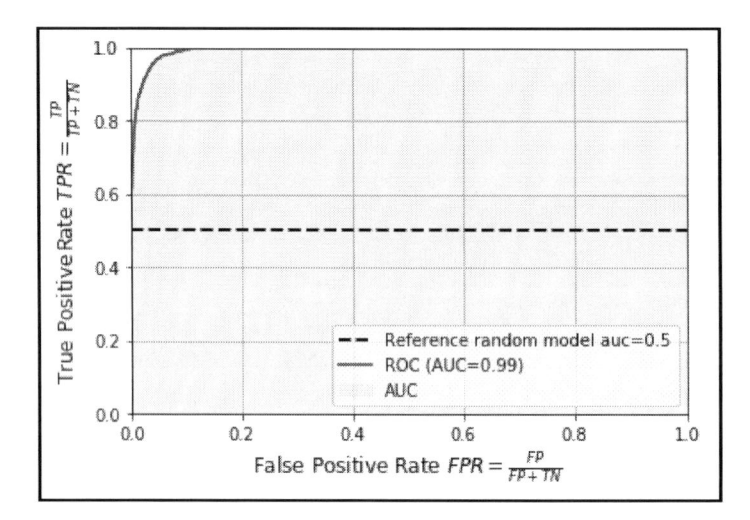

The result is illustrated on the following graphic:

As you can see from the preceding plot, our model is performing quite well and there are some thresholds for which we can achieve good performances both for TPR and FPR. We just need to choose this threshold to finish building our first link-prediction model.

Determining the optimal cutoff and computing performances

Choosing the threshold to use for classification depends on many parameters. Here, we are going to use a threshold that leads to the best trade-off between precision and recall:

```
precisions, recalls, thresholds = precision_recall_curve(y_train, X_train.score)
plt.plot(thresholds, recalls[:-1], label="Recall")
plt.plot(thresholds, precisions[:-1], label="Precision")
plt.legend()
plt.grid()
plt.xlabel("Threshold")
plt.show()
```

The generated plot is reproduced here, where the decreasing curve shows the recall and the increasing curve represents the precision:

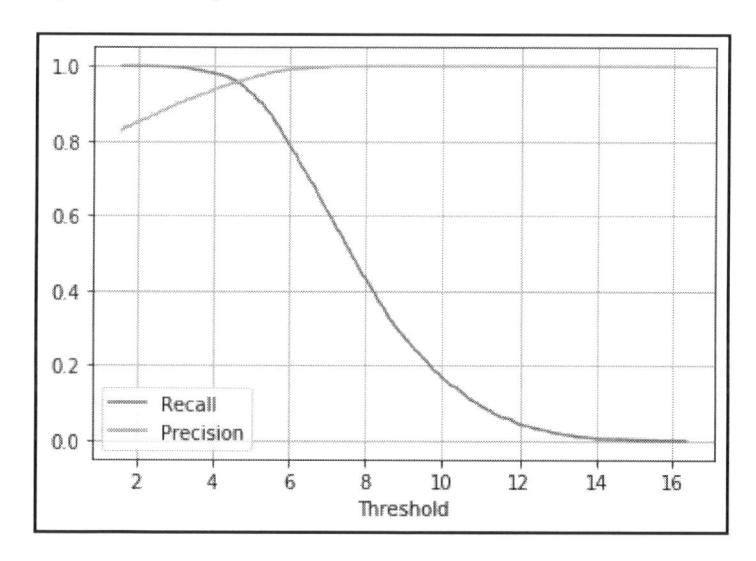

Choosing a threshold of 5 leads to the following confusion matrix:

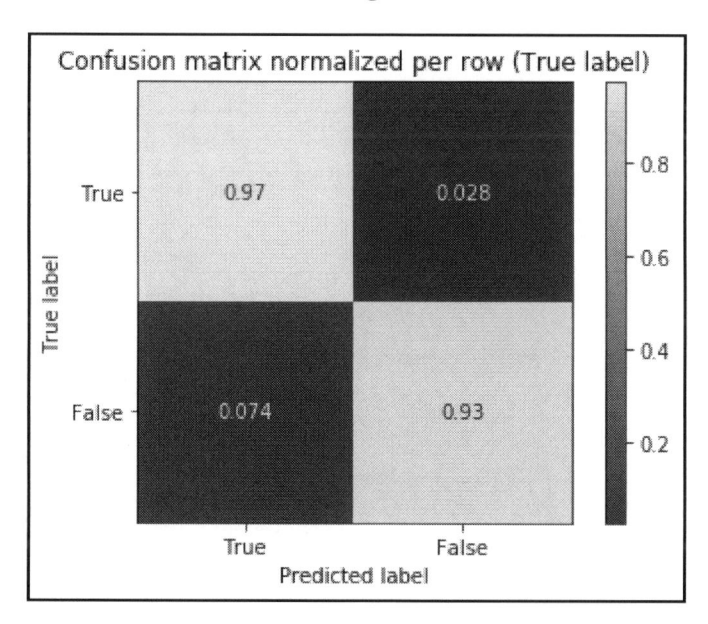

Among all existing edges at time t_2 (first row), 97% were correctly labeled as *True* by our algorithm. Similarly, for the non-existing edges, 93% were correctly classified as *False*.

Building a more complex model using scikit-learn

This first model, which uses only the Adamic-Adar score to make predictions, already works well, however, it only uses one feature. In the following section, we will extract more features from the graph, as we previously did in Chapter 8, *Using Graph-Based Features in Machine Learning*. Once the data is extracted into a DataFrame and we have the label properly set, we can imagine using any binary classifier, whether it be scikit-learn or another package.

Saving link prediction results into Neo4j

Once our model is ready and produces predictions, we can save them back into Neo4j for future use (see Chapter 11, *Using Neo4j in Your Web Application*). Regarding the link prediction problem, we will save a new relationship type, FUTURE_LINK, for each pair of nodes we identify as more likely to be connected in the future.

Let's start by writing the parametrized Cypher query that will perform this operation:

```
cypher = """
MATCH (u:Node {id: $u_id})
MATCH (v:Node {id: $v_id})
CREATE (u)-[:FUTURE_LINK {score: $score}]->(v)
"""
```

We merge all the required information into a single DataFrame:

```
df_test = df.loc[X_test.index]
df_test["score"] = pred
```

We can then iterate over this data and create one relationship per row having label=True:

```
with driver.session() as session:
    for t in df_test.itertuples():
        if t.label:
            session.run(cypher, parameters={
                "u_id": t.u_id,
                "v_id": t.v_id,
                "score": t.score
            })
```

The loop is now closed; after extracting data from Neo4j to perform our analysis, the results of this analysis are now back in the database. They can now be fetched by the backend or frontend application, for example, to show connection recommendations to users.

Before closing this topic, let's return to the topic of bipartite graphs, which are especially useful to make product recommendations, for example.

Predicting relationships in bipartite graphs

In the case of bipartite graphs, the previous methods don't work well. Indeed, the algorithms consisting of *closing the triangle* are not appropriate.

Consider, for instance, the following graph:

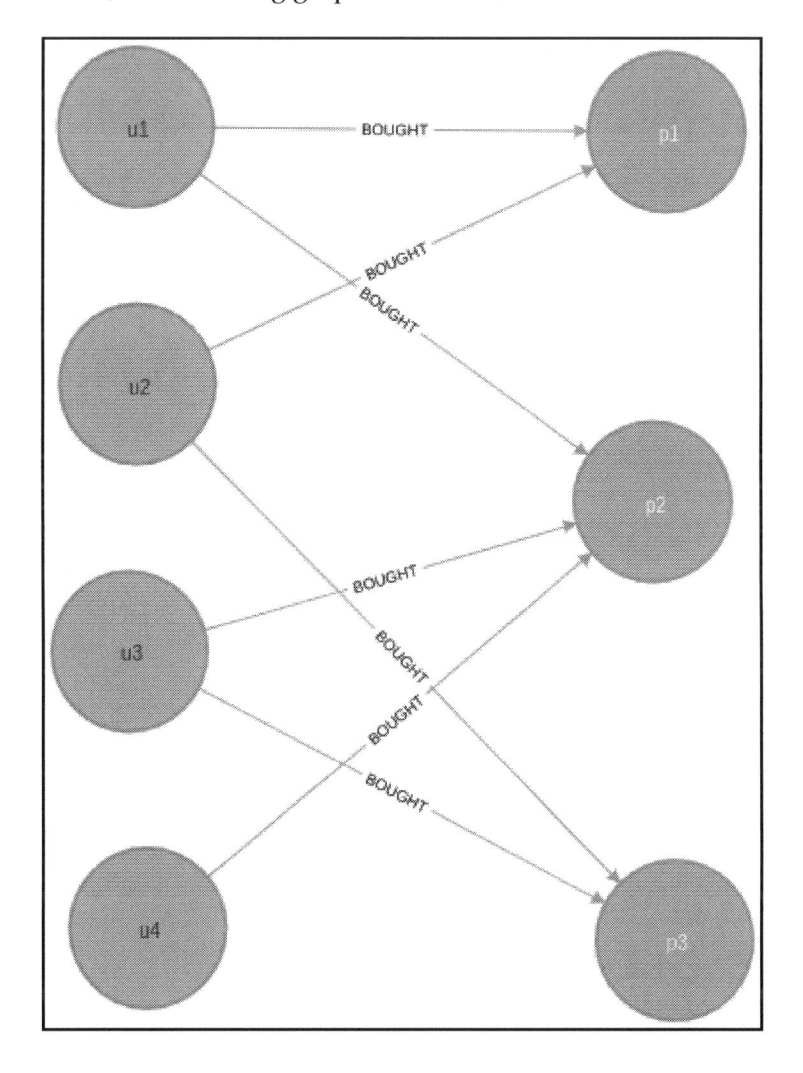

Predicting Relationships

This graph can be created using the following Cypher:

```
CREATE (u1:User {name: "u1"})
CREATE (u2:User {name: "u2"})
CREATE (u3:User {name: "u3"})
CREATE (u4:User {name: "u4"})

CREATE (p1:Product {name: "p1"})
CREATE (p2:Product {name: "p2"})
CREATE (p3:Product {name: "p3"})

CREATE (u1)-[:BOUGHT]->(p1)
CREATE (u1)-[:BOUGHT]->(p2)
CREATE (u2)-[:BOUGHT]->(p1)
CREATE (u2)-[:BOUGHT]->(p3)
CREATE (u3)-[:BOUGHT]->(p2)
CREATE (u3)-[:BOUGHT]->(p3)
CREATE (u4)-[:BOUGHT]->(p2)
```

Users `u1` and `u2` both bought product `p1`. `u1`, `u2`, and `p1` are therefore three corners of a possible triangle. However, closing this triangle by adding an edge between `u1` and `u2` is not possible since we cannot have a relationship between `u1` and `u2`.

The solution to this would be either to change our way of finding neighbors or to create some fake relationships in order to transform a bipartite graph into a monopartite graph. In the preceding graph example, we could create fake relationships between users by considering that users who buy the same product can be somehow connected.

A new relationship can be created using the following query:

```
MATCH (u1:User)-[:BOUGHT]->(:Product)<-[:BOUGHT]-(u2:User)
CREATE (u1)-[:LINKED_TO]->(u2)
```

The resulting graph made of the `User` nodes and the `LINKED_TO` relationship is reproduced in the following diagram:

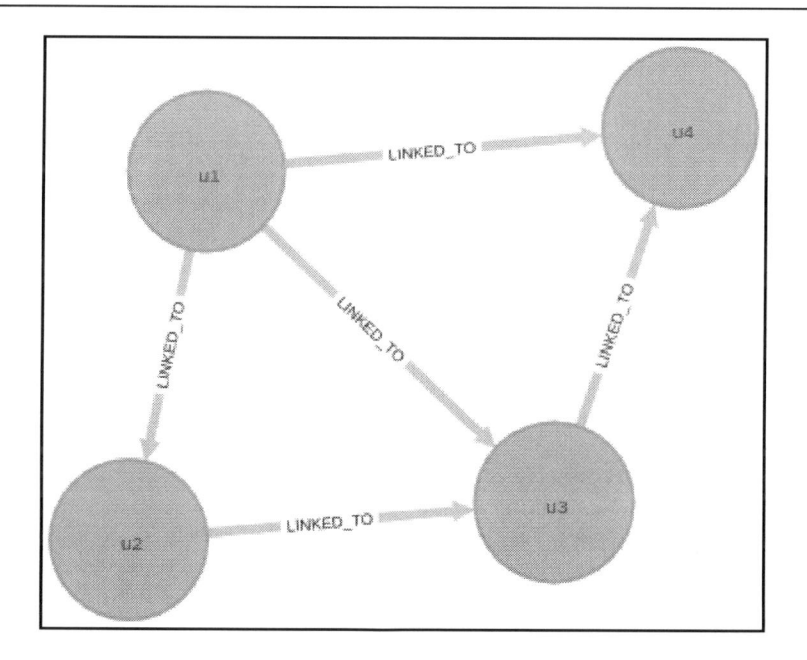

This new `LINKED_TO` relationship can be used as a parameter in the link prediction functions:

```
MATCH (u:User)
MATCH (v:User)
WHERE id(u) < id(v)
RETURN gds.alpha.linkprediction.commonNeighbors(u, v, {
    relationshipQuery: "LINKED_TO",
    direction: "BOTH"
})
```

Knowing that two users are likely to be connected by this fake relationship will give us an idea about the products they are likely to buy in the future. However, it is not yet a link prediction problem between a user and a product.

To make it so, we would need to create a new relationship between products and users, which is just the reverse of the BOUGHT relationship:

```
MATCH (p:Product)<-[:BOUGHT]-(u:User)
CREATE (p)-[:LINKED_TO]->(u)
```

Predicting Relationships

With these new relationships, our graph looks like this:

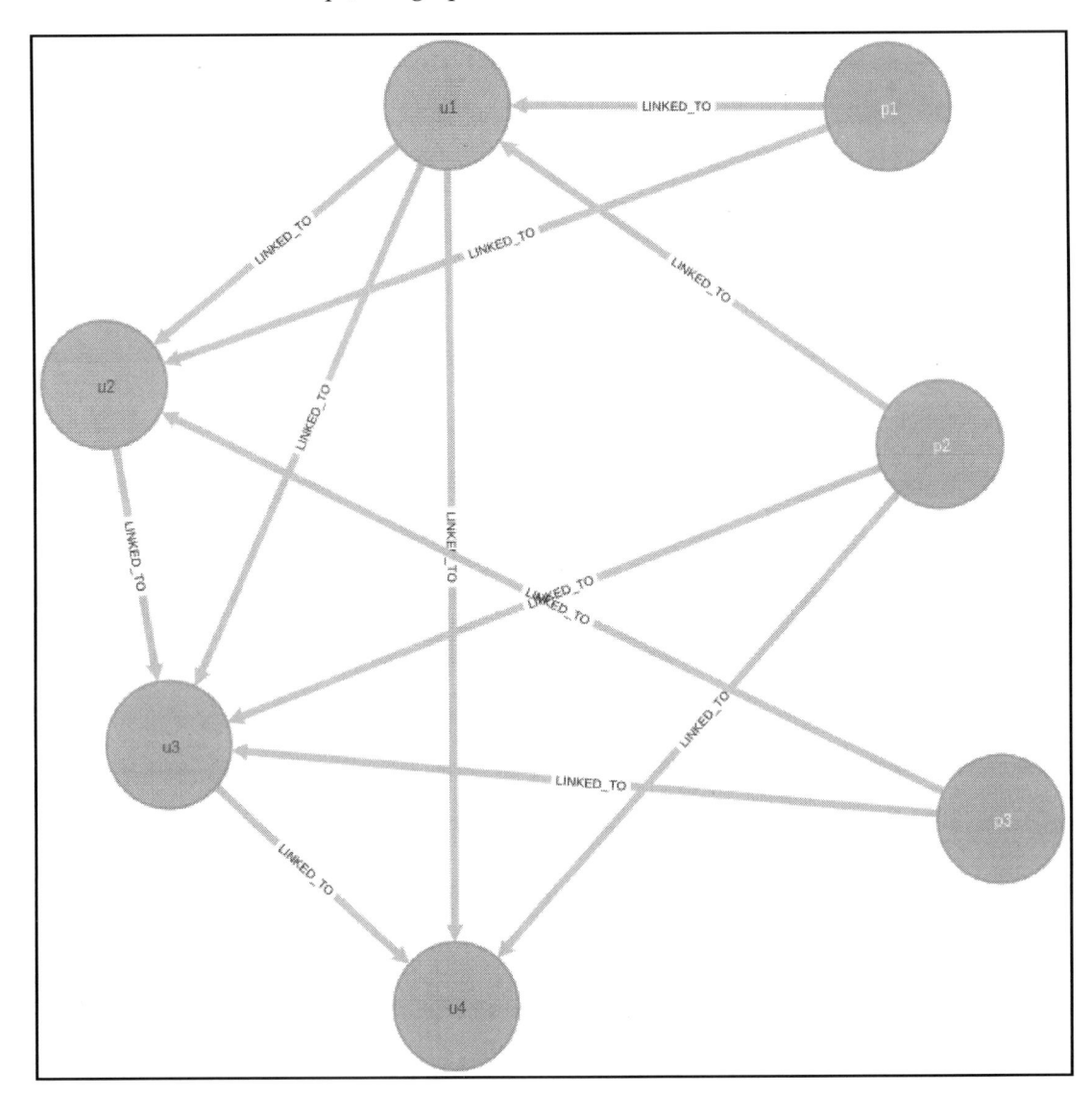

We can now use the following query to get a prediction score for the link between a user and a product:

```
MATCH (u:User)
MATCH (p:Product)
WHERE NOT EXISTS ( (u)-[:BOUGHT]->(p) )
WITH u.name as user, p.name as product,
gds.alpha.linkprediction.commonNeighbors(u, p, {
    relationshipQuery: "LINKED_TO",
    direction: "BOTH"
}) as score
RETURN user, product, score
ORDER BY score DESC
```

The result is reproduced in the following table:

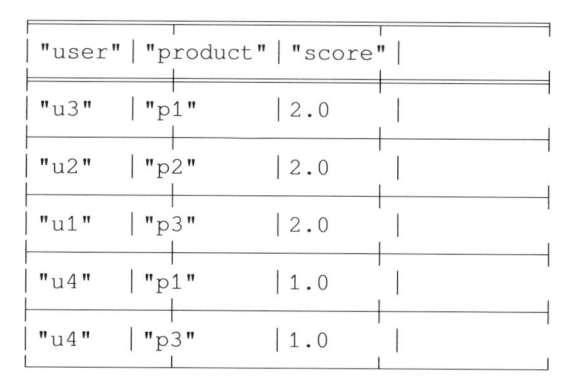

"user"	"product"	"score"
"u3"	"p1"	2.0
"u2"	"p2"	2.0
"u1"	"p3"	2.0
"u4"	"p1"	1.0
"u4"	"p3"	1.0

Let's analyze this result:

- u3 is connected to u2 and u1, who both bought product p1, so the number of common neighbors between u3 and p1 is 2.
- u4 and p1 have a single common neighbor, u1, since the other neighbor of p1 is u2 and u2 is not connected to p1, so the score of the relationship between u4 and p1 is 1.

We have used the `commonNeighbors` algorithm here because it is easier to analyze the results, but the same can be achieved with any of the other link prediction functions we have seen in this chapter.

Summary

After reading this chapter, you should have a clearer understanding of what link prediction means and how it can be used to tackle many graph-related questions. You should also know which kind of metric can be used to predict how likely a link is to appear between two nodes in the future. Finally, you have built from scratch a link prediction problem, understanding how it is different from a classical data science problem, and have learned how to successfully build a predictive model to foresee new relationships in a graph.

Until now, we have learned how to build features based on the fact that our data forms a graph structure. It is an important step to understand the graph structure and the prediction power of these features. However, modern machine learning techniques tend to avoid the feature engineering steps where algorithms automatically learn features called **embedding**. Applying this technique to graphs is the topic we will cover in the following chapter.

Questions

- Try other link prediction algorithms from the GDS plugin

Further reading

- Link Prediction in Complex Networks: A Survey: https://arxiv.org/abs/1010.0725
- A paper about link prediction for biology and gene-disease relations: https://bigdata.oden.utexas.edu/publication/prediction-and-validation-of-gene-disease-associations-using-methods-inspired-by-social-network-analyses/
- Link prediction in the context of crime: https://www.ncbi.nlm.nih.gov/pmc/articles/PMC4841537/
- Link prediction at twitter: *WTF: The Who to Follow Service at Twitter*: https://dl.acm.org/doi/10.1145/2488388.2488433
- Katz index computation (paper from 2019): https://arxiv.org/abs/1912.06525

10
Graph Embedding - from Graphs to Matrices

In this chapter, we will continue to explore the topic of graph analytics and address the last piece of the puzzle: feature learning through graphs via embedding. Embedding became popular thanks to the word embedding used in **Natural Language Processing** (NLP). In this chapter, we will first address why embedding is important and learn about the different types of analyses covered by the term **graph embedding**. Following that, we will start learning about embedding algorithms from a number of algorithms based on the graph adjacency matrix trying to reduce its size.

Later on, we will continue our journey by discovering how neural networks can help with embedding. Starting with the example of word embedding, we will learn about the skip-gram model and draw parallels with graphs with the DeepWalk algorithm. Finally, in the last section, we will talk about other graph embedding techniques and conclude with some words about a new promising type of algorithm: **Graph Neural Networks** (**GNNs**).

The following topics will be covered in this chapter:

- Why do we need embedding?
- Adjacency-based embedding
- Extracting embeddings from artificial neural networks
- Graph neural networks
- Going further with graph algorithms

Technical requirements

In this chapter, we will use the following technologies and libraries:

- Neo4j and the GDS
- Python (>= 3.6) with the following packages (all pip-installable):
    - Jupyter Notebooks (or Jupyter Lab)
    - Pandas, NumPy, Matplotlib
    - Networkx
    - Karateclub: https://github.com/benedekrozemberczki/karateclub

The code used in this chapter is available on GitHub at https://github.com/PacktPublishing/Hands-On-Graph-Analytics-with-Neo4j/ch10/.

Why do we need embedding?

Machine learning models are based on matrix calculations: our observations are organised into rows in a table, while the features are columns or vectors. Representing complex objects such as text or graphs as matrices of a reasonable size can be a challenge. This is the issue that embedding techniques are designed to address.

Why is embedding needed?

In Chapter 8, *Using Graph-Based Features in Machine Learning*, we drew the following schema:

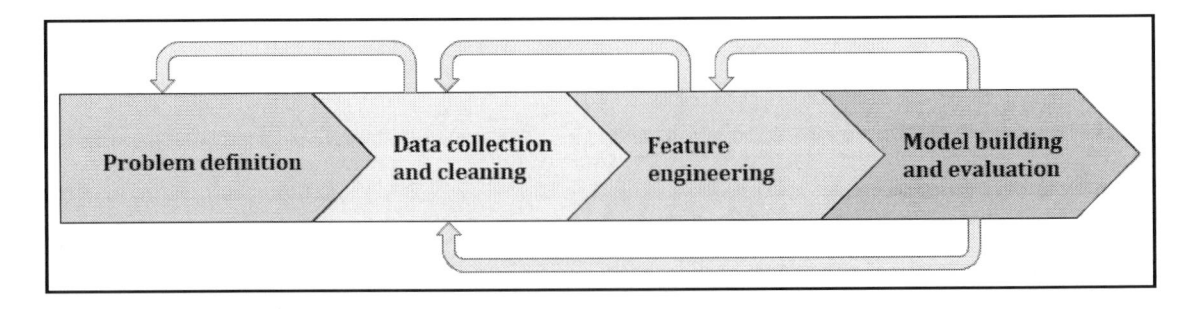

The **Feature engineering** step involves extracting features from our dataset. When this dataset consists of observations that already have numerical or categorical characteristics, it is easy to imagine how to build features from these characteristics.

However, some datasets do not have that tabular structure. In such cases, we need to create that structure before feeding the dataset into a machine learning model.

Take a text, such as a book, for example, that contains thousands of words. Now imagine that your task is to predict, from a given word, which word is more likely to come after. To create this model, we need to find a machine learning model such that:

$$Model(Word) = Next\ Word$$

However, machine learning models, from linear regression to artificial neural networks, work with feature vectors. Therefore, we need to find a list of features associated with each $V(Word)$, and then fit a model to these vectors:

$$Model(V(Word)) = V(Next\ Word)$$

The challenge is to find a *good V*. Prior to this, however, we need to define what a *good V* is.

One-hot encoding

Let's consider the following quotation, uttered by the famous character Detective Sherlock Holmes in the novel *A Study in Scarlett*, by Arthur Conan Doyle:

It is a capital mistake to theorize before one has data.

First, we will simplify this sentence by removing words that do not provide any information, such as *a* and *the* (known as stop words in NLP) and remove the conjugate form of the verbs:

be capital mistake theorize before one have data

In most cases, we would also order words, let's say into alphabetical order, and remove duplicates, which would leave us with the following words to encode:

be before capital date have mistake one theorize

In order to represent each word of this corpus with a vector, we can use the one-hot encoding technique. This involves creating a vector of size equal to the number of words in the corpus, with zeros everywhere except at the index of the word. This is illustrated in the following diagram:

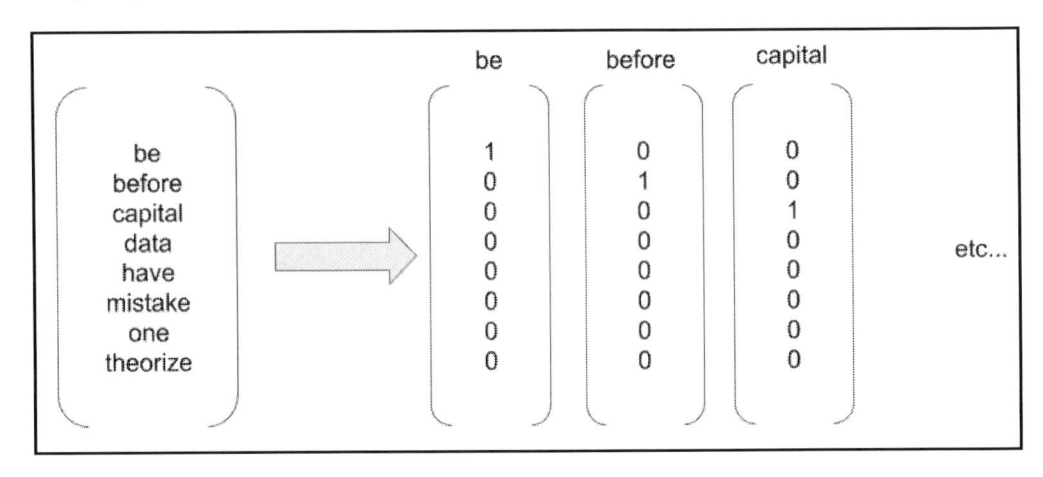

The word *be* is the first word in our corpus, so the vector representing this word has zeros everywhere except at the first position, where we put a 1.

Using this technique means each word has as many features as the number of words in the dataset. In a real text analysis application, a corpus can have several tens of thousands of words, so, as you can imagine, representing the whole dataset as discussed would be memory-inefficient. Even if we were to take advantage of the data sparsity and use sparse matrix representation, we might fall into the curse of dimensionality.

This issue arises when the number of observations makes it impossible to cover the whole feature space. Imagine you have one feature X, with values uniformly distributed between 0 and 10. If you want one point per bin of size 1, you will need roughly 10 observations. If you add another feature, Y, with the same distribution and want to cover the full 2D plane made of X and Y, meaning having at least one point in each square of size 1×1, then you will require 100 observations. And this number continues to grow as you add more features, until it becomes impossible for you to gather that many observations.

This is where embedding comes in. The embedding technique allows us to find a vector representation for each word, involving fewer dimensions than the total number of words. The features are chosen in a way that preserves key information about the initial dataset, such as word meaning.

Chapter 10

Creating features for words – the manual way

In a text corpus, each observation corresponds to a word and we need to find and quantify **characteristics** for each observation. It makes sense to create features so that words representing similar concepts will have similar features. As a first example, let's consider some characters from the *Star Wars* movies.

We can try and find a list of characteristics for each character. Here, three characteristics are identified: gender, species, and goodness (0 for bad, 1 for good). Using these three characteristics, we can build the following table:

Character	Gender	Species	Goodness
Darth Vader	1	1	0
Yoda	1	2	1
Princess Leia	0	1	1
R2D2	1	3	1

Darth Vader is a man from the Dark Side of the Force – the bad people in the saga, while Leia and Yoda are on the Light Side – the good people. While Darth Vader and Leia are both humans, R2D2 is a robot and Yoda is from an alien species.

We can conduct the same exercise for other categories of words. Let's consider colors as features, for example. If we choose three features – redness, greenness, and blueness, we can represent them using the following table:

Color	Redness	Greenness	Blueness
Red	1	0	0
Green	0	1	0
Blue	0	0	1
White	1	1	1
Yellow	1	1	0
Black	0	0	0
Orange	1	0.6	0
Violet	0.9	0.5	0.9

The first column (feature) encodes the level of redness of each color, while the second and third columns give information about its greenness and blueness.

[385]

Graph Embedding - from Graphs to Matrices

In this example, we see another interesting aspect of word representation. We can measure how close two real-number vectors are by using, for instance, a dot product. Hence, we can measure the closeness of *red* and *blue* using the vector representation from the previous table:

$$V(Red) \cdot V(Blue) = (1, 0, 0) \cdot (0, 0, 1) = 0$$

The closeness between *violet* and *blue* is much higher:

$$V(Violet) \cdot V(Blue) = (0.9, 0.5, 0.9) \cdot (0, 0, 1) = 0.9$$

Our vector representation of colors tells us that *blue* is much closer to *violet* than to *red*. This representation therefore looks good since it also carries some information about the colors that one-hot encoding cannot see. Indeed, the dot product of two one-hot encoded vectors will return either 1 (when the vectors are identical) or 0 (when the vectors are different), thereby hiding any shade of difference in between.

Now we have two sets of characteristics: [*Redness, Greenness, Blueness*] on one side, and [*Gender, Species, Goodness*] on the other. We can merge them to have a full set [*Redness, Greenness, Blueness, Gender, Species, Goodness*]:

Word	Redness	Greenness	Blueness	Gender	Species	Goodness
Red	1	0	0	0	0	0
Darth Vader	0	0	0	1	1	0

We also know that Yoda has a certain greenness, so we can fill in the color features for him:

Word	Redness	Greenness	Blueness	Gender	Species	Goodness
Yoda	0.4	0.6	0.3	0	0	0

This section has given you an idea about how we want the features to appear when representing words. As you can see, manually building features to represent all the words in a corpus is not feasible. However, we have discussed the important concept of similarity: embedding will not return random numbers but somehow **encode** the similarity between entities (words here).

Now, let's move on and learn how embedding techniques can solve our problem.

Embedding specifications

The goal of embedding is to encode words as a vector *V(word)* with dimension $d \ll N$, such that the word meaning is somehow preserved. So, starting with the one-hot encoded matrix representing words, we want to end up with a matrix with size $N \times d$, where *d* is small, as illustrated in the following diagram:

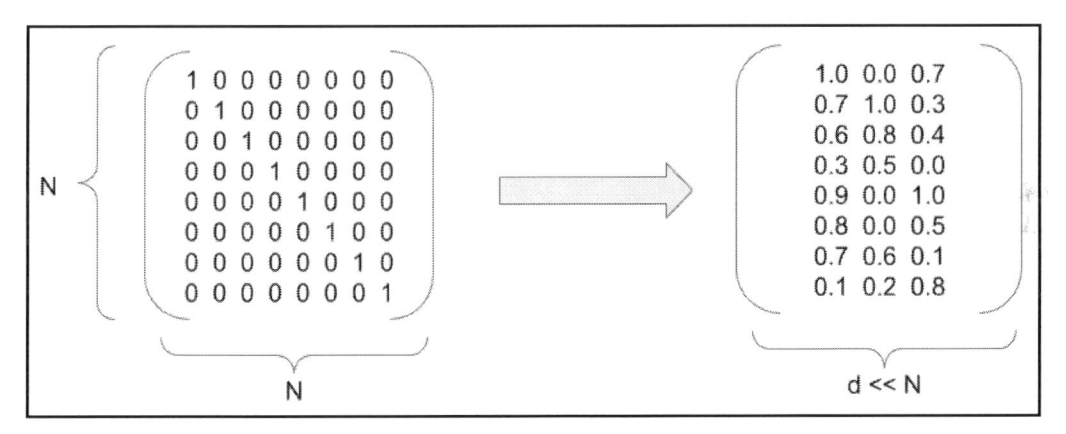

However, so far, all we have done is reduce the number of features. What it actually means to preserve the word meaning is illustrated by the following diagram:

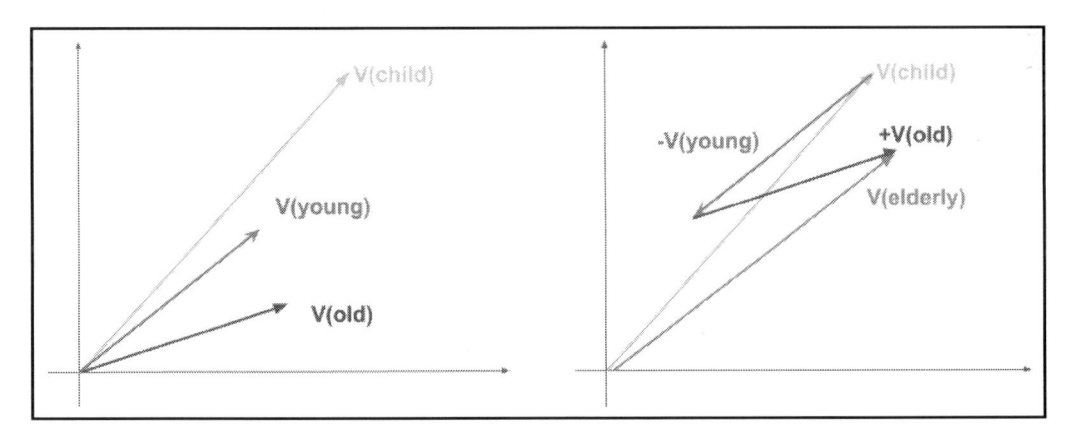

This diagram shows four words – *child*, *young*, *old*, and *elderly*, each represented by two-dimensional vectors. These vectors are related to each other as in the following equation:

$$V(child) - V(young) + V(old) \approx V(elderly)$$

Graph Embedding - from Graphs to Matrices

This means that if you take the vector representing the word *child* and remove from it the vector representing the word *young*, you have an intermediate vector representing a person without age. If you add to this vector the vector representation of the word *old*, then you must find the vector representing an *elderly* person.

In other words, embedding not only reduces the number of features needed to describe an entity, but also encodes some part of the problem so that two close entities in the real dataset are also close in the embedding space. The concept of similarity is therefore very important when talking about embedding; measuring how similar two entities are is crucial and badly represented entities will lead to poor results when used in a prediction problem.

While texts are a long sequence of words, graphs, even if not sequential, are a long list of nodes, connected to each other through edges. Since graphs are made up of several entities, nodes on one side and edges on the other side, *graph embedding* can actually refer to several types of algorithms, depending on the entity being encoded.

The graph embedding landscape

In the previous two chapters, we saw how to apply a traditional machine learning pipeline to graphs, using either nodes or edges as observations. We have discussed how to create the features to represent nodes and edges based on some node properties and graph structure (communities, node importance, neighborhood).

A graph contains two different types of objects, nodes and edges, and both can be the entity of interest for a given analysis and be represented as vectors. In Chapter 8, *Using Graph-Based Features in Machine Learning*, we were interested in nodes and studied how to perform some node classification. Similar to text, we can create N×N matrix representations of graphs, where N is the number of nodes, using an adjacency matrix. However, being able to find a lower dimensional vector of node representation while preserving the **structure of the graph** would be very useful.

In Chapter 9, *Predicting Relationships*, our observations were edges. Modeling edges with a matrix containing all possible edges between nodes would have N^2 elements.

To recap, graph embedding covers three types of algorithms:

- **Node embedding**: The objects being embedded are nodes, so the algorithm creates one vector per node. This can be used in node classification problems.
- **Edge embedding**: Here, we use the edges as main entities, and try to assign a vector to each of them like we manually did in the previous chapter (Chapter 9, *Predicting Relationships*) using the Adamic-Adar score.

- **Whole-graph embedding**: Finally, there is another embedding application where the whole graph can be represented as a single vector. One application of whole-graph embedding is in small graphs analysis (such as molecules where atoms are nodes connected to each other via chemical bonds). It can be useful to study graph evolution over time, and whole-graph embedding can give us information about the dynamic of the graph.

> Many authors will use the term *graph embedding* to refer to node embedding, so don't be surprised if you encounter this term very frequently.

In the rest of this chapter, we will focus on the most common graph embedding algorithm, which is the node embedding problem. Before doing so, let's focus on the main word embedding method, as this will help us understand the concept before applying it to graphs.

Adjacency-based embedding

Graphs can be represented as large matrices pretty easily. The first technique we are going to study that can reduce the size of this matrix is called **matrix factorization**.

The adjacency matrix and graph Laplacian

Similar to text analysis, graphs can be represented by a very large matrix encoding the relationships between nodes. We have already used such a matrix in the preceding chapters – the adjacency matrix, named M in the following diagram:

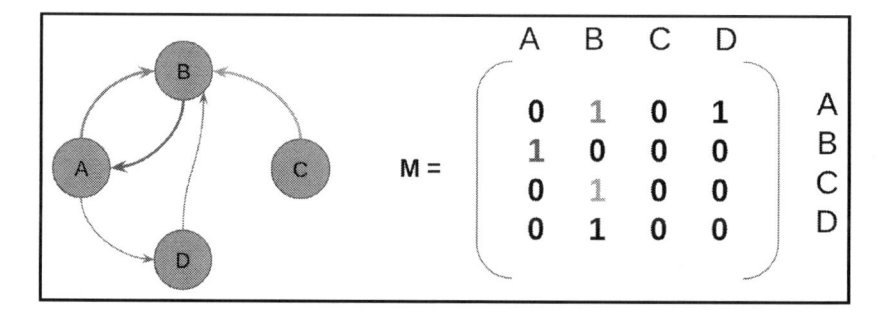

$$M = \begin{pmatrix} & A & B & C & D \\ 0 & 1 & 0 & 1 \\ 1 & 0 & 0 & 0 \\ 0 & 1 & 0 & 0 \\ 0 & 1 & 0 & 0 \end{pmatrix} \begin{matrix} A \\ B \\ C \\ D \end{matrix}$$

Other algorithms rely on the graph Laplacian matrix $L = D - M$ where D is the diagonal matrix containing the degree of each node. But the principles remain unchanged.

Eigenvectors embedding

One simple way of reducing the size of the matrix is to decompose it into eigenvectors, and use only a reduced number of these vectors as embedding.

An example of such graph representation can be seen when using graph **positioning**. Indeed, drawing a graph on a two-dimensional plane is a type of embedding. One of the positioning techniques that can be found in `networkx` is called `spectral_layout` and consists of decomposing the Laplacian matrix into its eigenvectors.

Locally linear embedding

Locally linear embedding (LLE) assumes that the vector representation of a node n_i, let's call it V_i, must be a linear combination of the vector representations of the neighbors of i, $N(i)$. It is encoded into the following equation, where the adjacency matrix is denoted by the letter M:

$$V_i = \sum_{j \in N(i)} M_{ij} \times V_j$$

Finding an embedding is hence reduced to an optimization problem where you are finding the vectors V_i such that the distance between V_i and the linear combination of its neighbors is as small as possible. In mathematical terms, we end up with a least-squares minimization problem, where the function to minimize is as follows:

$$\Phi(V) = \sum_i (V_i - \sum_{j \in N(i)} M_{ij} \times V_j)^2$$

This problem contains many variables since the unknown variables are the components of the V_i vectors – hence $N \times d$. However, it can be shown that the solutions to this problem are the first $d+1$ eigenvectors of the matrix $M' = (I-M)^T(I-M)$, hence, the problem is reduced to an eigenvector problem.

> LLE techniques can also be used outside of the graph context. Generally, neighbors are defined by a k-nearest neighbors approach, and the weights M_{ij} are learned in the first stage of the algorithm.

Similarity-based embedding

If we are unable to make any hypothesis about what the vectors look like in the embedding space, we can still assume that they need to preserve some sort of similarity.

High-Order Proximity preserved Embedding (HOPE)

Just as we did earlier when comparing similarity between colors using the dot product of their vector representation, we can measure embedded node similarity by computing the dot product of their vectors. However, we can also measure node similarity using other heuristics, like the ones we studied in Chapter 7, *Community Detection and Similarity Measures*. Jaccard or Adamic-Adar similarities are well-known examples of node similarity measures.

We can build a node embedding by trying to make the vector similarity of two nodes as close as possible. The node similarity in the vector space is measured by the dot product of the embedding vectors, $V_i \cdot V_j$, while the node similarity in the graph is measured by a scoring function, S_{ij}. This scoring function can be computed using any similarity measure (for instance Adamic-Adar). Reducing the difference between these two measures requires the following function to be minimized:

$$\Phi(V) = \sum_{i,j} (V_i \cdot V_j - S_{ij})^2$$

In this section, we have covered a number of embedding techniques, but many more can be found. In the following section, I will introduce the `karateclub` Python package that contains many implementations, along with links to the related papers.

Computing node embedding with Python

Node embedding algorithms are usually first implemented by researchers trying to find new ways to represent graphs in a low-dimensional space. There are many people working on this topic using different languages. Hopefully, when it comes to using graph algorithms such as embedding with Python, we can find packages aimed at harmonizing these implementations under a consistent API. Among them, we can quote the following:

- `scikit-networks`: Within the scikit toolbox, this uses the exact same API as `scikit-learn`, with fit/transform methods for each algorithm. Graphs need to be represented as adjacency matrices, using either `numpy` or `scipy` sparse matrices.

- `karateclub`: This uses a similar API even if not strictly identical to `scikit-learn`, except that it is based on the `networkx` package and its graph representation.

Even if `scikit-networks` is closer to the `scikit-learn` API by construction, it contains only a few embedding algorithms so far; that's why we are going to use the `karateclub` package in the rest of this section. Since `karateclub` is based on `networkx`, our first task is create a `networkx` graph object from a Neo4j graph.

> **TIP**
> Don't confuse the `karateclub` package with the karateclub graph: the karateclub graph is an example graph comprising 34 nodes, while the `karateclub` package contains graph algorithms that can be run on any graph.

Creating a networkx graph

There are many ways to create graph objects for `networkx`, from importing edgelist files to reading a pandas DataFrame. Here, we want to feed it from a Neo4j graph. We will therefore use `networkx.from_pandas_edge_list`, since we already know from previous chapters how to create a DataFrame from Neo4j.

The Neo4j test graph

In this section, we will use the well-known Zachary's karateclub graph (see `Chapter 7`, *Community Detection and Similarity Measures*). This is a very popular graph in the graph community and probably inspired the name of the package. The Cypher query to create this graph in Neo4j is provided in the code files associated with this book.

Extracting the edge list data from Neo4j

Extracting an edge list from Neo4j is quite straightforward since we only need two pieces of information: the source node and the target node, linked together by a relationship. Considering our graph is undirected, we can use the following Cypher query to extract the pair of nodes linked together through a relationship of the `LINK` type:

```
MATCH (n:Node)-[r:LINK]-(m:Node)
RETURN n.id as source, m.id as target
```

So, similar to what we did in the previous chapters, we can extract this data using the Neo4j Python driver:

```
from neo4j import GraphDatabase

driver = GraphDatabase.driver("bolt://localhost:7687", auth=("neo4j",
"<YOUR_PASSWORD>"), encrypted=False)
with driver.session() as session:
    res = session.run("""
            MATCH (n:Node)-[r:LINK]-(m:Node)
            RETURN n.id as source, m.id as target
        """)
```

The result object, `res`, can then be exploited to create a new DataFrame:

```
data = pd.DataFrame.from_records(res.data())
```

We can now use this DataFrame to create a graph, using the `networkx` structure.

Creating a networkx graph matrix from pandas

The first rows of the DataFrame we have just created are reproduced in the following diagram:

	source	target	weight
0	0	8	1
1	0	6	1
2	0	13	1
3	0	12	1
4	0	17	1

We can use this to create the `networkx` graph using the following function:

```
import networkx as nx

G = nx.from_pandas_edgelist(data)
```

Graph Embedding - from Graphs to Matrices

> **TIP**
> The name of the columns used as *source* and *target* are configurable. In the preceding code, I have used the default values, but I could have written the following command:
>
> ```
> G = nx.from_pandas_edgelist(data, source="source", target="target")
> ```

Now that we have our graph object, we can run algorithms on it, for instance, node embedding.

Fitting a node embedding algorithm

As an example, we will run the HOPE embedding algorithm. We first need to import it from `karateclub`:

```
from karateclub import HOPE
```

Then, similar to what we would do with `scikit-learn`, we can create the model instance:

```
hope = HOPE(dimensions=10)
```

The `dimension` parameter gives the size *d* of the resulting embedding.

Once the model is created, it can be fitted on a `networkx` graph:

```
hope.fit(G)
```

In order to extract the embedding from the fitted model, we need to use the `get_embedding` method:

```
embeddings = hope.get_embedding()
```

And here we are. You can check that the `embeddings` variable is a matrix of size 34 (*number of nodes*) × 10 (*dimension of the embedding vector*).

Finally, we can try and visualize the embedding vectors. Since visualization is easier in a two-dimensional space, a **Principal Component Analysis (PCA)** is performed on the embedding to reduce its size to 2 before plotting:

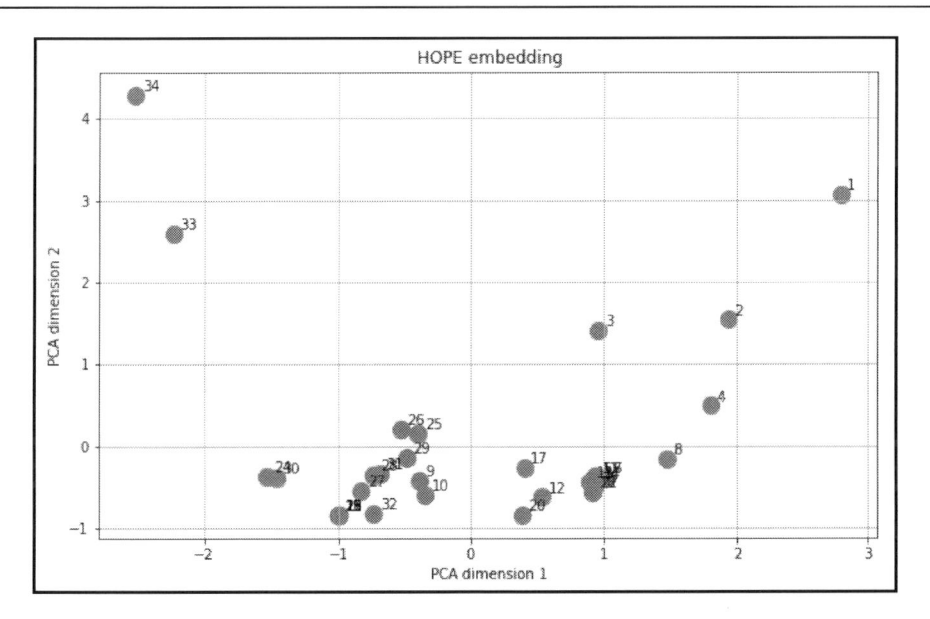

In order to evaluate the quality of the embedding, let's draw the graph and make the ground truth communities appear:

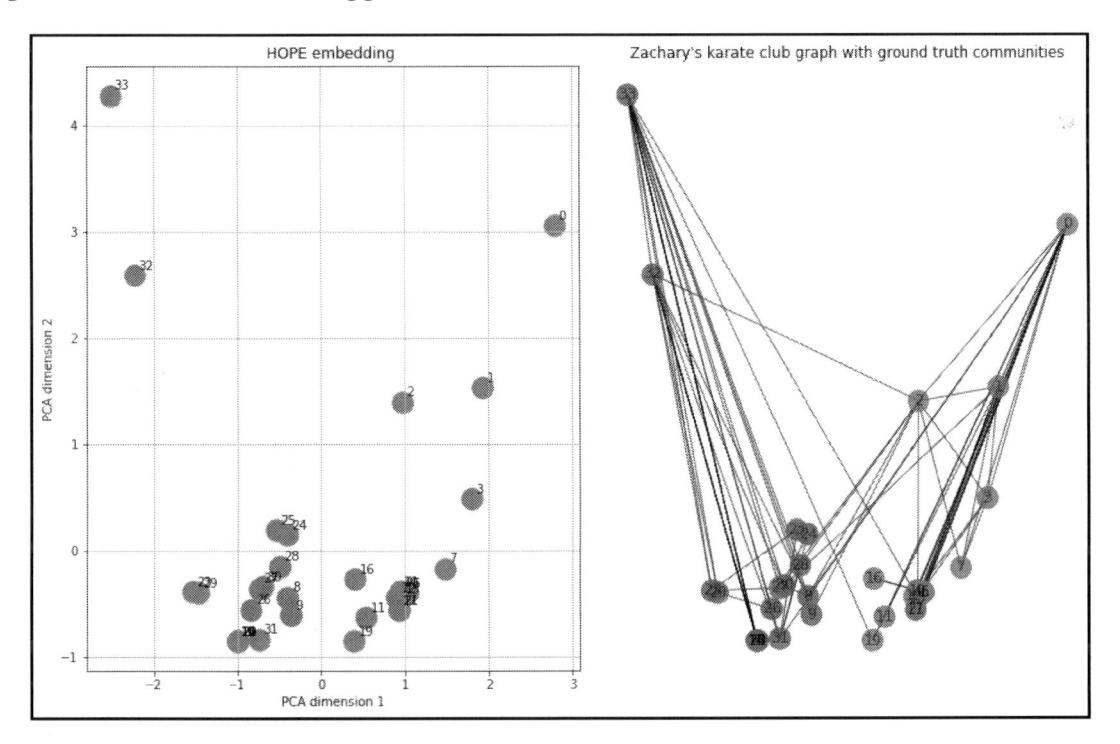

As you can see, the HOPE embedding performs quite well in splitting the graph into its two real communities. A clustering algorithm could give us some meaningful and more quantitative metrics on this result, but I'll leave this task up to you (refer to the *Questions* section).

The `karateclub` package contains many more algorithms with links to the associated paper. The one we are going to deal with now is probably one of the most famous node embedding algorithms, based on random walks through the graph.

Extracting embeddings from artificial neural networks

Neural networks are the new gold standard of models for machine learning. Thanks to this structure, impressive progress has been made, from image analysis to speech recognition, and computers are now able to perform increasingly complex tasks. One surprising application of neural networks is their ability to model complex objects, such as images, text, or audio records, with fewer dimensions, while still preserving some aspects of the original dataset (shapes in the image, frequencies in the audio, and so on). In this section, following a quick general review of neural networks, we will focus on one architecture called skip-gram, which was first used in the context of word embedding but can be extended to graphs as well.

Artificial neural networks in a nutshell

Artificial neural networks were inspired by the human brain, where millions of neurons are connected to each other through synapses. The human brain is clearly adept at learning and recognition. For example, once you have seen an example of a squirrel, you can recognize all squirrels, even if they are smaller, a different color, or if the camera angle is different:

Chapter 10

A reminder about neural network principles

Let's review some of the basic principles of neural networks, focusing on what is pertinent within the context of embedding.

Neurons, layers, and forward propagation

In order to understand how neural networks work, let's consider a simple classification problem with two input features, x_1 and x_2, and a single output class O, whose value can be 0 or 1.

A simple neural network that can be used to solve this problem is illustrated in the following diagram:

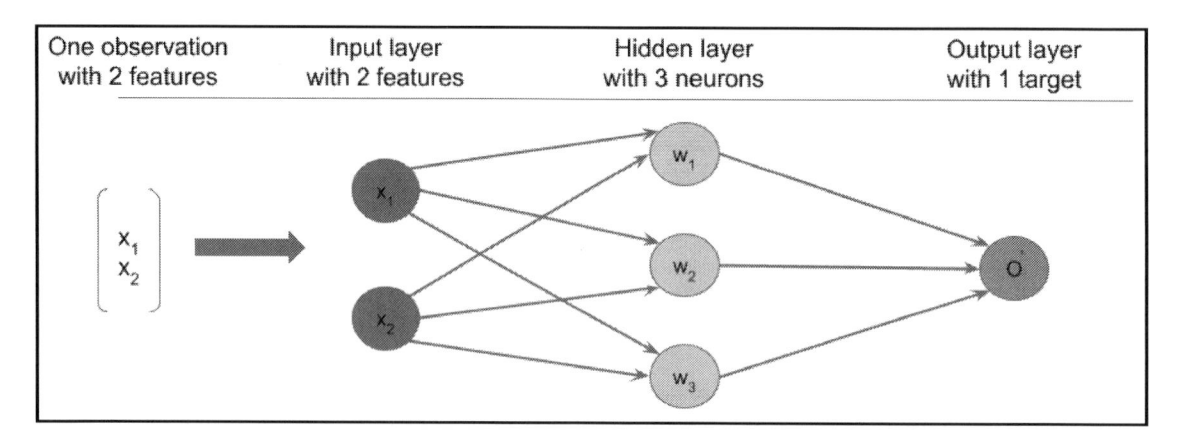

The neural network has a single hidden layer comprising three neurons (the middle layer) and the output layer (right-most layer). Each neuron of the hidden layer has a vector of weights, w_i, whose size is equal to the size of the input layer. These weights are the model parameter that we will try to optimize so that the output is close to the truth.

When an observation is fed into the network through the input layer, the following happens:

1. Each neuron of the hidden layer receives all the input features.
2. Each neuron of the hidden layer computes the weighted sum of these features, using its weight vector and bias. As an example, the output of the first neuron of the hidden layer would be as follows:

$$h_1 = (x_1, x_2) \cdot W_1 + b_1 = x_1 \times w_{11} + x_2 \times w_{12} + b_1$$

3. The output layer also performs a weighted combination of its inputs, which are the output of the last hidden layer:

$$o = (h_1, h_2, h_3) \cdot O + b_O = h_1 \times o_1 + h_2 \times o_2 + h_3 \times o_3 + b_O$$

4. This process is repeated with all the observations in the dataset.

5. An *error* metric, or loss function, is computed, comparing the network output and the expected label. Based on this loss function, weights in the hidden layer are adjusted (backpropagation).
6. Repeat the process until the loss function can no longer be significantly improved.

Hidden layers can be chained together. In this case, the output of the ith hidden layer is the input for the $(i+1)^{th}$ hidden layer, until the output layer. This makes this kind of structure highly customizable and, depending on the goal, many different ways of combining layers can be imagined.

> I won't go into the details of the activation functions, even if they are part of the neural network's magic, since they allow non-linearity to be introduced into the model. Check the *Further reading* section to learn more about them.

Different types of neural networks

Many different neural network architectures are possible depending on what you wish to achieve. Each architecture defines its own layers and how they transform the input values. The most famous types of neural network are the following:

- **Convolutional Neural Networks (CNNs)**: These are usually used for image analysis, and are very efficient at finding shapes within a two-dimensional image. They can be used for:
    - Image classification
    - **Optical Character Recognition (OCR)** for a computer to transform an image showing text into an editable text document
    - Object detection on images that can have applications, for example, in the following areas:
        - Healthcare with applications in breast cancer detection
        - Self-driving cars, which need to understand their environment, partly using images coming from on-board cameras, in order to choose the best trajectory

- **Recurrent Neural Networks (RNNs)**: These are very good at analyzing sequences of data, such as texts or time series. They can be used for the following application:
    - **Image captioning**: Finding a set of words that best describe an image
    - **Sentiment analysis**: Classifying a text as being positive or negative in tone
    - **Text translation**: Translating a text from one language to another

You will also find in the literature adversarial neural networks, which can be used to fill missing data and many more applications besides. In the last section of this book, we will even see how graphs can be related to neural networks via GNNs.

Understanding each of these structures is beyond the scope of this book. I am also not detailing here the concepts of loss function, backpropagation, or gradient descent, which are not important for the upcoming sections. Please refer to the *Further reading* section if you are interested in learning more about neural network architecture and how skip-graphs work.

In the next section, we will focus on a simple, yet powerful, type of neural network that will help us create the **skip-gram** model of embedding.

Skip-graph model

Artificial neural networks contain one or several hidden layers. Usually, the values of the weights of the hidden layers learned by the network are not particularly interesting: they are just parameters of the model and we only care about the model output. For instance, when using a CNN to predict whether your image is a dog or a cat, you just want to get the prediction out of your model. Embedding is the exact opposite; we are not directly interested in the model output, but in the weights learned by the hidden layer, which are the embedded words.

Fake task

In order to train a neural network like any other machine learning model, we need to define a task to be done, that is, the goal of the predictor; for example, classification based on some labels or text translation. In an embedding scenario, we are not really interested in the model output, but we still need to define it in order for the neural network to be trained. That's why we refer to a *fake task* in this context.

In the skip-gram model, the fake task is the following: given a word, look at the words nearby and return one of these words randomly. This task was chosen because we can assume that *similar words have similar context* – *cooking* and *kitchen* are more likely to be part of the same sentence than *kitchen* and *parachute*.

In practice, *nearby* is determined by a number N, and all words within the window of size N around the target word are considered to be in the target word neighborhood.

Input

Let's take a look at the shape of the training dataset and talk first about the word representation before embedding. We will then focus on the definition of the model target.

Word representation before embedding

One possible approach is to use **one-hot encoder** and create a matrix of size $N \times N$ where N is the number of distinct words in the text, also known as the dictionary. The value of each matrix element is either 0 or 1, as explained in the first section of this chapter.

Target

Remember that our fake task is to predict words within a window of given size around the word. So our target variable is also a word and our training set will be made up of pairs of words appearing within the same context. Context here is defined by the size of the window; the larger the window size, the bigger our dataset (we can create more pairs). However, if window sizes are larger, we start getting more irrelevant data in the training set, since we will get pairs of words appearing quite far away from each other.

Let's consider again the quotation from Sherlock Holmes:

> *It is a capital mistake to theorize before one has data.*

Considering a window size of 2, we will create the dataset in the following way (see the following diagram). Starting from the first word, the input, we can pair it with all the words within a 2-word window. Since we are considering the first word of the text, we can only move toward the right and encounter two words: *is* and *a*. Hence, we create two training samples: (*it, is*) and (*it, a*). By moving to the next word, *is*, we can pair it with the next two words, *a* and *capital*, but also with the previous word, *it*. So, we can create three pairs of training samples, and so on, until the final word:

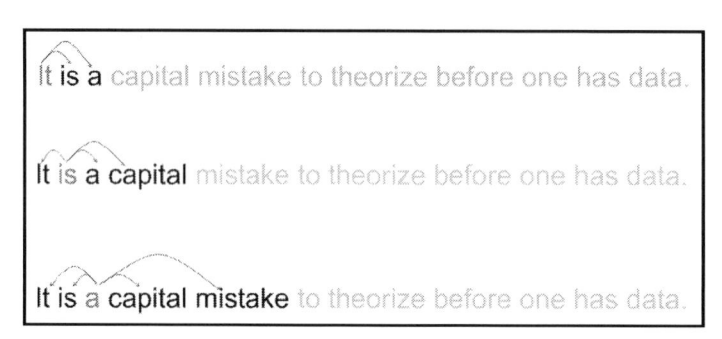

> It is a capital mistake to theorize before one has data.
>
> It is a capital mistake to theorize before one has data.
>
> It is a capital mistake to theorize before one has data.

So, when using a window size of *s*=2, the generated input dataset will contain the following pairs:

```
(it, is)
(it, a)

(is, it)
(is, a)
(is, capital)

(a, it)
(a, is)
(a capital)
(a mistake)
```
...

The first element of the tuple is the input, while the second element is one of the expected output. Since our words are one-hot encoded, the real input dataset will contains elements such as the following:

```
( (1, 0, 0, 0, 0, ...), (0, 1, 0, 0, 0, ...) )
( (1, 0, 0, 0, 0, ...), (0, 0, 1, 0, 0, ...) )
( (0, 1, 0, 0, 0, ...), (1, 0, 0, 0, 0, ...) )
```

Hidden layer

The skip-gram neural network architecture contains one single hidden layer. The number of neurons in that layer corresponds to the dimension of the embedding space or the number, *d*, of features following dimensionality reduction. The following diagram illustrates how we can go from the neuron weights in the hidden layer (one vector of length *N* for each of the *d* neurons, the vertical vectors) to the word embedding, *N* vectors of length *d* (the horizontal vectors on the right):

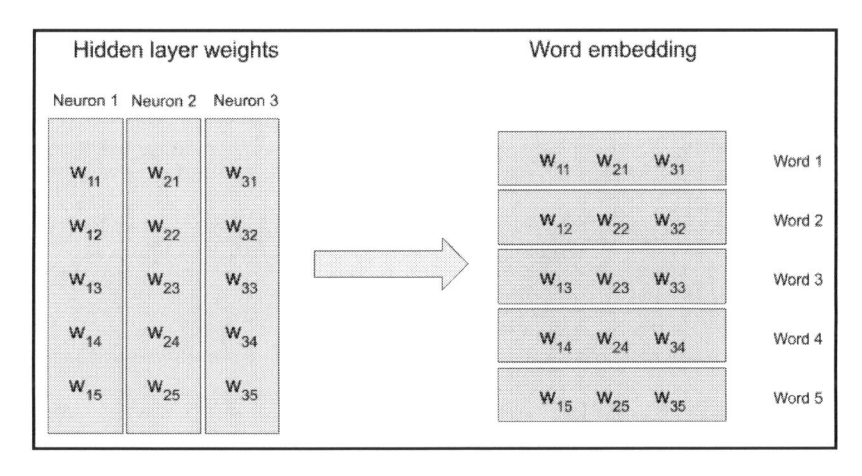

Since the skip-graph network has a single hidden layer, the next step in the calculation flow is the output layer.

Output layer

Remember our fake task: predicting a word within the same context (window) from the input word. This means that we are not trying to execute a binary classification (the example used in the introductory section about neural networks), but rather a classification with *N* classes, *N* being the number of words in the corpus. Hence, the output layer contains *N* neurons whose values are either 0 or 1: if the value of the neuron at index *i* is 1, the word *i* is the chosen word, meaning the network predicts that word *i* is within the same context as the input word. In practice, neural networks will use a softmax classifier, where the softmax function gives the *probability* of a word being in the same context as the input word:

$$softmax(i) = e^{o_i} / \Sigma_i\, e^{o_i}$$

In this formula, o_i is the output of the the ith neuron in the output layer.

This is the basic idea behind skip-gram. In practice, some care needs to be taken when implementing such a model:

- Certain words, such as *the*, will be over-represented, which makes them much more likely to appear close to any other word.
- With large corpus sizes, the number of weights to optimize grows quickly (remember that we have $N \times d$ weights in the hidden layer).

Solutions have been proposed to deal with both of these issues, by using sub-sampling and negative sampling techniques. Going into such details here goes beyond the scope of this book, but you will be able to dig deeper into the skip-gram model with the references listed in the *Further reading* section.

Now that we have a better understanding of the skip-gram model and how it can be used to create word embeddings, let's go back to the context of graphs and talk about the DeepWalk algorithm, a skip-gram-based node embedding technique.

DeepWalk node embedding

DeepWalk is probably one of the most famous node embedding algorithms, developed in 2014 by *Perozzi et al*. Its core concept is analogous to the word embedding algorithm we studied in the previous section, using random walks through the graph to generate sentences.

Generating node context through random walks

In the word embedding scenario, we generated the word context by pairing the word with all the words located close to it, within a given window size. However, graphs are not sequential, so how can we generate a context for nodes? The solution is to use random walks through the graph, with a given length.

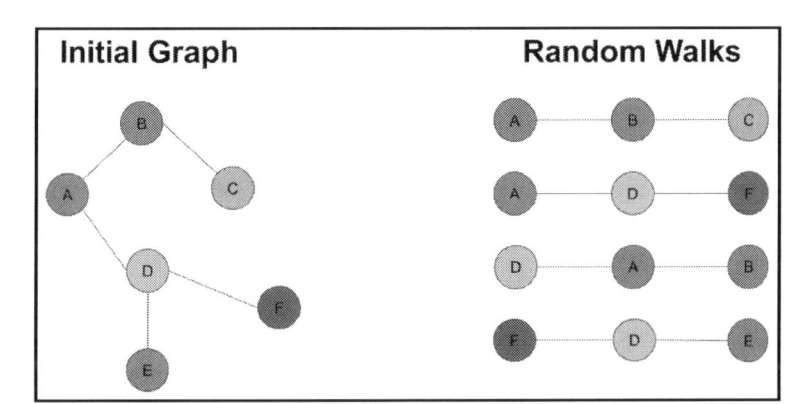

Consider the graph represented in the following diagram on the left:

Starting from node *A*, we can generate paths of length 3 going through *B* then *C*, or starting from *D* and continuing to *F* for instance. The paths represented on the right in this diagram are the equivalent of the sentences in the context of text analysis. Using these sequences of nodes, we can now generate a training set and train a skip-gram model.

Before moving on from the topic of DeepWalk, let's extract the random walks from the GDS.

Generating random walks from the GDS

In the GDS, random walks through a projected graph can be generated using the `gds.alpha.randomwalk` procedure in the following way (still using the karateclub graph from the previous sections as an example):

```
MATCH (n:Node {id: 1})
CALL gds.alpha.randomWalk.stream({
    nodeProjection: "*",
    relationshipProjection: {
        LINKED_TO: {
            type: "LINK",
            orientation: "UNDIRECTED"
        }
    },
    start: id(n),
    walks: 1,
    steps: 2
})
YIELD nodeIds
RETURN nodeIds
```

[405]

You can recognize the parameters we have already encountered earlier, to configure the number of walks (here it is equal to 1) and the number of hops to perform (equal to 2 in the preceding query).

The result of the preceding query is a list of node IDs similar to the following:

```
| "nodeIds" |
|-----------|
| [1,317,285] |
```

Here are the sentences needed to feed a skip-gram model.

In practice, it would be much easier to use existing implementations, which take care of everything for us, from the random walks to the neural network training. The karateclub package proposes such an implementation.

DeepWalk embedding with karateclub

In practice, if you are using GDS prior to version 1.3, embedding algorithms are not yet implemented. To train a model, you will have to extract data from Neo4j. We can do this with the karateclub package in a similar way to the previous section. For instance, we can use the following:

```
from karateclub import DeepWalk

dw = DeepWalk(walk_number=50, walk_length=15, dimensions=5)
```

For the DeepWalk algorithm, on top of the number of dimensions in the embedding space d, you can configure the following:

- The number of walks starting from the same node
- The length of each generated path
- The window size to use to generate pairs of nodes forming the training set
- Parameters for the neural network training, learning rate, and the number of epochs (iterations)

An alternative to DeepWalk, node2vec, adds two additional parameters to add more control to the random walk part of the algorithm.

Node2vec, a DeepWalk alternative

While the DeepWalk algorithm uses fully random walks, the node2vec alternative, proposed in 2016, introduces two new parameters to control whether the random walk will be performed depth-first or breadth-first, traditionally named p and q:

- p or the return parameter: A higher p will force the random walk to return to the previous node more often, thereby creating more localized paths.
- q or the in-out parameter: In contrast to the preceding, q gives the probability that the random walk will visit an unknown node further away, hence increasing the *distance* covered by each walk.

So, compared to DeepWalk, node2vec offers more control on the local versus global structure of a graph.

You can generate node2vec-like random walks from the GDS using the `inOut` and `return` parameters:

```
MATCH (n:Node {id: 1})
CALL gds.alpha.randomWalk.stream({
    nodeProjection: "*",
    relationshipProjection: {
        LINKED_TO: {
            type: "LINK",
            orientation: "UNDIRECTED"
        }
    },
    start: id(n),
    walks: 1,
    steps: 2,
    inOut: 0.2,
    return: 1.0
})
YIELD nodeIds
RETURN nodeIds
```

With this approach, you need to extract data from Neo4j to feed a skip-gram model or a function that will do the whole calculation for you (random walks and the model training, like `karateclub` is doing). Starting from version 1.3 of the GDS, it is also possible to compute node embedding without having to do this data extraction beforehand.

Node2vec from the GDS (≥ 1.3)

If you are using Neo4j 4, you are able to use the 1.3 release of the GDS that comes with a few node embedding algorithms. In particular, you can run the node2vec algorithm inside Neo4j. The output of the embedding procedures are the node embeddings themselves. As with any other procedures of the GDS, you first have to create a projected graph, and then you can extract embedding for the nodes in this projected graph with the following query:

```
CALL gds.alpha.node2vec.stream("projected_graph")
```

The `node2vec` procedure returns the embedding vector for each node. You can configure random walks and model training with the configuration map. For instance, let's change the embedding size from 100 (default value) to 20, and the number of generated random walks for each node from 10 to 2:

```
CALL gds.alpha.node2vec.stream("MyGraph", {walksPerNode: 2, embeddingSize: 10})
```

Let's now see how the results of these procedures can be used in a machine learning analysis.

> **TIP**
> As with the other procedures in the GDS, you can also use the write mode for embedding to write the result as a node property instead of streaming it back to the user directly:
> ```
> CALL gds.alpha.node2vec.write("MyGraph", {})
> ```

Getting the embedding results from Python

Computing embedding is usually not the end of the story. Once you have managed to get a vector representation of nodes, you can continue your machine learning task, such as node classification, with your favorite package (this can be scikit-learn to use decision trees or support vectors, for instance). We won't go into the details of such analysis in this book, but here is how to retrieve the computed vectors from Neo4j.

First, we need to create a Neo4j `driver` (check Chapter 8, *Using Graph-Based Features in Machine Learning*, if you don't know about the Neo4j Python driver):

```
from neo4j import GraphDatabase
driver = GraphDatabase.driver("bolt://localhost:7687", auth=("neo4j",
"<YOUR_PASSWORD>"))
```

Then, we can run an embedding procedure and get the results in a DataFrame:

```
import pandas as pd

with driver.session() as session:
    result = session.run(
        "CALL gds.alpha.node2vec('proj_graph')"
    )
    df = pd.DataFrame.from_records(result)
```

However, in `df`, the embedding will be stored as a list in a single column. If we want to extend this list such that each embedding feature is in a separate column, we can use the following code:

```
df = pd.DataFrame(df.tolist())
```

Now, `df` has as many columns as the embedding dimension, meaning each column is a feature. You can use this DataFrame to proceed with the rest of your analysis.

DeepWalk and node2vec embeddings are quite intuitive, but it is important to note that they are *transductive* algorithms. This means that each time a new node is added to the graph, the whole algorithm has to be trained again. From the random walk generations to the neural network training, the embedding of all nodes has to be relearned. This is where GNNs come in; these do not learn embedding themselves, but instead learn how to create the embedding from the graph structure.

Graph neural networks

GNNs were introduced in 2005 and have received a lot of attention during the last 5 years or so. The key concept behind them is to try to generalize the ideas behind CNNs and RNNs to apply them to any type of dataset, including graphs. This section is only a short introduction to GNNs, since we would require an entire book to fully explore the topic. As usual, more references are given in the *Further reading* section if you would like to gain a deeper understanding of this topic.

Extending the principles of CNNs and RNNs to build GNNs

CNNs and RNNs both involve aggregating information from a neighborhood in a special context. For RNNs, the context is a sequence of inputs (words, for instance) and a sequence is nothing more than a special type of graph. The same applies to CNNs, which are used to analyze images, or pixel grids, which are also a special type of graph where each pixel is connected to its adjacent pixels. It is logical therefore to try and use neural networks for all types of graphs (refer to the following diagram):

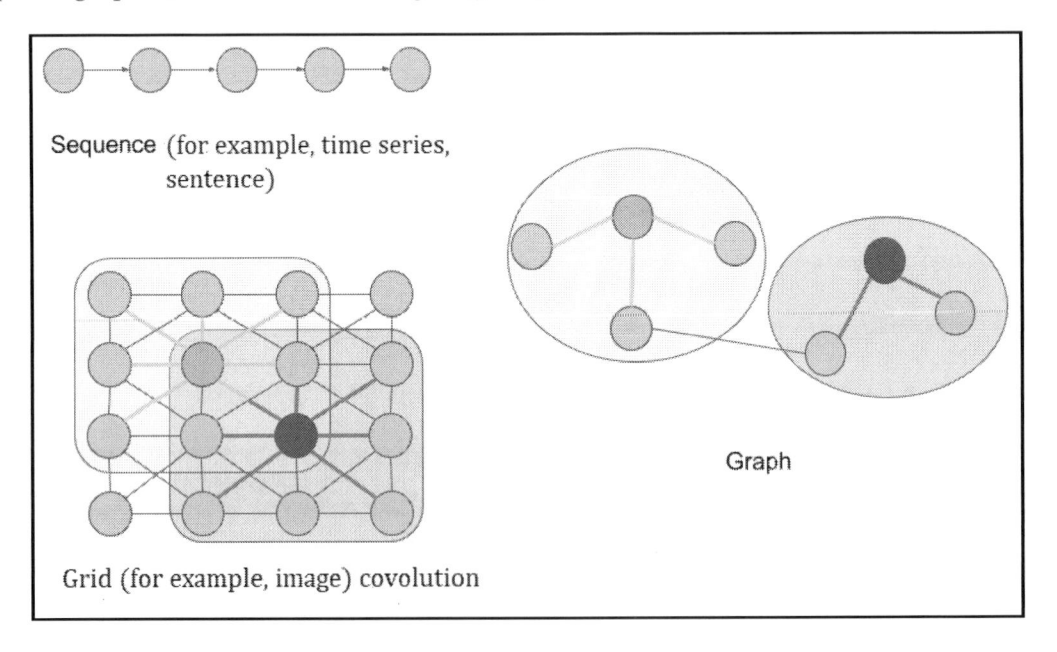

In order to find the embedding associated with each node, GNNs will use the data from that node but also from its neighbors in the graph.

Message propagation and aggregation

A GNN layer performs an aggregation of the *messages* sent by the neighbors of each node. Let's take a look at the following diagram:

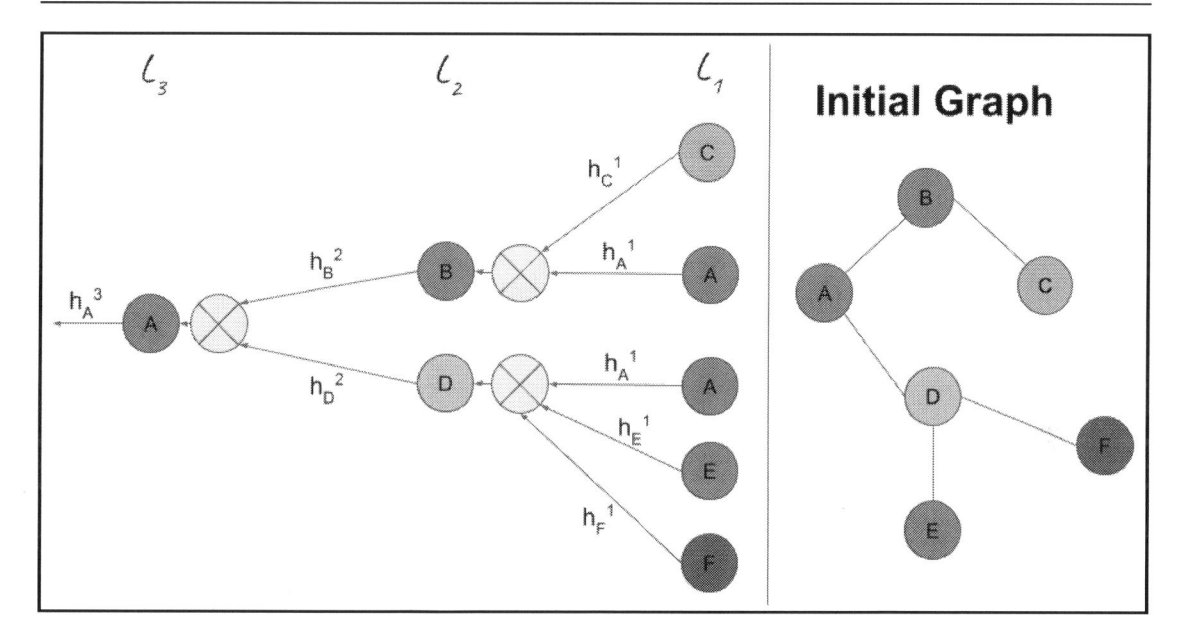

Consider the question:

> *How is the embedding of node A in the third layer, L_3, computed?*

By looking at the graph structure on the right-hand side of the diagram, you can see that A's neighbors are nodes B and D, hence the embedding h_A^3 of node A after layer three is a combination of the embedding of nodes B and D in the previous layer, L_2. The embedding of B and D in layer two is similarly computed using the embedding of their neighbors in the previous layer, L_1. This is summarized by the following equation, giving the embedding of node i in the $(k+1)^{th}$ layer:

$$h_i^{k+1} = \sigma(W_k \Sigma_j h_j^k + B_k h_i^k)$$

The second term of the equation is there to make sure the representation of i in the kth layer is also taken into account and σ is an activation function.

The most important thing to remember from this equation is that W_k and B_k are the parameters the algorithm will learn and **are identical among all nodes**. This means that once the network is trained, W_k and B_k are known, and, when adding a new node, you can compute its embedding using these parameters and its neighbors without having to rerun the full embedding algorithm.

GNNs are *inductive* and therefore *solve* one of the issues of the other embedding algorithms we studied earlier in this chapter.

The preceding equation is quite simple, and many more aggregation techniques have been proposed (replacing the gray crosses in the preceding diagram), which explains the extremely large variety of available layers when building a GNN.

Taking into account node properties

One of the other advantages of GNNs compared to the other node embedding algorithms we have seen in this chapter is their ability to take into account **node features** on top of the graph structure. Indeed, in the previous section, I have not given any details about the network input, h^0. If you do not have node features, you would simply use the one-hot encoded node ID or something similar. However, if your nodes have features, x_i, the input becomes as follows:

$$h_i^0 = x_i$$

You can then propagate this feature vector along the graph, using the graph structure as a propagation path. This is the best way to generate a vector representation of nodes carrying the characteristics of the entities, such as the age of a person or the price of a product, and the relationships between these entities, encoded in the graph structure.

Even though GNNs appeared in the machine learning landscape quite recently, they already had plenty of applications. In the next section, we will explore these applications and discuss how powerful they are.

Applications of GNNs

GNNs have already been proven to be extremely useful in many cases. Besides learning nodes, edges, and whole-graph embedding, they have already been used successfully in the following domains.

Image analysis

Incredible results in the field of image analysis have already been achieved without GNNs, from image classification to object detection. GNNs have been used to further improve this type of analysis.

Video analysis

For instance, GNNs are used to identify object interactions between video frames (interaction networks) or predict the future position of an object without using any physics simulator.

Zero-shot learning

A classification task requires the training dataset to have examples (observations) for all the target classes that will be observed in the test set. Let's just consider a classification task where you would like to extract an animal species from a picture, whatever the animal is. Recent estimates assume that there are around eight million species on the Earth. This means that we will have to build an image dataset with millions of images. In order not to reach these numbers, zero-shot learning tries to infer classes in the test set, **even if they are not in the training set**.

This is an ongoing research topic and several solutions have been proposed to tackle this problem. One approach using GNNs consists of the following idea. Starting from a knowledge graph where each node is a class, connected depending on some attribute's similarity, a GNN is trained whose task is to output a classifier for each class. In practice, the GNN learns the weights of the output layer of a pretrained CNN. Since GNNs are inductive, in order to add a new class, it will suffice to add a node in the class knowledge graph, without adding any image. In other words, a neural network is trained to learn another network's weights.

Text analysis

In the previous section, we used an analogy with words to build our first neural network to infer node embedding (the DeepWalk algorithm). Surprisingly enough, we can also obtain information about a text by turning it into a graph and applying GNNs to it.

To understand why graphs are important in NLP, look at the following diagram, which is repeated from `Chapter 3`, *Empowering Your Business with Pure Cypher*:

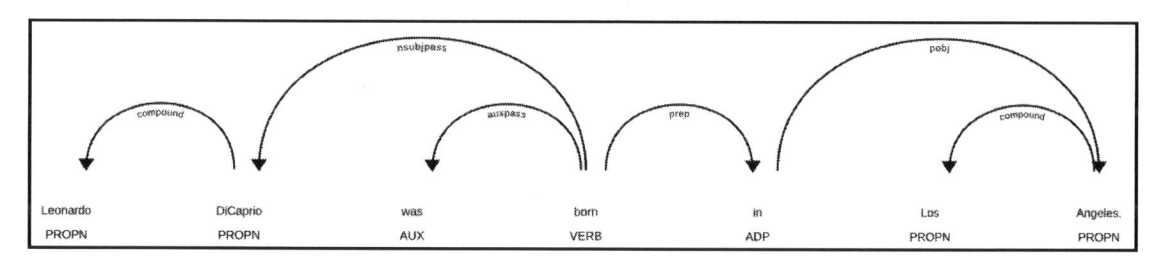

The preceding diagram shows the *relationships* between words in a sentence, and it is clearly not linear.

And there's more...

The applications of GNNs extend beyond image and text analysis. GNNs have, for instance, been used in combinatorial analyses, such as the *Traveling Salesman Problem* (discussed in `Chapter 4`, *The Graph Data Science Library and Path Finding*).

Following this short discussion of GNN applications, let's explore the use of GNNs in practice.

Using GNNs in practice

Several libraries already exist to provide a common API for all type of GNNs, like `scikit-learn` does for machine learning algorithms. In Python, you can refer to any of the following, depending on your favorite deep learning package:

- **PyTorch Geometric**: As the name suggests, this is a PyTorch extension that allows us to deal with complex datasets such as graphs with a new `Dataset` object. It also gathers tens of algorithm implementations (https://github.com/rusty1s/pytorch_geometric).
- **Graph Nets library**: Created by DeepMind, the company behind AlphaGo, the algorithm that was first that was able to beat a human player at Go. With Graph Nets, you will be able to build GNNs using TensorFlow (https://github.com/deepmind/graph_nets).
- **Deep Graph Library (DGL)**: Supporting both PyTorch and TensorFlow, DGL provides tools to build all types of GNNs (https://www.dgl.ai/).
- **GDS**: Starting from its version 1.3, the GDS contains implementations for some embedding algorithms, including one GNN architecture, as we will discuss in the next section.

GNNs from the GDS – GraphSAGE

Starting from its version 1.3, the GDS contains implementations for some embedding algorithms. One of these is the GraphSAGE algorithm, which is part of the GNN family. Invented in 2017 by a group of researchers from the University of Stanford, it is one of the mostly widely used GNN architectures today.

One specificity of GNNs is that they can take node properties into account to get their representation. In the GDS, this behavior is parameterized using the `nodePropertyNames` property. If you prefer not to use properties, you will have to explicitly tell the algorithm to initialize itself with the node degrees with the `degreeAsProperty` property. So, here are two examples to run GraphSAGE from the GDS:

- Without using node properties is done as follows:

    - `CALL gds.alpha.graphSage.stream("proj_graph", {degreeAsProperty: true})`

- Using node properties is done as follows:

    - `CALL gds.alpha.graphSage.stream("proj_graph", {nodePropertyNames: ['x', 'y']})`

Similar to the `node2vec` procedure, the `graphSage` procedure returns a vector for each node, which can be imported into a DataFrame for further analysis.

Before closing this chapter, which also closes the part of this book strictly related to graph algorithms, we will explore a broad overview of the graph algorithms landscape, without restricting ourselves to Neo4j and the GDS, and look at some pieces of advice to help us stay up to date with the state-of-the-art algorithms.

Going further with graph algorithms

Graphs and graph algorithms are hot research topics, and new papers are published every week proposing new approaches to community detection, dynamic graph evolution, anomaly detection in networks, and so on. In this section, we will detail several ways to keep learning about graph algorithms and learn about the latest progress that makes them even more powerful.

State-of-the-art graph algorithms

Published papers about graphs can be found in dedicated journals such as the *Journal of Graph Algorithms and Applications* (http://jgaa.info). *Papers with code* also do amazing work collecting papers where the code is publicly available. The graph section (https://paperswithcode.com/area/graphs) provides a nice overview of the top current research topics regarding graphs.

Graph Embedding - from Graphs to Matrices

However, if you can't afford to read multiple papers a week, you can still extend your knowledge about graphs and stay up to date with the latest advances by regularly checking packages dedicated to graphs. The Neo4j Graph Data Science plugin is an example of such a package.

When your graph is stored in Neo4j, the GDS is very important and already provides many interesting algorithms. However, not all of them are implemented and some applications, such as graph embedding or overlapping community detection, may require other types of algorithms. To get an overview of the existing graph algorithms, I encourage you to check the algorithms implemented in the main packages that deal with graphs.

In Python, we have already talked about the main three packages used for graph analysis in data analysis, science, and research communities:

- `networkx`: https://networkx.github.io/
- `karateclub`: https://karateclub.readthedocs.io/en/latest/index.html
- `scikit-network`: https://scikit-network.readthedocs.io/en/latest/

Graph structures are also used in other languages (of course!). R, for instance, has the `igraph` package, while Java developers may find `JGraphT` interesting.

Summary

This chapter provided an overview of the graph embedding algorithms. Starting with adjacency-based methods using similarity metrics, we moved to a neural network-based approach. After gaining an understanding of the skip-graph model using word embedding as an example, we drew a parallel with graphs using DeepWalk to generate sentences. We also studied a variant of DeepWalk called node2vec, where the traversal is configured by two parameters to enhance local or global graph structures. The following table provides a short summary of the assumption about the graph structure made in each of the algorithms studied:

Algorithm	Hypothesis
Adjacency matrix	The higher the weight of the edge between nodes *i* and *j*, the more similar nodes *i* and *j* are.
LLE	Node embedding is a linear combination of its neighbors' embeddings.
HOPE	Similarity between nodes in the graph can be measured by a metric such as the Adamic-Adar score.
DeepWalk	The similarity between two nodes is given by the probability that node *j* is found in a random walk from node *i* with maximum *k* hops.

Finally, we considered the future of graph analysis using graph neural networks and some tricks for staying up to date with the latest advances in the field.

This chapter ends our long series about graph algorithms. In the next chapter, we will learn how to use Neo4j to build a web application that runs into production, learning about Graph Objects Mapper and the GraphQL query language to build reusable APIs.

Questions

- Run a clustering algorithm such as K-means on the `karateclub` graph embedding. What do you think of the results?
- Use the `karateclub` package to generate a node embedding with the DeepWalk algorithm.

Further reading

- *A Tutorial on Network Embeddings*, H. Chen *et al.*: https://arxiv.org/abs/1808.02590
- *Asymmetric Transitivity Preserving Graph Embedding*, M. Ou *et al.*: https://www.kdd.org/kdd2016/papers/files/rfp0184-ouA.pdf
- The paper behind `karateclub`:
  An API Oriented Open Source Python Framework for Unsupervised Learning on Graphs, B. Rozemberczki *et al.*: https://arxiv.org/abs/2003.04819
- Paper introducing DeepWalk: *Online Learning of Social Representations*, B. Perozzi *et al.*: https://arxiv.org/abs/1403.6652
- *node2vec: Scalable Feature Learning for Networks*, A. Grover *et al.*, ACM SIGKDD International Conference on Knowledge Discovery and Data Mining (KDD), 201: https://arxiv.org/abs/1607.00653
- You will find a deeper introduction to GNNs in:
    - Chapter 13 of *Advanced Deep Learning with Python*, I. Vasilev, Packt Publishing.
    - *Graph Neural Networks: A Review of Methods and Applications*, J. Zhou *et al.*: https://arxiv.org/abs/1812.08434
    - *A Comprehensive Survey on Graph Neural Networks*, Z. Wu *et al.*: https://arxiv.org/abs/1901.00596

- *GraphSAGE*: All the related information can be found on the SNAP (Stanford Network Analysis Project) page at `http://snap.stanford.edu/graphsage/`.
- GNN applications in zero-shot learning:
  Rethinking Knowledge Graph Propagation for Zero-Shot Learning, M. Kampffmeyer *et al.*: `https://arxiv.org/abs/1805.11724`

Section 4: Neo4j for Production

So far, we've only interacted with Neo4j through the web browser, other Neo4j desktop applications, or Jupyter. In this section, we will detail several techniques to automate the data analysis process we have set up. Two aspects will be covered: integrating Neo4j in an existing application with Graph Object Mappers (the graph equivalent of ORMs), and building a new application from scratch using the GRAND stack. We will also briefly discuss the challenges of using Neo4j for big data.

This section consists of the following chapters:

- Chapter 11, *Using Neoj4 in Your Web Application*
- Chapter 12, *Neo4j at Scale*

11 Using Neo4j in Your Web Application

In this book, we have learned a lot about Neo4j capabilities, including graph data modeling, Cypher, and link prediction using the Graph Data Science Library. Almost everything we have done required writing Cypher queries to extract data and/or store the results in Neo4j. In this chapter, we will discuss how to use Neo4j in a real-world web application, using either Python and the Flask framework or the React JavaScript framework. This chapter will also give you the opportunity to play with GraphQL in order to build a flexible web API.

The following topics will be covered in this chapter:

- Creating a full-stack web application using Python and Graph Object Mappers
- Understanding GraphQL APIs by example – the GitHub API v4
- Developing a React application using GRANDstack

Let's get started!

Technical requirements

In this chapter, you will require the following technical tools:

- Neo4j ≥ 3.5
- Python:
- `Flask`: A lightweight but powerful framework used to build web applications.
- `neomodel`: A graph object mapper for Python that's compatible with Neo4j.
- `requests`: A small Python package used to make HTTP requests. We will use it to test a GraphQL-based API.
- JavaScript and `npm`

Creating a full-stack web application using Python and Graph Object Mappers

There are different ways to programmatically interact with Neo4j. In the previous chapters, we used the Neo4j Python driver, from which we have been able to execute Cypher queries and retrieve the results, especially for creating DataFrames in a data science context. In the context of a web application, manually writing a Cypher query each time we want our program to perform an action on the graph would be a very time-consuming and laborious task involving repeating code. Fortunately, **Graph Object Mappers (GOMs)** have been created to interface Python code to Neo4j without us having to write a single Cypher query. In this section, we are going to use the `neomodel` package and use it alongside `Flask` to build a web application that displays information from Neo4j.

Our context is similar to GitHub: we have users that can own and/or contribute to repositories.

Toying with neomodel

`neomodel` is a Graph Object Mapper for Python whose syntax is very close to Django's **object-relational mapping (ORM)**. For instance, in order to retrieve the user whose ID is 1 from a `User` table (SQL), in Django, you would write the following:

```
User.objects.get(id=1
```

The same goal can be achieved with `neomodel` to retrieve the node with the `User` label, whose `id` property is 1, with the following code:

```
User.nodes.get(id=1)
```

In both cases, this statement returns a `User` object whose `id` is 1. How we define this object in the case of Neo4j is the topic of the upcoming subsection.

The previous statement is equivalent to the following Cypher query:

```
MATCH (u:User {id: 1}) RETURN u
```

By using this package, you can also traverse relationships, which is the purpose of graphs!

Defining the properties of structured nodes

Neo4j does not have a schema for node properties. You can basically add whatever you want as a property for nodes with any label. However, in most cases, you know what your data must look like and at least some of the fields are mandatory. In this case, you need to define a `StructuredNode`. If, on the contrary, you do not have any constant properties for your nodes, then a `SemiStructuredNode` will meet your requirements.

StructuredNode versus SemiStructuredNode

In `neomodel`, we will create a *model* for each node label in our graph. A model is a class that will declare the properties that are being attached to a given node label.

We can choose to create `StructuredNode` or `SemiStructuredNode`. A `StructuredNode` will have to declare all properties that can be attached to it. You will not be able to add properties to a node if these properties have not been declared. On the other hand, `SemiStructuredNode` offers more flexibility.

In this chapter, we will always use `StructuredNode` since the graph schema will be clear from the beginning. The minimal code to create a `User` model is as follows:

```
from neomodel import StructuredNode

class User(StructuredNode):
    pass
```

The next step is to declare the properties for this model.

Adding properties

Properties have types. In `neomodel`, all the basic types are available:

- `String`
- `Integer`
- `Float`
- `Boolean`
- `Date`, `DateTime`
- `UniqueID`

Apart from that, there are other extra types that exist as well, as follows:

- `JSON`
- `Email` (a string with extra checks for its format)
- `Point` (the Neo4j spatial type)

Each of these properties is created with some optional parameters to define; for instance, whether they are required or not.

For our purposes, let's create a `User` model with the following properties:

- `login` (String): Required and a primary key
- `password` (String): Required
- `email` (Email): Optional
- `birth_date` (Date): Optional

The `User` model should look like this:

```
class User(StructuredNode):
    login = StringProperty(required=True, primary=True)
    password = StringProperty(required=True)
    email = EmailProperty()
    birth_date = DateProperty()
```

Now that our model exists, we can use it to create and retrieve nodes, without writing any Cypher queries.

Creating nodes

The simplest way to create a user is by creating an instance of the `User` class:

```
u = User(login="me", password="12345")
```

To save the object, or create it in Neo4j, you just have to call the `save` method on that instance:

```
u.save()
```

If you want to use a `MERGE` statement instead, you will have to use a slightly different method:

```
users = User.get_or_create(
    dict(
        login="me",
        password="<3Graphs",
        email="me@internet.com",
        birth_date=date(2000, 1, 1),
    ),
)
```

> Be careful as the `get_or_create` method can create several nodes at once (adding more arguments after the first `dict`) and return a list of nodes.

Now, go ahead and add a few more users to the graph. Once we have some users in the graph, we can retrieve them.

Querying nodes

If you want to see all the nodes in the graph, you can use the following code:

```
users = Users.nodes.all()
```

This is equivalent to the following:

```
MATCH (u:User) RETURN u
```

users is a list of User objects. We can iterate through it and print the user properties:

```
for u in users:
    print(u.login, u.email, u.birth_date)
```

Next, we'll look at filtering nodes.

Filtering nodes

GOM also allows you to filter nodes based on their properties:

- `User.nodes.get`: This is when a single node is expected to match the requirements. If no node is found, a `neomodel.core.UserDoesNotExist` exception is raised.
- `User.nodes.filter`: This is when you expect several nodes to match the requirements. Similar to the `User.nodes.all()` method, the `filter()` method returns a list of User.

Nodes can be filtered when their properties match. For instance, you can filter all users whose birth date is January 1, 2000, with the following:

```
users = User.nodes.filter(birth_date=date(2000, 1, 1))
```

The equivalent Cypher for this statement is as follows:

```
MATCH (u:User)
WHERE u.birth_date = "2000-01-01"
RETURN u
```

However, you can also use other filters by adding a __<filter_name>=<value> suffix to the property name in the filter clause. The available filters are limited and listed at https://neomodel.readthedocs.io/en/latest/queries.html#node-sets-and-filtering. For instance, we can filter users born after January 1, 2000, by asking for a birth date **greater than** 2000-01-01:

```
users = User.nodes.filter(birth_date__gt=date(2000, 1, 1))
```

You are now able to create (check the previous section) and retrieve nodes from Neo4j. However, GOM doesn't stop here and also allows you to model relationships between nodes.

Integrating relationship knowledge

First, let's create another `StructuredNode` to represent repositories. In this exercise, repositories are only characterized by their name, so the `Repository` class only contains one property:

```
class Repository(StructuredNode):
    name = StringProperty()
```

Next, we are going to let `neomodel` know about the relationships between users and repositories. This is done in order to filter users or repositories depending on whether a relationship between them exists.

We want to keep track of both repository ownership and repository contributions. Regarding the contributions, we want to know when the user contributed to that repository. Therefore, we will create two relationship types: `OWNS` and `CONTRIBUTED_TO`.

Simple relationship

Let's start with the ownership relationship. In order to materialize it in our user, we need to add the following line:

```
class User(StructuredNode):
    # ... same as above
    owned_repositories = RelationshipTo("Repository", "OWNS")
```

This allows us to query the repositories from the users:

```
User.nodes.get(login="me").owned_repositories.all()
# [<Repository: {'name': 'hogan', 'id': 47}>]
```

If we also need to perform the operation the other way around – that is, from the repositories to the users – we also need to add the opposite relationship to the `Repository` model:

```
class Repository(StructuredNode):
    # ... same as above
    owner = RelationshipFrom(User, "OWNS")
```

We can also get the owner from the repository:

```
Repository.nodes.get(name="hogan").owner.get()
# <User: {'login': 'me', 'password': '<3Graphs', 'email':
'me@internet.com', 'birth_date': datetime.date(2000, 1, 1), 'id': 44}
```

Using Neo4j in Your Web Application

The OWNS relationship does not have any attached properties. If we want to add properties to the relationship, we will have to create models for the relationships as well.

Relationship with properties

For the contribution relationship, we want to add a property that will save the relationship when these contributions happen; let's call it contribution_date. This can also be achieved in neomodel using StructuredRel:

```
class ContributedTo(StructuredRel):
    contribution_date = DateTimeField(required=True)
```

This class can be used to create the required relationship in the model class:

```
class User(StructuredNode):
    # ... same as above
    contributed_repositories = RelationshipTo("Repository",
"CONTRIBUTED_TO", model=ContributedTo)


class Repository(StructuredNode):
    # ... same as above
    contributors = RelationshipFrom(User, "CONTRIBUTED_TO",
model=ContributedTo
```

With a relationship model, we can filter patterns by relationship properties using the math method. For instance, the following query returns users contributing to the hogan repository after May 5, 2020, at 3 p.m.:

```
Repository.nodes.get().contributors.match(
    contribution_date__gt=datetime(2020, 5, 31, 15, 0)
).all()
```

The preceding code is equivalent to the following Cypher query:

```
MATCH (u:User)-[r:CONTRIBUTED_TO]->(:Repository {name: "hogan"})
WITH u, DATETIME({epochSeconds: toInteger(r.contribution_date)}) as dt
WHERE dt >= DATETIME("2020-08-10T15:00:00")
RETURN u
```

You are now able to use neomodel to model your Neo4j graph.

In the following section, we will use the model we have created in this section to retrieve data from Neo4j and create new nodes and relationships through a simple user interface built with Flask.

Building a web application backed by Neo4j using Flask and neomodel

In this section, we are going to use one of the popular web frameworks for Python, `Flask`, in order to build a fully functional web application using the `neomodel` models we created earlier.

Creating toy data

First of all, let's copy the preceding code into a `models.py` file. The equivalent file in the Packt GitHub at `https://github.com/PacktPublishing/Hands-On-Graph-Analytics-with-Neo4j/blob/master/ch11/Flask-app/models.py` contains a few extra lines. They contain some instructions we can use to create example data that we will play with in the following section. To execute it, just run the following command from the root directory:

```
python models.py
```

The created nodes and relationships are illustrated in the following diagram:

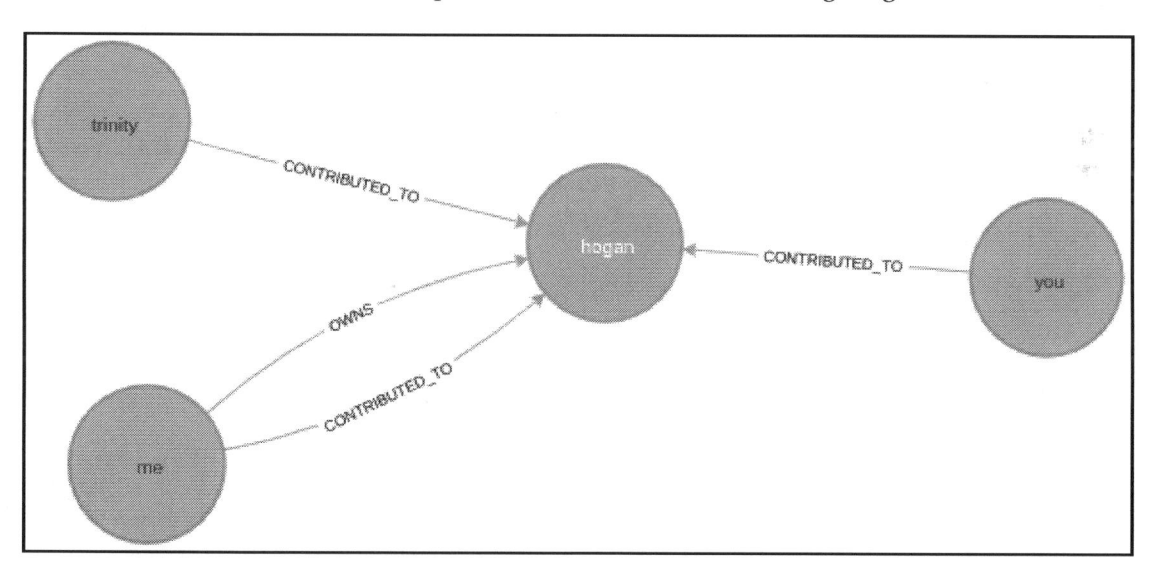

We have one repository called `hogan`, owned by a user whose name is `me`. The user `me` also contributed to this repository. Two more users, `you` and `trinity`, also contributed to the same repository.

Let's start writing our first web page.

Login page

To begin with, we will create a login page in our application so that we can authenticate users. For this, we will rely on the `Flask-login` package, which will take care of saving the user data in the browser session, for instance. However, we still need to create the form and link it to our `User` model.

Creating the Flask application

Let's go ahead and create the Flask application in a new `app.py` file:

```
app = Flask(__name__)
```

Since our application will use various `forms` and `POST` variables, we need to add **Cross-Site Request Forgery (CSRF)** protection:

```
csrf = CSRFProtect(app)
```

To use the `Flask-login` plugin, we also need to define a `SECRET` variable and instantiate the login manager:

```
app.config['SECRET_KEY'] = "THE SECRET"

login_manager = Flask_login.LoginManager()
login_manager.init_app(app)
```

With that, our `Flask` app has been created and we can run it with the following code:

```
Flask run
```

However, we have not created any routes yet, so for now, all our URLs will result in a `404, Not found` error. We will add the `/login` route in the following paragraphs.

Adapting the model

In order to use our `User` class with `Flask-login`, we need to add a few methods to it:

- `is_authenticated`: Determines whether the user authentication succeeded.
- `is_active`: Can be used to deactivate users (email address not validated, subscription expired, and so on).
- `is_anonymous`: This is another way to detect unauthenticated users.
- `get_id`: Defines the unique identifier for each user.

Since these methods are common to almost all web applications, they have been implemented in a `UserMixin`, which we can add to our `User` class to access these methods. The only method we need a custom behavior for is the `get_id` method since our model does not have an `id` field; here, the primary key role is taken by the `login` field:

```
class User(StructuredNode, Flask_login.UserMixin):
    # ... same as above

    def get_id(self):
        return self.login
```

The login form

In order to manage form rendering and validation, we will use another Flask plugin called `wtforms`. This plugin requires that the form is defined in a dedicated class, so let's go and create a login form. This form requires the following:

- **A username/login**: This is a required text input that can be created with the following line:

    ```
    login = StringField('Login', validators=[DataRequired()])
    ```

- **A password**: This is also a required text input with a hidden value (we do not want our neighbor to read the password on the screen). On top of `StringField` with a `DataRequired` validator, we will also specify a custom widget for this field:

    ```
    password = StringField('Password', validators=[DataRequired()],
                           widget=PasswordInput(hide_value=False)
    )
    ```

- **A submit button**:

    ```
    submit = SubmitField('Submit')
    ```

The full code for the login form is as follows:

```python
class LoginForm(FlaskForm):
    login = StringField('Login', validators=[DataRequired()])
    password = StringField('Password', validators=[DataRequired()],
                    widget=PasswordInput(hide_value=False)
    )
    submit = SubmitField('Submit')
```

Let's continue our implementation and create the login template that will render this form.

The login template

On the login page, which will be accessible via the /login URL, we want to display the login form; that is, the login and password input fields and the submit button. Flask, like many web frameworks, uses a template generator, allowing us to dynamically display variables on the page. The template generator used by Flask is called Jinja2. The following Jinja2 template allows us to display a simple login form with two text inputs (login and password) and a submit button:

```html
<form method="POST" action="/login">
    {{ form.csrf_token }}
    <div class="form-field">{{ form.login.label }} {{ form.login }}</div>
    <div class="form-field">{{ form.password.label }} {{ form.password }}</div>
    {{ form.submit }}
</form>
```

This template can be added to the templates/login.html file, after we've added the basic HTML tags (see https://github.com/PacktPublishing/Hands-On-Graph-Analytics-with-Neo4j/blob/master/ch11/Flask-app/templates/login.html). You will notice that I have used another interesting feature of Jinja2: template inheritance. The base.html template contains all the constant parts across pages. In our case, I have only included a header, but you can also place a footer or a navigation sidebar, for instance. It also contains an empty block:

```
{% block content %}
{% endblock %}
```

This block can be seen as a placeholder, where the code from derived templates will be written.

In the `login.html` template, we then tell `Jinja2` that it needs to be included inside the base template with the following instruction:

```
{% extends "base.html" %}
```

We also tell `Jinja2` where to put the form inside the base template by surrounding our form with the following instructions:

```
{% block content %}
    /// FORM GOES HERE
{% endblock %}
```

In the form template, we assume that the page context contains a `form` variable that consists of a `LoginForm` instance. We are now going to inject this variable into the context to be able to see the login page.

The login view

So, let's create a simple `/login` route that will add a `LoginForm` instance to the application context. Then, we'll render the `login.html` template:

```
login_manager.login_view = 'login'

@app.route('/login')    # URL
def login():            # name of the view
    form = LoginForm()    # create a LoginForm instance
    return render_template('login.html', form=form)    # render the
login.html template with a form parameter
```

Now, you can navigate to `http://localhost:5000/login`. You should see the following form:

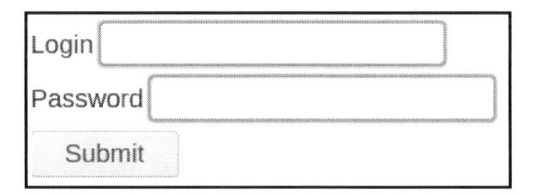

However, at the moment, clicking on the form will raise an error because `POST` requests are, by default, not allowed on our view. To make them allowed, we have to modify the `app.route` decorator on our view so that we can add the allowed methods:

```
@app.route('/login', methods=["GET", "POST"])
def login():
```

[433]

Using Neo4j in Your Web Application

Now that we are able to make POSTs to this view, we can handle them. Here are the steps we will follow:

1. Validate the form data with the `form.validate_on_submit()` method. This method performs the following checks:
    - **ecks that the required fields are there**: This is configured by the field validators.
    - **Checks that the provided login/password corresponds to a real user**: Here, we need to implement our own logic in order to check that a `User` node with the given login/password exists in Neo4j.

2. After doing this, two possible scenarios can occur:
    - f the form is valid and the user exists, call the `Flask_login.login_user` function to manage the session.
    - Otherwise, render the login form again.

These operations are performed in the view by the following piece of code:

```
form = LoginForm()
if form.validate_on_submit():
    if Flask_login.login_user(user):
        return redirect(url_for("index"))   # redirect to the home page
return render_template('login.html', form=form)
```

In order to check the existence of a `User` with the given credentials, we need to add a `validate` method to our form:

```
class LoginForm(FlaskForm):

    # ... same as before

    def validate(self):
        user = User.nodes.get_or_none(
            login=self.login.data,
            password=self.password.data,
        )
        if user is None:
            raise ValidationError("User/Password incorrect")
        self.user = user
        return self
```

For convenience, the authenticated user is saved in the `self.user` form attribute. This allows us to retrieve the user in the login view, without performing the same request again.

Reading data – listing owned repositories

You can try this on your own. The results are presented in the following paragraphs.

The view will use the `current_user` object saved by `Flask_login`. This current user is already of the `User` type, so we can directly access its members, such as `contributed_repositories` and `owned_repositories`. The full code for the view is as follows:

```
@app.route('/')
@Flask_login.login_required
def index(*args):
    user = Flask_login.current_user
    contributed_repositories = user.contributed_repositories.all()
    owned_repositories = user.owned_repositories.all()
    return render_template(
        "index.html",
        contributed_repositories=contributed_repositories,
        owned_repositories=owned_repositories,
        user=user
    )
```

You may have noticed the use of a new function decorator, `@Flask_login.login_required`. This will check that the user is already logged in before rendering the view. If not, the user will be redirected to the login view.

In the HTML template, we will simply loop over the contributed and owned repositories in order to display them in a bullet list:

```
<h2>User {{ user.login }}</h2>
<p><a href="/logout">Logout</a></p>
<h3>List of repositories I contributed to:</h3>
<ul>
{% for r in contributed_repositories %}
<li>{{ r.id }}: {{ r.name }} (on {{ user.contributed_repositories.relationship(r).contribution_date.strftime('%Y-%m-%d %H:%M') }})</li>
{% endfor %}
</ul>
<h3>List of repositories I own:</h3>
<ul>
{% for r in owned_repositories %}
<li>{{ r.id }}: {{ r.name }}</li>
{% endfor %}
</ul>
```

Using Neo4j in Your Web Application

The following screenshot shows what the list of repositories will look like after running the preceding snippet:

Flask app using Neo4j graph

User me
Logout

List of repositories I contributed to:
- 47: hogan (on 2020-05-31 17:02)
- Add a new contribution

List of repositories I own:
- 47: hogan
- Create new repository

> Index page at the end of this section – I added a little styling that you can find in the GitHub repository for this book

In this subsection, we have read data from the graph. Now, let's learn how to add data to it.

Altering the graph – adding a contribution

In this exercise, we are going to let the authenticated user add a contribution to an existing repository. Again, we will use the WTForm Flask extension to manage HTML forms. Our form is even more simple than the login form since it contains only one text input: the name of the repository the user contributed to:

```
from models import Repository

class NewContributionForm(FlaskForm):
    name = StringField('Name', validators=[DataRequired()])
    submit = SubmitField('Submit')
```

The provided repository name is validated to make sure a `Repository` node with that name already exists, and raise a `ValidationError` otherwise:

```
    def validate_name(self, field):
        r = Repository.nodes.get_or_none(name=field.data)
        if r is None:
            raise ValidationError('Can ony add contributions to existing repositories')
```

Now, let's build the template that will render this form. This template should not be surprising to you since it is very similar to the login page template:

```
<form method="POST" action="{{ url_for('add_contribution') }}">
{{ form.csrf_token }}
<div class="form-field">
    {{ form.name.label }} {{ form.name }}
</div>
{{ form.submit }}
</form>
```

Let's add another piece of information to this page: the validation errors reported by the form. We'll do this to let the user know what happened. This can be achieved thanks to the following code. This code needs to be added before the `<form>` tag shown in the previous code snippet:

```
{% for field, errors in form.errors.items() %}
<div class="alert bg-danger">
{{ form[field].label }}: {{ ', '.join(errors) }}
</div>
{% endfor %}
```

We also need to add a link to our new page from the index page. At the end of the contribution list, add the following item:

```
<li><a href="{{ url_for('add_contribution') }}">Add a new contribution</a></li>
```

Now, let's focus on the view. Once the user is logged in and the form has been validated, we can find the repository that matches the name entered by the user and add this repository to the `contributed_repositories` section of the authenticated user:

```
@app.route("/repository/contribution/new", methods=["GET", "POST"])
@Flask_login.login_required
def add_contribution(*args):
    user = Flask_login.current_user
    form = NewContributionForm()
    if form.validate_on_submit():
        repo = Repository.nodes.get(
            name=form.name.data,
        )
        rel = user.contributed_repositories.connect(repo,
{"contribution_date": datetime.now()})
        return redirect(url_for("index"))
    return render_template("contribution_add.html", form=form)
```

Using Neo4j in Your Web Application

Now, you can navigate to `http://www.localhost:5000/repository/contribution/new`. You will see something similar to the following:

Flask app using Neo4j graph

Add a contribution

Name [   ]

Submit

With that, we have built a web application using Neo4j as the backend. We are able to read data from Neo4j (the login and index pages) and create new relationships in the graph. The full code for this section is available at `/Flask-app`. This directory contains an extra view that allows the user to create a new repository. I recommend that you try and implement it on your own before looking at the code.

This is one way to interact with Neo4j using Python. The same exercise can be repeated using another popular web framework called Django. You can check the *Further reading* section to find references for the `neomodel` and `Django` integration.

Throughout the rest of this chapter, we will use another way to interface an application with Neo4j – by building a GraphQL API. However, first, we are going to become more familiar with GraphQL by using the GitHub API v4.

Understanding GraphQL APIs by example – GitHub API v4

While in the previous section we used Python to build a full web application whose backend database is Neo4j, in this section, we will remove the dependency on Python and build an API directly accessible from the Neo4j server.

When building APIs, a very popular framework is **Representational State Transfer** (**REST**). Even though this approach is still possible with a graph database (check, for instance, the `gREST` project), a different approach is becoming more and more popular – GraphQL, a query language for API.

In order to understand GraphQL, we will again use the GitHub API. In previous chapters, we used the `REST` version (v3). However, v4 uses GraphQL, so we should build a few queries. To do so, we can go to `https://developer.github.com/v4/explorer/`, which is the traditional GraphQL playground. After providing GitHub login credentials, there is a two-part window; the left panel is where we will write the query, while the right panel will display the query result or error messages.

In order to get started with an unknown GraphQL API, the **< Doc** button (top-right of the screen – see the following screenshot) is key. It will list the available actions, both for querying the database and performing mutations (creating, updating, or deleting objects). Let's start by just reading the data with the `query` part:

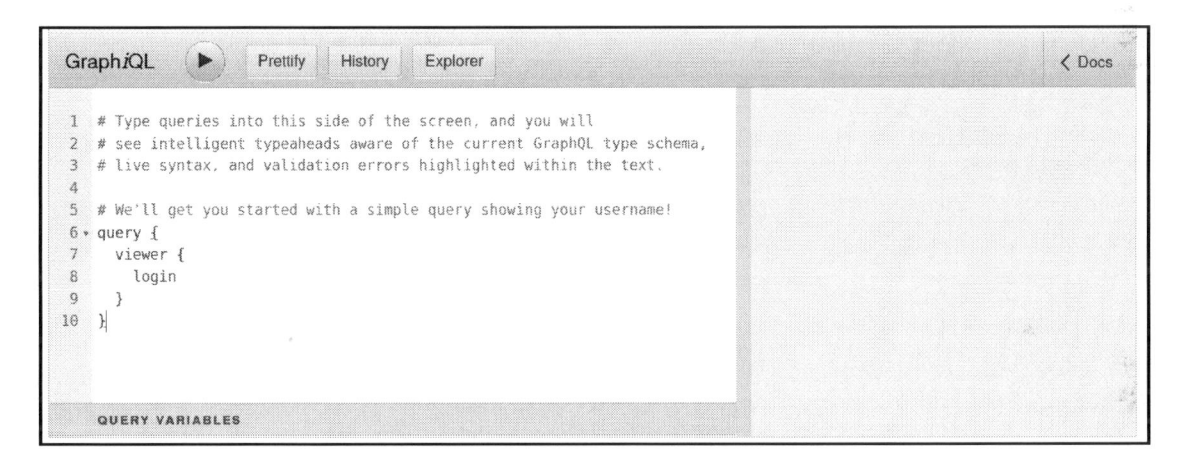

```
GraphiQL    ▶    Prettify    History    Explorer                                    < Docs

1   # Type queries into this side of the screen, and you will
2   # see intelligent typeaheads aware of the current GraphQL type schema,
3   # live syntax, and validation errors highlighted within the text.
4
5   # We'll get you started with a simple query showing your username!
6 ▸ query {
7     viewer {
8       login
9     }
10  }

QUERY VARIABLES
```

The preceding screenshot is what you will see when you navigate to the GitHub GraphQL API for the first time. It is prefilled with an example query. We will analyze this in the following sections.

Endpoints

Let's start by building a query. We'll do this by choosing an endpoint. One of them is called `viewer` and, according to the documentation, will give us information about the currently authenticated user. To use this endpoint, we have to write the following in the query builder:

```
{
    viewer {

    }
}
```

[439]

If we try and run this query, it will return a parse error message. The reason for this is that we are still missing an important piece of information – the parameters about the viewer that we want the API to return.

There is an optional query keyword that can be placed in front of a query request, like this:

```
query {
    viewer {

    }
}
```

Returned attributes

One of the advantages of GraphQL is that you can choose which parameters are returned. It is a good way to reduce the size of the data that's received from an API and speed up how it's rendered for the user. The list of available parameters is defined in the GraphQL schema; we will look at this in more detail later in this chapter. A valid query can be written like so:

```
{
  viewer {
    id
    login
  }
}
```

This query will return the `id` and `login` information of the viewer. The result of this query is the following JSON:

```
{
  "data": {
    "viewer": {
      "id": "MDQ6VXNlcjEwMzU2NjE4",
      "login": "stellasia"
    }
  }
}
```

[440]

This query is quite simple, especially because it doesn't involve parameters. However, most of the time, the API response depends on some parameters: the user ID, the maximum number of elements to be returned (for pagination), and so on. It is worth focusing on this feature since it is crucial for any API to be able to send parameterized requests.

Query parameters

In order to understand how query parameters work, let's consider another endpoint, organization. Through the GitHub API, let's say you send the following query:

```
{
  organization(login) {
    id
  }
}
```

You will receive an error message in return:

```
"message": "Field 'organization' is missing required arguments: login"
```

This means the query has to be updated to the following:

```
{
  organization(login: "neo4j") {
    id
  }
}
```

By requesting more fields, such as the creation date or the organization's website, the resulting data will be similar to the following:

```
{
  "data": {
    "organization": {
      "name": "Neo4j",
      "description": "",
      "createdAt": "2010-02-10T15:22:20Z",
      "url": "https://github.com/neo4j",
      "websiteUrl": "http://neo4j.com/"
    }
  }
}
```

Using Neo4j in Your Web Application

Much more complex queries can be built; simply browse the documentation to see which information can be extracted. For instance, we can build a query that returns the following:

- The current viewer's login.
- Their first two public repositories, ordered by creation date in descending order, along with the following for each of these repositories:
  - Its name
  - Its creation date
  - The name of its main language:

```
{
  organization(login: "neo4j") {
    repositories(last: 3, privacy: PUBLIC, orderBy: {field: CREATED_AT, direction: ASC}) {
      nodes {
        name
        createdAt
        primaryLanguage {
          name
        }
      }
    }
  }
}
```

The result is displayed in the following screenshot:

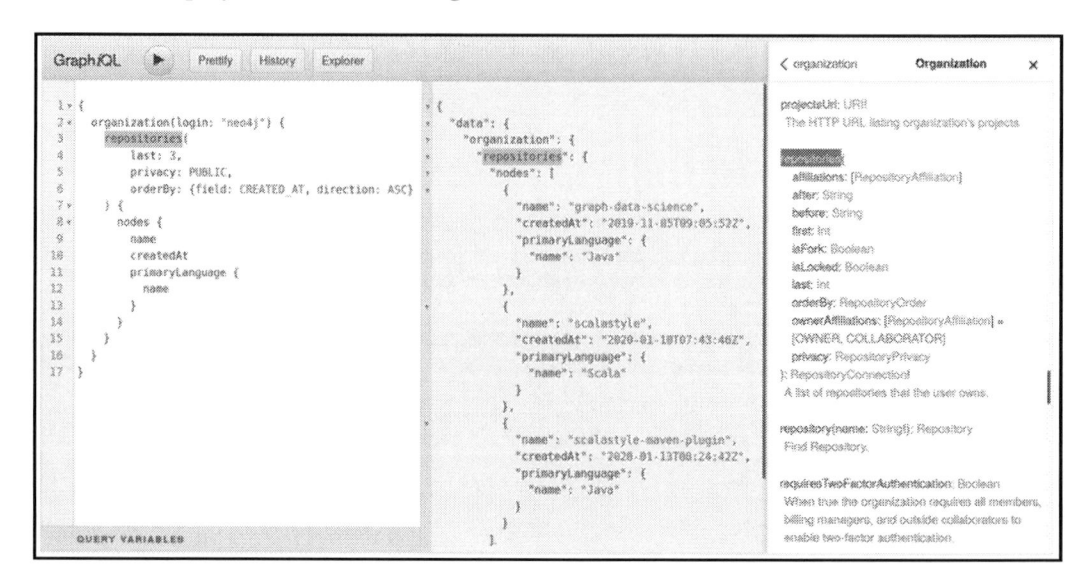

[442]

Queries are used to *retrieve* data from the database. In order to alter the data, we need to perform another type of operation called a **mutation**.

Mutations

Let's study an example of a mutation allowed by the GitHub API: adding a star to a repository. This mutation is called addStar and accepts a single input parameter: the repository ID to be starred. It can return information of the Starrable type ("*Things that can be starred*" according to the documentation). The full query is written as follows:

```
mutation {
  addStar(input: {starrableId: "<REPOSITORY_ID>"}) {
    starrable {
      stargazers(last: 1) {
        nodes {
          login
        }
      }
    }
  }
}
```

Similarly to the queries, the arguments and returned parameters for each mutation are defined in the GraphQL schema, whose documentation is accessible through the right panel in the GraphQL playground.

We will see more examples of mutations in the next section.

> Despite its name, GraphQL is not tied to a graph database and can be used with a SQL database backend. With Python, check the graphene module to learn more.

> Neo4j used to maintain the neo4j-graphql plugin, which was integrated with the Neo4j server and exposed a /graphql/ endpoint under port 7474 (same as the browser). However, this plugin has been deprecated since the introduction of Neo4j 4.0 and replaced by more mainstream tools, such as the GraphQL JavaScript package.

The Neo4j GraphQL JavaScript package is part of GRANDstack, which we will cover in the following section.

Developing a React application using GRANDstack

GRANDstack is the best thing to use if you are creating an application using Neo4j nowadays. In this section, we are going to build a small application similar to the one we created with Python in the first section of this chapter.

The full documentation for GRANDstack can be found at https://grandstack.io/.

GRANDstack – GraphQL, React, Apollo, and Neo4j Database

GRAND is actually an acronym for the following:

- GraphQL
- React
- Apollo
- Neo4j Database

We explored Neo4j throughout this book and GraphQL in the previous section. React is a JavaScript framework used to build web applications. Apollo is the block that will glue together the GraphQL API and the React frontend. Let's see how these things work.

In order to initiate a project using the GRANDstack, we can use the following code:

```
npx create-grandstack-app <NAME_OF_YOUR_APPLICATION>
```

The script will ask for our Neo4j connection parameters (bolt URL, username, password, and whether to use encryption or not) and create a directory by using the name of our application. This will contain, among other things, the following elements:

```
.
├── api
├── LICENSE.txt
├── package.json
├── README.md
└── web-react
```

As the name suggests, the `api` folder contains the code for the GraphQL API, while the `web-react` folder is where the frontend React application lives.

> Actually, it is also possible to use Angular for the frontend. See `https://github.com/grand-stack/grand-stack-starter/tree/master/web-angular` for more details.

Creating the API

The starter app has already done almost all of the work for us. The `api` folder's structure is as follows:

```
.
├── package.json
├── README.md
└── src
    ├── functions
    ├── graphql-schema.js
    ├── index.js
    ├── initialize.js
    ├── schema.graphql
    └── seed
```

The only file we will need to modify to meet our application goals is the `schema.graphql` file.

Writing the GraphQL schema

Still in the context of users owning or contributing to repositories, we are going to write the GraphQL schema that will be used to create the same frontend pages that we created in the first part of this chapter.

Defining types

Let's start with the `User` nodes. We can define the properties with the following code:

```
type User {
  login: String!
  password: String!
  email: String
  birth_date: Date
}
```

We can also add more data to the user, such as the following:

- **Their owned repositories**:

    ```
    owned_repositories: [Repository] @relation(name: "OWNS",
    direction: "OUT")
    ```

- **The repositories they contributed to**:

    ```
    contributed_repositories: [Repository] @relation(name:
    "CONTRIBUTED_TO", direction: "OUT"
    ```

- Their total number of contributions (to all repositories). Here, we have to define this field from a custom Cypher statement to write the COUNT aggregate:

    ```
    total_contributions: Int
       @cypher(
         statement: "MATCH (this)-[r:CONTRIBUTED_TO]->(:Repository)
    RETURN COUNT(r)"
        )
    ```

Similarly, the repositories can be described with the following schema:

```
type Repository {
  name: String!
  owner: User @relation(name: "OWNS", direction: "IN")
  contributors: [User] @relation(name: "CONTRIBUTED_TO", direction:
"IN")
  nb_contributors: Int @cypher(
      statement: "MATCH (this)<-[:CONTRIBUTED_TO]->(u:User) RETURN
COUNT(DISTINCT u)"
    )
}
```

You can add as many fields as you think are necessary for your application.

Starting the application

Starting the application is as simple as doing the following:

```
cd api
npm run
```

By default, the application runs on port `4001`. Now, we will look at two ways we can test whether everything works as expected; namely, the GraphQL playground and sending direct requests to the API.

Testing with the GraphQL playground

When the application is running, we can visit `http://www.localhost:4001/graphql/` and find the GraphQL playground for this application.

> **TIP**
> By default, the dark theme is enabled. You can disable it by changing the following line in the settings:
> `"editor.theme": "dark",`
> Change it to the following:
> `"editor.theme": "light",`

Let's write a query that will gather the information we need to create the login page of our application (see the *Creating the Flask application* section). We want to display, for the authenticated user, their login, the repositories they own, and the repositories they have contributed to. Therefore, we can use the following query:

```
{
  User(login: "me") {
    login
    owned_repositories{
        name
    }
    contributed_repositories{
        name
    }
  }
}
```

Similarly, to get the number of contributors and the owner of a given repository, use the following query:

```
{
  Repository(name: "hogan") {
    nb_contributors
    owner {
      login
    }
  }
}
```

The API is now totally up and running and you can send requests to it from your favorite tool (curl, Postman, and so on). In the following section, I'll demonstrate how to query this API from Python using the `requests` module.

Calling the API from Python

In order to make HTTP requests from Python, we are going to use the pip installable `requests` package:

```
import requests
```

Then, we need to define the request parameters:

```
query = """
{
    User(login: "me") {
        login
    }
}
"""

data = {
  "query": query,
}
```

Finally, we can post the request using a JSON-encoded payload:

```
r = requests.post(
    "http://localhost:4001/graphql",
    json=data,
    headers={
    }
)

print(r.json())
```

The result is as follows:

```
{'data': {}}
```

Using variables

The query we are using contains one parameter: the username. In order to make it more customizable, GraphQL allows us to use variables. First, we need to change the way we format the query slightly by adding the parameter definition:

```
query($login: String!) {
```

The parameter is called $name, is of the String type, and is mandatory (hence the final exclamation mark !). This declared parameter can then be used in the query, like so:

```
User(login: $login) {
```

So, the final query looks as follows:

```
query = """
query($login: String!) {
    User(login: $login) {
        login
    }
}
"""
```

However, we now have to feed the parameter into the query in the API call. This is done using the `variables` parameter. It consists of a dictionary whose keys are the parameter names:

```
data = {
    "query": query,
    "variables": {"login": "me"},
}
```

After doing this, we can post this query once more using the same `requests.post` code we used previously.

Now, let's learn how to build a frontend application that consumes the GraphQL API using React.

Mutations

As we have already seen with the GitHub API, mutations alter the graph, thereby creating, updating, or deleting nodes and relationships. Some mutations are automatically created from the types declared in the GraphQL schema; they can be found in the following documentation:

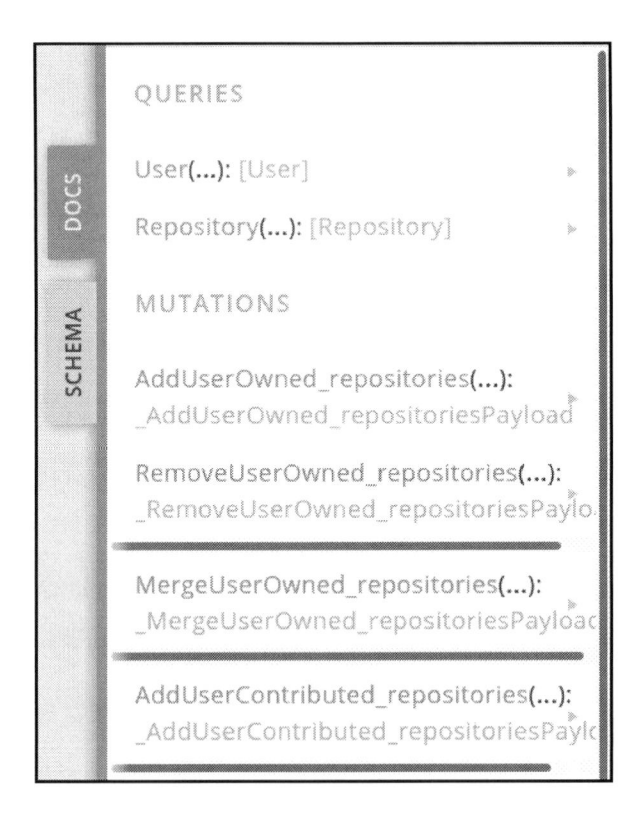

```
QUERIES

User(...): [User]

Repository(...): [Repository]

MUTATIONS

AddUserOwned_repositories(...):
_AddUserOwned_repositoriesPayload

RemoveUserOwned_repositories(...):
_RemoveUserOwned_repositoriesPaylo

MergeUserOwned_repositories(...):
_MergeUserOwned_repositoriesPayload

AddUserContributed_repositories(...):
_AddUserContributed_repositoriesPaylo
```

Let's create a new user and add a contribution to the hogan repository. To create a user, we need to use the `CreateUser` mutation, with parameters containing at least the two mandatory parameters: login and password. As for any GraphQL query, we also need to list the parameters that we want the API to return in the second part of the request:

```
mutation {
  CreateUser(login: "Incognito", password: "password123") {
    login
    email
    birth_date {year}
  }
}
```

We can also create the relationship between the newly created user and the hogan repository:

```
mutation {
  AddUserContributed_repositories(
    from: { login: "Incognito" }
    to: { name: "hogan" }
  ) {
    from {login}
    to {name}
  }
}
```

We can check the result in the Neo4j browser, or use the same GraphQL API to check that the User node and the CONTRIBUTED_TO relationships were created properly:

```
{
  User(login: "Incognito") {
    contributed_repositories {
      name
    }
  }
}
```

This should result in the following output:

```
{
  "data": {
    "User": [
      {
        "contributed_repositories": [
          {
            "name": "hogan"
          }
        ]
      }
    ]
  }
}
```

When creating a new repository, we may want to add its owner to the same query. This can be achieved with GraphQL by chaining mutations:

```
mutation {
  CreateRepository(name: "graphql-api") {
    name
  }
  AddUserOwned_repositories(
    from: { login: "Incognito" }
    to: { name: "graphql-api" }
  ) {
    from {
      login
      email
      total_contributions
    }
    to {
      name
      nb_contributors
    }
  }
}
```

In the preceding query, first, we perform a `CreateRepository` mutation by adding the `graphql-api` repository. Then, the `AddUserOwned_repositories` mutation is performed. We do this by adding a relationship between the `Incognito` user we created earlier and the newly created `graphql-api` repository.

You should now be able to build your own GraphQL API and query it to fetch and alter data in the graph. The next step is to plug this API into a frontend application.

Building the user interface

The UI is using React. The code shipped with the `grand-stack-starter` app contains a lot of features but is also quite complex for beginners, which is why we are going to rewrite part of it using a simpler approach. Our goal here is to build an application that will show a list of users on the home page.

In order to make our components use the API, we have to connect them to the GraphQL application we created in the previous section.

Creating a simple component

Let's start by building the home page and creating a component that will list all users.

Getting data from the GraphQL API

In order to retrieve all registered users, we will use a query that requests all users without using any parameters, like so:

```
query Users {
  User {
    login
    email
    total_contributions
  }
}
```

This can be tested in the GraphQL playground to check that it returns all the users in the Neo4j graph.

> **TIP:** Here, we are using a very small dataset containing two to four users. If your dataset contains more, which is very likely, you may need to use pagination instead. Refer to the GRANDstack application starter to see an example of such a feature:
> https://github.com/grand-stack/grand-stack-starter/blob/master/web-react/src/components/UserList.js

Writing a simple component

The `UserList` component will be implemented in the `src/components/UserList.js` file. We start by importing the necessary tools:

```
import { useQuery } from '@apollo/react-hooks'
import gql from 'graphql-tag'
```

Then, we define the query that we need to use to retrieve the data we need for this component:

```
const GET_USERS = gql`
  query Users {
    User {
```

Using Neo4j in Your Web Application

```
            login
            email
            total_contributions
        }
    }
}
```

After this, we can create the component using function notation. The function has to return the HTML code that will be displayed in the browser.

Before that, however, we need to fetch the data. This is where the `useQuery` function from Apollo is used. Let's start with a simple implementation where we will just log the results of the `useQuery` function in the console and return an empty string as HTML:

```
function UserList(props) {

    const { loading, data, error } = useQuery(GET_USERS);
    console.log("Loading=", loading);
    console.log("Data=", data);
    console.log("Error=", error);

    return "";
};

export default UserList;
```

> `useQuery` is a React hook.

We will also need to create the `src/App.js` file in order to use the `UserList` component. Ensure it contains the following content:

```
import React from 'react'

import UserList from './components/UserList';


export default function App() {
  return (
      <div>
        <h1>My app</h1>
        <UserList />
      </div>
  );
}
```

[454]

Once these two files have been saved, we can start the server by running `npm start` in the `web-react` folder and visiting `http://localhost:3000`. The HTML is not showing anything, but the interesting information is in the console, which you can open with *Ctrl + I* or by pressing the *F12* key (Firefox and Chrome). You should see something similar to the following:

```
Loading= true
Data= undefined
Error= undefined
▶ XHR POST http://localhost:3000/graphql
▶ GET http://localhost:3000/favicon.ico
Loading= false
Data= ▶ Object { User: (4) […] }
Error= undefined
```

As you can see, our logs are displayed twice. The first time this happens, the `loading` parameter is true and both the `data` and `error` variables are undefined. The second time this happens, the result of the POST request that was performed by our GraphQL API is received. This time, we have `loading=false`, and `data` actually contains some data.

The `data` object can be explored even further. You will see something similar to the following:

```
Data= ▼ {…}
       ▼ User: (4) […]
          ▶ 0: Object { login: "me", email: "me@internet.com", totalContributions: 1, … }
          ▶ 1: Object { login: "you", totalContributions: 1, typename: "User", … }
          ▶ 2: Object { login: "trinity", totalContributions: 1, typename: "User", … }
          ▶ 3: Object { login: "Incognito", totalContributions: 1, typename: "User", … }
            length: 4
```

So, let's modify our `UserList` function and replace the empty string return statement with some meaningful data.

Using Neo4j in Your Web Application

We have to consider three cases:

- If we do not have data from the API yet, then `loading=true`. In this case, we would just render the `Loading...` text:

  ```
  if (loading) {
    return <p>Loading...</p>
  }
  ```

- The API returned some errors, `error !== undefined`. Here, we would display the raw error message:

  ```
  if (error !== undefined) {
    console.error(error);
    return <p>Error</p>
  }
  ```

- The API didn't return and error and we received some data. In such a case, we would iterate over the `data.User` array and display its login, its email, and its total number of contributions for each element.

  The last step is achieved thanks to the following code:

  ```
  return (
      <table>
        <thead>
        <tr>
          <th>Login</th>
          <th>Email</th>
          <th>Total contributions</th>
        </tr>
        </thead>
        <tbody>
  {data.User.map((u) => {
          return (
            <tr key={u.login}>
              <td>{u.login}</td>
              <td>{u.email}</td>
              <td>{u.total_contributions}</td>
            </tr>
          )
  })}
        </tbody>
      </table>
  )
  ```

After saving the new version of `UserList.js`, visiting `http://localhost:3000` again will display a table of existing users in Neo4j.

> In order to see some proper results, you have to have three components up and running:
> - Neo4j
> - The API from the previous section
> - The `web-react` application

Now, let's add some complexity with navigation. This will enable us to see more information about our user when we click on their login.

Adding navigation

From the home page, which lists all users, it would be nice to be able to navigate to another page showing details about a specific user. To make this possible, let's start by modifying the `UserList` component and add a link for the user login:

```
<td><Link to={`/user/${u.login}`}>{u.login}</Link></td>
```

Now, clicking on such a link will redirect us to `http://localhost:3000/user/me`. This just shows a blank page since our application has not been configured yet.

Let's go ahead and configure the application. The content of the `App` component has to be replaced with the following code. We will use a `Router` object to do so:

```
export default function App() {
  return (
      <Router>
         <div>
            <h1>My app</h1>
         </div>

         <Switch>
             <Route exact path="/" component={UserList} />
             <Route path="/user/:login" component={User} />
         </Switch>
      </Router>
  );
}
```

[457]

Using Neo4j in Your Web Application

The router defines two routes:

- `"/"`: This will render the `UserList` component.
- `"/user/<login>"`: This will render a new `User` component (we are going to create this now). The login is a parameter of the route, which we will be able to retrieve in the component.

So, let's create the `User` component in `src/components/User.js`; this will show the list of owned repositories for the user. The query to get this data is as follows:

```
const GET_USER_DATA = gql`
    query($login: String!) {
        User(login: $login) {
            owned_repositories {
                name
            }
        }
    }
`;
```

In this query, we have defined a `$login` variable that we will have to feed to the GraphQL endpoint, together with the query, to get a result. The beginning of the `User` component is as follows:

```
function User(props) {
    let login = props.match.params.login

    const { loading, data, error } = useQuery(GET_USER_DATA, {
        variables: {
            login: login
        }
    });
```

The login variable is read from the URL because the user page's URL is `/user/<login>`.

The rest of the `User` component is quite straightforward; we add loading and error handling and then show a list of repositories:

```
        if (loading) {
            return <p>Loading...</p>
        }

        if (error !== undefined) {
            return <p>Error: {error}</p>
        }
```

[458]

```
        let user = data.User[0];
        return (
            <ul>
                {user.owned_repositories.map((r) => {
                    return (
                        <li key={r.name}>{r.name}</li>
                    )
                })}
            </ul>
        )
};

export default User;
```

Now, navigating to `http://localhost:3000/user/me` will display a list of repositories owned by the user with the `me` login.

The following subsection will show us the missing piece that is needed for writing a fully usable application: **mutations**.

Mutation

For simplicity's sake, we will implement this mutation in a new component and a new URL.

So, first, let's add a link to this new page in the router (in `src/App.js`):

```
<Route path="/user/:login/addrepo" component={AddRepository} />
```

We also need to add the possibility for the user to reach that page by adding a link to our new page at the end of the repository list of the `User` component (`src/components/User.js`):

```
<li><Link to={`/user/${login}/addrepo`}>Add new repository</Link></li>
```

Then, we can create the `AddRepository` component in `src/components/AddRepository.js`. First, let's define the mutation in terms of GraphQL:

```
const CREATE_REPO = gql`
mutation($name: String!, $login: String!) {
  CreateRepository(name: $name) {
    name
  }
  AddRepositoryOwner(from: { login: $login }, to: { name: $name }) {
    from {
```

Using Neo4j in Your Web Application

```
      login
    }
    to {
      name
    }
  }
}
`;
```

Similar to what we have done for queries, we will create a mutation with two variables: the user login and the new repository name.

The following task consists of creating a mutation object with the following code:

```
import { useMutation } from '@apollo/react-hooks';
const [mutation, ] = useMutation(CREATE_REPO);
```

Once the mutation has been created, we can use it in the callback when the form is submitted with `onFormSubmit`:

```
function AddRepository(props) {
    let login = props.match.params.login;

    const [mutation, ] = useMutation(CREATE_REPO);

    const onFormSubmit = function(e) {
        e.preventDefault();
        mutation({variables: {
                login: login,
                name: e.target.name.value,
            }
        });
 props.history.push(`/user/${login}`);
    };

    return (
        <form onSubmit={onFormSubmit}>
            <input type={"test"} name={"name"} placeholder={"New repository name"}/>
            <input type={"submit"}/>
        </form>
    )
}

export default AddRepository;
```

The `onFormSubmit` callback contains an extra line in order to redirect the user to the main user page after the operation is complete:

```
props.history.push(`/user/${login}`);
```

If we run this code now, we will see that the form is properly submitted, but the list of repositories in `/user/<login>` has not changed. However, the mutation works! (This can be checked in the database.) The issue is that the `UserList` component has not been refreshed. We can trigger this refresh in the mutate function, as we will see now.

Refreshing data after the mutation

In order to refresh the queries affected by the mutation, we need to use the `refreshQueries` parameter of the `mutate` function, as follows:

```
import {GET_USER_DATA} from './User';

// .....
        mutation({
            variables: {
                login: login,
                name: e.target.name.value
            },
            refetchQueries: [ { query: GET_USER_DATA, variables: {login: login} }],
        });
```

Now, if we try and add a new repository, we will see it appear in the list of owned repositories for the user.

You should now be able to read data from Neo4j using GraphQL queries and insert data into the graph using mutations.

Summary

In this chapter, we discussed how to build a web application using Neo4j as the main database. You should now be able to build a web application backed by Neo4j using either Python, its `neomodel` package, and the `Flask` framework to build a full-stack web application (back and frontend); GraphQL, to build an API out of Neo4j that can be plugged to any existing frontend; or GRANDstack, which allows you to create a frontend application for retrieving data from Neo4j using a GraphQL API.

Even though we have specifically addressed the concepts of users and repositories, this knowledge can be extended to any other type of object and relationship pretty easily; for example, repositories can become products, movies, or posts written by the user. If you have used a link prediction algorithm to build a *followers* recommendation engine, as we did in Chapter 9, *Predicting Relationships*, you can use the knowledge you've gained in this chapter to show a list of recommended users to follow.

In the next and last chapter, we will deal with big data and learn how to use Neo4j at scale.

Questions

- What is GOM?
- Practice: In the Flask application, add the possibility for a user to add a new repository, noting the following:
    - A repository is characterized by its name only.
    - We can't have several repositories with the same name owned by the same user.
- GraphQL:
    - Add the total number of owned repositories in the User type.
    - Add a new parameter in the User type that will return the recommended repositories.
- GRANDstack:
    - Update the UserList component to also show the number of owned repositories.

Further reading

- More details about neomodel and Flask or Django can be found in the book entitled *Building Web Applications with Python and Neo4j*, S. Gupta, Packt Publishing.
- All you need to know about GraphQL and Neo4j can be found in the book entitled *Full-stack GraphQL*, W. Lyon, Manning Publications.
- Learn how to use React with no prior experience with the following series of videos: *The Complete React Developer Course (with Hooks and Redux)*, A. Mead, Packt Publishing.

12
Neo4j at Scale

Now that we are able to use Neo4j and graph algorithms to answer many questions, it is time to worry about how Neo4j manages data of different sizes. Neo4j versions prior to 4.0 were already able to deal with huge amounts of data (billions of nodes and relationships), only limited by disk size. But Neo4j 4.0 has overcome these limitations (almost) by introducing **sharding**, a technique that spans a graph across several machines. This chapter will provide an introduction to sharding, both in terms of shard definition and a new Cypher statement that was introduced especially to query such graphs. In the last section, we will investigate the GDS performances of large graphs.

The following topics will be covered in this chapter:

- Measuring GDS performance
- Configuring Neo4j 4.0 for big data

Let's get started!

Technical requirements

While the first section of this chapter can still be done with Neo4j 3.x, the last section will use sharding, which was only introduced in version 4 of Neo4j. Thus, the following configuration is required for this section:

- **Neo4j ≥ 4.0**
- GDS ≥ 1.2

Measuring GDS performance

The Graph Data Science library has been built for big datasets; graph representation and algorithms are optimized for big graphs. However, for efficiency's sake, all operations are performed in the heap, which is the reason why having an estimation of the memory requirements to run a given algorithm on a given projected graph can be important.

Estimating memory usage with the estimate procedures

GDS algorithms are run on an in-memory *projected* graph. The library provides helper procedures, which can be used to predict the memory usage required for storing a projected graph and running a given algorithm. These estimations are performed via the `estimate` execution mode, which can be appended to graph creation or algorithm execution procedures.

Estimating projected graph memory usage

Projected graphs are stored entirely in-memory (in the heap). In order to know how much memory is required to store a projected graph with the given nodes, relationships, and properties, we can use the following procedures:

```
gds.graph.create.estimate(...)
// or
gds.graph.create.cypher.estimate(...)
```

There are several ways to use this procedure, but in all cases, it will return, among others, the following parameters:

- `requiredMemory`: The total required RAM
- `mapView`: A detailed description about which entities require more memory between nodes, relationships, and properties
- `nodeCount`: The total number of nodes in the projected graph
- `relationshipCount`: The total number of relationships in the projected graph

Let's study a few examples.

Fictive graph

The projected graph stores the following:

- A node as the Neo4j internal identifier (id(n))
- Relationships as a pair of node IDs
- Properties, if requested, as floating-point numbers (8 bytes)

This means that the memory requirements can be estimated as soon as we know how many nodes, relationships, and properties the projected graph is about to contain by using the following query:

```
CALL gds.graph.create.estimate('*', '*', {
 nodeCount: 10000,
 relationshipCount: 2000
})
```

The mapView field looks as follows:

```
{
  "name": "HugeGraph",
  "components": [
    {
      "name": "this.instance",
      "memoryUsage": "72 Bytes"
    },
    {
      "name": "nodeIdMap",
      "components": [
          ...
      ],
      "memoryUsage": "175 KiB"
    },
    {
      "name": "adjacency list for 'RelationshipType{name='__ALL__'}'",
      "components": [
          ...
      ],
      "memoryUsage": "256 KiB"
    },
    {
      "name": "adjacency offsets for 'RelationshipType{name='__ALL__'}'",
      "components": [
          ...
      ],
      "memoryUsage": "80 KiB"
    }
```

```
    ],
    "memoryUsage": "511 KiB"
}
```

This tells you that the total memory usage of your graph will be around `511KB` (last line). It also helps you identify which parts consume most of this memory so that, eventually, you can reduce the size of the graph to the bare minimum for your needs.

Graph defined by native or Cypher projection

Estimating the memory requirement for a projected graph defined with Cypher projection is achieved thanks to the following syntax:

```
CALL gds.graph.create.cypher.estimate(
    "MATCH (n) RETURN id(n)",
    "MATCH (u)--(v) RETURN id(u) as source, id(v) as target"
)
```

Note the difference compared to real graph creation with Cypher projection, which would be as follows:

```
CALL gds.graph.create.cypher(
    "projGraphName",
    "MATCH (n) RETURN id(n) as id",
    "MATCH (u)--(v) RETURN id(u) as source, id(v) as target"
)
```

> **TIP**: The graph name parameter has to be skipped in the `estimate` scenario.

Knowing how much memory is required by a projected graph is one thing. But usually, we create projected graphs to run some algorithms on them. Therefore, being able to estimate the memory consumption of algorithms is also crucial to determining the size of the machine we will need to use.

Estimating algorithm memory usage

For each algorithm in the production quality tier, the GDS implements an estimate procedure similar to the one studied in the preceding paragraph for projected graphs. It can be used by appending `estimate` to any algorithm execution mode:

```
CALL gds.<ALGO>.<MODE>.estimate(graphNameOrConfig: String|Map,
configuration: Map)
```

> The algorithms in the alpha tier do not benefit from this feature.

The returned parameters are as follows:

```
YIELD
    requiredMemory,
    treeView,
    mapView,
    bytesMin,
    bytesMax,
    heapPercentageMin,
    heapPercentageMax,
    nodeCount,
    relationshipCount
```

The parameter names are self-explanatory and similar to the projected graph estimation procedure. By estimating the memory usage of both the projected graph and the algorithms you want to run on them, you can get a fairly good estimate of the heap required and use a well-sized server for your analysis.

The stats running mode

Another interesting feature introduced by the GDS (compared to its predecessor, the Graph Algorithms Library) is the `stats` mode. It runs the algorithm without altering the graph, but returns some information about the projected graph and the algorithm's results. The list of returned parameters is the same as the one from the `write` mode.

In the following section, we are going to study an example of both graph and algorithm memory (`estimate`) and execution (`stats`) estimations.

Measuring time performances for some of the algorithms

When using the algorithm write procedure, which means writing the results back into the main Neo4j graph, the procedure will return some information about its execution time:

- `createMillis`: Time to create the projected graph
- `computeMillis`: Time to run the algorithm
- `writeMillis`: Time to write the results back

Let's use these parameters to check the PageRank or Louvain algorithms' performances with a slightly larger graph compared to the one we've used so far. To do so, we are going to use a social network graph provided by Facebook during a recruiting Kaggle competition. The dataset can be downloaded from https://www.kaggle.com/c/FacebookRecruiting/overview. It contains 1,867,425 nodes and 9,437,519 relationships. You can import it into Neo4j using your favorite import tool (LOAD CSV, APOC, or the Neo4j command-line import tool). In the rest of this example, I'll use `Node` as the node label and `IS_FRIEND_WITH` as the relationship type.

In order to use the GDS, we need to create a projected graph that contains all our nodes and undirected relationships:

```
CALL gds.graph.create(
    "graph",
    "*",
    {
        IS_FRIEND_WITH: {
            type: "IS_FRIEND_WITH",
            orientation: "UNDIRECTED"
        }
    }
)
```

Then, we can execute the Louvain algorithm with the following command:

```
CALL gds.louvain.write.estimate("graph", {writeProperty: "pr"})
```

This tells us that only around 56 MB of the heap is required to run the algorithm.

Now, run the following command:

```
CALL gds.louvain.stats("graph")
```

This will give us an estimate regarding the required time to run the Louvain algorithm.

> **TIP**: Even the estimation can take quite a long time, so be patient.

Now, you should be able to estimate how much memory is required by your graph to execute a given algorithm. You should also be able to estimate how much time it will take for an algorithm to converge on your data.

In the next section, we will come back to Neo4j and Cypher and learn about the novelties introduced in version 4.0 for very large graphs.

Configuring Neo4j 4.0 for big data

Neo4j 4.0 was announced in February 2020. Among other new features, it is the first version that supports sharding to split a graph across several servers. We will discuss this further in the following section. First, let's review some basic settings that can improve Neo4j's performance before thinking about complex solutions.

The landscape prior to Neo4j 4.0

Neo4j 3.x is already an incredibly powerful database that can manage billions of nodes and relationships. One of the first settings you learn to tune when getting the Neo4j certification is the allocated memory.

Memory settings

Memory is configured by several settings in the `neo4j.conf` file. The default values are quite low and it is often recommended to increase them, depending on your data and usage. Neo4j has a utility script that's used to estimate the memory required by your graph instance. The script is located in the `bin` directory of your `$NEO4J_HOME` path. When using Neo4j from Neo4j Desktop, you can open a Terminal from your graph management tab and it will automatically open in that folder. Then, you can execute `memrec` with the following `bash` command:

```
./bin/neo4j-admin memrec
```

The output of this command contains the following block:

```
dbms.memory.heap.initial_size=3500m
dbms.memory.heap.max_size=3500m
dbms.memory.pagecache.size=1900m
```

You can use these indications to update `neo4j.conf` (or graph settings in Neo4j Desktop) and then restart your database.

Neo4j in the cloud

It has been possible to run Neo4j in the cloud in a completely automated and managed way for a long time now. In fact, Neo4j provides images to be used in Google cloud or AWS.

Since 2019, Neo4j has also had its own Database-as-a-Service solution with Neo4j Aura, an all-in-one solution used to run a Neo4j database without the need to worry about infrastructure. Check the deployment guide for more information and links: https://neo4j.com/developer/guide-cloud-deployment/.

Sharding with Neo4j 4.0

Sharding is a technique that involves splitting a database across multiple servers when the amount of data to be stored is larger than a single server's capacity. This only happens with very large datasets, since the current hardware capacities for a single server can reach several terabytes of data. An application would have to generate GBs of data per day to reach these limitations. Now, let's address how to manage these big datasets using Neo4j.

Neo4j has developed another tool that can be used especially for this purpose called `fabric`.

If you create a new graph using Neo4j 4.0 in Neo4j Browser, you will notice that the *active* database is now highlighted next to the query box.

Defining shards

The first thing to do when dealing with shards is to define how to split the data. Indeed, sharding is powerful, but it is not without its limitations. For instance, an important limitation of sharding is the inability to traverse a relationship from one shard to another. However, some nodes can be duplicated in order to avoid this situation, so it all depends on your data model and how you are querying it. Imagine we have data from an e-commerce website that's registering orders from customers all around the world. Several dimensions can be considered for sharding:

- **Spatial-based**: All orders coming from the same continent or country can be grouped together in the same shard.
- **Temporal-based**: All nodes created on the same day/week/month can be saved in the same shard.
- **Product-based**: Orders containing the same products can be grouped together.

The last situation assumes that there are clear partitions between ordered products; otherwise, we would have to duplicate almost all the product nodes.

Once we have a better idea of how to split our data and how many databases will be needed, we can proceed to the configuration in neo4j.conf. As an example, we will use two local databases that can be configured by adding the following lines to neo4j.conf:

```
fabric.database.name=fabric

fabric.graph.0.name=gr1
fabric.graph.0.uri=neo4j://localhost:7867
fabric.graph.0.database=db1

fabric.graph.1.name=gr2
fabric.graph.1.uri=neo4j://localhost:7867
fabric.graph.1.database=db2
```

Before we move on, we need to do one more thing: create the two databases (db1 and db2).

Creating the databases

In Neo4j Browser, from the left panel, navigate to the **Database Information** tab (see the following screenshot):

There, you can choose which database will be used. While the default is `neo4j`, we will connect to the `system` database in order to be able to create new ones. Here, select **System** from the drop-down menu. Neo4j Browser will let you know the following:

> *"Queries from this point on are using the database system as the target."*

Here, you can create the two databases needed for this section:

```
CREATE DATABASE db1;
CREATE DATABASE db2
```

Now, you can switch to the main entry point for our cluster: the database called `fabric` (again, from the left menu).

Now that we have told Neo4j that the data will be split across several clusters and that we have created these clusters, let's learn how to tell Cypher which cluster to use.

Querying a sharded graph

The last Cypher version introduced a new keyword, `USE`, which we can use to query a sharded graph. Together with the `fabric` utilities, this allows us to query data from different shards using a single query.

The USE statement

The USE Cypher statement was introduced in Neo4j 4.0 to tell Cypher which shard to use. For instance, we can add some data to one of our databases with the following query:

```
USE fabric.gr1
CREATE (c:Country {name: "USA"})
CREATE (u1:User {name: "u1"})
CREATE (u2:User {name: "u2"})
CREATE (u1)-[:LIVES_IN]->(c)
CREATE (u2)-[:LIVES_IN]->(c)
CREATE (o1:Order {name: "o1"})
CREATE (o2:Order {name: "o2"})
CREATE (o3:Order {name: "o3"})
CREATE (u1)-[:ORDERED]->(o1)
CREATE (u2)-[:ORDERED]->(o2)
CREATE (u2)-[:ORDERED]->(o3)
```

We can retrieve data from this shard using the following code:

```
USE fabric.gr1
MATCH (order:Order)<--(:User)-->(country:Country)
RETURN "gr1" as db,
       country.name,
       count(*) AS nbOrders
```

The preceding query will use only nodes in the gr1 database, as defined in the fabric configuration section in neo4j.conf. You can run the same query with USE fabric.gr2 and get no result since we have not created any data in gr2 yet. If you are interested in all your data, without filtering on a specific database, this is also possible using fabric, as we will see now.

Querying all databases

To query all known shards, we will have to use two other functions:

- fabric.graphIds(), which returns all the known databases. You can test its result with the following command:

    ```
    RETURN fabric.graphIds()
    ```

- fabric.graph(graphId) returns the name of the database with a given ID, directly usable in a Use statement.

This will essentially allow us to perform a loop over all our shards:

```
UNWIND fabric.graphIds() AS graphId
CALL {
  USE fabric.graph(graphId)
    WITH graphId
    MATCH (order:Order)<--(:User)-->(country:Country)
    RETURN "gr" + graphId as db,
           country.name as countryName,
           count(*) AS nbOrders
} RETURN db, countryName, sum(nbOrders)
```

Here is the result of the preceding query:

"db"	"countryName"	"sum(nbOrders)"
"gr1"	"USA"	3

Here, we can see the three orders from the USA that we created earlier in this section in `gr1`.

Now, let's say you add some data to `gr2`, for instance:

```
USE fabric.gr2
CREATE (c:Country {name: "UK"})
CREATE (u1:User {name: "u11"})
CREATE (u2:User {name: "u12"})
CREATE (u1)-[:LIVES_IN]->(c)
CREATE (u2)-[:LIVES_IN]->(c)
CREATE (o1:Order {name: "o11"})
CREATE (o2:Order {name: "o12"})
CREATE (u1)-[:ORDERED]->(o1)
CREATE (u2)-[:ORDERED]->(o2)
```

By doing this, the preceding MATCH query returns the following:

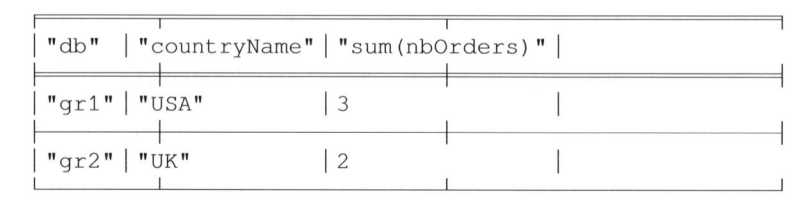

"db"	"countryName"	"sum(nbOrders)"
"gr1"	"USA"	3
"gr2"	"UK"	2

With this, you should now understand that sharding provides infinite possibilities for data storage, both in terms of volume and in terms of realization, with the latter depending on the queries that will be run against the database.

Summary

After reading this chapter, you should be able to deploy a Neo4j database either on a single server or using cluster and sharding techniques. You should also be aware of the best practices for using the GDS with big data and the limitations of this plugin.

With this chapter, we have closed the loop we started in `Chapter 1`, *Graph Databases*, where you first started learning about graphs, graph databases, and Neo4j. `Chapter 2`, *The Cypher Query Language*, taught you how to insert data into Neo4j and query it using the visual query language known as Cypher. `Chapter 3`, *Empowering Your Business with Pure Cypher*, gave you the opportunity to use Cypher to build knowledge graphs and to perform some **natural language processing (NLP)** using a third-party library built by Graph Aware.

In `Chapter 4`, *The Graph Data Science Library and Path Finding*, you learned about the basics of the Graph Data Science library. Developed and supported by Neo4j, this plugin is the starting point for data science on graphs using Neo4j. In the same chapter, you learned how to perform shortest path operations without having to extract data from Neo4j. The following chapter, `Chapter 5`, *Spatial Data*, then taught you how to use spatial data in Neo4j. Here, you discovered the built-in spatial type, `Point`, and learned about another plugin, `neo4j-spatial`. You saw that spatial data is well integrated into Neo4j and can even be visualized thanks to Neo4j Desktop applications.

In the rest of the chapters in the *Graph Algorithms* section, you discovered the centrality (`Chapter 6`, *Node Importance*) and community detection (`Chapter 7`, *Community Detection and Centrality Measures*) algorithms. You also learned about tools such as `neoviz`, which is used to create nice graph visualizations.

With this new knowledge, you then learned how to use these graph algorithms in machine learning. First, in `Chapter 8`, *Using Graph-based Features in Machine Learning*, you built a simple classification model. By turning your data into a graph and adding graph-based features, you were able to increase the model's performance. In `Chapter 9`, *Predicting Relationships*, you got more familiar with a machine learning problem specific to graphs: predicting future links between nodes in a time-evolving graph. In `Chapter 10`, *Graph Embedding—from Graphs to Matrices*, you moved even further into the graph analysis stage by learning about the different types of algorithms available in order to automatically learn the features that are used to represent nodes in vector format.

Finally, in the last section of this book, you learned how to interface Neo4j with a web application using Python or GraphQL and React, thanks to GRANDstack (`Chapter 11`, *Using Neo4j in Your Web Application*), as well as how to tune Neo4j and the GDS for really big data.

The path we have traveled down since the beginning of this book has been impressive, but remember that there is no end of the road toward knowledge. Keep reading, learning, experimenting, and building amazing things!

Other Books You May Enjoy

If you enjoyed this book, you may be interested in these other books by Packt:

Learning Neo4j 3.x - Second Edition
Jérôme Baton, Rik Van Bruggen

ISBN: 978-1-78646-614-3

- Understand the science of graph theory, databases and its advantages over traditional databases.
- Install Neo4j, model data and learn the most common practices of traversing data
- Learn the Cypher query language and tailor-made procedures to analyze and derive meaningful representations of data
- Improve graph techniques with the help of precise procedures in the APOC library
- Use Neo4j advanced extensions and plugins for performance optimization.
- Understand how Neo4j's new security features and clustering architecture are used for large scale deployments.

Leave a review - let other readers know what you think

Please share your thoughts on this book with others by leaving a review on the site that you bought it from. If you purchased the book from Amazon, please leave us an honest review on this book's Amazon page. This is vital so that other potential readers can see and use your unbiased opinion to make purchasing decisions, we can understand what our customers think about our products, and our authors can see your feedback on the title that they have worked with Packt to create. It will only take a few minutes of your time, but is valuable to other potential customers, our authors, and Packt. Thank you!

Index

A

A* algorithm
  heuristic function, defining 150, 151
  principles 150
  shortest path, finding 149
  using, within Neo4j GDS plugin 152
acyclic graphs
  versus cyclic graphs 29
adjacency matrix 389
aggregation functions
  about 54
  AVG(expr) 54
  COUNT(expr) 54
  SUM(expr) 54
  using 53, 54
algorithm memory usage
  estimating 467
all-pairs shortest path algorithm 155
anonymous projected graphs 125
ant colony optimization (ACO) 159
APOC utilities
  used, for importing CSV files 65
  used, for importing JSON files 66, 67, 69
  used, for imports 64, 65
arrows tool
  URL 26
ArticleRank 222, 223
artificial neural networks
  about 396
  Convolutional Neural Networks (CNNs) 399
  embedding, extracting from 396
  forward propagation 397, 398, 399
  layers 397, 398, 399
  neurons 397, 398, 399
  Optical Character Recognition (OCR) 399
  principles 397

Recurrent Neural Networks (RNNs) 400
  types 399, 400

B

betweenness centrality 231, 232
binary classification model performance
  computing 372, 373
  DataFrame, creating 369, 371
  features, extracting 368
  labels, extracting 368
  measuring 363
  measuring, with ROC curve 364, 365, 366, 367, 368
  optimal cutoff, determining 372, 373
  ROC curve, drawing 369
  ROC curve, plotting 371, 372
bipartite graphs
  relationships, predicting 375, 376, 377, 379
bounding box 176
bridging node 208

C

centrality algorithms, applying to fraud detection
  about 234
  fraud, detecting with Neo4j 234
  projected graph, creating with Cypher projection 236, 237, 238
centrality algorithms
  about 123
  applications 239
  used, for assessing fraud 235, 236
classification problems, examples
  cancer detection 299
  hand-written digit classification 300
  sentiment analysis 300
  spam detection 299
classification problems

versus regression problem 299
Clique Percolation Method (CPM) 282
closeness centrality algorithm 230
closeness centrality
  about 228
  computing, from shortest path algorithms 228, 229, 230
  formula 228
  using, in multiple components graphs 231
clustering 19
clusters of nodes
  identifying 245
column definition
  categorical feature 303
  numerical feature 303
command line
  data, importing from 64
communities
  visualizing 249, 251
community detection method, applications
  about 246
  clusters of products 246
  clusters of users 247
  fraud detection 247
  properties or links, predicting 247, 248
  recommendation engines 246
  targeted marketing 246
community detection techniques
  overview 248, 249
community detection
  about 244
  applications 244
  clusters of nodes, identifying 245
  overlapping 278, 281
community-based metrics 355
connected graphs
  versus disconnected graphs 31
convergence 266
Convolutional Neural Networks (CNNs)
  about 399
  principles, extending to build GNNs 410
cosine similarity 288, 289
criminal rings 234
critical node 207, 208
CSV files with headers
  importing, with LOAD CSV 58, 59, 61, 62
CSV files without headers
  importing, with LOAD CSV 58
CSV files
  data, importing from 56
  importing, with APOC utilities 65
  importing, with LOAD CSV 58
  used, for reviewing steps of machine learning project 300
cyclic graphs
  versus acyclic graphs 29
Cypher projections 127
Cypher queries
  building, manually 103, 104
Cypher query planner 72, 74
Cypher, data importing from
  about 56
  eager operations 62, 63
  file location 56, 57
  import folder configuration 58

D

data retrieval 48
data science project, data characterization
  about 301
  columns 303, 304, 305
  data visualization 306, 307
  dataset size, quantifying 301
  labels 301, 302, 303
data science project, data cleaning
  about 308
  correlation between variables 311
  missing data 310
  outliers detection 308, 310
  outliers detection, reasons 308
data science project, model
  building 313
  cross-validation 313, 314
  performances, evaluating 316, 317, 318
  train and test samples, creating with scikit-learn 314, 315
  train/test split 313, 314
  training 315
data science project
  building 296, 297

data enrichment 311
data, cleaning 300
data, obtaining 300
feature engineering 312
problem definition 297, 298
data
  importing, from command line 64
  importing, from CSV 56
  importing, from JSON 56
  importing, from web API 69
  testing 49, 50
  using, as graph 19
databases
  managing, with Neo4j Desktop 36, 37
  querying 473, 474, 475
Deep Graph library
  about 414
  reference link 414
DeepWalk node embedding
  about 404
  node context, generating through random walks 404, 405
  random walks, generating, from GDS 405, 406
  with karateclub 406
degree 11
degree centrality results
  versus PageRank results 222
degree centrality
  computing 209
  computing, in Neo4j 210, 211
  formula 209
degree of separation 18, 130
dense graphs, versus sparse graphs
  about 30
  graph traversal 30
Dijkstra's shortest paths algorithm
  about 131, 136, 137
  example implementation 135
  full path from A to E, displaying 138, 139
  graph representation 135
  purpose 131
  relationship direction 146, 147, 149
  running, on simple graph 132, 133, 134
dimensions, sharding
  product-based 471

spatial-based 471
temporal-based 471
directed acyclic graphs (DAG) 29
directed graphs
  versus undirected graphs 28
disconnected graphs
  versus connected graphs 31
Django 438
document object model (DOM) 198
document-oriented databases 20
dynamic graphs 348, 349
dynamic networks 282

E

edge embedding algorithm 388
eigenvector centrality
  about 224, 227
  computing, in GDS plugin 227
eigenvectors embedding 390
embedding
  extracting, from artificial neural networks 396
  features, creating for words 385, 386
  need for 382, 383
  one-hot encoding 383, 384
  results, obtaining from Python 408, 409
  specifications 387, 388
English, automating to Cypher translation
  about 104
  with NLP 104, 105, 106, 107
  with translation-like models 107, 108, 109
euclidean distance 287, 288
Eulerian cycle 11

F

False Positive Rate (FPR) 366
flask and neomodel, used for building web application
  about 429
  data, reading 435
  flask application, creating 430
  graph, altering 436, 438
  login form 431, 432
  login page 430
  login template 432, 433
  login view 433, 434

model, adapting 430
  toy data, creating 429
fraud detection
  centrality algorithms, applying to 234
friend-of-friend example 77, 78, 79
full-stack web application
  creating, with Graph Object Mappers 422
  creating, with Python 422
  relationship knowledge, integrating 427
  structured nodes, properties 423
functions
  about 121
  versus procedures 121, 122

G

GDS performance
  measuring 464
  memory usage, estimating with estimate procedures 464
  time performances, measuring for algorithms 468, 469
GDS results
  writing, in graph 254, 255
gene algorithms (GA) 159
geographic coordinate systems 168, 170, 171, 172
GeoJSON 198, 199, 200, 201
geometry layer
  creating, with neo4j-spatial plugin 175
GitHub API v4 439
Global Positioning System (GPS) 129
GRANDstack
  about 444
  URL 444
  used, for developing React application 444
graph algorithms
  about 415
  reference link 415
graph components
  detecting 249, 251
graph connected components, versions
  strongly connected components 249
  Weakly Connected Component (WCC) 249
Graph Data Science (GDS) plugin
  about 120, 414

eigenvector centrality, computing 227
function, writing 123
function, writing in Neo4j 122
Label Propagation algorithm, using from 267, 268
library content 123, 124
Louvain algorithm, using 273
Neo4j, extending with custom functions and procedures 121
path-related algorithms 152
projected graph, defining 124
projected graph, mutating 128
results, streaming 128, 129
results, writing to Neo4j graph 128, 129
used, for assessing PageRank centrality in Neo4j 221
used, for computing incoming degree 212
used, for computing outgoing degree 211, 212
graph databases models 20
graph databases, types
  document-oriented databases 20
  key-value stores 20
  relational databases 20
graph databases
  figurative representations 21
graph definition 10, 12
graph embedding landscape
  about 388, 389
  algorithms 388
  edge embedding algorithm 388
  node embedding algorithms 388
  whole-graph embedding algorithm 389
graph Laplacian 389
graph machine learning, graph characterization
  about 321
  number of components 323, 324
  number of nodes and edges 322, 323
graph machine learning
  about 319
  data, importing into Neo4j 321
  external data source, using 321
  graph, building 319
  graph-based features, extracting 325, 326
  relationships, creating from existing data 319
  relationships, creating from Neo4j 320

[482]

relationships, creating from relational data 319, 320
graph modeling, considerations in Neo4j
    about 31
    nodes 32
    relationship orientation 32
Graph Nets library
    about 414
    reference link 414
graph neural networks (GNNs)
    about 409
    account node properties 412
    applications 412, 414
    building, by extending principles of CNNs to 410
    building, by extending principles of RNNs to 410
    message aggregation 410, 411, 412
    message propagation 410, 411, 412
    running, from GDS 414, 415
    text analysis 413
    used, for zero-shot learning 413
    using 414
    using, for image analysis 412
    using, for video analysis 413
Graph Object Mappers (GOMs)
    full-stack web application, creating 422
    nodes, creating 425
    nodes, filtering 426
    nodes, querying 425
graph optimization problems
    about 157
    spanning trees 160
    traveling salesman problem 158, 159
graph properties 27
graph theory 10
graph traversal
    about 30, 50
    number of hops 51
    orientation 50, 51
    variable-length patterns 52
graph-based feature creation, automating with Python
    about 331
    GDS procedures, calling 334, 335
    projected graph, creating 332, 333
    projected graph, dropping 338

results, writing back to graph 335, 336, 338
graph-based features creation
    automating, with Neo4j Python driver 328
graph-based features, extracting from Neo4j Browser
    about 326
    algorithms, running 327
    data, extracting 328
    projected graph, creating 327
    projected graph, dropping 328
graph-based features
    extracting 325, 326
    using, with pandas 326
    using, with scikit-learn 326
graph-based search
    about 101
    Cypher queries, building manually 103, 104
    English, automating to Cypher translation 104
    methods 101, 102, 103
GraphML 185
GraphQL APIs
    about 438
    endpoint 439
    mutations 443
    query parameters 441, 442
    returned attributes 440
graphs visualization 12, 14
graphs, examples
    about 14
    computer networks 16
    networks 14
    road networks 14, 16
    social networks 16, 18, 19
graphs
    examples 10
    GDS results, writing 254, 255
    used, for optimizing processes 157
    visualizing, with neovis.js 256, 257, 258
GraphSAGE algorithm 414, 415
GraphSAGE algorithm, running from GDS
    examples 415
Gremlin
    reference link 36
guilt by association 238

[483]

H

haversine equation 150
heuristics approach 149
High-Order Proximity preserved Embedding (HOPE) 391

I

imbalanced 303
import methods 72
incoming degree, computing with GDS plugin
  about 212
  anonymous projected graph, using 213, 214
  named projected graph, using 212, 213

J

JavaScript Neo4j driver
  about 197
  used, for visualizing shortest paths 196
Journal of Graph Algorithms and Applications
  URL 415
JSON files
  data, importing from 56
  importing, with APOC utilities 66, 67, 69

K

k-clique 282
k-shortest path algorithm 153
karateclub
  DeepWalk embedding with 406
  reference link 416
Key Performance Indicator (KPI) 298
key-value stores 20
knowledge graphs
  about 84
  building, from structured data 85, 86
  building, from unstructured data with NLP 86
  context, adding from Wikidata 92
  definition, attempting 84, 85
  enhancing, from semantic graphs 99, 101

L

Label Propagation algorithm
  results, writing to graph 269, 270
  running 262
  seeds, using 268, 269
  using, from GDS plugin 267, 268
Label Propagation, versus Louvain algorithm
  on Zachary's karate club graph 276, 278
Label Propagation
  defining 263
  implementing, in Python 264, 265, 267
  nodes relationships 264
  semi-supervised learning 264
  weighted nodes 264
latitude 168
layer 177
layers, creating with polygon geometries
  about 179, 181, 182
  data, obtaining 179, 181
Leaflet 198, 199, 200, 201
linear optimization 157
link prediction algorithm
  used, for making recommendations 352, 353, 354
link prediction metrics
  about 360
  community-based metrics 355
  creating, from Neo4j 354
  instability 360
  local neighborhood information, using 358
  newness weakness 360
  path-related metrics 355
  reciprocity 360
link prediction model
  building, with ROC curve 361
  building, with scikit-learn 374
link prediction
  applications 350
  need for 348
  used, for fighting crime 350
  used, for making product recommendations 351, 352
  used, for making recommendations 350
  used, for recovering missing data 350
  used, for representing social links 351
  using, for research 350
list of objects
  creating 55
LOAD CSV statement

used, for importing US states 75, 76
local neighborhood information
  Adamic-Adar score 359
  common neighbors 358
  preferential attachment 360
  total neighbors 359
  using 358
locally linear embedding (LLE) 390
longitude 168
Louvain algorithm, drawbacks
  about 278
  resolution limit 279, 280
Louvain algorithm, in GDS plugin
  about 273
  aggregation method, in relationship projection 274, 275
  syntax 273
Louvain algorithm
  about 270
  alternatives 280
  intermediate steps 275, 276
  modularity 270, 271
  reproducing, steps 273

M

matrix factorization 389
Mean Square Error (MSE) 316
MERGE keyword 43
modularity, Louvain algorithm
  all nodes in own community 271
  all nodes in same community 271
  optimal partition 272
modularity
  defining 270, 271

N

Named Entity Recognition (NER) 87, 90
named projected graphs
  about 125
  creating 125, 126
Natural Language Processing (NLP)
  about 86
  Neo4j tools 87
  used, for building knowledge graph from unstructured data 86

Neo4j 3.x 469
Neo4j 4.0
  configuring, for big data 469
  sharding 470
Neo4j Browser
  graph-based features, extracting from 326
Neo4j built-in spatial types
  points, creating 172, 173
  querying, by distance 174, 175
  using 172
Neo4j Desktop
  databases, managing with 36, 37
Neo4j GDS plugin
  A* algorithm, using 152
Neo4j graph
  minimum spanning tree, finding 162
Neo4j indexing 75
Neo4j Python driver
  discovering 329
  graph-based features creation, automating with 328
  transactions, creating with 330, 331
  usage 329, 330
Neo4j test graph 392
Neo4j tools, for NLP
  about 87
  graph, enriching with NLP 90, 91, 92
  GraphAware NLP library 87, 89
  test data, importing from GitHub API 89, 90
Neo4j translator 26
Neo4j, fundamentals
  about 24
  nodes 25
  properties 25
  relationships between nodes 25
neo4j-spatial plugin
  about 175
  download link 175
  spatial indexes 176
  used, for creating geometry layer 175
Neo4j
  about 23, 24
  custom function, writing 122, 123
  data, exporting to pandas 338, 339, 340
  databases, creating 472

degree centrality, computing 210, 211
documentation, reference link 123
extending, with custom functions and procedures 121, 122
geometry layer, creating with neo4j-spatial 175
graph modeling, considerations 31
in Cloud 470
link prediction metrics, creating from 354
link prediction results, saving 374
memory settings 469
PageRank centrality, assessing with GDS plugin 221
shortest path algorithm, using 139, 142, 143, 144
use cases 27
used, for visualizing spatial data 194
neomap
  nodes, visualizing with simple layers 195
  paths, visualizing with advanced layer 195, 196
  URL 194
neomodel
  properties, adding 424
  working with 422
neovis.js
  graph, visualizing with 256, 257, 258
networkx graph matrix
  creating, from pandas 393, 394
networkx graph
  creating 392
  edge list data, extracting from Neo4j 392, 393
  Neo4j test graph 392
networkx
  reference link 139, 416
NEuler, usage
  for community detection visualization 259, 260, 262
NEuler
  using 258
node embedding algorithms
  about 388
  computing, with Python 391
  fitting 394, 395, 396
node importance
  defining 206, 207
node labels
  updating 45

node property
  deleting 46
node2vec algorithm
  about 407
  from GDS (≥ 1.3) 408
nodes similarities, measuring techniques
  about 283
  set-based measures 283
  vector-based measures 283
nodes similarities
  set-based similarities 283
  vector-based similarities 286
nodes
  all properties, updating 44, 45
  creating 36, 37, 38, 39
  deleting 44
  filtering 39, 40
  influencer concept 207
  properties, returning 40
  selecting 39
  updating 44

O

object-relational mapping (ORM) 422
objective function 157
objects
  deleting 47
  existing property, updating 44
  new property, creating 44
  unnesting 55, 56
  updating 44
one-hot encoding 383, 384
Optical Character Recognition (OCR) 399
optimal solution 157
optional matches 53
outgoing degree
  computing, with GDS plugin 211, 212

P

PageRank algorithm
  about 214
  damping factor 216
  formula, building 215
  implementing, with Python 219, 220
  normalization 216

running, on example graph 217, 218, 219
PageRank formula
  rebuilding, with adjacency matrix 224, 225
  rebuilding, with eigenvector centrality 227
  rebuilding, with matrix notation 225, 226
PageRank results
  versus degree centrality results 222
PageRank, variants
  about 222
  ArticleRank 222, 223
  eigenvector centrality 224
  personalized PageRank 223, 224
pandas
  data, exporting from Neo4j 338, 339, 340
  networkx graph matrix, creating from 393, 394
path-based centrality metrics
  about 227
  betweenness centrality 231, 232
  closeness centrality 228
  comparing 232, 233
path-related algorithms, GDS plugin
  all-pairs shortest path 155, 157
  k-shortest path 153
  SSSP algorithm 154, 155
path-related metrics
  about 355
  distance between nodes 356, 357
  the Katz index 357, 358
pathfinding applications
  about 130
  GPS navigation 129
pattern matching 48, 49
personalized PageRank 223, 224
polygon geometries
  used, for creating layers 179
Prim's algorithm 161, 162
procedures
  about 121
  versus functions 121, 122
product similarity recommendations
  about 109, 110
  ordering 113
  products, bringing together frequently 112
  products, in same category 110, 111
projected graph memory usage

  Cypher projection 466
  estimating 464
  fictive graph 465, 466
projected graph
  Cypher projections 127
  defining 124
  native projections 125, 126
Python
  embedding results, obtaining from 408, 409
  full-stack web application, creating 422
  graph-based feature creation, automating with 331
  Label Propagation, implementing 264, 265, 267
  used, for computing node embedding 391
  used, for implementing PageRank algorithm 219, 220
PyTorch Geometric
  about 414
  reference link 414

Q

Question and Answer website
  join table 21
  relationship, between tags and questions 22
  SQL 21
  whiteboard model 23

R

React application, with GRANDstack
  API, calling from Python 448
  API, creating 445
  application, starting 446
  component, creating 453
  data, obtaining from GraphQL API 453
  data, refreshing after mutation 461
  GraphQL schema, writing 445
  mutations 450, 452, 459, 461
  navigation, adding 457, 458
  simple component, writing 453, 455
  testing, with GraphQL playground 447
  types, defining 445
  user interface, building 452
  variables, using 449
React application
  developing, GRANDstack used 444

recall 317
Receiver Operation Characteristics (ROC) curve 363
recommendation engine 109
Recurrent Neural Networks (RNNs)
  about 400
  principles, extending to build GNNs 410
regression problem
  versus classification problem 299
relational databases 20
relationships
  creating 36, 40, 41, 42
  deleting 44
  selecting 42
  simple relationship 427
  updating 44
  with properties 428
Representational State Transfer (REST) 438
resolution limit problem 280
Resource Description Framework (RDF) 92, 93
ROC curve, used for building link prediction model
  about 361
  binary classification model performance, measuring 363
  data, importing into Neo4j 361, 362
  graphs, splitting 362, 363
  link prediction results, saving into Neo4j 374
  relationships, predicting in bipartite graphs 375, 376, 377, 379
  score for edge, computing 362, 363
routing algorithms 130
routing engine, building
  about 184
  data, importing 185, 186, 188
  data, preparing 186
  shortest path algorithm, running 188, 190, 192, 194
  spatial layer, creating 188
  specifications 184

S

scikit-learn model
  centrality features, using 343, 344
  community features 341, 342, 343
  community features, using 343, 344
  training 341
scikit-learn
  used, for building link prediction model 374
semantic graphs
  knowledge graph, enhancing from 99, 101
semi-supervised learning 264
set-based measures
  mathematical definition 283, 284
  user similarity, quantifying in GitHub graph 284, 285
set-based nodes similarities, variants
  about 283
  Jaccard similarity 286
  overlapping 283
Seven Bridges of Königsberg problem 10, 11
sharded graph
  querying 472
sharding
  with Neo4j 4.0 470
shards
  defining 471
shortest path algorithm
  path visualization 146
shortest path algorithms
  importance 129
  in social network 130
  path visualization 145
  reference link 141
  running 188, 190, 192, 194
  using, within Neo4j 139, 142, 143, 144
shortest path, based on distance
  finding 184
similarity-based embedding
  about 391
  High-Order Proximity preserved Embedding (HOPE) 391
Single Source Shortest Path (SSSP) algorithm 154, 155
sinks 216
skip-gram model
  creating 400
  fake task 401
  input 401
  target 401, 402
  word representation, before embedding 401

skip-gram neural network architecture
  hidden layer 403
  output layer 403, 404
social graphs, analyses
  community detection 19
  link prediction 19
  node importance 19
social recommendations 113, 114
spanning trees 160
SPARQL 92, 93
sparse graphs
  versus dense graphs 30
spatial attributes
  geographic coordinate systems 168, 170, 171, 172
  representing 168
spatial data visualization
  JavaScript Neo4j driver, used for visualizing shortest paths 196
  neomap, using 194
  with Neo4j 194
spatial data
  LINESTRING 178
  POINT 178
  POLYGON 178
  type, defining 178
  visualizing, with Neo4j 194
spatial indexes 176
spatial layer of points
  creating 177
spatial layer
  defining 177
  points, adding 178
spatial queries, performing
  about 182
  distance between two spatial objects, finding 182, 183
  objects contained within other objects, finding 184
spatial.importShapefile 181
spatial.withinDistance 182
state-of-the-art graph algorithms 415, 416
stats running mode 467
stratification 314
strongly connected components 252, 253

structured data
  knowledge graph, building from 85, 86
Structured Query Language (SQL) 20
StructuredNode
  versus SemiStructuredNode 423
supervised learning
  about 298
  versus unsupervised learning 298

T

the Katz index 357, 358
Tile layer 198
tokenization 90
traveling-salesman problem (TSP) 157, 158, 159
True Positive Rate (TPR) 366

U

undirected graphs
  versus directed graphs 28
unsupervised learning
  about 298
  versus supervised learning 298
unweighted graphs
  versus weighted graphs 28, 29
use cases, pathfinding applications
  scientific fields 130
  video games 130
Use statement 473

V

vector-based similarities
  about 286
  cosine similarity 288, 289
  euclidean distance 287, 288

W

Weakly Connected Component (WCC) 251, 252, 323
web API, data importing from
  about 69
  GitHub web API, calling 70, 71
  parameters setting 69
weighted graphs
  versus unweighted graphs 28, 29

Well-Known Text (WKT) 179
whole-graph embedding algorithm 389
Wikidata
  importing, into Neo4j 96, 97, 98
  querying 93, 94, 95
World Geodetic System 1984 (WSG84) 171

Y
Yen's algorithm 153

Z
Zachary's karate club graph
  Label Propagation, versus Louvain algorithm 276, 278

Printed in Great Britain
by Amazon